Nascent Proletarians

Studies in Social Discontinuity

General Editor   *Charles Tilly, The New School for Social Research*

Studies in Social Discontinuity began in 1972 under the imprint of Academic Press. In its first 15 years, 53 titles were published in the series, including important volumes in the areas of historical sociology, political economy, and social history.

Revived in 1989 by Basil Blackwell, the series will continue to include volumes emphasizing social changes and non-Western historical experience as well as translations of major works.

Published:

The Perilous Frontier
Nomadic Empires and China
Thomas J. Barfield

Regents and Rebels
The Revolutionary World of an Eighteenth-Century Dutch City
Wayne Ph. te Brake

Nascent Proletarians
Class Formation in Post-Revolutionary France
Michael P. Hanagan

In preparation:

Modern French Anti-Semitism
A Political History
Pierre Birnbaum

Coffee and Contention
Political Change in Modern Brazil
Mauricio Font

Rites of Revolt
The War of the Demoiselles in Ariege, France (1829–1831)
Peter Sahlins

Nascent Proletarians

Class Formation in Post-Revolutionary France

Michael P. Hanagan

Basil Blackwell

Copyright © Michael P. Hanagan 1989

First published 1989

Basil Blackwell Ltd
108 Cowley Road, Oxford, OX4 1JF, UK

Basil Blackwell Inc.
3 Cambridge Center
Cambridge, Massachusetts 02142, USA

British Library Cataloguing in Publication Data

A CIP catalogue record for this book is
available from the British Library.

Library of Congress Cataloging in Publication Data

Hanagan, Michael P., 1947–
    Nascent proletarians: class formation in post-revolutionary
France / Michael Hanagan.
        p.   cm. – (Studies in social discontinuity)
    Bibliography: p.
    Includes index.
    ISBN 1-55786-041-6
    1. Social classes–France–Saint-Etienne Region
(Loire)–History–19th century. 2. Labor and laboring
classes–France–Saint-Etienne Region (Loire)–History–19th
century. 3. Saint-Etienne Region (Loire, France)–Social
conditions.   I. Title.   II. Series: Studies in social
discontinuity (Basil Blackwell Publishers)
HN438.S242H36 1989
305.5'0944'581–dc19   89-27 CIP

Typeset in 10 on 11.5 pt Ehrhardt
by Vera-Reyes Inc., Philippines.
Printed in Great Britain by T. J. Press, Padstow

In memory of my parents,
Berenice Henke Hanagan and
Francis Patrick Hanagan

Contents

Preface		ix
1	Class Formation and Workers' Families in the Region of Saint-Etienne, France	1
2	Capital Concentration and Industrial Employment in the Stéphanois: 1780–1880	29
3	The Formation of a Permanent Proletariat: 1840–1880	57
4	Patterns of Life-Cycle Employment in Industry: Miners and Metalworkers	95
5	The Working-Class Family Economy in the Industrial City	134
6	Proletarians and Protest in the Stéphanois: the Origins of the Modern Labor Movement	182
Conclusion		208
Appendix	The Manuscript Census Sample: Measurement Problems	213
Select Bibliography		216
Index		239

Preface

As is the case with many second books, this one traces its roots to my first book, *The Logic of Solidarity: Artisans and Industrial Workers in Three French Towns, 1871–1914*. Although the first work dealt with the relations between artisanal and industrial workers, several reviewers commented on the richness of the material on artisans compared with that on industrial workers. While continuing to believe in the particular strategic importance of artisanal workers fighting for changes in the organization of work, I also believe that historians find themselves unusually attracted to artisans because of their literacy and their extensive written culture. But how to study groups of workers who left few records, particularly during the crucial early period when their identities were first being formed?

Because of the lack of written sources, some of the best work on the new industrial working class has been studies such as those of Michael Anderson, Joan Scott and Louise Tilly, Tamara Hareven, and Michael Katz which focus on the family and on the life course of working-class men and women. One of the goals of this study has been to use the methods and concepts of family history to help enrich our understanding of labor history.

In the process of writing this book, I learned a lot and have incurred obligations to colleagues and to students who taught me many things. The present work would never have been possible without a training fellowship from the Social Science Research Council that allowed me to study demography at the Population Studies Center of the University of Pennsylvania. Pennsylvania proved a very stimulating intellectual environment, and I thank Etienne and Francine van de Walle, Richard Easterlin, Ann Miller, and Samuel Preston for their patience with a neophyte and for their willingness to give me wise counsel. Vanderbilt University Research Council, the American Philosophical Society, and Columbia University Research grants made it possible for me to spend many summers in France gathering material and doing research. An American Council of Learned Societies Research fellowship allowed me to make much progress in the writing of the manuscript.

Along the way, I was fortunate to obtain generous and thoughtful assistance. Yves Soulingeas, Director of the Archives of the Haute-Loire, and F. Leclercq, Directress of the Archives of the Puy-de-Dôme were very helpful. Especially and continually helpful was Eliane Viallard, Directress of the Archives of the Loire. When the difficulties involved in microfilming a census in one archive seemed nearly insurmountable, Professor Yves Lequin graciously intervened to help with the microfilming. At Vanderbilt University, both graduate and undergraduate students helped code censuses and marriage records. Eugene Pizetta III, Hugh Phillips III, Jeff Schneider, Valerie A. Dobiesz, and George D. Tooley all proved intelligent and conscientious coders; they called my attention to many problems and suggested solutions that often proved fruitful. Chuck Stangor did most of my programming, and also gave me valuable advice. Since graduate school, I have been fortunate to find good friends with the patience to read my work and the intelligence to provide thoughtful criticism. Indeed, it seems to me that one of the chief benefits of academic life is the opportunity to exchange comment and criticisms with one's peers. While I was researching and writing this book, my own family was being formed; my daughters, Nora and Julia, who were born during this period, continue to inspire me. My wife, Miriam Cohen, continues to be my most valued critic; taking time from her own work, she has enriched mine. Time and again, Charles Tilly has given his thoughtful advice. During my research and in the writing, Yves Lequin has given insightful and helpful comment. George Alter, Elinor Accampo, Ron Aminzade, Jim Lehning, John Merriman, Leslie Page Moch, Jean-Luc Pinol, and Len Smith read all or large portions of the manuscript and helped me to significantly improve the final work.

1

Class Formation and Workers' Families in the Region of Saint-Etienne, France

Between 1840 and 1880, a permanent and largely hereditary industrial proletariat developed in the Stéphanois region of France. The Stéphanois region, often labeled the "cradle of the Industrial Revolution in France," consists of those cities, towns and villages lining the coal basins on both sides of the city of Saint-Etienne in the southeast of France. In 1840, the number of full-time, permanent industrial proletarians in the Stéphanois was small and confined to two or three urban enclaves. By 1880, industrial proletarians dominated the local economy in urban centers which had grown with breakneck speed. In the crucial years between 1840 and 1880, the proletarian population grew rapidly and, even more critically, the proletarian family established itself as a major social institution in the region. In the decades to come, these families would produce succeeding generations of proletarians. By 1880, the population of the industrial region had begun to stabilize, and for the whole period between 1880 and 1914, most industrial workers were the sons and daughters of local industrial workers, often residents of the same cities as their parents, overwhelmingly from the same small region.[1] Between 1840 and 1880, a new social class came into existence in this region of France.

To fully understand the process of class formation, it is necessary to explore the relationship between the growth of the proletarian work force, the emergence of the working-class family, and the large-scale economic trends that so completely transformed the Stéphanois region of France in the years between 1840 and 1880. It is also vital to look at the connection between the growth of the industrial working-class family and the early forms of political organization and militant action that developed in the region. The relationship between the demographic and familial aspects of class formation and its political aspects needs emphasizing because labor history and family history have developed so separately that, until recently, it was easy to forget that they often concern the same people. In the Roman world, "proletarian" referred to both social status and reproductive capacity. A "proletarian" was a "citizen of the lowest class, but regarded as useful as being a parent."[2] By neglecting the reproductive aspects of proletarian behavior, eighteenth- and nineteenth-century social thinkers ignored a crucial factor in the shaping of the modern industrial working classes. To nineteenth-century industrial workers, both work and family were key elements of social identity and important guides to social action. As we shall see time and again, putting industrial relations in the context of a family setting improves our insight into the meaning of workers' struggles.

This study focuses on three small industrial cities on the outskirts of Saint-Etienne: Le Chambon-Feugerolles, Rive-de-Gier, and Saint-Chamond. In addition to being smaller, more easy to study than Saint-Etienne and more purely working class, these communities offer the opportunity to analyze two key groups of industrial workers during different phases of economic development. These cities witnessed the growth of two industries that produced typical industrial proletarians of the late nineteenth century – metalworkers and miners. Because the pace of industrial growth proceeded unevenly in the Stéphanois, faster in Rive-de-Gier in the period 1840 to 1860, faster in Saint-Chamond and in Le Chambon-Feugerolles in the period 1860 to 1880, a look at several cities enables us to study the most rapidly growing urban centers during both phases of industrial expansion. Rive-de-Gier was an original center of the Industrial Revolution in France, an early coal mining town that evolved in the direction of metalworking and glassworking. Saint-Chamond was a garment city that developed into a capital of the metal industry. Starting as a village of ribbonweavers and miners, Le Chambon-Feugerolles turned into an important coal mining and metalworking town. Employment opportunities and demographic factors among Stéphanois cities varied substantially. A multi-city study has the virtue of providing a comparative context for judging the effects of these forces.

Comparing the new industrial proletariat with other groups engaged in industrial work helps to identify its distinctive features. At the very beginning of the period under study, 1840, skilled artisans and their families predominated in most of the larger urban centers. Except for Rive-de-Gier, where a coal mining population was just developing, artisanal workers, particularly ribbonweavers and arms makers, were the major component of the settled urban working classes. In all the area cities, families of artisans passed skills and often bits of property from generation to generation.

Sharing the burden of manual labor within the region, there were large numbers of less-skilled proletarians. In the early 1840s, clusters of domestic workers, such as nailmakers, cutlers, and plain silk ribbonweavers, who also engaged in agriculture lived in the small villages and hamlets of the Stéphanois valley. Some branches of these domestic industries were highly skilled but the vast majority demanded little skill. Outside the cities and small towns in the valley were tens of thousands of country folk who, like the inhabitants of the villages in the industrial valley, alternated between domestic industry in their cottage and agriculture.

Alongside these stable populations were transient unskilled and semi-skilled workers – sawyers, construction workers, and day laborers – who were seasonal or temporary migrants from the country. Between 1780 and 1840, most unskilled laborers in the industrial city were involved in what Olwen Hufton has labeled an "economy of makeshifts": they worked in local mills and manufactories for part of the year, in agriculture for another part of the year. Between mill and field, they might work as wood cutters, charcoal burners, ragpickers, masons, hawkers, navvies, and thatchers; in the interim, or when all else failed, they turned to begging.[3] These casual laborers were the "vagabonds" and "beggars" that figured so prominently as a disciplinary problem in eighteenth-century elite political debates.[4] In the case of many young migrant men and women who were saving for a return to the countryside or waiting to gain admittance to a trade, such an economy of "makeshifts" was a necessary but temporary step toward a secure place in society. For them, proletarianization only served as an apprenticeship which would end when they married, returned to the countryside, and raised children in peasant cottages.

Because proletarianization occupied an early stage in the life-cycle, few proletarians had children. Proletarians who did have children found the going rough, and their children were liable to be sentenced to the almost certain death of the foundling hospital. For proletarians, the presence of children made it less likely that they would ever attain the degree of social security that most sought; pregnant proletarian females often found themselves deserted. With little hope of being able to support children, single mothers as well as proletarian couples were often forced to abandon illegitimate children to those foundling hospitals which, whether their parents recognized it or not, were really institutions for legalized infanticide. Such institutions were agents of "death control" that dealt summarily with infants and young children. They were, as Harris and Ross have shown, part of a system, prevalent in pre-industrial societies, for eliminating the economically burdensome young.[5] Nothing is known about those who abandoned children at the *Hôpital de la charité* at Saint-Etienne but in nearby Lyon, between 1812 and 1861, seamstresses, domestic servants, textile workers and day-laborers were the chief occupations of women abandoning their children.[6]

A new industrial proletariat, employed mainly in mining and metalworking, developed in the coal basin around the city of Saint-Etienne between 1840 and 1880. This new proletariat was different from any social group that had existed previously in the region; it was more dependent on the employer than the artisan but more stable and permanent than the casual laborers. Unlike the artisans, this new industrial workforce lacked any collective control over skill; industrial proletarians usually possessed a degree of skill but their skills were taught by the employer or picked up on the job in the factory or the mine. This lack of collective control was the distinctive feature of "semi-skilled" and "skilled" industrial proletarians; the supply of industrial proletarians did not depend on internal regulation by customary institutions or on workers' organizations but on the cost to employers of training workers for the job or of recruiting able-bodied workers if job turnover was high. Unlike non-artisanal workers, the new industrial proletarians were engaged in full-time, year-round, industrial employment.

Another contrast with those seasonal or temporary migrants who had performed so much unskilled labor in the cities in the past was that an important segment of the new industrial proletarians comprised heads of families living in the city or people who lived in households headed by industrial proletarians. The role of industrial proletarians as heads of urban households was a new one in the Stéphanois region. The appearance of *families* of industrial proletarians is of utmost significance, because the creation of the industrial proletarian family is a crucial element in the process of industrial proletarian class formation. At its most basic level, class self-awareness builds on the expectation or the realization of class membership as a permanent condition. As Frank Parkin has noted, "Without the long-term continuity provided by the kinship link it would still be possible for inequality to persist, but not class stratification in the conventional meaning of the term."[7] Although his focus is overwhelmingly on male labor force activity and on masculine work experience, Edward Thompson gives a glancing recognition of the centrality of the family to the development of the class consciousness of both men and women when he notes that "class experience is largely determined by the productive relations in which men are born – or enter involuntarily."[8]

Both Parkin and Thompson agree that class is not simply a question of employment at a given point in time, but a genuinely historical category that must be defined over time. Class is not primarily about "empty places in the social structure that are filled by individuals," as a sociologist once defined it. Class involves projections about future conditions as well as present circumstances. Membership in a class depends on a worker's estimate of a life-time "trajectory" based on experience, expectations, and judgements.[9] Both the pauperized proletariat of the early decades of the nineteenth century and the relatively stable proletarians of later decades occupied the same empty places in the social structure. They both hauled the same heavy loads, followed the barked orders of the same supervisor, and drew the same pay every two weeks. But men beginning to identify themselves as "miners" and as "metalworkers" and gradually accustoming themselves to permanent residence in the city reacted differently to the conditions in industry than those who saw factory labor as a winter's work or as a way to pay off the mortgage on the farm. The extreme occupational instability of the first proletarians to enter Stéphanois factories had consigned them to membership of a socially amorphous pauper underclass which had very little sense of group consciousness.

In the course of the nineteenth century, an enduring industrial working class emerged alongside and finally replaced this underclass of proletarianized paupers. But in order for a class of industrial proletarians to develop a social identity and to organize and act collectively it had first to establish roots in the industrial city. This key transition, the settling of industrial workers in the city, must be understood in order to truly comprehend the making of a working class.

Both political and economic factors made the region in the nineteenth century an especially important unit of analysis for the discussion of class formation in nineteenth-century France. To a surprising extent between 1840 and 1880, centralized institutions such as the church and the state severely limited their efforts to relieve regional social problems; generally, regions were expected to care for the sick, the aged, and the impoverished on their own. Workers trying to plan for the future or to protect themselves against personal adversity had mainly to take account of local institutions, such as employers' policies, municipal aid, parish charities, or workers' mutual aid societies.

The spread of the fertility decline in France in this period also strengthened the regional character of labor recruitment. As one region of France after another witnessed a fertility decline, the competition for migrant labor heightened. Competing with regions such as Paris or nearby Lyon, the Stéphanois had little chance of attracting large numbers of long-distance proletarian migrants to its mines and mills. While France possessed a number of declining rural regions that might supply migrants, it did not possess the equivalent of an Ireland or of Germany's provinces east of the Elbe, whose seemingly inexhaustible supply of landless laborers would migrate long distances to wherever work was available. The bulk of the labor force had to be found nearby.[10]

The appearance of proletarian families was required for the reproduction of an enduring industrial working-class presence, because families in nineteenth-century society provided a variety of services that were practically unavailable elsewhere. In the nineteenth century, it was the family that raised children, nurtured the sick and injured, cared for the aged, and provided assistance to family members during times of decreased earnings. The working-class family economy was often a carefully balanced mechanism, the viability of which depended on the different contributions of each of its members.[11]

The growing recognition of the importance of social reproduction has sometimes tempted students of social change to portray reproduction as simply a reflection of the needs of the productive order, as the tool of exploitative ruling classes, or as a conquest of class struggle.[12] That social reproduction must be studied as the product both of human agents and of economic circumstances is only a recent discovery of historians and sociologists. The proletarian family was the creation of economic development providing wages and living conditions enabling an urban proletarian population to survive, of employers who wanted a stable labor force, and of workers who married and raised children in an urban environment. More important, however, demographic and familistic behavior are part and parcel of larger social behavior, and the integration of our different modes of viewing popular behavior embodied in disciplines such as demography, family history, and labor history is a necessity.[13] A central theme of this book is that the same set of long-term perspectives that promoted and shaped semi-skilled workers' collective consciousness also promoted and shaped their demographic behavior and the manner in which they lived in families.

These new, long-term perspectives characterizing this new industrial proletariat however can only be meaningfully understood in their historical context. Proletarian families arose in many regions of Europe in the nineteenth century but they responded to the process of class formation in a variety of ways. To understand the differences as well as similarities of this process, Stéphanois class formation must be located in a particular point in time, in the mid-nineteenth century, at a period when the state refused to assume substantial responsibility for social welfare, the church was relatively weak, and industrialization was still largely an unknown force. Stéphanois class formation also occurred within a particular national context. Although the region enjoyed an unusual degree of autonomy, it was far from independent. Class formation in the Stéphanois occurred in the France of Napoleon III, in a country where the labor movement was repressed, where the government searched to build popular support, and where the ruler was committed to military intervention.

In the Stéphanois between 1840 and 1880, a key force in the development of proletarian families was a vast increase in capital concentration in industry. Capital concentration demanded steady, year-round economic activity and permitted employers to pursue managerial strategies that benefited the firm over the long haul. By creating long-term employment opportunities, capital accumulation also made it possible for workers to organize their lives and those of family members on the basis of the requirements and working conditions of urban industrial employment.[14] As soon as workers began regarding themselves as miners or metalworkers, living in a specific urban *milieu*, they were able to build expectations about the conditions of old age, sickness, and accident based on their knowledge of employer policies. Once established in an industrial city, workers could judge their children's chances of surviving to maturity based on their own experience in the city and that of their friends and neighbors. Furthermore, looking around them, they could see what services growing children might be able to provide for their families and with what kinds of education it would be necessary to furnish their children.

While capital concentration created the economic basis for the rise of a new kind of working class in the Stéphanois region, managerial and employer strategies struggled to shape the direction in which the new labor force would develop. Inevitably, employer benefits brought dangers to the family as well as advantages. The more employers sought to intervene to encourage the development of families, the more they strengthened their control and authority over a crucial area of their workers' lives. Families' responses to employer policies and to the conditions of urban industrial life were absolutely crucial to the survival and growth of the industrial proletarian family. In important ways, the destiny of the nineteenth-century industrial working-class family was intertwined with epochal changes in demographic behavior and labor-force participation that altered the patterns of family life among the popular classes in France.

An analysis of the relationship between proletarianization and family life is especially significant because of the particular saliency of family ties to the social cohesion of industrial proletarians. Of course family relations are of great psychological and sentimental importance to everyone. Family is one of those central social relations that is connected to almost everything. Yet, however important family ties were to artisans and peasants, they were part of a many-stranded social relationship in which family ties, property relations, and skill were bound up with one another. Among these groups, land, skill, and kin ties all mutually reinforced one another and together helped to create a sense of collective consciousness and group identity.[15] Deprived of land and skill, the social unity wrought by the industrial proletarian family was a more single-stranded relationship. Their more complete reliance on family ties for the forging of a sense of collective solidarity made industrial proletarians especially sensitive to employer efforts to manipulate family life.

In the middle decades of the nineteenth century in France, conflict was particularly likely to arise in the strategically valuable but unmarked terrain occupied by the industrial proletarian family. This was a crucial period when the basic "rules of the game" *vis-à-vis* industrial work and the proletarian family were being shaped by employers and workers. Some recent labor historians have described the working-class family as a privatistic institution that diverted workers' attentions away from political struggles.[16] By increasing workers' responsibilities and obligations, the development of family institutions may have exerted a conservatizing influence. But in so far as the decision to marry and have children indicated a permanent commitment to urban industrial life, and in so far as the family crystallized workers' loyalties and sentiments and served to generate needs and interests distinct from their employers, the family could also incite workers to battle against their employers. Conservatives have more accurately understood the capacity of family sentiments to mobilize men and women than have radicals. Although he was hardly thinking about industrial workers, Edmund Burke had an important insight into the roots of solidarity when he noted that "we begin our public affections in our families. No cold relation is a zealous citizen."[17]

Often, when issues of class reproduction are placed into a historical context, they reveal that the familistic rhetoric of employers and workers could be a source of class tension and conflict. The neat overlay between the interests of workers and some employers in sponsoring the working-class family broke down because the family served different purposes for workers and employers.

A useful and important illustration of many of the most sensitive issues in the relationship between the proletarian family and the process of class formation emerges in the case of coal miners in the small Stéphanois town of Rive-de-Gier in the 1840s. For reasons discussed in the next chapter, the coal miners of Rive-de-Gier were the earliest permanent proletarians to develop in the Stéphanois region, though their relative newness still needs to be kept in mind. The year 1840 marked the bare beginnings of growth, and during the stormy years between 1844 and 1849, the majority of settled Ripagérien miners had probably not been at work for a decade. The issues raised by the miners of Rive-de-Gier in the 1840s would be raised by industrial proletarians throughout much of the Stéphanois region in subsequent decades.

But while the issues raised for the first time in the 1840s would recur and grow more prominent – for they were endemic problems of class formation – many of the solutions proposed at that time would fade away. The decade of the 1840s was characterized by a search for alternatives to the new industrial order of unparalleled dimensions. The era that culminated in the Second Republic marks both a beginning and an end. Gareth Stedman Jones's analysis of the early English labor movement holds doubly true for France: "there was no belief in the inevitability of industrial capitalism in the 1830s and 1840s . . . For workers the precariousness of the new system, however terrible, offered sources of hope."[18] The failure of the Second Republic forced workers to realize that there was no way to avoid the regime of industrial capitalism. Workers' experiences in the factory and in the industrial city were not temporary but enduring features of an industrial order of prodigious strength and power. Precisely this realization of the rootedness of the industrial order, however hated and despised, formed the background for the development of family life and work experience in the succeeding decades. Recognizing the reality of capitalist power, the next generation of proletarian rebels would develop its fundamental criticisms from within the new system.

If a look at the battles of Ripagérien coal miners in the 1840s reveals the salience of family to an understanding of proletarian conflict, it also identifies some problematic aspects of the relationship between family and the development of a class orientation. An analysis of these events helps to locate issues that had to be resolved for a broader, more class-oriented political program to emerge. Clarifying the issues at stake, first involves examining the coal company's efforts to promote the development of a stable proletarian labor force, and then examining the growth and culmination of a proletarian response.

THE ADVENT OF A NEW INDUSTRIAL ORDER IN THE STÉPHANOIS

Fundamental political questions concerning relationships between the industrial working-class, the proletarian family, and the new capitalist economic order were posed very early and with extraordinary clarity in the Stéphanois region in the 1840s. A number of large companies had begun to encourage proletarians to form families in the area, but the most ambitious efforts to establish a program for the long-term welfare of workers and their families was that instituted by the powerful coal monopoly that gradually established its hold between 1836 and 1846. The company's efforts to promote family membership among its work force was necessary because the company's size and financial strength enabled it to transform the work process; this transformation increased its need for a stable workforce. Under the able leadership of a one-time Saint-Simonian, Gustave Delahante, the monopoly, known as the Compagnie des mines de la Loire, connected and coordinated the separate mining pits, closing the least productive mines but dramatically expanding production in the richer ones.[19]

In the process of modernizing the mines, the company took new responsibilities for recruiting the labor force. It removed the recruitment of workers from the control of overseers drawn from the ranks of coal miners. Both for recruitment and in terms of setting the base rate of pay, university-trained engineers were put in charge of each pit and became the major sources of authority in a more centralized administrative structure. As the mines expanded, horses replaced children in drawing the coal carts and subsequent installation of rails in the mines allowed the horses to draw heavier loads; this transformation dramatically reduced the demand for child labor in the mines. The coordination of the mines and their extension also lengthened the time it took miners to get to the coal face. Since pay was based on productivity, time spent getting to the coal face was entirely uncompensated. In the older mining areas, particularly in Rive-de-Gier, the oldest mining area in the region, the time spent getting to work was often over an hour. The company's failure to compensate workers for their long underground journey to work combined with the new role of the engineer in hiring and setting the basic rates of payment enraged many miners. Hiring outsiders unfamiliar with established work practices was one way of putting pressure on the established miners. At a time when job opportunities for children were becoming much scarcer the person in charge of bringing in new workers to the work group was a stranger to mining practices and often unfamiliar with local methods.[20]

Veteran miners lamented the disappearance of the informal relations that they claimed had bound the old overseers and their workers. An old-hand regretted that "formerly we had masters . . . who talked familiarly with us, who cared about us, who liked us. But today they treat you as less than a dog. It is necessary to do what they order you without saying a word or they fire you." The breakup of the system of sub-contracting may also have destroyed the recruitment networks, which practiced preferential hiring for the children of coal miners. In any case, the miners charged that "strangers" were given preferential treatment in hiring.[21] Furthermore, the miners particularly resented the engineers, who they believed did not know very much about the work. According to one miner,

in the old days [*anciennement*] it was the *gouverneur* who set the length of the day, the workers were less loaded down than today, because the *gouverneur* was a man who, having been a worker himself was acquainted with the work, while an engineer having never handled anything but a quill, never suspected how hard the work was.[22]

While reducing miners control over their work, the company offered the workers rudimentary social benefits. In order to promote the development of a stable workforce, the company attempted to ease the burden that confronted families in the industrial city. The prospect offered by company spokesmen was one of a secure future for workers and their families protected by sickness and accident insurance and eventually by retirement benefits. Almost from its inception the monopoly began constructing hospitals, expanding the available medical care to include family members, and enlarging sickness and accident pay so as to better support workers' dependants.[23] The company wanted to maintain workers and their families in the Stéphanois but on terms that kept workers and their families immediately dependent on company benevolence. Writing in the 1860s, a careful student of company insurance funds cited one of the principal reasons for their inauguration: "The fund would attract workers, render the owners more competitive, while giving them a greater degree of authority and power over the whole work force."[24]

The other side of the company's policy of extended benefits to its workforce and members of their families was a policy of wage reduction which made its work force more dependent on company benefits and "generosity." By dominating local production, the monopoly could dictate wages. In 1844, a local author summarized the reasons for the miners' suspicions:

Unless one supposes the miners possess a stupidity more than bestial, does one pretend that they do not see preparing itself . . . an organization within which they will not longer have the least security for their existence or that of their families? Are they able to doubt that a unified administration would reduce, as much of their wages as it wants, when it wants, today 50 centimes, the day after tomorrow as much, up to the extreme limit of their strength and of their patience, until hunger, until death?[25]

Their fears were soon realized. The massive strike that brought 2,000 workers out in April and May of 1844 was provoked chiefly by the last in a series of successive wage reductions. The "hungry forties" was an uncertain economic era and the new company responded to fluctuating demand by cutting production, lowering wages and so holding prices steady. While the strike began in response to lowered wages, demands soon arose for a fixed wage schedule, a *conseil de prudhommes* to settle disputes in the mines, and an accident insurance fund administered by the workers. Thanks to vigorous government intervention, the strike was defeated after two months of bitter conflict.[26]

In the aftermath of the 1844 strike, the victorious coal monopoly revealed its own strategy for preserving the existence of working-class families during times of crisis. Agricultural crisis due to poor harvests in 1846 and 1847 led to an industrial depression that desolated most local industries and their workers. Throughout the region, the situation of the working classes became desperate as food prices rose. In October 1847, an alarmed prefect reported that

Already misery has begun to reach the majority of families. Jewelry, furniture, even looms have been sold to buy bread. Many have already spent everything they possess. Thus in order to procure the necessities some have resorted to begging during the day, but the greater part beg during the night . . .[27]

But the miners were spared the worst effects of a disaster that might have emptied the mining region. In 1845 and 1846, the miners' real wages, already reduced as a result of the 1844 cuts, plummeted due to the rapid rise of bread prices. But in early 1847, the Compagnie des mines took action; it promised that it would completely subsidize the price of bread whenever it rose above 45 centimes per loaf. Since bread had already passed this price in late 1846, the company announcement really represented a wage increase. Tokens to be redeemed by the coal company were issued that could be presented to bakers by coal miners and their families.[28] Single men who were not members of families, probably migrants living in boarding houses, grumbled about the company's measures. The majority of single men paid for their food at the boarding house and had no time to stand in line to redeem their tokens; many single men were probably willing to sacrifice bread to increase the cash savings they were accumulating so that they could return to the countryside. As a result, the company's measures did not satisfy them, and their wages continued to fall. But the evident satisfaction of miners' families and the disastrous economic conditions did not favor a strike.[29]

In 1847, the company succeeded in aiding its workers with families without conceding an across-the-board wage increase. The overall reduction of workers' income that occurred in the 1840s makes it difficult to identify the monopoly's strategy as one of paternalism, but it did differentiate and privilege the position of its stable employees and those who had families. Despite economic crisis, the company was determined to maintain workers with families in order to preserve for itself an experienced and stable workforce and also to insure its future supply of workers.

ALTERNATIVES TO THE NEW INDUSTRIAL ORDER

Toward the end of 1844, an eloquent and idealistic young lawyer, M. Sain, explained to a crowded courtroom why a group of several hundred residents of a mining town, including women and children, threw rocks at troops escorting arrested strikers during the miners' strike of May and June of that year. He explained, "The authorities should have avoided transporting [the prisoners] in open carts in broad daylight in the midst of crying mothers and wives, those poor workers that they knew at the bottom of their heart to be in the right . . ."[30] Sain clearly hoped that the court would recognize family loyalty as an extenuating circumstance for social violence. While the court ignored Sain's pleas and imposed severe sentences on the miners, there was still a logic to his argument. Although saying so would have won no credit with middle-class audiences, family concerns in the 1840s helped to make proletarian coal miners a sympathetic audience for radical social doctrines. One reason new political ideas appealed to workers is that they offered alternatives to the relationship between the world of the family and the world of work from that so recently espoused by their employers. In opposition to the company's efforts to use workers' families as one more tool for increasing the monopoly's control over their lives, workers drew on radical ideas to fashion a program for rendering the working-class family less dependent on the employer.

The strikes and battles of the 1840s are crucial to an understanding of the actions of proletarian miners in the decisive confrontation of 1848 and to the analysis of workers' initial response to permanent proletarianization. During the struggles of the 1840s, reformers and radicals propagandized the working classes in an effort to win them as political allies. In the process, they widened workers' conceptions of alternatives to the new order. The visits of outside radicals and the subsequent appearance of Parisian reform periodicals were important to working-class political thinking which matured and developed in relation to, and partially in response to, the ideas of radicals and reformers.[31] During the revolutionary period that followed the successful uprising of February 1848, Stéphanois workers responded to the challenge of industrial capitalism by taking bits and pieces of the reform ideas offered to them in the preceding decade and reshaping them to suit their own purposes.

The 1844 strike first helped to spread new ideas among the miners. The national concern with the growth of the Stéphanois coal monopoly, the militant miners' strike of 1844, and the proximity of the city of Lyon (perhaps the most radical city in France in the 1830s and early 1840s) all put Rive-de-Gier and other Stéphanois towns on the itinerary of French radicals. During the miners' strike, Flora Tristan visited Saint-Etienne and Rive-de-Gier and argued for her plan to unite the miners and all workers into a workers' union. Brochures by Jules Leroux, the brother of the working-class Saint-Simonian Pierre Leroux, were distributed in large quantities to the miners urging them to unite with other workers as the first step in the creation of associations that would include both workers and employers. A frightened local administration claimed that "communist ideas" were spreading among the miners; indeed, followers of Etienne Cabet had already established a following in Rive-de-Gier before 1844, and the strike allowed them to win new recruits. In Paris, the Fourierist newspaper *La Démocratie Pacifique* developed local contacts who, for the next four years, periodically reported on events in Rive-de-Gier.[32]

One of the common themes that emerged from all these propaganda efforts was the importance of "association," one of those magic words in the decade before 1848. Like that other great magic formula, "the organization of work," "association" was a success because it encompassed so many kinds of disparate phenomena. In the early 1840s, "association" could be used to describe producers' and consumers' cooperatives, insurance societies of all description, recreational clubs and even limited stock companies which in turn included the collective workshops of highly skilled workers and the mutual aid societies of less-skilled migrants to the city. Almost all reformers of the 1840s were in favor of associations. Middle-class republicans saw "associations" as the best hope for the working class, but so did Saint-Simon, Tristan, Fourier, and Cabet.[33]

At the moment when radicals from throughout France came to Rive-de-Gier to preach the virtues of associationism, the workers of Rive-de-Gier were already surrounded by artisanal workers organizing associations of all types in Saint-Etienne and Lyon. A wave of associationism had swept the region in the early 1830s, as Stéphanois and Lyonnais silkweavers organized associations that were crushed with brutal force and a loss of working-class lives. Between 1840 and 1844, new efforts to form associations of silkworkers in Lyon and Saint-Etienne were again repressed.[34]

In 1848, the mutual disillusionment and outrage that resulted when reformers tried to legally implement their conflicting concepts of "associationism" is well known. Less well known however is the cross-fertilization within the labor movement that the debate over the nature of associationism produced in the years before 1848. As workers politicized and rallied around the republican banner in the 1840s, second-generation followers of Saint-Simon and Cabet attempted to adapt their masters' principles in the direction of workers' associations. Because of the dominance of the large coal monopoly and the nation-wide interest it attracted as an example of modern industry, many efforts were made to apply the radical principles of associationism to this large enterprise. The young Proudhon, living in Lyon and strongly influenced by Cabet, visited Rive-de-Gier and himself sketched out a project for creating associations in the mines.[35]

In 1844 in Rive-de-Gier, followers of Cabet were apparently the most important of the radical groups. Cabet advocated the adoption of a "transitional" regime, that might last 50 or 100 years, before the full institution of communism. During the transitional regime, private property would be allowed to exist but 500 million francs would be spent each year to "provide work to workers and lodging for the poor." The public domain would be "transformed into city, villages, or farms, that would be turned over to a portion of the poor," as a form of poor relief. And "the education of new generations will be one of the principal objects of the public solicitude." Each year French society would move in the direction of republican control over all industry and the creation of a regime where everyone would work and where the republic would assume responsibility for the care of the aged and the young.[36]

The most well-worked out scheme for the Ripagérien mines was that of the Fourierist, Victor Hennequin, who frequently visited the Lyonnais area.[37] Claiming that Fourierist ideas were very well known in the department of the Loire (the department that included the Stéphanois region), Hennequin published a series of articles in a Fourierist newspaper in 1846 describing a scheme for organizing the mines into an association; the pieces were published shortly thereafter by the Fourierist publishing house.

Hennequin drew on Fourier's ideas for first principles and described a plan for restructuring and reorganizing the mining monopoly that refined Fourier's conception of a transitional stage between a corrupt and decadent "civilization," and a perfected and completed future state of "harmonism." To prepare the way for "harmonism," Fourier foresaw the establishment of large agricultural colonies that would provide security for industrial workers during times of unemployment; gradually these agricultural colonies would be transformed into

Phalanges, Fourier's term for his ideal settlements. The predominantly agricultural *Phalanges* would occupy most of the lives of their residents, who would spend only a few years working in the mines. As we shall see, at the time he was writing, Fourier's vision of a rural-based working class that spent several years in urban industry was far from unrealistic; indeed, Fourier visited the Stéphanois several times and may have drawn on his observations in that region when he wrote on organizing work in the mines. Always anxious to distinguish his own plan for social reorganization from that of socialists, Fourier had no desire to destroy the difference between proletarians and capitalists and envisaged these distinctions continuing to exist in the *Phalanges*. But Fourier emphasized that the poorest member of a *Phalange* would be better off than the most wealthy member of contemporary French society.

In the pamphlet he published and circulated, adapting Fourier's plans specifically to the Stéphanois, Hennequin discussed only those reforms needed to proceed toward the intermediate stage of "guaranteeism." The beauty of Hennequin's pamphlet was that it took Fourier's large-scale plans and related them to local needs and grievances. Hennequin emphasized that "we do not demand of the companies actually exploiting the mines of the Loire that they actually realize our ideals, but only of moving toward them, in the measure of their good will and of their ability."[38] Although Fourier himself was suspicious of large-scale industry, Hennequin defended the integrity of the mining monopoly against those who would decentralize it. Perhaps drawing on Saint-Simonian ideas, Hennequin explained that large-scale industrial organization was far more efficient than the regime of small-scale production that had preceded the monopoly. Although Hennequin wanted to involve workers in the management of the monopoly, his proposals never went beyond giving workers a share in management which would still have given capitalistic stockholders disproportionate influence in the company; here, Hennequin faithfully followed Fourier's ideas.

Working-class family problems figured prominently in Hennequin's scheme. Here he showed Fourier's influence in his concern with the concrete details of daily life among coal miners and his attention to the workers' life-cycle. As Barbara Taylor has shown, the penchant of social thinkers such as Fourier, Cabet, and Saint-Simon for detailing the conditions of future society often made them more sensitive to gender, age, and life-cycle issues than did the Marxist concentration on the organization of production.[39] Hennequin transformed Fourier's scheme to supplement industrial work with agricultural work into a program that addressed the concrete needs of Ripagérien coal miners caused by the lack of work for females and for young males; due to the difficult terrain adjacent to the city, unlike other miners in the region, few miners in Rive-de-Gier owned land where their families could garden or maintain small farms, and there were no industries that employed females in that city.[40] He proposed that the wives and children of miners be given access to land in the countryside that they could till. Periodically, the miners themselves would exchange places with agricultural workers in order to relieve the monotony and physical hardships of mining by working in the fields. Not emphasized in the brochure on coal mining were Fourier's plans for the abolition of most of the traditional aspects of family life including monogamy and parental authority.

Besides his plans for reorganizing work, Hennequin suggested a variety of proposals for changes in the organization of working-class family life. Clearly, he hoped that the coal mining association he advocated would assume the burden for many responsibilities currently in the hands of the working-class family. The coal mining association that he planned to form would be an extraordinarily powerful organization on a much larger scale than those envisaged by Fourier. Hennequin emphasized the need to form a unified coal mining association in the Loire that would have equal representation from the mining company, the coal miners, and local coal consumers. For the workers, he promised

Minimum [wage] assured to the miners . . . Organization of day nurseries [*crèches*], child shelters [*salles d'asile*], schools, infirmaries, hospitals and old age pensions: aid to widows and orphans, dividends paid to the workers from the profits of the exploitation, spirit of property developed and satisfied among them. Conservation of the miners' health by a diminution of the hours of work in the pits and galleries, and by their participation in industries organized on the surface of the earth.[41]

But as the Lyonnais followers of Cabet became increasingly divided in 1846 and as Cabet turned more and more in the direction of founding colonies in the United States, the influence of the Fourierists seems to have increased. In any case, both the followers of Cabet and the followers of Fourier agreed that the triumph of the republic would mean a giant step forward for the cause that they served.

ASSOCIATION AND REPUBLICAN POLITICS IN RIVE-DE-GIER IN 1848

The collapse of the July Monarchy and the on-going weakness of the governments that held power in 1848 and 1849 created a national power vacuum and led to confrontation between workers and their employers in the Stéphanois. In the course of 1848, the economic and social policy of large-scale industrialists in the Stéphanois was challenged by an alternative policy developed by industrial workers, which drew on local experiences and on the writings of social critics. These struggles enable us to get some idea of the workers' grievances against the company and the means that workers thought should be used to remedy the situation. Equally important, the outcome of these struggles influenced the whole subsequent history of the Stéphanois region. Among those many aspects of working-class life that were powerfully shaped by this battle was the course of industrial proletarian family life.

The spread of new social doctrines among Stéphanois coal miners in the 1840s had a powerful impact on workers' behavior during the Second Republic. As demonstrated in 1848, the spread of republicanism, Fourierism, and Cabetian communism, combined with the workers' own experiences and knowledge, encouraged the development of a political program among local workers. Working-class politicization encouraged workers to construct organizations and institutions that ultimately challenged the existing political structure with arms.

At the same time the political program of these workers was not a class program; it discouraged workers as a class from confronting capitalists as a class. Indeed, in the 1840s, there was little basis for the development of class consciousness among Stéphanois miners. The majority of coal miners had been employed in the mines for less than a decade. In the city, miners were surrounded by artisanal workers attempting to form associations joining together skilled workers and small-scale employers. Both artisans and workers were propagandized by social critics who unanimously agreed that workers and employers must advance together along the path of social progress. Indeed, what Stéphanois coal miners were fighting in 1848 was not so much a class struggle as a struggle to reverse the developments that were working to make them permanent proletarians. In Adam Przeworski's terms, 1848 in the Stéphanois was more a battle "about class" than a class struggle.[42]

The Second Republic witnessed a remarkable outbreak of popular militancy in Rive-de-Gier, the scope of which extends far beyond that of the present analysis. News of the outbreak of insurrection in Paris on February 23, 1848, and of the departure of Louis-Philippe and the formation of a provisional government on February 25, quickly spread through a Stéphanois region that was already near boiling point due to the growing opposition to the coal monopoly. In the early morning of February 27, in Saint-Etienne, officials noted nervously that the "workers received their [bi-weekly] pay last night and this leads us to fear that the day may not pass peacefully."[43] In fact, on February 26, a crowd had already forced the municipality to hoist a red flag over the city hall. In the evening a crowd burned a mannequin outside the city hall that was labeled "Vachier" and "Escoffier," the names of two City Councilmen known as defenders of the mining company. Also attached to the mannequin was the placard "Goodbye to the Mines." As the mannequin burned, there were cries of "Down with the Monopoly!"[44]

The anti-monopoly spirit that quickly surfaced in the Stéphanois in 1848 had been growing throughout the region in the final years of the July Monarchy. It was not opposed by the new political coalition of professional men and master artisans that led the popular upsurge. David Gordon has identified the members of this new coalition as "artisans, and lawyers, doctors and engineers."[45] They were, however, less sympathetic to strikes. On February 28, some miners of Rive-de-Gier tried to launch a strike against the coal monopoly. The newly appointed Prefect, M. Sain, the lawyer who had defended the miners in 1844, dispatched troops to end the strike. The approach of troops broke up efforts to call a strike but during the next day all the influence of the now Sub-Prefect Tristan Duché (another lawyer who had defended the miners against Orleanist prosecutions) was necessary to convince miners not to go out on strike.[46]

Local authorities worried about the turn of events in Rive-de-Gier appointed a mayor who could be counted on to preserve order. However, one of the major activities of this mayor was to bombard the military with the news that events were getting out of hand and with requests for troops. The military reported:

Rive-de-Gier causes uneasiness. Communism has made progress there and the formation of the national guard presents some difficulties. One would not very well want to arm the citizens who belong to this sect but it is to be feared . . . that they will commit excesses or disorder if one does not arm them as [one arms] other citizens.[47]

During April, the coal company reduced the working week from six to four days and asked for the required government authorization to close some of the least productive pits.[48] New and existing company provisions for workers' families and the increased wage rates conceded in 1848 seemed a farce when the company threatened to discharge workers wholesale. The projected closing of pits and the reduction of the working week undermined all the company's prior efforts at conciliation. Although local miners were quite familiar with wage reductions, they had suffered very little from unemployment. In 1844, a student of local mining had noted that " in this respect, the miners have a condition less bad than that of the greater part of manufacturing workers, who are liable to be thrown out of work from one day to another during a crisis. A crisis diminishes the salary of the mine worker but it rarely leaves him without any resources."[49] By September 1844, the Prefect was able to extort a promise from the company to further reduce its workforce only by attrition.[50]

Rumors of the projected mine closings seems to have stimulated miners to militant actions. On April 9, 1848, republicans planted liberty trees in Saint-Etienne and Rive-de-Gier; within the week, miners in Saint-Etienne and Rive-de-Gier began to plant the liberty tree in the coal mines themselves.[51] Sensing a "very serious" situation, the conservative economist Adolphe Blanqui traveled to the region to investigate. He observed that in April,

imitating of Paris, after the revolution of February, the workers chased away the old supervisors, the old engineers as (if these employees were) the dethroned dynasty, and they gave orders to the most powerful industrial society, notified by proclamations like the following:

The French Republic.
Liberty, Equality, Fraternity
We, the undersigned, members of the committee of pits Grangette, called Basseville, N. 5, considering that it is urgent to replace the supervisor *in a legal manner* have

proposed and do propose:
1. There exists in each pit a different way of working. 2. The workers knowing all (these ways) will chose better than anyone who should govern.
As a consequence, after having maturely examined that which is best for us, we have named citizens L., C. and N., to replace Citizen E., the present supervisor, and wishing to conform to the present government, we name him only the provisional supervisor, giving the company the choice of choosing which one of the three they wish . . .[52]

Blanqui commented that "is it not a curious importation from politics into industry, these provisional governments and these pit presidents, named in a revolutionary manner, without speaking of company agents fired by their workers?"[53]

The election of supervisors blended together a variety of traditions and ideas that had spread among local miners in the 1840s. In those few local mines that were too small to join or to concern the coal monopoly, authority in the mines was still exercised by men recruited from the ranks of miners. Allowing the company some role in the selection of the supervisor recalls the propaganda of the Fourierists who had preached the need for workers to participate alongside the capitalists in the administration of the mines. Cabetian communists had spread the idea that the republicans should control industry and that republican principles should be practiced within industry.

The election of supervisors continued in Saint-Etienne and in Rive-de-Gier for only about four months but it left a lasting impression. In 1884, a parliamentary committee investigating a proposal that safety delegates should be elected by miners elicited the following recollections from the Stéphanois mining representatives:

The oldest of our directors of the mines of the Loire still has memories [of elected representatives in 1848] . . . The difficulties multiplied, spirits grew embittered, the least details became the occasion for demands carried solemnly and imperiously to the directors by these delegates. The smallest efforts of these latter [refers to the elected representatives] and often the most unfortunate, was followed breathlessly by the workers, considering the success of their representations as a question of honor. The menace of a cessation of work appeared immediately to support it.
In fact, the delegates were becoming the masters of the mines and substituting themselves to the engineers, who . . . were on the point of quitting the field.[54]

Despite the June Days in Paris and the entry of a military column into Rive-de-Gier to disarm their National Guard, the miners of Rive-de-Gier were still not beaten. Miners participated enthusiastically in the meetings to elect delegates to the inquiry on agriculture and industry mandated by the government. The police commissioner noted that "the miners attach very much importance to this convocation, and they are proposing to request an authorization for the reconstitution of their club."[55]

The reports from the miners of Rive-de-Gier prepared in September 1848 gave miners a rare chance to enunciate fully their program of industrial reform. The responses to the government inquiry from several mines in Saint-Etienne and Rive-de-Gier were similar and indicate a degree of coordination among miners in the center and the eastern basin. As some Stéphanois miners and the Ripagérien miners saw it, the answer to their problems was association: "it would be of the greatest importance for all industries as well as for the heads of workshops that the worker be associated with them and share in the profits."[56] With association, the workers would be the employers as well, "the number of buckets of coal would be seriously counted and the interior work would be treated with very much more care." Under the association, supervisors would be elected by those experienced workers whose "practical knowledge would better enable him to direct the works with more intelligence."[57] Meanwhile the republican government in Paris would regulate the length of the working week, the duration of the work day, and the minimum wage.

The workers' responses to the administration inquiry stressed their dilemma as family members and particularly as fathers of families. The workers pleaded for support "for the household where there are 4, 5, and 6 children who are not yet able to work . . . These poor children are covered with rags and sometimes go barefoot for lack of money to buy shoes."[58] The miners reiterated their complaints that the company's policy of wage reductions had had a particularly devastating effect on fathers of families: "one has seen, during this sad period, poor mine workers and chiefly fathers of families who, in order to provide bread for their children and in order not to displease a supervisor, have exposed themselves to dangers that these latter [the supervisors] have not had the experience to recognize."[59] A further complaint was that "Fathers of families are obliged to impose on themselves rigorous deprivations which are yoked to the duration of their work. It results that they are quickly worn out and that while still young they become incapable of working."[60] A later chapter will explore miners' life-cycle experience in greater detail, but it is also notable that already in 1848 miners were considering long-term effects of mining on the workers' health in framing their demands.

One of the most important concerns of miners however was to withdraw from their employers' control those aspects of work life that affected the workers' families. The miners complained of discrimination and niggardliness in the company's administration of the sickness and accident fund. They believed that the solution was for representatives elected by the workers to watch over these funds and to invest them with some "honest capitalists" (*de quelques honnêtes gens capitalistes*).[61]

Concurrently with their efforts to share the administration of the enterprise with their employers, Ripagérien miners tried to limit the participation of non-native workers in their association. The association was conceived almost as a new type of corporation, with native working-class membership based on apprenticeship and family ties. Miners justified the need of apprenticeship for two reasons:

The workers of other industries have been able to find a means of throwing back [*rejetter*] hands from the countryside by putting very severe conditions on their mode of apprenticeship in imposing on the apprentices a long period of time and a considerable sum for their indemnity and by this means they have been able to throw into our industry that which renders us more miserable . . . also, a large number of veteran workers have perished due to the lack of knowledge concerning safety of men who enter without knowing how to work . . .[62]

To insure their wage levels and to provide for their safety, the miners intended to create a formal apprenticeship system in mining and to require indemnities for workers who were "strangers to the locality and to the industry." Miners' children entering the mines as youths would not be expected to pay an indemnity and as they reached the required age they would enter freely into the apprenticeship system.

The miners' concerns for their families and their suspicion of migrants reflected the views of coal miners whose position in industry was becoming permanent. Many of the recent migrants whose presence might have modulated these sentiments were no longer around in September of 1848. By September, the contraction of mining jobs had sent many young migrants back to the countryside, and the decision of the Ripagérien City Council to purge non-natives from the Municipal Workshops had further decreased the migrant population. Certainly, the 1848 *enquêtes* throughout the Stéphanois reveal the bitter hostility against migrant workers that was widespread in 1848. Such sentiments emerged only a few months after gangs of French workers in Lyon had attacked foreign workers.[63] More than a trace of urban prejudice against rural dwellers can be seen in the miners' arguments. The miners alleged that restrictions on outsiders would benefit agricultural production which they claimed was suffering because too many rural dwellers were swarming into the mining communities. In the miners' opinion, migrants dazzled by city ways (Rive-de-Gier had a population of almost 12,000 in 1846) and unaccustomed to mining ways soon "wished that they had never set foot in the mines."[64]

The inquiry of September 1848 is one piece of detailed evidence concerning Ripagérien miners' political outlook. After December 1848, because of the growing climate of repression, the Ripagérien workers' movement went increasingly underground, though it reappeared in time to contribute to the left-wing triumph in the department, in July 1849, that sent a majority of left-wing republicans to the chamber.[65] The lack of government interest in the miners' proposals and the increased atmosphere of repression strengthened the hands of those local republicans belonging to longstanding secret societies that had their center in the adjacent Lyonnais. The republican movement in Rive-de-Gier crested in June 1849. In Paris, left-wing republican deputies (the so-called *Montagnards*) committed an act of extraordinary political folly on June 13, when, after the failure of Ledru-Rollin's efforts to impeach President Louis Napoleon Bonaparte for sending French republican troops to crush Italian republicans, they issued a call to revolution but actually planned only a peaceful demonstration in Paris. There was little response to such a confused appeal in Paris, but on June 15, barricades arose in the Croix-Rousse suburb of Lyon and bloody conflict ensued.[66] When news reached Rive-de-Gier that there was an uprising in Lyon, the local republicans, many of them armed, marched in a band of 150 men towards Lyon in order to aid their embattled comrades. At the outskirts of Lyon they were informed that the insurrection had been defeated. However, Ripagérien republicanism was hopelessly compromised by its association with this armed rising. The repression that followed resulted in the imprisonment or exile of dozens of local leaders, and most deputies elected from the Loire fled into exile from Paris.[67]

By the end of June 1849, whatever republican currents still existed in Rive-de-Gier had been driven so deeply underground that their political program – indeed their existence – escape the historian. But between 1849 and 1851, several large and militant strikes occurred in the Ripagérien mines, and great disaffection with Louis Napoleon remained. The rate of abstentions in the plebiscite of 1851 ratifying Louis Napoleon's *coup d'état* was among the highest in France.[68] Despite being underground, republicanism was to remain deeply rooted within the Stéphanois working classes. At every opportunity throughout the 1850s and in the early 1860s, Stéphanois workers indicated their opposition to the Empire and their continuing allegiance to the republican *!* cause.

CLASS FORMATION AND WORKING-CLASS FAMILIES: THE STÉPHANOIS REGION

Despite their extreme combativeness, the coal miners of Rive-de-Gier in 1848 and 1849 retained their associationist faith that, by working together with the aid of government, workers and employers could create equity in the work place and sustain the workers' families. Eventually, the miners hoped, profit-sharing, the participation of workers in administration, and the regulation of working conditions would dissolve the distinction between employer and workers. To place the events of 1848 and 1849 within a framework of class struggle would be easy; but the question that needs to be addressed is why the participants themselves did not place their actions within this framework, since 25 years later, workers not a bit more daring and combative than these miners would unhesitatingly do so. Why were the miners of 1848 so militant yet so conciliatory? Why would the miners of the 1870s be more class-oriented? Why would other local proletarian workers in the 1870s also move towards the adoption of a class orientation?

An analysis of the development of the proletarian family and the services that it provided for its members can contribute to understanding the movement of workers in the direction of class action between 1848 and the late 1860s and

1870s. A look at the events of 1848 shows that family considerations were important to miners and were an important motive in workers' efforts to restructure the entire industrial system. But these same family considerations remained in the wake of the Second Republic and it is necessary to understand the ways in which they continued to influence workers who recognized the viability of the new industrial regime. A longer view and a closer attention to the changing conditions of working-class life can provide a better understanding of these effects. It hardly seems coincidental that the miners of Rive-de-Gier – the first permanent proletarians to establish themselves and their families in the region – were so militant. Yet established workers' suspicion of migrants and their efforts to privilege their male children at the migrants' expense certainly limited the field of class action.

Relationships between collective identity and the structure of family life call attention to the fundamental character of the social change occurring in the Stéphanois between 1840 and 1880, that is to the nature of the class formation process. The case of Rive-de-Gier in the 1840s should help sharpen and concretize the historical questions that need to be posed concerning class formation and the growth of the proletarian family in the Stéphanois. But what were the circumstances that created the basis for the existence of a permanent proletariat? Why did a stable work force become necessary for employers, and for which employers? Where did proletarians come from and why did they come to urban industry? A look at the relationship between the development of local industry and agriculture and the development of the permanent proletarian family may provide insights into the conditions for both the growth of class identity, and the sources of class disunity. For instance, those workers who belonged to established families in the city in 1848 exhibited a good deal of suspicion and hostility toward migrant workers. Can the examination of family formation and the relationship between class membership and migration provide any understanding of how these differences were overcome in the 1860s and 1870s?

Also, although something has been seen of employers' and workers' conceptions of the purposes and functions of the proletarian family, so far nothing has been seen of actual existing families. How did an industrial proletarian family economy arise that could survive and reproduce itself in the industrial city from one generation to another? Between 1840 and 1880, Stéphanois workers and their families were confronted with see-sawing prices, a murderous urban environment, and the slowing down of industrial growth. Yet under these circumstances a migrant, temporary proletarian workforce transformed itself into an established, permanent proletariat that was able to sustain itself. To what extent did changes in fertility, mortality, and the opportunities for female and child employment affect workers' ability to survive in the city? How did workers respond to high urban mortality and its secular decline? Was working-class fertility influenced by industrial conditions? How did changes in the distribution of paid and unpaid labor within working-class families affect working-class behavior? Equally important in this debate is the fact that industrial development ultimately proved beyond the calculation and control of even the mightiest industrialists. Industry was rocked by depression and stagnation that threatened the entire local economy. How could the working-class family survive in the chaotic and tumultuous years that followed rapid economic growth?

Of parallel concern here are the content of class identity and issues of reproduction. In the 1840s, in order to increase their hold over workers, the coal company provided an array of welfare services to workers and their families: sickness and accident funds, retirement benefits and assistance in old age, including company charity, spread widely throughout those local industries employing large numbers of proletarians who headed families. The outbreak of massive workers' protest in the 1840s and in the 1860s and 1870s shows that these programs were not uniformly successful in making the workers dependent on the company. To explain why not, the concrete operation of these programs and their contribution to working-class welfare need to be explored. Were company welfare programs ineffectual or did they themselves generate protest?

Finally, the social doctrines and political programs that appealed to Ripagérien workers in the 1840s, already described, need to be compared with those of the 1860s and 1870s, and the conceptions of the role of families embodied in them need to be identified and compared. Did the more class-oriented politics of the later period contain analyses of family life that better fitted workers' current experiences than those of the earlier period? Did their vision of family life play any role in predisposing workers towards the new class doctrines? Did workers' visions of family life change over time, and did workers' conceptions of the family continue to affect strike struggles and political programs as they had in 1848?

The following chapters address these issues. Chapters 2 and 3 discuss the economic forces that made possible the growth of a permanent proletariat and the proletarian family, and how both contributed to the development of a class identity. Chapter 2 focuses on developments in the industrial city, and the next chapter explores developments in the countryside and the relationship between migrants and the rural world. Chapter 2 describes economic forces in the industrial region that created those long-term economic opportunities that laid the basis for industrial family life. But the creation of long-term employment opportunities was only half the battle; chapter 3 shows how permanent pro-letarians were found to occupy long-term jobs. Tracing the rural background of industrial proletarians, it looks at how changes in the nature of rural life affected migrants' participation in urban working-class culture and politics.

Having examined the processes within town and country, industry and agriculture, that brought together long-term jobs and permanent proletarians, it is then possible to analyze how continuous employment in a particular industry shaped the lives of individual workers and their families. Chapters 4 and 5 deal with some of the characteristics of class identity among those proletarians who formed families, and with issues of class reproduction. Chapter 4 discusses the efforts of employers in mining and in metalworking to provide welfare services that would increase their control over the workers, and discusses workers' responses to employers' efforts. Chapter 5 considers the proletarian family economy and shows the importance of the welfare services it provided to its individual members. Drawing together evidence from mortality and fertility trends and from employment patterns, it examines how differences in the urban environment helped or hindered the functioning of the family economy.

Chapter 6 looks at the effects of long-term employment and permanent proletarianization on the labor movement. It explores the outbreak of strike militancy in 1869 and the spread of republicanism, socialism, and trade unionism in the 1870s. Placing the development of a permanent proletariat and issues of reproduction in the context of the spread of republican and socialist doctrines, as well as the formation of new local political coalitions, it analyzes the birth of class consciousness and action among proletarians in the Stéphanois.

A brief final chapter summarizes the conclusions and sets them in a broader context of class formation in nineteenth-century France.

NOTES

1 Between 1880 and 1914, a surprising percentage of inhabitants of the Stéphanois industrial cities were natives of the city or of the very nearby region. The percentage of natives and migrants from the department of the Loire (almost certainly most of these were from the *arrondissement* of Saint-Etienne) is large. Many of those born in the department of the Loire were industrial workers from other Stéphanois valley towns who found jobs in a nearby community. (See table 1.1.)

Table 1.1   Percentage of origins of the population: census of 1891

	Natives	Born in department of Loire	Total
Le Chambon-Feugerolles	77.4	11.3	88.7
Rive-de-Gier	53.0	19.3	72.3
Saint-Chamond	40.4	36.6	77.0

There are substantial differences in the proportion of natives in the individual community. These differences will be explored in the course of this study. Information on nativity in 1891 was found in ADL 47/M/20. Writing about the Stéphanois labor force in the 1930s, Maxime Perrin noted: "It is *homogeneous*: more than three quarters of the inhabitants have their origin in the region" (*La région industrielle de Saint-Etienne* (Tours, Arrault, 1937), p. 351). Studying the origins of the population of Saint-Etienne between 1872 and 1946, Jacques Schnetzler also notes that it was "strongly indigenous" (*autochtone*), "L'evolution démographique de la région de Saint-Etienne de 1876 à 1946," in *Etudes foréziennes* 4 (1971), pp. 157–96, 193.

2 Walter W. Skeat, *An Etymological Dictionary of the English Language*, New Rev. Edn (Oxford, Clarendon Press, 1946), p. 478.

3 Olwen H. Hufton, *The Poor of Eighteenth-Century France, 1750–1789* (Oxford, Clarendon Press, 1974).
4 On these debates in the Lyonnais see the magnificent work of Jean-Pierre Gutton, *La société et les pauvres, l'exemple de la généralité de Lyon 1534–1789* (Paris, Société d'édition "Les Belles Lettres", 1969).
5 Marvin Harris and Eric B. Ross, *Death, Sex, and Fertility: Population Regulation in Preindustrial and Developing Societies* (New York, Columbia University Press, 1987).
6 Janet Ruth Potash, "The Foundling Problem in France, 1800–1869: Child Abandonment in Lille and Lyon," unpub. diss., Yale University, 1979. p. 255.
7 Frank Parkin, *Class Inequality and Political Order: Social Stratification in Capitalist and Communist Societies* (New York, Praeger Publishers, 1971), p. 14.
8 E. P. Thompson, *The Making of the English Working Class* (New York, Vintage Books, 1966), p. 1.
9 Erik Olin Wright, *Class Structure and Income Determination* (New York, Academic Press, 1979) pp. 20–1.
10 For a comparative discussion of the effects of fertility trends on the development of the labor movement see my unpublished paper, "Fertility Trends, Rural Social Structure, and the Labor Movement in the Regions around Birmingham and Saint-Etienne: 1800–1880," paper presented to the Conference on the European Fertility Decline, Toronto, May 1988.
11 On the workings of the "family economy" in industry, see Louise Tilly and Joan Scott, *Women, Work and Family* (New York, Holt, Rinehart and Winston, 1978); Martha May, "The Historical Problem of the Family Wage: The Ford Motor Company and the Five-Dollar Day," *Feminist Studies* 8 (2) (Summer, 1982), pp. 399–424; Ruth Milkman, "Redefining 'Women's Work': The Sexual Division of Labor in the Auto Industry during World War II," *Feminist Studies* 8 (Summer 1982), pp. 337–72.
12 Some important structuralist views of the family are: Manuel Castells, *The Urban Question: A Marxist Approach* (Cambridge, Mass., MIT Press, 1979); David Harvey, *The Limits to Capital* (Chicago, University of Chicago Press, 1982); and Claude Meillassoux, *Femmes, greniers, et capitaux* (Paris, Maspero, 1979). Also the debate between Heidi Hartmann, "Capitalism, Patriarchy, and Job Segregation by Sex," *Signs* 1(3) (Spring, 1976), pp. 137–69 and Jane Humphries, "Class Struggle and the Persistence of the Working-Class Family," *Cambridge Journal of Economics* 1 (1977), pp. 241–58, and "The Working-Class Family, Women's Liberation and the Class Struggle: The Case of Nineteenth-Century British History," *Review of Radical Political Economics* 9 (3) (Fall, 1977), pp. 25–41.
13 On the need to integrate historical demography and family history see David Levine, *Reproducing Families: The Political Economy of English Population History* (Cambridge, Cambridge University Press, 1987).
14 An important discussion of the effects of capital concentration on the division of labor in heavy industry is Ruth Milkman, *Gender at Work: The Dynamics of Job Segregation during World War II* (Urbana, Ill., University of Illinois Press, 1987).
15 On the relations between property and family in peasant households see the important discussion by Richard M. Smith, "Some Issues Concerning Families and their Property in Rural England 1250–1800," in *Land, Kinship and Life-Cycle*, ed. Richard M. Smith (Cambridge, Cambridge University Press, 1984), pp. 1–86; and

Martine Segalen, *Love and Power in the Peasant Family* (Chicago, University of Chicago Press, 1983).

16 On the conservatism of family life, John Bodnar, "Immigration, Kinship, and the Rise of Working-Class Realism in Industrial America," in *Journal of Social History* 14 (1) (Fall, 1980), pp. 45–65; Heidi Hartmann and Ann R. Markusen, "Contemporary Marxist Theory and Practice: A Feminist Critique," *Review of Radical Political Economics* 12 (2) (Summer, 1980), pp. 87–94; and Evelyn Frankford and Ann Snitow, "The Trap of Domesticity," *Socialist Revolution* 10 (2) (July–Aug., 1972), pp. 83–94. For an important discussion of the relationship between family and protest and a good summary of major schools of sociological thinking about the family, see Kathleen Marie Blee, "The Impact of Family Settlement Patterns on the Politics of Lake Superior Communities, 1890–1920," unpub. diss., University of Wisconsin, 1982.

17 Edmund Burke, *Reflections on the Revolution in France* (Garden City, New York, Anchor Press, 1973), p. 213.

18 Gareth Stedman Jones, "Class Struggle and the Industrial Revolution," in *Languages of Class: Studies in English Working-Class History, 1832–1982* (Cambridge, Cambridge University Press, 1983), pp. 25–75, see esp. pp. 59–60.

19 Pierre Guillaume, *La compagnie des mines de la Loire, 1846–1854: Essai sur l'apparition de la grande industrie capitaliste en France* (Paris, Presses Universitaires de France, 1966), pp. 63–5.

20 *La Démocratie Pacifique*, November 12, 1846; Guillaume, *La compagnie des mines*, pp. 116–20, 144–46; "Enquête de 1848 – mineurs de Rive-de-Gier," AN C/956.

21 Eugène Tarle, "La grande coalition des mineurs de Rive-de-Gier en 1844," *Revue Historique* (1936), pp. 249–78, p. 252.

22 *La Démocratie Pacifique*, November 12, 1846.

23 Guillaume, *La compagnie des mines*, pp. 150–2.

24 Ibid., p. 150.

25 Anselme Petetin, "Situation industrielle du bassin houiller de la Loire," *Economie Politique* 3 (1844), pp. 321–33, 327.

26 On the 1844 strike see, Michael Hanagan, "Proletarian Families and Social Protest: Production and Reproduction as Issues of Social Conflict in Nineteenth-Century France," in *Work in France: Representations, Meaning, Organization, and Practice*, ed. Steven Laurence Kaplan and Cynthia J. Koepp (Ithaca, NY, Cornell University Press, 1986), pp. 418–56.

27 *Préfet*, October 13, 1847, AN F/12 4476B.

28 Jean-Pierre Aguet, *Grèves sous la monarchie de Juillet* (Geneva, 1954) p. 352.

29 *Procureur général*, February 15 and 19, 1847, AN BB/18 1450.

30 AN BB/18 1420.

31 On this point see, Lynn Hunt and George Sheridan, "Corporatism, Association, and the Language of Labor in France, 1750–1850," *Journal of Modern History* 58 (Dec., 1986), pp. 813–44.

32 On Flora Tristan's visit to Rive-de-Gier, *Procureur général*, April 8, 1844, AN BB/18 1420: the authorities reported that her trip was a failure; her speech at Rive-de-Gier is not mentioned in her travel log. The authorities paid a great deal more attention to the distribution of Jules Leroux's brochure, *Le bourgeois et le prolétaire*, AN BB/18

1420. The liberal paper, *Le Mercure ségusien*, printed long excerpts from this pamphlet as evidence of its subversive character, May 1, 1844. From 1844 onward, there are dozens of references to "communists" in the correspondance of the mayor and the police authorities. By "communism," the authorities usually meant the doctrine of Cabet. On February 19, 1847, the *procureur général* reported on militant miners that, "one notices that the workers who show themselves animated with the worst dispositions are those among whom one knows that communism has made the most progress" (AN BB/18 1450). Judged by the frequent references of the authorities and by the character of their references, "communism" was undoubtedly viewed by the authorities as the most widespread and influential of local doctrines. Nevertheless, the Fourierist journal, *La Démocratie Pacifique* provided information on Rive-de-Gier that indicated local contacts there; the Fourierists seem to have been quite intellectually influential among the ribbonweavers of the region, and the ribbonweavers' responses to the government inquiry of 1848 reveal many Fourierist phrases.

On popular Cabetian communism, the definitive work is Christopher H. Johnson, *Utopian Communism in France: Cabet and the Icarians* (Ithaca, New York, Cornell University Press, 1974). More study needs to be done on how disciples of Saint-Simon and Fourier translated their master's ideas into concrete political programs. French historians have only recently begun to study the ways in which the doctrines of Cabet, Fourier, and Saint-Simon were cast into popular form and exerted mass political influence.

33 On associations in the first half of the nineteenth century, John M. Merriman, *The Agony of the Republic: The Repression of the Left in Revolutionary France, 1848–1851* (New Haven, Conn., Yale University Press, 1978); and William Sewell Jr, *Work and Revolution in France: The Language of Labor from the Old Regime to 1848* (Cambridge, Cambridge University Press, 1980).

34 On the artisanal movement in Lyon see, Mary Lynn Stewart-McDougall, *The Artisan Republic: Revolution, Reaction, and Resistance in Lyon 1848–1851* (Kingston and Montreal, McGill–Queen's University Press, 1984).

35 P. J. Proudhon, *Carnets* (Paris, Marcel Rivière, 1960), vol. 1, carnet no. 3, September 1846. Proudhon wrestled with schemes for reorganizing the Stéphanois mines and the early notes contain numerous references. This is the most elaborate.

36 Etienne Cabet, *Voyage en Icarie* (Paris, Populaire, 1848), pp. 358–9.

37 Victor Hennequin, *Féodalité ou association: types d'organisation du travail pour les grands établissements industriels à propos des houillères du bassin de la Loire* (Paris, Librairie Sociétaire, 1846). This is a compilation of a series of articles appearing in *La Démocratie pacifique* in 1846.

38 Ibid., p. 43.

39 See Barbara Taylor, *Eve and the New Jerusalem: Socialism and Feminism in the Nineteenth Century* (New York, NY, Pantheon, 1981).

40 Hennequin, *Féodalité ou association*, p. 27.

41 Ibid., p. 28.

42 Adam Przeworski, "Proletariat into a Class: The Process of Class Formation from Karl Kautsky's *The Class Struggle* to Recent Controversies," in *Politics and Society* 7 (1977), pp. 343–401, esp. p. 385.

43 Général, commandant la 7 division militaire, February 27, 1848, MdG F/1 2.
44 L.-J. Gras, *Histoire économique générale des mines de la Loire* (Saint-Etienne, Theolier, 1922), vol. 1, p. 346.
45 David Gordon, *Merchants and Capitalists: Industrialization and Provincial Politics in Mid-Nineteenth-Century France* (Alabama, University of Alabama Press, 1985), p. 46.
46 Général, subdivision de la Loire, March 1, 1848, MdG F/1 2.
47 Général, subdivision de la Loire, March 5, 1848, MdG F/1 3. On March 4, 9, 10, and 13, military men reported the Mayor of Rive-de-Gier's uneasiness and his desire to maintain a strong military garrison in that town.
48 Miners' petition in *Le Mercure ségusien*, May 21, 1848.
49 Petetin, "Situation industrielle," p. 324.
50 *Préfect*, September 10, 1848, ADL 1/M440.
51 *La Voix du peuple*, April 11, 1849.
52 Adolphe Blanqui, "Des classes ouvrières en France pendant l'année 1848," in *Petits traités publiée par l'academie des sciences morales et politiques* (Paris, Firmin-Didot, 1849), pp. 162–3.
53 Ibid., p. 164.
54 Rapport A. Girard, Chambre des députés, n. 2760, Séance du 3 avril 1884, p. 698.
55 Commissaire de police de Rive-de-Gier, September 25, 1848, ADL 92/M/7.
56 "Enquête de 1848 – mineurs de Rive-de-Gier," AN C/956.
57 Ibid.
58 Ibid.
59 Ibid.
60 Ibid.
61 Ibid.
62 Ibid.
63 Stewart-McDougall, *The Artisan Republic*, p. 52. The municipal workshops in Rive-de-Gier employed 401 workers, employing fathers of families at higher rates than single men (see ADL 1/J/440). Given the size of the town, the percentage of workers in the workshop as a proportion of the working population was one of the highest in France. See Thomas R. Christofferson, "The French National Workshops of 1848: The View from the Provinces," in *French Historical Studies*, 11 (4) (Fall, 1980), pp. 505–20.
64 "Enquête de 1848 – mineurs de Rive-de-Gier," AN C/956.
65 Claude Latta, *Un républicain méconnu: Martin Bernard, 1808–1883* (Saint-Etienne, Centre d'études Foréziennes, 1980), p. 142.
66 Stewart-McDougall, *The Artisan Republic*. pp. 116–34.
67 For a comprehensive report on this incident, "Evenements de Saint-Etienne et Rive-de-Gier pendant les journées des 15 juin et 16, 1849," ADL 10/M/30.
68 The best guide to political events in the Stéphanois during the Second Republic is Yves Lequin, *Les ouvriers de la région lyonnaise (1848–1914)* (Lyon, Presses Universitaires de Lyon, 1977), vol. 2, pp. 157–203. The history of the Second Republic in Rive-de-Gier still remains to be told.

2

Capital Concentration and Industrial Employment in the Stéphanois: 1780–1880

A look at the Stéphanois case confirms some of the most important findings of recent economic and social historians as to the continuity of economic development. Contemporary research in economic history emphasizes the variety of technologies and industrial organizations found both in the eighteenth century and over the whole of the nineteenth century, and stresses the continuity of patterns of development in nineteenth-century industrial Europe.[1] But an examination of the Stéphanois also reveals that industrial changes were sometimes associated both with dramatic alterations in working-class social identity and with the reformation of family life. In the Stéphanois between 1780 and 1880, technological innovation had little direct effect on the daily life of most workers and transformations of work structures only had impact when they were viewed as threatening jobs seen as life-time occupations. While inventions and the reorganization of work did create the preconditions for large-scale capital investment in industry, it was capital concentration that most immediately and directly transformed the character of everyday life for many local proletarians.

Once underway, large-scale capital accumulation had a logic of its own, a logic with serious repercussions for working-class life. While large investments in producers' goods could yield tremendous economies of scale, they also required the routinization and stabilization of production, and enormous amounts of resources were devoted to securing these objectives. Capital concentration demanded a large and reliable group of workers possessing physical strength and a degree of skill. The tremendous financial resources of the newly created enterprises enabled employers to recruit and train their own workers. The need to pay out dividends regularly and to keep expensive machines rolling obligated employers to keep their workforce together all year round and through difficult times. As a result, capital concentration enabled workers who were not highly skilled to find year-round, permanent employment. Unlike every other kind of proletarian work, these new jobs were full-time occupations that workers could, if willing and able, expect to retain for their entire working lives. These new opportunities allowed workers to develop a sense of industrial identity different from that of previous groups of artisanal or unskilled workers. As will be shown in later chapters, capital concentration, in conjunction with other economic developments, also made it possible for proletarian workers to form families.

The significance of these newly redefined jobs in metalworking and coal mining for the development of working-class social and political life was enormous. Almost from the beginnings of worker protest, embattled industrial proletarians in the region appear with firm industrial identities, as "metalworkers," and as "miners"; during the entire period, no other industrial proletarians developed so sharp a sense of identity. For the whole of the nineteenth century, these industrial occupations were vital elements of proletarian identity, and all efforts to unite workers used these industrial solidarities as vital building blocks.

Unlike most other aspects of Stéphanois social and economic development, the emergence of new employment opportunities for proletarians in mining and metalworking after 1840 was relatively sudden and sweeping. Economic and technological change did not occur in the Stéphanois, "suddenly, like a thunderbolt from the clear sky," but had deep historical roots.[2] Nevertheless, contemporaries saw that a fundamental social transformation was going on in the Stéphanois in the decade or so after 1840, and realized that in some obscure way it was related to the enormous increase in capital concentration.

Already, in the earliest stages of this Industrial Revolution, the great historian Jules Michelet had a clear sense of the transformation. In 1839, Michelet boldly risked his life by taking a ride on the newly built and highly accident-prone railway from Lyon to Saint-Etienne. He was shocked both by the physical conditions of the industrial cities and by the spirit of ruthless competition that seemed to dominate:

In advancing in the direction of Rive-de-Gier, agriculture gradually disappears. Scrub covers the mountains. Black and smoking factories, emitting the thick and stinking . . . coal fumes. . . . On the very peaks arise high chimneys which indicate the presence of coal mines. On one side of them, extinguished, surrounded by ruined buildings, are revealed mines that have been abandoned. They are tacit witnesses to false speculations, ruined investments, fortunes vanished in smoke, doubtless also indiscrete exploitations, the reciprocal joining of industrial struggles and competition, deep in the earth . . . I returned completely preoccupied with this spectacle.[3]

Michelet's prior suspicion of industrialism must have been strongly reinforced by his visit to the Stéphanois, but the full measure of Michelet's horror can only be judged by his later reference. Michelet took France's defeat in the Franco-Prussian War of 1870–1 as a severe personal blow, which may have hastened his death. In his last work, describing the sudden decline of French fortunes, he could summon no more powerful metaphor than the change he had witnessed, 30 years before, going through a tunnel from the "friendly Lyonnais" to the "world of mines, crude slag, and the black carbons of the Forez."[4]

Writing in 1869, reflecting on the changes that had occurred, a Stéphanois native, Jules Janin, a well-known Parisian literary critic, remarked that "without any doubt this black earth contains a revolution comparable to the French Revolution, Ah! poor Gagas! ['Gaga' was the patois name for native Stéphanois] powerful and hardworking men."[5] Janin described the Stéphanois for his Parisian audience:

At Saint-Etienne there are no casual laborers [*profession de hasard*] as at Paris, no officious vagabonds, always ready to serve as guides, at eight o'clock in the morning, you would be fortunate to find someone to point out an inn to you . . . One acts at Saint-Etienne, as if in a vast barracks, at the tap of the drummer boy: an army in battle has no more precision. Last night, we entered into the city to the methodical noise of thirty thousand hammers falling in cadence on fifty thousand anvils, you went to sleep to the sound of twelve hundred carts carrying packages to foreign countries; in the morning you will find the same order and precision.[6]

The historian and the literary critic both sensed that dramatic change was going on in this Stéphanois region, sometimes labeled the "cradle of the Industrial Revolution in France." Michelet saw the economic results of the enormous financial struggle that witnessed the triumph of outside capitalists and large-scale capital in the region's economy; Janin observed the social results of this struggle, the formation of a new large-scale method of organizing labor. Because a rapid restructuring of the character of industrial employment and social life occurred in an old industrialized area, a look at the Stéphanois provides a special opportunity to scrutinize the nature of the transition from those rich and complex pre-industrial systems of labor to the early emergence of the large-scale, year-round, disciplined work environment that was to spread so widely in the course of the nineteenth century.

This chapter focuses on three phases in the development of proletarian labor in the Stéphanois region: the age of manufacture, 1780–1820; the era of the Industrial Revolution, 1820–40; and the period of the growth of long-term employment opportunities, 1840–80. It will distinguish the situation of the semi-skilled worker from that of the many other proletarian industrial workers that existed in the region between 1780 and 1880, and it will identify the timing of the appearance of large numbers of semi-skilled workers in the Stéphanois.

THE AGE OF MANUFACTURE: 1780–1820

Long before the Stéphanois region felt the impact of the Industrial Revolution the area was already a center of industrial work; industrial work in the region engaged not simply highly skilled artisans who exerted control over the work hierarchy, but many unskilled industrial proletarians who had little control over the organization of their labor. The truly remarkable feature of the different systems of labor organization that existed in the Stéphanois during this period is that, while they offered employment to tens of thousands of industrial proletarians, none of these systems offered full-time industrial employment to large numbers of unskilled industrial proletarians but only to artisans.

In the years before 1820, in such major industries as hardware production, silk weaving, and coal mining, a variety of systems for organizing proletarian labor existed in the Stéphanois. Already by 1820, an extensive division of labor existed within some of these industries and substantial progress towards mechanization had occurred in several industries. Overall, a large industrial workforce had grown up in the area; the distinguishing characteristics of this workforce before 1820 were the small-scale of individual enterprises and the seasonality of production.

Before 1820, most industrial labor was performed by temporary, seasonal workers who were also active in agriculture. As far back as 1788, Messance, the pseudonym of a noted eighteenth-century demographer who was employed in tax collection in the Stéphanois, had noted that in the mountainous areas surrounding the Stéphanois valleys, "there are no houses where there are not one or several looms for weaving ribbons."[7] In 1778, when Roland de la Platière visited the region, he commented that "in the countryside, when agricultural work ceases, all the men are forgers, principally nail forgers; the women make ribbons and the girls sell the products, returning or selling the fabricated products and bringing back the raw materials."[8] He added that when flooding or summer heat forced the miners of Rive-de-Gier to abandon the mine, they returned to their homes and occupied themselves "at the forge, making nails, locks and other hardware."[9] In 1826, Captain Lappier de Gemeaux noted that:

in every village, manufacturing is carried on and the cottages are turned into workshops which supplement the products of Saint-Etienne. The different branches of industry which are exercised there occupy in all more than 20,000 workers spread over city and countryside. These last are at the same time farmers and artisans, they pass from one work to the other and quickly return to their fields when commerce stagnates.[10]

The largest single component of the early industrial work was ribbonweaving, a highly seasonal industry. Ribbonweaving was a fashion industry and dependent on a demand that changed seasonally and rapidly. Subject to the seasonal swing of fashion, in early spring and again at the beginning of the winter, commissions poured in from Paris to Stéphanois silk manufacturers, who feverishly rushed orders to their labor force in city and countryside; for most unskilled workers, off-season in ribbonweaving lasted for three or four months.[11] Since the dead season in the ribbon industry was almost the reverse of that in agriculture, where a frenzied pace in the early summer and in the fall was followed by relative quiet, ribbonweaving found a natural source of labor in the countryside.

While the demands of fashion yielded seasonality in ribbonweaving, the seasonality of production and employment in local metalworking was the natural consequence of the dominance of waterpower. In this area too, industrial demand for laborers did not compete with agricultural demand. Waterpowered mills came to a stop for a month or so every winter when the streams froze and, more importantly, they stopped for several months in the summer, usually between July and September, when water levels fell drastically. Millowners and millworkers could count on being without work for three or four months every year. Local millowners viewed with envy their counterparts in the neighboring Basse Isère which, unlike the Stéphanois, was included in the Alpine watershed and received abundant water all year round, even in August.[12] Some idea of the fluctuations in the water supply is given by monthly averages of the rate of flow of the Loire near Saint-Victor-sur-Loire, a few kilometers from Saint-Etienne. The average rate of flow from November through May is 68.7 cubic meters per second. This drops to an average monthly rate of flow from June through October of 23.9 cubic meters per second, almost one-third of the previous figure. The monthly average for August is only 9 cubic meters per second.[13] The Loire itself was not an important source of waterpower but its flow does indicate seasonal rainfall patterns. Beside the seasonality of waterpower, the irregularity of waterpower also needs to be stressed. An unusually hot summer or an especially cold winter could extend mill unemployment by several months. In the Stéphanois, workers as well as farmers surveyed the skies in the morning and watched the temperature carefully in order to judge their economic futures. When the mills for cutting bars into rod iron, the "slitting mills," shut down, pig-iron could not be processed for forging or polished for export, and local metalworking was generally threatened. As late as 1848, 3,000 metalworkers were unemployed in the area around Le Chambon-Feugerolles because of the failure of water power.[14]

Even so typically modern an industry as coal mining had a strong seasonal component. Sustained rain brought flooding to all the local mines. The heavy dependence of coal mining on water transportation also oriented many coal employers towards seasonal production. On the eastern edge of the coal basin, the canal was unreliable in both winter and summer; constructed in 1780, between Rive-de-Gier and the Rhône, it froze in winter and dried up during the summer drought. In 1809, a reservoir was constructed at Couzon which made it possible to use the canal all summer; this move towards freeing transportation from its seasonal bonds was a very important reason for the rapid growth of Rive-de-Gier in the early years of the century.

Transport difficulties were still more severe for coal producers in the western coal field. The steep Loire–Rhône watershed between Rive-de-Gier and Saint-Etienne rendered technically unfeasible the canal's extension to the richer and less exploited western portion of the coal basin. As a result, the two sections of the coal basin belonged to different markets. Through the Givors canal and its connection to the Rhône, Rive-de-Gier sold cheap coal to customers in Lyon and Marseilles. But in the western portion of the basin, the transport situation was desperate and remained so during the entire period before 1820. Coal was hauled from the basin to Saint-Just-sur-Loire where coal stocks accumulated awaiting the brief periods, five or six times a year, when coal barges could be sent down the Loire; their major market was distant Paris, where they had to compete with northern coal.[15] Still, the western edge of the coal basin was a major supplier of the Parisian market during the first half of the century; when prices were low in Paris and the roads permitted, coal from the eastern half of the basin made its way to the west.[16]

Seasonality is often associated with a primitive division of labor and crude methods of production. But as manufacturing and coal mining in the Stéphanois show, seasonality was perfectly compatible with sophisticated productive techniques and extensive industrial development.

An exceptionally complicated division of labor coexisted with seasonal production in hardware which, along with silk weaving and gunsmithing, represented one of the major industries in the Stéphanois in the half-century before 1820. Cutlery and nail making were the most important of the many branches of the hardware trade. The organization of labor in cutlery was similar to that in other large branches of hardware production and also to that in gunsmithing. Cutlery production itself was dominated by domestic industry and by small shops that employed between two and six workers. The numerous water-powered mills that processed iron products for various aspects of the hardware trade employed small numbers of workers; in 1818, sharpening mills employed on average between five and six workers.[17] The best-known cutlery product was the small and cheap *Eustache* knife produced in large numbers for a mass market. Merchant cutlers steered their commodity through an elaborate series of stages of manufacture. Each knife was worked on by eighteen separate workers who made the haft, smeltered the iron, and forged, polished, and tempered the blade.[18]

Seasonality also coexisted with the complex division of labor in ribbonweaving. In addition, this complexity was increased by the division of labor between urban and rural ribbonweaving; the industry's size made this division of rural and urban labor of central significance to the economic relationship between city and country. Throughout the century 1760 to 1860, ribbonweaving was by far the largest single industrial employer in the *arrondissement* of Saint-Etienne. In the cities that were the centers of the ribbon industry, Saint-Etienne and Saint-Chamond, silk weaving was a highly skilled, artisanal industry.[19] From these centers, silk merchants established local branches for the distribution of silk to the countryside and to neighboring communities. In the countryside around Saint-Etienne and Saint-Chamond, workers used simpler, easy to operate, looms *à la basse lisse*, to weave unpatterned ribbons of blended fabrics; these much less skilled workers called themselves "*rubaniers*" to distinguish themselves from the highly skilled, "*passementiers*".[20] Frequently, mothers taught the weaving of unpatterned ribbons to their daughters, sometimes fathers possessed the requisite knowledge, and sons learned ribbonweaving, but this was less common. When parents or their household residents could not teach children the trade, neighbors usually could. In such cases, children were typically apprenticed to neighboring families who obtained the child's labor free for three or four months while the child learned basic skills.[21] Then the child might remain with the family in order to earn enough money to buy a loom, or the child's family or silk merchants might supply the required sum.

The division of labor in coal mining was not so extensive as it would later become, the small size of individual enterprises placing limits on the division. In 1788, the total number of miners employed underground in the Stéphanois region was 800.[22] In the years between 1780 and 1810, mining expansion was slowed down by a bitter contest over the right to exploit the mines. The battle was a three-cornered one among the owners of the land that contained the minerals, the *concessionnaires* who had been given the right to exploit the minerals by the state, and local coal-consuming artisans who had been guaranteed by law that a portion of the coal field would be exclusively devoted to production for local industrial consumption.[23] By 1810 the struggle between landowners and *concessionnaires* was finally settled in favor of the latter, and the way was opened for rapid expansion, but this development did not result in an immediate change in the basic conditions of coal production. The *concessionnaires*, even the holders of the largest and richest concessions, such as the Marquis d'Osmond who controlled the mines of Roche-la-Molière et Firminy, sublet their concessions to a variety of small-scale miners, who, it was claimed, were really "peasants."[24] During the years between 1780 and 1820, the average size of the individual mining enterprise grew, but even at the end of the period most mining operations employed only a handful of workers as coal cutters, haulers, and a few weighmen. The largest mines employed 80 to 100 workers.[25]

In the case of hardware manufacturing, seasonality proved compatible not only with a sophisticated division of labor but with considerable mechanization as well.[26] Hardware merchants centered in Stéphanois imported pig-iron into the area and, during its various stages of preparation, consigned the metal to local processors and workmen. The small mills to which the merchants "put out" the unfinished metal contained machines for polishing, forging, and grinding metal. Small slitting, grinding, and polishing mills which catered to the metal trade multiplied during the eighteenth and nineteenth centuries. In 1788, in the course of his studies of local industry, Messance noted the growth of water-powered metalworking mills and workshops along streams that flowed through Saint-Etienne, Rive-de-Gier, Saint-Chamond, and Le Chambon-Feugerolles. All told, he counted 11 slitting mills, 26 hammering mills, 47 trimming mills, 287 sharpening mills, and 104 polishing mills along streams in the Stéphanois valley.[27]

The extensive division of labor, progress of mechanization, and improvements in transportation in the Stéphanois region in the years before 1820 led to a growth of a large industrial workforce in the area. The size of the labor force in the pre-industrial revolution period is remarkable. Describing the first decade of industrialization between 1820 and 1830, a geographer has noted that: "within little more than a decade the whole region, from Rive-de-Gier to Le

Table 2.1 Estimates of workers employed in principal industries, as a percentage of total estimated population in the election of Saint-Etienne and *arrondissement* of Saint-Etienne

	Workers in principal industries as % of total population	Ribbonworkers as % of total population	Population of *arrondissement* of Saint-Etienne
1788	34.5	—	115,966
1828	32.8	18.9	145,165
1836	29.4	16.8	163,576
1847	36.2	16.9	191,734
1872	32.2	16.7	268,917

Chambon was transformed into one of the busiest and fastest developing industrial areas in Europe."[28] Yet even in this period – and indeed over the whole course of Stéphanois' industrialization – although the absolute size of the industrial work force grew, there is no evidence of an increase in the *proportion* of the region's population employed in industrial labor.

In 1788, the early student of population, Messance, studied the region and prepared his own estimates of the population and of the labor force. At a time when the total population of Saint-Etienne was around 28,000, Le Chambon 2,200, Saint-Chamond 4,100, and Rive-de-Gier 3,000, he estimated that around 40,000 people were involved in industrial labor for the silk and metalworking industries in the subdelegation of Saint-Etienne.[29] The election or subdelegation of Saint-Etienne to which Messance refers is roughly coterminous with the later *arrondissement* of Saint-Etienne, which includes the lower third of the department of the Loire, and is the approximate equivalent of an American county.[30]

Those estimates of the number of workers in major industries as a proportion of the work force suggest a secular decline in the proportion of the population employed in major industries. Table 2.1 shows a number of estimates derived from a variety of sources. The principal industries included are: mining, machine construction, hardware manufacture, armor making, braid weaving, and ribbonweaving.[31] Over time, a decline in the proportion of seasonal workers in industrial production was counterbalanced by an increase in the proportion of the worker's time devoted to industrial production. The overwhelming number of industrial workers indicated in the earliest estimates were seasonally employed workers who returned to agriculture when industrial employment ceased. By 1876, full-time, year-round proletarians had become a majority.

THE INDUSTRIAL REVOLUTION: 1820–1840

If the first phase of regional economic development was characterized by seasonality and small-scale production, the second phase, in the years between

1820 and 1840, was notable for the introduction of foreign technologies and competition and the appearance of the first small groups of semi-skilled workers. During this period, aided by the tariffs of 1821 and 1822, Stéphanois entrepreneurs adapted themselves relatively successfully to these new challenges compared with many other French capitalists. In the years after 1820, the Industrial Revolution hit the Stéphanois with full force. By 1840, the region was surely one of the half-dozen most technically advanced regions in all of continental Europe. But although a new category of worker, the semi-skilled worker, began to slowly expand its numbers, the first 20 years of Industrial Revolution still had little effect on the social composition of the workforce. Seasonality still dominated the work patterns of the overwhelming number of less skilled workers.

The presence of developed coal deposits, cheap and abundant labor available in domestic industry, and a local market for metal products attracted knowledgeable and ambitious outsiders to the area. The ease with which new technologies spread to the Stéphanois is an impressive demonstration of the close ties within the European economy of the first half of the nineteenth century.[32] In 1814, the French government paid a substantial sum of money to the English industrialist, James Jackson, to introduce the cementation and crucible steel-making processes in France, and Jackson chose the Stéphanois as his theater of operations. Numerous local industrialists and engineers spent time in England or in developing metalworking regions of France and returned to the Stéphanois to set up mechanized shops.[33] The flood of new technologies into the Stéphanois also stimulated local inventors. Many local inventors either taught at the *Ecoles des mines* of Saint-Etienne, founded in 1816, or were the products of this school. In 1827, in Saint-Etienne, Benoît Fourneyron perfected and patented the water-powered turbine engine – one of the great technical accomplishments of the nineteenth century.[34]

The new technologies introduced into local metalworking and the expanding demand for coal led to an increase in the size of metalworking and mining enterprises, but in the years before 1840 increases in establishment size were generally modest compared with its monster growth in the succeeding period. In 1820, the average coal mine employed about 36 workers, in 1832, the average rose to 84.[35] In 1833, in mechanized braid weaving, the average mill employed only 55 workers.[36] In metalworking, many of the most important local firms, those that would dominate the industry in the 1850s and 1860s and employ thousands of workers, also remained relatively small. Between 1823 and 1826, in addition to James Jackson and his sons, the Jackson steelworks and forge employed between 17 and 21 workers. In 1840, Jacob Holtzer employed only 8 workers in his steel plant. In 1836, the average steel-making plant employed 60 workers, and the average forge 250.[37]

The average size of forging enterprises was increased by a handful of exceptions to the dominance of small-scale metalworking enterprises in the period 1820 to 1840. These exceptions were the half-dozen plants with blast furnaces established in the *arrondissement* of Saint-Etienne in the 1820s. These plants were built on the widespread belief that substantial ore deposits existed in the Loire near the coal field. The relatively rapid exhaustion of Stéphanois ore deposits constituted a severe check to ironmaking and smelting in the region. Subsequently, ironmakers were required to import iron ore from outside, and several ironmakers went out of business when business depression hit the metal industry in 1826 and 1827.[38] The plant at Terrenoire, founded in 1822, was the most significant survivor of these early plants. Unlike its early rivals, the Terrenoire firm possessed its own iron ore mines in the Ardèche. Terrenoire grew rapidly, partly because it expanded by purchasing its bankrupt rivals, and as early as 1826, it had a workforce of 200 people.[39]

Despite the pioneering role of the Stéphanois region in the introduction of new technologies in France, why did the size of industrial enterprises grow so slowly? Why did the introduction of cunning new inventions – some seen for the first time on the continent of Europe – not result in the immediate growth of a large proletarian workforce? In textiles an important reason for the slow transformation of the labor force was that the benefits of economies of scale were less substantial than in other industries. In silk weaving, the sophistication of the Jacquard loom, the presence of many highly skilled silk weavers and the difficulties of further mechanizing silk weaving, combined with the erratic nature of the market for ribbons, enabled local ribbon producers to forestall mechanization. With the exception of braid weaving, which will be discussed separately, local textiles did not experience a movement towards factory production comparable to that taking place during the early Industrial Revolution in English textiles.

The enormous expense of reorganizing coal mining, the costs of many of the new technologies in metalworking, and the difficulty of obtaining access to outside capital also slowed the restructuring of local industry. The difficulty of attracting sufficiently large-scale investment rather than technological problems proved the major obstacle to the growth of coal mining. In 1836 the largest employers of steam engines were not mills or factories but the coal mines themselves. The replacement of wood by coke as fuel and the enormous amounts of coal needed to make wrought iron and steel everywhere forced metalworks to locate near coal fields. Faced with expanding demand in local industry and a growing market outside the region, the mines extended ever deeper into the earth; this in turn increased the risk of flooding. The danger was partially overcome by the introduction of horse-powered pumps and steam engines. In 1836, about 60 percent of all steam engines employed in the area were used in coal mining.[40] The cost of pumps and steam engines necessitated larger capital outlays.

The partial and incomplete development of those energy and transportation technologies that most strongly facilitated routinized, year-round production was one reason for the reluctance of outside capitalists to invest heavily in the reorganization of local industry. Although Stéphanois industrialists were among the first to introduce steam engines on the continent, the steam engine did not immediately bring about a revolution. Even in a region with abundant and cheap coal, the early steam engines produced by James Watt and his imitators were expensive and relatively inefficient.[41] However, the steam engines introduced into the Stéphanois did not even measure up to Watt's early standards. In 1836 the presence of steam power was noted by one observer, who remarked that the machines "are low pressure and average 20 horsepower. These machines are very much less costly and, frankly, very much less sophisticated [*bien moins perfectionnées*] than those used in England."[42] Steam power spread slowly in local metalworking industries, although the enormous amount of energy consumed in the rolling mills encouraged the largest metal companies to turn to steam. As late as 1851, when the age of water-power was receding quickly, a departmental survey found 718 water-powered establishments along the principal streams of the coal basin.[43] At mid-century, had the ghost of Messance walked alongside local streams such as the Ondaine, the Furan, or the Gier, his spirit would still have felt at home along banks thick with water-powered mills.

The growing demand for coal inspired the growth of the first French railways, and although the Stéphanois is renowned for having introduced the first continental railways, it took several decades before railways became a truly reliable form of transportation. Drawn by horses, the first railway in France connecting Saint-Etienne to Andrezieux (a port town on the Loire) opened in 1827. In 1830, a route was completed connecting Saint-Etienne to Lyon. Only when the coal-carrying contracts negotiated by the railways proved unprofitable, after their first few years of operation, did the railways decide to expand their services to passenger transportation. Between 1831 and 1842, steam engines gradually took the place of horses,[44] but even after the complete mechanization of the mines, engineering problems remained that for years caused frequent accidents and railway transportation was still hazardous.

The most dramatic change in the nature of industrial employment occurred in one sector of the textile industry, braid weaving, where mechanization and the complete triumph of factory production occurred almost simultaneously. In 1806, a silk wholesaler from Saint-Chamond, Charles-François Richard-Chambovet, visited the Duchy of Berg, where he saw braid weaving machines, and in the next year he introduced these machines and the textile mill into Saint-Chamond.[45] Braid weaving proved tractable both to mechanization and to rapid factory organization, because the costs of mechanization in braid weaving were much less than those in metalworking or coal mining. Early in the century, average factory size in braid weaving was also relatively small and remained so throughout the whole of the century. Also the costs and uncertainty of local transportation were not such important factors in textiles as in coal and metalworking.

Because Stéphanois industrial production was so subject to seasonality and to the irregularities of the weather, many distant investors felt it was too risky, and capital for industrial production was dependent on the limited financing made possible by small local investors. Only a few local enterprises obtained substantial financial backing from outside the region: the Frèrejean family, foundrymen from Lyon, played a leading role in local metalworking almost from the beginning; the Marquis d'Osmond, a leader in mining, was also an outsider. But during the first phase of industrial development, these were the exceptions that proved the rule.[46] Bertrand Gille has noted the "very divided" (*très partagé*) investments in one important local metalworks which was supported by many, local small investors.[47] Gille stressed the role played by financiers and merchants in the early development of the iron and steel industry generally, and there is some evidence that they played the same role in both mining and metalworking in the Stéphanois. Silk merchants often doubled as bankers and were important investors in both mines and metal works. Prominent ribbon merchants, such as the Neyrands, Thiollière, and Royet, invested in local metalworking in the 1820s. Other native ribbon merchants such as the Palluats obtained mining concessions in the 1820s. The manufacture of arms for the military was organized as a monopoly, and several of the holders of this monopoly – the most well known were the locally prominent Brunons – invested in machine construction.[48]

Some of the capital for development was also generated internally in metalworking, by internal financing from the profits of the many companies started by owners of small local forges or foremen in forges who introduced new techniques in small workshops they established on their own. Throughout the entire period 1820 to 1840, for those with technical skills and some managerial experience, entry into many aspects of local metalworking remained relatively easy, as was the case of Claudinon, the Morels, and Holtzer. In 1837, Hippolyte Petin and Jean-Marie Gaudet put together their savings to start a forge in Rive-de-Gier; their total capital was 500 francs, a small sum even at the time.[49]

The very important technological and industrial accomplishments of the early decades of the nineteenth century all prepared the field for the headlong expansion of investment in the decades after 1840. From the perspective of economic history, innovation and industrial organization exhibit continuity. But once organization and invention had largely eliminated old-fashioned dependence on the weather and seasonality, they created the basis for the growth of a new kind of industrial organization which had a revolutionary impact on the social life of industrial proletarians. Between 1820 and 1840, the small core of year-round, full-time production in some sections of metalworking, coal mining, and textiles gradually introduced and stimulated the development of transportation and energy technologies that finally transformed working-class life in coal mining and metalworking. By 1840, the prevention of flooding in the mines required constant vigilance and on-going expenditures that were beyond the resources of small mining companies. The skilled workers employed in puddling in the metalworks had to be kept in the region if wrought-iron production was to be maintained. Steam hammers and rolling mills depreciated whether they were used or not. Indeed, in 1828, reports compiled on the prospects for French metalworking reported the lament of the traditional metal producers who complained that, during times of economic crisis such as existed at the time of the inquiry, the mechanized firms contributed to a further lowering of the price of metal goods because their high fixed costs forced them to maintain production – even when the cost of production exceeded their revenues.[50]

By 1840, the mechanized metal producers' need to maintain year-round production was greatly facilitated by the extension of railway transportation and the spread of steam power in the Stéphanois. The chief advantage of the rail transportation available in the 1830s was not its price but its dependability. As Alfred Chandler Jr points out, "The railroad's fundamental advantage" is "its ability to provide a shipper with dependable, precisely scheduled, all-weather transportation of goods."[51] Until the early 1850s, it remained cheaper to ship coal from Rive-de-Gier to Givors by canal than by rail. Only the nation-wide extension of the railway, which rendered superfluous the costly transfer of coal from canal barge to steamboat at Givors, and rail transportation down the Rhône, finally destroyed the economic basis of the canal. But the presence of the railway assured shippers that, if they were willing to pay a bit more, they could have as much coal as they wanted whenever they wanted it. The fundamental advantage of the stationary steam engine was quite similar to that of the railroad. Explaining his motives for introducing steam engines into the braiding industry in 1807, Richard-Chambovet wrote "my mill (*fabrique*) had 30 looms, I decided to double their number but I lacked the means to keep them active all the time as freezing temperatures and drought diminished the volume of the water. In order to keep them active, I employed a high-pressure steam engine."[52]

THE GROWTH OF LONG-TERM EMPLOYMENT OPPORTUNITIES:
1840–1880

From the perspective of technological change, the years between 1820 and 1840 were among the most exciting in the whole history of the Stéphanois. But from the perspective of the formation of an industrial proletariat, these years were only preparatory for the decades between 1840 and 1880. What was distinctive about industrial organization in the Stéphanois in this period was the rise of the large, capital-intensive, individual industrial establishment, an institution which includes the large coal mine as well as the factory, and the growth of year-round employment opportunities for a large unskilled and semi-skilled work force.

After 1840, both the size of the average enterprise and the size of the workforce increased rapidly in both mining and metalworking. Between 1836 and 1846, a multitude of competitive small-scale coal producers were united into a great monopoly, the largest company in France, the Compagnie des mines de la Loire, which welded the mines into a coordinated and unified mining operation. In the period 1817–19 when systematic records were first

Table 2.2   Workers in machine construction and metalworking in three Stéphanois towns

	1839–43	1851	1856[a]	1876[a]
Rive-de-Gier	360	654	735–1,625	945–1,875
Saint-Chamond	288	395	633–733	895–1,565
Le Chambon-Feugerolles	25	259	480–544	640–853
Total	673	1,308	1,848–2,902	2,480–4,293

[a] Estimates of workforce size for 1856 and 1876 come from manuscript censuses. The first figure is for those people who identify themselves formally as metalworkers and machine construction workers; the second figure includes those who identify themselves as daylaborers.

compiled, the mining work force averaged around 1,889 workers. Average employment increased in the decade 1820–29 to 2,509. But a marked increase in labor force growth occurred between 1836 and 1840 as the mining monopoly began to take shape. Between 1832 and 1838, the mining workforce jumped by almost two-thirds, from 2,875 to 4,741. Average employment in the decade 1830 to 1839 was 3,940 and in the decade 1840 to 1849, 5,872. By the decade 1870 to 1879, it would be 17,200.[53]

Most of the major metalworking enterprises that developed in the *arrondissement* of Saint-Etienne in the second half of the nineteenth century were founded or transformed themselves into large enterprises between 1845 and 1856. In 1852, Jacques Claudinon took over a plant in Le Chambon-Feugerolles, and by 1856 the place had become a major employer in machine construction. In 1854, the Petin–Gaudet works merged with Jackson Brothers and the new company greatly increased in size. In 1848, Petin–Gaudet had opened a works in Saint-Chamond to supplement production of their plant in Rive-de-Gier, and after its expansion in the mid-1850s the great factory in Saint-Chamond became the center of their operations.[54] By 1862, the plant in Saint-Chamond alone employed some 2,000 workers.[55]

In contrast to coal mining, information on the growth of metalworking employment is difficult to come by. Table 2.2 shows some estimates of the growth of the workforce in iron and steel making and machine construction in three Stéphanois towns between 1839 and 1876. The lower estimates show a four-fold increase in the number of metalworkers; the higher estimates, which are probably more accurate, show a seven-fold increase.[56]

The years between 1840 and 1880 were the great period of capital-concentration in the Stéphanois. Given the availability of a power source and of transportation on a steady, year-round basis, the major forces behind this extraordinary accumulation of capital were the growing benefits accruing to economies of scale and the resulting changes in the demand for labor in heavy industry, the intervention of outside capital, and the special protection the French state gave to industrial corporations in strategic areas.

In the case of Stéphanois coal mining, the roles played by state intervention and economies of scale are interdependent. In 1838, the French state intervened to save the coal fields, the very existence of which was threatened by continued small-scale operation. The railroad's opening of the western coal field to Lyonnais markets had resulted in fierce competition among coal producers. In order to offer coal at the cheapest possible price, small owners were forced to scrimp on maintenance; the ferocity of competition made the owners of adjacent mines reluctant to cooperate in even the most necessary task of mining drainage. In 1838 flooding occurred in numerous pits and threatened the existence of large portions of the mining system. As a result of this, a law was passed in April of that year encouraging the consolidation of mine concessions and forbidding the subleasing of mining concessions. This subleasing of large concessions among many small-scale operators was a major, contributing force to the disastrous system of mining that collapsed in 1838.[57]

The move toward concentration, encouraged by the law of 1838, resulted in the formation of a near total monopoly of local coal production by 1845. The monopoly employed a corps of technically trained engineers and spent large sums of money to deepen the mines and to improve underground transportation. The result of the new coordination of mining was to consolidate mining into a smaller number of pits. The average number of workers employed per pit grew rapidly; between 1846 and 1850, the company closed down around 25 percent of the pits it had taken over, while it increased the size of the workforce.[58] The abandoned pits that Michelet saw from his train in 1839 were the end of the era of competition. A comparison of these figures with production figures suggests that many of the new labor force were probably involved in coordinating and repairing the delapidated individual pits, since it took several years for increases in employment to yield increases in production. Comparing average annual coal production in the five-year period 1836–40 with average annual production in the period 1841–45 reveals a 60 percent increase; this was the largest average annual increase in any five-year period between 1821 and 1876, although nearly every five-year period before 1876–81 witnessed an increase in average annual mining production of ten percent or more.[59]

At least in part, the growing size of Stéphanois metal establishments resulted from the nature of demand. The market for small quantities of highly tempered steel was quickly overtaken by the demand for large quantities of steel and wrought iron. The growth of railways in the 1840s created a demand for rails that required technical capacity far exceeding that of small producers. Increasingly, the local steel and wrought iron producing industries concentrated on producing large and costly metal parts for government consumption in ordnance, railway equipment and naval armor. The new products demanded a great deal of fitting and finishing to meet exacting government specifications. Finishing necessitated the employment of a great many workers familiar with the use of lathes, files, and riveters in machine construction and metalworking.[60]

The high cost of new metal technologies and the large supply of labor they required increased establishment size, and the new kinds of tasks involved in these technologies redefined industrial employment. Capital-intensive machinery such as the steam hammer, the crucible, the Bessemer converter, and the Siemens–Martin ovens, helped make the Stéphanois a center for the forging of large metal objects.[61] The forging of large pieces greatly expanded the need for unskilled labor: gangs of some 50 unskilled workers were needed to maneuver large pieces of metal. Semi-skilled workers were also needed to assemble a completed product.

The introduction and the growing efficiency of steam power combined with the growing efficiency of steam engines encouraged metal producers to combine a variety of previously separated stages in the manufacture of steel and wrought iron and the transformation of these metals. Steam-powered factories housing a variety of machines gradually replaced the water-powered workshops devoted to specialized machine production. In the 1840s most of the forges and steelmaking plants converted to steam. By 1856, 74 percent of all machines in metalworking were steam-powered, and steam engines produced 84 percent of total machine horsepower. By 1876, 95 percent of the machines employed in metalworking were steam-powered, generating 97 percent of machine horsepower.[62]

In metalworking as in mining, the French state played an important role in promoting the growth of large-scale enterprises. The government had shaped the course of regional development since it recruited James Jackson in 1814, but its role was to prove even more decisive at mid-century. The modest metalworks of the early period lacked the power and capital resources of the mining monopoly. In 1848, without state aid, the infant Stéphanois heavy metalworks would have been forced into bankruptcy. An observer in 1889 noted that "in 1848 orders ceased brusquely in the region's factories and the resulting crisis obliged the forgemasters to seek new outlets by creating new products. It was then that Petin and Gaudet had the idea of forging, following Armstrong's designs, an iron cannon for the Navy."[63] With state investment in armaments, local metal employers were able to maintain their workforce and continue in existence. There was nothing unusual about the promotion of the Petin–Gaudet works by the republic: throughout the crisis of 1848–50, the *Banque de France* loaned huge sums of money to large-scale metal establishments and, as far as it could, the government continued to aid industry by continuing to expand the railways during the crisis years.[64]

The character of new technologies combined with the government's encouragement of heavy industry created a favorable climate for the large-scale entry of outside capital into the Stéphanois. In coal mining, outside capital took complete charge. While a prominent local family of silk wholesalers and bankers, the Palluat, played an important early role in the consolidation of the coal monopoly, their company was soon taken over by outsiders. By 1854 only 9 percent of the capital in the coal mining monopoly belonged to natives of the Stéphanois, while 49 percent belonged to Lyonnais, 28 percent to Parisians, and 10 percent to Genevans.[65] A similar, though less complete, transformation occurred in metalworking. The large company dominated by the Lyonnais Frèrejean soon took control of the native company comprising largely small

Stéphanois investors. Where small metalworks had grown into large ones, as in the case of the Claudinons, Morels, or Holtzers, self-financing provided some room for the growth of powerful local producers who retained their independence. But even where self-financing and the investments of local silk merchants did play an important role, as in the case of the Petin–Gaudet works, great success could lead to the same results as failure – to the inflow of outside capital and the loss of local control. Between 1870 and 1885, through a series of mergers, the Petin–Gaudet works was transformed into the Compagnie de la marine et des chemins de fer with ore mines scattered throughout France and Italy and major plants in the Loire, in Paris, and in the Parisian *banlieue*; the main office of the company was in Paris.[66]

Even ribbonweaving, which remained a small-scale enterprise, felt the currents of change. If the large-scale enterprise did not develop in ribbonweaving, the dispersion of weaving between city and countryside lessened, and ribbonweaving became more urban and tended to concentrate in Saint-Etienne. The advent of the railway centralized high-fashion ribbonweaving in Saint-Etienne. Saint-Chamond, which had shared the trade with the larger city, lost its importance in highly skilled ribbonweaving in the years after 1840. The restructuring of the silk trade that occurred after 1856, reinforced this trend. During the late 1850s and early 1860s a number of serious crises hit ribbonweaving. The American Civil War cut off an important market in the Southern states. After the fall of Napoleon III and his Empress, a trend set in against elaborate ribbons on women's dresses that proved durable. The decline of the trade in fashion led to industrial reorganization. An increasingly large proportion of even unskilled ribbonweaving centered in Saint-Etienne, where skilled workers, lacking fancy ribbons, proved willing to work on plain ribbons and blended patterns.[67]

Elsewhere in the Stéphanois, ribbonweavers tended increasingly to congregate in small towns. Communes like Saint-Just-Malmont began to urbanize around the mid-century because of the concentration of silk weaving there; ribbonweaving also maintained itself in some urban centers in the coal mining region, cities like Le Chambon-Feugerolles where miners' wives and children were engaged in the trade. Some households in Saint-Just-Malmont depended on the combination of farming and ribbonweaving, but the number of households in which nearly everyone worked in ribbonweaving was undoubtedly growing.[68]

THE DEVELOPMENT OF LARGE-SCALE ENTERPRISE AND A SEMI-SKILLED WORKING CLASS

The dramatic technological changes and increases in the scale of industrial enterprise that had occurred in the Stéphanois between 1780 and 1840 had had little effect on the nature of industrial work itself. Industrial work was still divided between highly skilled artisans who worked full-time in industry and lived in cities, and unskilled workers who labored part-time in industry and either lived in the country or migrated to the city on a temporary basis. Only after 1840 did the appearance of technologies that promoted routinized labor and the creation of companies large enough to sustain such labor permit the creation of a fundamentally new work experience and a new kind of worker in important local industries. Because of the tendency of unskilled metalworkers to identify themselves as "day laborers" it is difficult to estimate the proportion of the metalworking work force that was semi-skilled; judging from those towns that seem to have had the most complete industrial registration, it is likely that semi-skilled workers composed around one-third of the metalworking labour force in 1856 and around one-half in 1876; in both years, the proportion of semi-skilled workers was probably higher in Le Chambon than in the other cities, and lower in Saint-Chamond.

The appearance of large numbers of semi-skilled workers in the Stéphanois was less a product of technological requirements generated at the shop floor than of a managerial strategy aimed at securing enhanced profitability. The technological requirements of the work floor hardly required the creation of the semi-skilled workers. For two decades the new technologies of the Industrial Revolution had been operated successfully by highly paid skilled workers working alongside poorly paid, transient, unskilled workers. To cite a prominent example, James Jackson had brought along a crew of skilled workers from England who were paid high wages with signed individual contracts stipulating the payment of very substantial bonuses to those who remained with Jackson between six to sixteen years.[69]

However, as the size of investments in plant equipment grew and as routinized production became more crucial to the realization of profits, employers became leery about the extent of their dependence on skilled metalworkers and on mining subcontractors who might prove as rebellious as other French skilled workers, and on large groups of unskilled workers who might seasonally desert the factory for high-paying harvest jobs. The employers' response was to train workers themselves, to replace supervisors from the working class with university-trained engineers, and to expand hiring practices so as to recruit workers from outside the traditional working-class *milieux*. In order to prevent the workers they had trained from abandoning their jobs to take higher paying positions elsewhere, companies fostered benefit programs which effectively penalized workers for leaving their job.

In 1848, the Ripagérien miners' attempt to institute apprenticeship in the mines represented the first working-class response to the companies' measures. From the beginning, miners forcefully opposed employers' efforts to create a class of permanent industrial workers whose bargaining position would be much weaker than that of the urban artisans who lived beside them in the city. Semi-skilled workers were permanent proletarians who developed their own occupational identity, yet these workers lacked those traditional institutions for defending workers' occupational interests possessed by artisanal workers; they lacked those customary regulations, contractual agreements, craft organizations, or family workshops that enabled workers, either individually or collectively, to limit or regulate access to the industry. The creation of the semi-skilled worker also had profound repercussions on the transmission of employment opportunities within families. Unlike artisans, semi-skilled workers could not transmit skills to their children and the decision of the Ripagérien mine owners to recruit outsiders weakened workers' ability to even informally pass job opportunities to their children. Semi-skilled workers could now only assure their children's future by formal education or by good relations with the employer.[70]

Although the position of the semi-skilled worker was portrayed as modern and efficient in contrast to the "traditionalism" of the highly skilled worker, its real defining character was its dependence on the employer. Dependence combined with the relative cheapness of its implementation made the organization of semi-skilled work a nearly irresistible managerial strategy. A local metal employer explained why employers needed to pay special attention to this category of workers:

All the transformations by which the raw material must pass in order to become iron bars are operated by the workers themselves . . . These are very delicate operations whose success no surveillance no matter how active is able to assure.
  The labor of workers is therefore of an enormous importance . . . yet . . . the work force represents only 15 percent to 20 percent of the value of the product; all the remainder represents the cost of material or fixed costs.[71]

For the purposes of this study, workers who obtained skills from employer-controlled training programs or, less frequently, through schools open to all, are classified as "semi-skilled." In the Stéphanois "semi-skilled" occupations included the following: "forgemen," (*forgeurs*) "miners," (*mineurs*) "fitters," (*ajusteurs*) and "riveters" (*raboteurs*).[72] The semi-skilled worker could only have come into existence in a large-scale enterprise because small-scale enterprises were typically unwilling to pay the cost of training workers. Customs and craft unions performed the dual function of training workers as well as organizing them. Small employers needed these institutions to guarantee workers' skills and turned to them for a supply of skilled workers, which was forthcoming, at the cost of strengthening workers' independence and autonomy. Only large firms that needed dependable workers had both the incentive and the capital to train their own workers. When employers took over job training, they generally broke up highly skilled jobs into a number of less-skilled or "semi-skilled" jobs. Subdividing skilled tasks meant that less time was spent training individual workers, who could then be more easily replaced.[73]

Metal employers set up special workshops for the purpose of training semi-skilled workers. In metalworking the companies recruited the semi-skilled, from the teams of unskilled haulers that, under the supervision of the forgemaster, helped to manipulate large metal pieces in the forging process. In 1848 the large forging establishments proudly proclaimed that as a matter of policy they did not enter into private engagements to train apprentices. Instead they selected from the pool of their employees those who were able and displayed "good conduct." They explained their purpose as making job training a form of "encouragement" for their workers.[74]

The organization of work was somewhat different in mining. Mine employers divided the job into several specialties and rewarded steady workers who remained on the job with access to many high-paying jobs. In the mines, the majority of workers were semi-skilled. Already by 1848, workers responding to a government inquiry answered that there was no apprenticeship in the mines.[75] When labor force requirements demanded, the companies hired inexperienced adult males directly into the better-paid timbering and packing jobs (*boiseurs* and *remblayeurs*). The only really highly skilled workers in the mines were those coal cutters who drilled holes and filled them with blasting powder to shake loose coal from the seam and those timbermen who had to judge the direction of the cutting and the extent of shoring required to support it. These specialists were a small minority of both coal cutters and timbermen, and they were generally recruited from those who had spent long years in the mine.[76]

The major requirements for the majority of cutters, timbermen, and packers were physical strength, an ability to perform exhausting manual labor in the cramped and close quarters of the frequently narrow Stéphanois coal seams, and a basic respect for some fundamental safety regulations. The underground division of labor had grown with the emergence of large-scale mining. As shafts deepened and the crosscuts lengthened, the need grew for large numbers of workers to devote their time to hauling, timbering, and packing. In the first half of the nineteenth century – before the formation of the coal monopoly and the extension and reorganization of the coal mines – the majority of underground workers spent their time cutting coal. In 1844 around half the underground miners were coal cutters, but by 1869 this figure had dropped to one-quarter.[77] Most adult male workers spent several years as timberers or packers before advancing into relatively high-paying coal-cutting, because companies needed large numbers of workers for the lower-paying job categories and used most coal-cutting jobs to reward more stable workers. The companies did not try to train "coal cutters" but expected them to have acquired their training by observation and emulation during the period when they worked as timberers or packers alongside the cutters; the companies let "piece rate" serve as incentive for workers to improve their performance.

Because employers had invested their resources in training semi-skilled workers and because of their need for large numbers of these workers, employers sought to keep these workers on the job, and to protect them from the fluctuations of the market. An 1871 report on local industrial conditions commented on the case of the machine construction industry:

Actually, even in times of unemployment, it is rare that a factory decides to fire all or part of its personnel, for the personnel, once dispersed, the factory will not be able to take them back when it is useful to do so. It is generally preferred to retain all the workers and to diminish the hours of work or the amount of the work assigned to different groups.[78]

The mines also tried their best to maintain year-round production. A look at bi-weekly fluctuations in the wage bill of the Montrambert mines in 1856 and in 1876 shows very little bi-weekly fluctuation in salary payments.[79]

It was the ability of large employers to sustain the greater part of their workforce even during periods of economic crisis that really favored the growth of a stable workforce of semi-skilled workers. For both workers and employers, the great economic crisis of the years 1848–50 proved a tremendous test of the stability of employment opportunities for the new category of workers just coming into existence. One of the consequences of the revolution of 1848, and the specter of social revolution that increased after February 1848, was a crisis of business confidence that led to a severe business downturn. As always in bad times, ribbonweaving and hardware manufacture contracted and left their workers to fend for themselves.

Not so with mining and metalworking. Sheltered from competition by a government-promoted monopoly, the mines contracted their hours of operation and lowered wages, but they provided some employment for most workers. In 1850, the Prefect of the Loire wrote, "the *Compagnie de la Loire* amassed mountains of coal while industry demanded only the smallest quantities . . . it has powerfully seconded my efforts during the bad times."[80] The distinctive character of development in local coal mining is revealed in tables 2.3 and 2.4 which give the number of days worked and the average yearly wage in coal mines in the Loire, the Gard, and the Nord. In 1849 and 1850, the mines of the

Table 2.3   Average yearly salary (in francs) of miners in the Loire, Gard, and Nord: 1847–1854

	1847	1848	1849	1850	1851	1852	1853	1854
Loire	796	705	790	755	776	740	822	861
Gard	756	765	101	92	690	627	615	1,320
Nord	531	510	515	536	535	531	566	613

Table 2.4   Average number of days worked per year by miners in the Loire, Gard and Nord: 1847–1854

	1847	1848	1849	1850	1851	1852	1853	1854
Loire	300	245	278	290	271	271	286	285
Gard	306	288	44	40	333	288	284	444
Nord	276	257	266	255	271	273	286	308

Gard simply let their workers go. In the Nord, the mines paid a much lower salary than in the Loire; the migrant component of the northern labor force was very substantial in this period, and mines there may still have been able to make do by depending on a temporary workforce of single men who did not support families. The 444 days per worker in 1854 in the Gard includes double shifts imposed on workers during a time of labor shortage.[81] Like their counterparts in mining, the metal employers also kept their plants and machines running. In Assaily, a small village between Saint-Chamond and Rive-de-Gier, the Jackson brothers proudly recorded that although they had difficulty finding the specie to keep their steelworks operating they had been able to do so during the whole of the year 1848.[82]

After 1840, industrial work in the Stéphanois was no longer divided between highly skilled artisans with a firm industrial identity who were members of a self-conscious worker elite with memories of the corporations, and unskilled workers who moved between one industry and another, between urban and rural labor, participants in Olwen Hufton's "economy of makeshifts."[83] The emergent semi-skilled working class was a product of a managerial strategy that itself was based on the growth of large enterprises in metalworking and mining, the need of these enterprises for workers with special qualifications, and their financial ability to pay a premium to stabilize the workforce that they required so urgently. In 1846 an observer of the Stéphanois coal miners attempted to capture some of the distinctive aspects of this new semi-skilled workforce and to explain to contemporaries the difficulty of their situation in those economically depressed years:

But, people say, if one reduces their wages, the miners will easily find employment in numerous above-ground industries . . . Don't these people know that they [the miners] identify themselves with their profession, that it has become for them a second nature. . . . Does one really believe that it is easy for workers to change their profession? To prepare themselves for another kind of work? . . . In any case, they will only be able to devote themselves to those trades that demand the least apprenticeship and as a result are the least well paid . . .[84]

This passage well indicates the plight of the dependent and permanently proletarianized semi-skilled worker beginning to appear in the Stéphanois in the 1840s. After the failure of the Second Republic and the vast expansion of their numbers in the 1850s, attempts to better the semi-skilled workers' position by assimilating it to that of the artisan came to seem hopelessly inadequate. Yet their situation was less a product of industrialization than of industrial capitalism, and it was only by confronting industrial capitalists that their lot could be improved. Fashioning a solution to the new problems that beset semi-skilled workers was to be a foremost task of the labor movement of the late nineteenth century and of semi-skilled workers and their families.

NOTES

1 Pioneering critics of the emphasis on the rapidity of industrial change, the so-called "Industrial Revolution hypothesis", are: Franklin Mendels, "Proto-industrialization: The First Phase of the Industrialization Process," *Journal of Economic History* 32 (1972), pp. 241–61; and Charles Tilly and Richard Tilly, "Agenda for European Economic History in the 1970s," *Journal of Economic History* 31 (1971), pp. 184–98. Some recent studies that emphasize the continuity of the industrialization process are: *Industrialization before Industrialization*, ed. Peter Kriedte, Hans Medick, and Jürgen Schlumbohm, (Cambridge, Cambridge University Press, 1981); *Manufacture in Town and Country before the Factory*, ed. Maxine Berg, Pat Hudson, and Michael Sonenscher (Cambridge, Cambridge University Press, 1983); and *The Historical Meanings of Work*, ed. Patrick Joyce (Cambridge, Cambridge University Press, 1987).

2 Charles Beard cited in David Cannadine, "The Present and the Past in the English Industrial Revolution 1880–1980," *Past and Present* 10 (May, 1984), pp. 131–72, esp. p. 139.

3 Jules Michelet, *Journal 1828–1848*, vol. 1, 4th edn (Paris, Gallimard, 1959), p. 300.

4 Jules Michelet, *Révolution française – origines des Bonapartes*, vol. 8 (Paris, Calmann-Levy, 1925) pp. xiv–xv. Michelet had visited England in 1834 and was concerned about the effects of child labor on the future development of the working classes, see *Journal 1828–1848*, p. 152. A decade later Michelet repeated the same reservations about the developing French factory proletariat: "The factory worker carries all his life a heavy burden – the burden of his childhood that weakened him early and often corrupted him," *The People* (Urbana, Ill., University of Illinois Press, 1973 (1846)), p. 51.

5 Jules Janin, *Les révolutions des pays de Gagas* (Lyon, Scheuring, 1869), pp. 41–3.

6 Jules Janin, *Mélanges et variétés* (Paris, Librairie des Bibliophiles, 1876), vol. 1, pp. 79–81.

7 M. Messance, *Nouvelles recherches sur la population de la France* (Lyon, Frères Perisse, 1788), p. 116.

8 Jean-Marie Roland (de la Platière), *Lettres écrites de Suisse, d'Italie, de Sicile et de Malthe, en 1776, 1777, et 1778* (Amsterdam, 1780), vol. 6, pp. 450–1.

9 Ibid., p. 456.

10 M. Lappier de Gemeaux "Mémoire militaire – sur le lever à vue de Saint-Etienne à la Loire," MdG/MR/1266.

11 Antoine Limousin, *Enquête industrielle et sociale des ouvriers et des chefs d'ateliers rubaniers acceptée par la majorité des délégués* (Saint-Etienne, Pichon, 1848) p. 22.

12 M. Devun, "L'utilisation des rivières du Pilat par l'industrie," *Revue de géographie alpine*, 32 (fasc. 2) (1944), pp. 241–305. Devun notes that "continuous work was exceptional. Unemployment nearly always lasted several weeks – sometimes as much as six months." See pp. 276–7. On the watersheds in the Massif Central and in the Isère, see Maxime Perrin, *La région industrielle de Saint-Etienne: étude de géographie économique* (Tours, Arrault, 1937), p. 196.

13 Information on the rate of flow of the Loire is presented in M. Devun, *Géographie du départment de la Loire* (Grenoble, Les éditions françaises nouvelles, 1944) p. 21.

14 "Enquête de 1848 – Loire – Canton du Chambon-Feugerolles," AN-C956.

15 Etienne Fournial, *Saint-Etienne: Historie de la ville et de ses habitants* (Roanne, Horvath, 1976), p. 184.

16 Alphonse Peyret, *Statistique industrielle du département de la Loire* (Saint-Etienne, Chez Delavie, 1835), p. 93; and L.-J. Gras, *Essai sur l'histoire de la quincaillerie et petite métallurgie* (Saint-Etienne, Theolier, 1904), p. 198.

17 Ibid., p. 104.

18 Ibid., pp. 92–3.

19 On "*passementiers*" see James Condamin, *Histoire de Saint-Chamond* (Paris, Alphonse Picard, 1890); L.-J. Gras, *Histoire de la rubanerie et des industries de la soie* (Saint-Etienne, Theolier, 1906); and in the 1848 *enquête*, the report of the "Chefs d'ateliers du rubans-Saint-Chamond," AN-C956.

20 On "*rubaniers*" see Louis Reybaud, *Etudes sur le régime des manufactures* (Paris, Michel Levy, 1859), pp. 215–33; and in the 1848 *enquête*, the report from the "canton du Chambon-Feugerolles," AN-C956.

21 On apprenticeship in ribbonweaving, "Enquête de 1848 – Loire – Canton du Chambon-Feugerolles," AN-C956.

22 L.-J. Gras, *Histoire économique générale des mines de la Loire*, 2 vols (Saint-Etienne, Theolier, 1922), vol. 1, p. 182.

23 Ibid., p. 116.

24 Pierre Guillaume, "Les débuts de la grande industrie houillère dans la Loire: les mines de Roche-la-Molière et de Firminy sous la restauration," *Cahiers d'Histoire* 4 (2) (1959), pp. 147–66, esp. p. 148.

25 Ibid. In 1817, at one of the larger pits in the western field, the La Roche pits, only 92 workers were employed.

26 For an interesting survey of some different systems of labor organization in the early Industrial Revolution in England, see Maxine Berg, *The Age of Manufactures, 1700–1820* (Totowa, NJ, Barnes and Noble, 1985). On hardware manufacture in domestic industry in England, Marie B. Rowlands, *Men and Masters in the West Midland Metalware Trades before the Industrial Revolution* (Manchester, Manchester University Press, 1975).

27 Messance, *Nouvelles recherches*, p. 122.

28 N. J. G. Pounds, *An Historical Geography of Europe 1800–1914* (Cambridge, Cambridge University Press, 1985), p. 417.

29 Messance, *Nouvelles recherches*, pp. 115, 119.

30 Messance's "Election" of Saint-Etienne includes most of the modern-day *arrondissement* of Saint-Etienne, plus much of the modern-day cantons of Givors and Condrieu in the department of the Rhône.

31 Estimates of the principal industries are from very different sources and are extremely rough, but, from one source to another, they demonstrate a great deal of consistency. The 1788 estimates are from Messance, *Nouvelles recherches*, p. 122; these are the vaguest references of all. The 1828 estimates are from, "Notice sur l'industrie de l'arrondissement de Saint-Etienne au commencement de 1828," *Bulletin Industriel*, vol. 4 (1828) p. 15. The 1836 estimates are from Philippe Hedde, *Revue industrielle de l'arrondissement de Saint-Etienne* (Saint-Etienne, chez Janin, 1836), p. 34. The 1847 estimates are from "Rapport fait à la société industrielle et agricole de Saint-Etienne par la commission chargée d'étudier la question du libre échange au point de vue des intérêts généraux et de ceux particuliers de l'arrondissement," in *Bulletin de la société industrielle et agricole de Saint-Etienne* (1845–7), vol.

20, pp. 249–90. The 1872 estimates are from, P. Heritier et al., *150 ans de luttes ouvrières dans le bassin Stéphanois* (Saint-Etienne, Editions le champ du possible, 1979), p. 27. All estimates for the population of the *arrondissement* of Saint-Etienne for non-census years were linearly interpolated. For 1788, Messance's estimates were used for the subdelegation of Saint-Etienne.

32 On the easy communication among European nations in the first half of the nineteenth century see Sidney Pollard, "Industrialization and the European Economy," *Economic History Review*, 26 (1967), pp. 636–48. A very interesting and provocative discussion of the course of European industrialization, one that discusses the Stéphanois, is by Charles Sabel and Jonathan Zeitlin, "Historical Alternatives to Mass Production: Politics, Markets and Technology in Nineteenth-Century Industrialization," *Past and Present* (Aug., 1985), pp. 132–76. However, the treatment of the Stéphanois in this article is one-sided and misleading.

33 M. L. Babu, "L'industrie métallurgique dans la région de Saint-Etienne," in *Annales des Mines*, neuvième série, 15 (1899), pp. 357–462, esp. pp. 371–6.

34 Ibid., p. 380.

35 Peyret, *Statistique industrielle*, p. 155.

36 Lucien Thiollier, *La chambre de commerce de Saint-Etienne et les industries de sa circonscription 1833–1890* (Saint-Etienne, Theolier, 1891), p. 61.

37 W. F. Jackson, *James Jackson et ses fils* (Paris, chez l'auteur, 1893), p. 73; Hedde, *Revue industrielle*, pp. 24, 34.

38 Babu, "L'industrie métallurgique," pp. 375–9. Many of the workers who were needed to run these new metalworking establishments undoubtedly came from those workers engaged in hardware manufacture. An 1848 report from Saint-Chamonnais hardware workers, written by nailers, complains that urban hardware workers were leaving the trade en masse because adult males could find much more remunerative work in urban industry. The report found that the industry was increasingly confined to rural domestic workers who grew their own food and could supplement their inadequate incomes with agricultural work. See "Enquête de 1848 – Loire – Cloutiers de Saint-Chamond," AN-C956.

39 On the consolidation of Terrenoire, see Bertrand Gille, *Recherches sur la formation de la grande enterprise capitaliste (1815–1848)* (Paris, SEVPEN, 1959), pp. 73–6.

40 Hedde, *Revue industrielle*, pp. 24–5.

41 On the early steam engines, G. N. von Tunzelman, *Steam Power and British Industrialization* (Oxford, Clarendon Press, 1978).

42 Hedde, *Revue industrielle* p. 24.

43 Claude Liogier, *Les Constructeurs* (Saint-Etienne, Union departementale des syndicats CGT de la Loire, 1946) p. 84.

44 Alfred Dunham, "Railroads," *The Industrial Revolution in France* (New York, Exposition Press, 1955), pp. 50–7, p. 66; and Fournial, *Saint-Etienne*, pp. 190–2.

45 L.-J. Gras, *Histoire de la rubanerie et des industries de la soie suivie d'un historique de la fabrique de lacets de Saint-Chamond* (Saint-Etienne, Theolier, 1906), pp. 702–4.

46 Pierre Cayez, *Métiers jacquard et hauts fourneaux aux origines de l'industrie lyonnaise* (Lyon, Presses Universitaires de Lyon, 1978), pp. 235–40, Fournial, *Saint-Etienne*, pp. 139–40, and Guillaume, "Les débuts de la grande industrie houillère."

47 "Enquête de 1848 – Loire – Canton du Chambon-Feugerolles," AN-C956. For a

fascinating discussion concerning the relationship between domestic industry and industrial development, see Joel Mokyr, *Industrialization in the Low Countries, 1795–1850* (New Haven, Yale University Press, 1976).

48 On changes in the nature of the industrial elite and their relations see, David Martin Gordon, "Merchants and Capitalists: Industrialists and Provincial Politics at Reims and Saint-Etienne under the Second Republic and Second Empire," unpub. diss., Brown University, 1978, esp. pp. 6–26, 151–76.

49 C. Chomienne, *Histoire de la ville de Rive-de-Gier du canton et de ses principales industries* (Saint-Etienne, 1912), pp. 311–16; and Babu, "L'industrie métallurgique," pp. 389–91. A very interesting discussion on the origins of industrial development capital in the West Riding is by Pat Hudson, *The Genesis of Industrial Capital: A Study of the West Riding Wool Textile Industry c.1750–1850* (Cambridge, Cambridge University Press, 1986).

50 Bertrand Gille, *La sidérurgie française au XIXe siècle: Recherches historiques* (Geneva, Librairie Droz, 1968), pp. 116–20.

51 Alfred D. Chandler, Jr, *The Visible Hand: The Managerial Revolution in American Business* (Cambridge, Mass., Belknap, 1977) p. 86.

52 Gras, *Histoire de la rubanerie*, p. 707.

53 Figures on coal employment are found in Service éducatif, *La mine et les mineurs* (Saint-Etienne, CDDP, 1981).

54 In 1849 the Deflassieux Brothers forge in Rive-de-Gier was opened. In 1853 the Morel Brothers abandoned Saint-Martin-la-Plaine and created an enlarged forge in Rive-de-Gier. On concentration in Stéphanois metalworking, see Gille, *La sidérurgie française*, pp. 174–9.

55 C. Lallemand, "Les industries du bassin de la Loire: usine de Saint-Chamond," in *L'illustration, Journal universel* 3 (1002) (1862), p. 299.

56 Manuscript censuses for Le Chambon-Feugerolles, Rive-de-Gier, and Saint-Chamond for 1856 and 1876 were consulted at the Archives départementales de la Loire. Samples were drawn from these censuses; the size and reliability of these samples will be discussed extensively in chapter 4.

Some respondents to the census questionnaire identified themselves as metal-workers or as engaged in one or another metalworking trade. Other respondents identified themselves simply as "day laborers": although most day laborers worked in machine construction, there were several industries, particularly in Rive-de-Gier, that also employed day laborers. The lower figure for the machine construction workforce is based on the inflated sample estimate of all those who identified themselves as engaged in one or another aspect of metalworking; the higher figure also includes those who identified themselves as day laborers.

57 Gras, *Histoire économique générale des mines de la Loire*, vol. 1, pp. 269–73.

58 Pierre Guillaume, *La compagnie des mines de la Loire 1846–1854* (Paris, Presses universitaires de la France, 1966), pp. 111–12.

59 A refined analysis of change in Stéphanois coal production can be found in François Simiand, *Le salaire des ouvriers des mines de charbon en France* (Paris, Cornely, 1907).

60 On the demand for iron and steel in France, see François Caron, "French Railroad Investment, 1850–1914," in *Essays in French Economic History*, ed. Rondo Cameron (Homewood, Ill., Irwin, 1970) pp. 315–40. For a discussion of French demand for iron and steel, although centered mainly in the period after 1880, Ann Wendy Mill, "Comment and Debate, French Steel and the Metal-Working Industries: A Contri-

bution to Debate on Economic Development in Nineteenth-Century France," *Social Science History* 9 (3) (Summer, 1985), pp. 307-38.

61 On the steam hammer, see Jean-Paul Bravard, *L'Ondaine: vallée du fer* (Saint-Etienne, Henaff, 1981), p. 11; Babu, "L'industrie métallurgique," pp. 357–462; and Gille, *La sidérurgie française*, pp. 102–6.

62 In 1840 Grand and Jullien requested official permission to introduce a steam-powered tilt hammer in Rive-de-Gier and in that same year Jacob Holtzer introduced the steam engine into the valley of the Ondaine. In 1843, Petin and Gaudet received authorization to use steam-powered machines in the small forge they opened in Rive-de-Gier, and in 1845 Chaleyer obtained authorization to use steam-powered machinery in making crucible steel in Firminy, near Le Chambon-Feugerolles.

On steam power in metalworking in 1856 and in 1876, see Ministère des travaux publics, *Statistique de l'industrie minérale et des appareils à vapeur en France et en Algerie* (Paris, Imprimerie impériale, 1856); and Ministère des travaux publics, *Statistique de l'industrie minérale* (Paris, Imprimerie nationale, 1876).

63 Babu, "L'industrie métallurgique," p. 390.

64 Gille, *La sidérurgie française*, p. 45.

65 Guillaume, *La compagnie des mines de la Loire*, p. 45.

66 On the Frèrejeans, see Pierre Cayez, *Métiers jacquard et hauts fourneaux aux origines de l'industrie lyonnaise* (Lyon, Presses Universitaires de Lyon, 1978), pp. 234–40; and on the transformation of the Petin–Gaudet company into the Forges et Aciéries de la Maine, see Chomienne, *Histoire de la ville de Rive-de-Gier*, pp. 311–16.

67 Gras, *Histoire de la rubannerie.*

68 On the population growth in Saint-Just-Malmont and its connection to weaving, Jean Vigouroux, *Saint-Just-Malmont: Jadis Naguère* (Firminy, Guzot, 1981).

69 Contracts were signed for 6, 12 and 16 year periods. See Jackson, *James Jackson*, pp. 37–8, 63–6.

70 For an elaboration of this definition of skill see my essay on, "Industrial Workers," in *Historical Dictionary of the Third French Republic, 1870–1914*, ed. Patrick H. Hutton, (Westport, Conn., Greenwood Press, 1986), vol. 2, pp. 1079–92. See also Mark Granovetter and Charles Tilly, "Inequality and Labor Processes," research paper no. 939, Graduate School of Business, Stanford University.

71 J. Euverte, "De l'organisation de la main d'oeuvre dans la grande industrie," *Journal des économistes* 19–20 (Sept., 1870), pp. 340–89, esp. p. 350.

72 "Semi-skilled" workers were those mentioned in the 1848 *enquête* as receiving company training and those mentioned in an 1891 study as going through company-run training schools. See Charles Benoist, "Le travail dans la grande industrie," *Revue des deux mondes*, 12 (Dec., 1902).

73 On this point, Arthur Stinchcombe, "Bureaucratic and Craft Administration: A Comparative Study," *Administrative Science Quarterly* 4 (Sept., 1959), pp. 168–87.

74 "Enquête de 1848 – Réponses aux questions d'enquête faite par les délégués des gros forges," AN-C956.

75 "Enquête de 1848 – Mineurs de Rive-de-Gier," AN-C956.

76 On skill classification in mining, Louis Simonin, *La vie souterraine: les mines et les mineurs*, 2nd edn (Paris, Hachette, 1867); and George Jared Lamb, "Coal Mining in France, 1873 to 1895," unpub. diss., University of Illinois, 1976, pp. 158–62, 203–12.

77 Occupational distributions in various Ripagérien mines are found in Meugy's "Historique des mines de Rive-de-Gier," *Annales des Mines*, 12 (série 4) (1847), pp. 177–86. The 1869 occupational distribution for the mines of Roche-la-Molière-Firminy is in ADL 15/J/2655.

78 "Rapport sur la situation industrielle et commerciale de l'arrondissement de Saint-Etienne," Chambre de commerce de Saint-Etienne, March 7, 1871, ADL F/12 4511B.

79 In 1856 the coefficient of variation for bi-weekly pay rolls was 0.1160, in 1876 0.0707. Bi-weekly pay roll figures were found in the *Journal*, vols 1 and 9, of the Société anonyme des houillères de Montrambert et de la Beraudière, in ADL 15/J/2199.

80 Guillaume, *La compagnie des mines*, p. 141.

81 These tables are derived from Guillaume, *La compagnie des mines*, p. 141.

82 Jackson, *James Jackson et ses fils*, p. 73.

83 Olwen Hufton, *The Poor of Eighteenth-Century France, 1750–1789* (Oxford, Clarendon Press, 1974), pp. 69–127.

84 A. Clement, "De la concentration des enterprises industrielles," *Economie politique* 7 (1846), pp. 187–98, esp. p. 195.

3
The Formation of a Permanent Proletariat: 1840–1880

In the years after 1840, long-term industrial employment opportunities for semi-skilled workers developed rapidly within the Stéphanois, but the mere existence of long-term employment opportunities did not necessarily mean that workers accepted them on a long-term basis. An important distinction needs to be made between characteristics of jobs and characteristics of workers. This distinction is an old one that goes back to Karl Marx's discussion of the process of capital accumulation.[1] Marx pointed out that the process of capital accumulation has two components: one requires dramatic increases in the amount of capital in the hands of capitalists, the accumulation of sufficient capital to introduce machines and to organize factories; the other necessitates the creation of a labor force, the loss of capital on the part of sufficient numbers of people to create a permanent workforce. Marx believed that in England the permanent proletariat had been created well in advance of the era of mechanization, however the accuracy of his description of English proletarianization has been hotly debated.[2] But whatever the relationship between proletarianization and mechanization in England, a different relationship existed between the rise of factory industry and the creation of a permanent proletariat in the Stéphanois. There the mechanization of urban industry partly coincided with and partly preceded the formation of a permanent proletariat.

The slow formation of a permanent proletariat in the Stéphanois did not mean that urban industrial jobs went begging. As in France generally, wages were very low in local agriculture and rural domestic industry. A thickly populated countryside with small landholdings, like the Stéphanois, could provide abundant labor to industry. But many of these laborers were also small landowners, or expected to inherit land when their parents or in-laws died. They would work in industry only as long as was required in order for them to be able to return to peasant agriculture. While their immediate social position was that of urban proletarians, their anticipated social destination was to become, by the end of their lives, rural landowners.

How did temporary migration affect migrants' integration into the urban working class? Did it contribute to the native workers' hostility towards migrants that was revealed so strongly in 1848? Did changes in the nature of migratory flows significantly influence migrants' participation in urban working-class society and culture in the years between 1840 and 1880? Why did the migration issue disappear so completely from working-class politics by the early years of the Third Republic? In an attempt to answer such questions, this chapter weighs the effects of changes in rural society and the ties binding the worker to the countryside as well as the forces drawing the migrant into the urban world. A single-minded concentration on the rural migrant's position in urban industry ignores too many constraints on migrants' behavior to yield much insight into the actions of different groups of migrant workers. The position of the migrant depended on events occurring in the sending area, in the receiving area, and in the kinds of linkages that connected the migrant to urban jobs and rural homelands.

Throughout the years of the creation of a large factory work force in the Stéphanois, between 1840 and 1880, the wildly fluctuating migration flow was by far the most important source of population growth *and decline* in the three cities. On balance, migration was a powerful force for urban growth, but it is too often forgotten that, particularly in the period before 1860, emigration from the industrial city served to stabilize the urban economy during periods of economic slowdown. Using registers of births and deaths and quinquennial census returns, it was possible to compare *annual rates* of net migration (NMR), crude natural increase (CRNI) and intercensal growth (IGR). They show that the intercensal growth rate, which represents the rate of growth of the total urban population, is only loosely related to the rate of crude natural increase, the balance of births and deaths, but is closely related to the net migration rate. In all three cities, declining rates of net migration were highest in the years between 1830 and 1860. Severe economic crises during the 1840s and exceptional prosperity during the 1850s made these three decades exceptionally unstable.[3]

To discover possible differences in background or expectations between the early and later migrants and the effect of these differences on their urban living patterns, the areas where the migrants came from must be identified and social and economic conditions in the different "sending" areas must be compared. Marriage records from the industrializing cities were used as a means of getting at the background of migrants. From marriage records of the industrial cities, six "sending" communities were selected, three in 1856 and three in 1876, and manuscript censuses for the "sending" communities were analyzed in conjunction with the information furnished by the marriage records. All the communities studied disproportionately provided migrants to the three industrializing cities of Le Chambon-Feugerolles, Rive-de-Gier, and Saint-Chamond. The years 1856 and 1876 were chosen because census materials for these years were the most complete and reliable of those in the periods of interest.[4] An economic and demographic profile based mainly on manuscript census material from the selected sending communes was constructed to give some sense of the individual village and small-town communities that produced migrants. Finally, the

Figure 3.1   The Stéphanois region and its hinterland: administrative areas

number of migrants in any one year from a sending commune to a single area of destination, or "receiving" city, was sometimes small; thus, marriage records of the receiving community for each year between 1856 and 1876 were searched for migrants from the selected sending communities. This yielded a profile of migrants from individual rural communities and small towns who went to each industrial city over a two-decade period.

Discussing economic change in six communes during two time periods is too unwieldly for a single chapter. For the purposes of this chapter, examples will be confined to two of the three selected towns in each period. Thus omitted is the town from each time period with the least number of migrants to the receiving city over the period 1856 to 1876.[5] For the period 1840 to 1860, the two sending areas for 1856 are Saint-Amant-Roche-Savine in the Puy-de-Dôme and Saint-Julien-Chapteuil in the Haute-Loire; for the period 1860 to 1880, the two selected communities for 1876 are Saint-Christo-en-Jarez and Pavezin, both in the department of the Loire (see figure 3.1).

THE GROWTH OF THE LABOR FORCE: 1840–1860

Examining regions and some individual communities that sent migrants to the Stéphanois cities in the early period of industrial transformation – the years between 1840 and 1860 – may help to explain why the tide of migration might seem threatening to the cause of worker militancy in 1848. As was shown in chapter 1, organized Stéphanois workers displayed hostility towards rural migrants in that revolutionary year. In 1856, a little under 60 percent of all non-natives of each of the three towns migrated from the northwestern, western, and eastern areas within a 60 kilometer radius of their receiving city. Excluding the department of the Loire and the department of the Rhône with its great city of Lyon, the most important sending area was in the west. The departments of the Haute-Loire and the Puy-de-Dôme together contributed 16.1 percent of all non-native brides and grooms in 1856.[6]

In the decades before 1840, tens of thousands of inhabitants of the *arrondissement* of Saint-Etienne in the Loire, of the *arrondissements* of Yssingeaux and Le Puy in the Haute-Loire, and of the *arrondissement* of Ambert in the Puy-de-Dôme had commonly participated in a regional economy that combined seasonal industrial work with agriculture (see figure 3.1). Rye was the overwhelmingly dominant grain crop in all three *arrondissements* which were situated on the eastern slopes of the Massif Central. The agricultural schedule complemented the requirements of industrial employers since the conditions for rye cultivation determined that the large manpower requirements of the harvest season were concentrated in July, August, and September.[7] The months of idleness in the mountain cantons created a thriving opportunity for rural industry. Ribbonweaving, lacemaking, cutlery and hardware production were concentrated in these rye-growing areas.

Between 1820 and 1840, the seasonal rhythm of the agricultural year also fit in well with the requirements of part-time industrial work in the cities and villages of the early Industrial Revolution. As was shown in the last chapter, even in the coal-producing Stéphanois region, fast-flowing streams long remained the major source of power for many mills. The summer drought thus closed the majority of water-powered mills at the harvest period, the months of July, August, and September, when agricultural demand for labor was at its height.[8] Moreover, the migrants to the industrial city came from rye-producing areas and continued to eat rye bread, creating an urban market for the products of the countryside at a time when urban dwellers were increasingly abandoning rye for wheat bread.[9]

Beginning around 1840, the expansion of local coal mining and the rise of large factory industries provided vast new opportunities for both seasonal and non-seasonal employment. Although the need for unskilled labor increased, the industrial production schedule was no longer coordinated with that of agriculture; seasonal work, though available, no longer coincided conveniently with the inactive period of the agricultural year, as it had in the past.

The impact of changing employment opportunities caused by the growth of large-scale urban industry can be seen in both Saint-Amant-Roche-Savine and Saint-Julien-Chapteuil, the two selected sending communes for 1856 (see figure 3.1). Saint-Amant, a small rural commune of just under 2,000 people, lies in the center of a high and rocky plateau, 12 kilometers northwest of Ambert, the capital of its *arrondissement* in the Puy-de-Dôme, and 69 kilometers northwest of Saint-Chamond, the city to which it sent a number of its sons and daughters (see figure 3.2). Also located in rough terrain is Saint-Julien-Chapteuil, a commune of 2,600 inhabitants, perched high on mountain slopes in the *arrondissement* of Le Puy in the department of the Haute-Loire. Saint-Julien is situated 61 kilometers to the southwest of Rive-de-Gier, where a number of migrants from Saint-Julien settled.

The economies of the two communes differed greatly. Saint-Amant was a marginal farming area that for generations had depended on seasonal labor for survival. An 1848 survey stated that all men participated in migratory industrial labor, either in sawyering or in rag picking, and claimed that "all our workers are simultaneously landowners who occupy themselves in the field upon their return [from migrant laboring]."[10] Dispersed holdings and seasonal migration had enabled the Puy-de-Dôme to support a large population but one that was always precariously poised on the edge of poverty. Located in one of the 15 most populous *arrondissements* in all of France, residents of Saint-Amant, responding to the 1848 enquiry, estimated that the harsh weather left agriculturalists with four idle months every year.[11] In 1856, 27 percent of all household heads were employed in seasonal sawyering while 47.2 percent were employed in farming. Sawyers doubtless pioneered the migration path to the industrial city. Coal mines required large amounts of lumber for mine timbering, and this generated employment for sawyers; a survey of migration made during the First Empire recorded that 100 sawyers from the Puy-de-Dôme annually traveled to the department of the Loire.[12]

In contrast, in Saint-Julien, seasonal labor was also widespread but played a more subordinate role in a basically agricultural economy. Here, seasonal labor opportunities existed *within* local industry as well as outside the region, through seasonal migration. Because the roads connecting Saint-Julien to the larger world were in very poor condition, the milling industry that had developed in the area was small-scale and localized; the many small mills that ground corn, wheat, and rye and sawed wood for export were water-powered and thus mainly seasonal industries. For generations, seasonal migration had occurred among day laborers from local agriculture who had sought jobs in the Stéphanois region during the wintertime.[13] The regional patois referred to the departure "either for the season . . . or for some years" as going "*à la marre.*" The "*marre*" was the pickaxe used by day laborers in roadwork and construction; migrants often departed carrying pickaxes on their shoulder.[14]

Figure 3.2   Saint-Amant-Roche-Savine, 1983

In both communes, by 1856, traditional seasonal industries were giving ground. In Saint-Amant, seasonal migration remained very important. Unlike other manuscript censuses for sending communes, the 1856 census for Saint-Amant specifically identifies seasonally absent migrants, who were counted as part of the commune's population. Analysis of this sawyering population shows widespread participation in seasonal industry. While some household heads, men in their forties and fifties, were sawyers, as many unmarried men, many of them sons of full-time farmers, were also employed in seasonal sawyering. In 1856, 32.4 percent of the total male population aged 20 to 29, and 19.4 percent of all household heads were listed as seasonally absent.

Alongside seasonal migration, new forms of migration were developing. Even in the industrializing cities, a number of male migrants retained their traditional occupational identities and perhaps their seasonal migration patterns; five sawyers from Saint-Amant and two rag pickers show up in industrial Saint-Chamond in the years between 1856 and 1876. But a larger proportion of male migrants from rural Saint-Amant, 10 out of 21, were attracted to the rapidly expanding machine-construction factories, where wages were much higher than among sawyers. Both men and women from Saint-Amant found employment in Saint-Chamond. The majority of the single female migrants from Saint-Amant, 17 out of 30, worked in the textile mills, and almost all of these stayed in company-run textile dormitories. Most of the rest of the female migrants were engaged in ribbon manufacture or in domestic service.

In Saint-Julien, the severe mid-century economic crisis and the displacement caused by the region's growing integration into the national market destroyed local seasonal industries and increased the need for seasonal migration. Moreover, for a time, the severity of the crisis prolonged the duration of the migration period and even threatened to create massive permanent emigration. After the 1840s, the expansion of roads, and later of rail·oads, in the Haute-Loire facilitated the dire∴ export of agricultural prcducts without processing. Betwee⌐ 1846 and 1881, the number of industrial e⌐∴blishments and, more importa∴tly, the total taxable value of processing establishments decreased sharply. Because of the severity of the crisis of 1848–50 in the Haute-Loire, the values of industrial establishments sank to their lowest point in 1851.[15] Jean Merley cites Saint-Julien as a commune that witnessed the "collapse of industrial establishments."[16] The 1856 census shows little trace of industrial employment: 86 percent of all economically active household heads listed themselves as engaged in farming. Between 1841 and 1856, the growth that had characterized the commune's population in the preceding 20 years ceased and its population declined by 15.2 per cent.

In the 1850s, migration to the Stéphanois region, pioneered by seasonally migrant agricultural day laborers, was swelled by the addition of many non-seasonal migrants, primarily displaced, and local industrial workers who had engaged in seasonal industrial work within the region of Saint-Julien. In 1848, the miners of Rive-de-Gier complained that "the greater part of the strangers [migrating to the local mines] come from Piedmont and from the Haute-Loire.

Emigration is always more frequent at the beginning of the winter; the greater part are settling down in the area."[17] The changing nature of migration also prompted concern in the Haute-Loire. In 1853 the *Conseiller Général* noted that "emigration . . . is no longer temporary [*momentanée*] as it used to be . . . the emigrant passes his summers and his winters, and no longer returns to his home except at intervals . . . "[18]

In 1856 in Saint-Amant, seasonal migration was giving way to permanent migration and to non-seasonal forms of temporary migration. Migrants no longer returned to the fields in time to sow and harvest, but went home only after several years – or did not return at all. In Saint-Julien too, the decline of local seasonal industry led to increased seasonal migration and to forms of temporary migration that might presage permanent migration. In the 1850s, migration to industrial cities such as Rive-de-Gier and Saint-Chamond from villages such as Saint-Amant and Saint-Julien was temporary, in the sense that migrants returned to their place of origin after many months or after a few years. Given the generations of temporary migrants from these same villages that had proceeded to and from these same industrial cities, many migrants in the 1850s must have arrived with the intention, or at least the expectation, of returning to the countryside. Temporary migrants might return to their homes upon inheriting land, after accumulating a target sum of money, or after contracting a marriage.

The massive agricultural survey of 1866 provides much evidence that natives of Saint-Amant and the *arrondissement* of Ambert frequently returned from proletarian labor in the industrial city to become landowning peasants. Exaggerating the earning capacity of urban workers, a landowner from Ambert claimed that "after six or eight months the emigrant brings back a sack of 1,000 francs, then he buys a bit of land."[19] A landowner from Saint-Amant-Roche-Savine testified to the government committee concerning the dire effects of returning migrants on local agriculture: "Ten years from now there will only be small proprietors. Upon the death of the father of the family, the children sell everything piecemeal in order to situate themselves in the industrial regions . . . They return with their savings and buy a small piece of land but do not improve it."[20]

After the severe economic crisis at mid-century, return migration also resumed its importance in the Haute-Loire. The extension of a railway line through the southern Haute-Loire, opening the hitherto relatively inaccessible plateau region to commerce, greatly increased the export capacity of local agriculture and fueled a decade of agricultural prosperity during which both the population of Saint-Julien and the populations of the *arrondissements* of Le Puy and of Yssingeaux grew steadily.[21] Possibly agricultural prosperity even encouraged the return of some emigrants from urban industry. An analysis of a sample of the 1876 census for Rive-de-Gier, the sole census in the study that recorded place of birth in 1876, shows that, of the 20 percent of the Ripagérien population sampled, 86.8 percent listed a birthplace (N = 2,917) and not a single person came from Saint-Julien. According to Jean Merley, in the southern *arrondissements* of the Haute-Loire, truly massive and permanent out-migration did not occur until the last years of the Second Empire.[22]

Exchanges of letters and visits between migrant children and their non-migrating parents in the countryside helped to preserve the migrants' contacts with village society. Among nearby rural communities, market-day in the industrial city must often have served as an occasion for the reaffirmation of rural and urban contacts, while the less frequent agricultural fairs that were held in the industrial cities might have served the same purpose for more distant villagers. The frequent return to the country of industrial workers during the harvest season or the departure of young urban children to serve as shepherds must have often involved the reassertion of workers' ties to old contacts and friends as well as increasing the income of workers and their families.

A more roundabout confirmation of the continuity of relations between rural and urban laboring populations in the years between 1840 and 1860 can be derived from the demonstration that rural–urban ties were *least* ruptured in this period. One indication of the rupture of ties between sending area and receiving city is the departure of the brides' and grooms' parents from the sending area. This is indicated by the presence outside the native commune of parents of sufficient age to have marriageable children. Of the 90 parents of children who migrated from Saint-Amant to Saint-Chamond between 1856 and 1876 for whom evidence exists, only 30 percent either were living outside Saint-Amant or had died outside their native commune at the time of their child's marriage. This was the lowest percentage of non-residing parents of any of the six sending communes studied. Many migrants to Saint-Chamond maintained a living parent in Saint-Amant. Others had lost both parents both whom were buried in Saint-Amant, but some of these had doubtless also inherited a piece of land which tied them anew to their commune of birth. The crisis nature of the flight of workers from Saint-Julien had constituted some-what more of a break but substantial contact remained; the comparable figure for the 24 parents from Saint-Julien on whom information exists is 37.5 percent, living or dead outside the commune.

The retention of ties to the sending villages clearly facilitated temporary migration. But the most fundamental condition for temporary rather than permanent migration was the existence of expanding opportunities in agriculture in the sending areas. In 1856, the dominant trends in agriculture in all of the *arrondissements* were increases in the proportion of farmers who owned their land and did not employ labor, and in the number of farmers who owned their land and worked part-time as day laborers. In 1852, these two categories included more than 70 percent of all those engaged in agriculture in the three departments. Most of those working in agriculture did own property, yet most farms were small. The overwhelming number of farms were under ten hectares in size – 87 percent in the Puy-de-Dôme, 76 percent in the Haute-Loire, and 68 percent in the Loire.[23]

The processes promoting the proliferation of ownership are well described in the 1866 report for the department of the Haute-Loire, which noted the complaints of large- and medium-sized landowners concerned by the "ever increasing wages of domestics and agricultural workers."[24] The rising cost of day laborers was caused partly by the permanent departure of agricultural workers to work in the city. Another factor contributing to labor scarcity was the return from the industrial city of former agricultural laborers and small landowners who had previously worked part-time for others but who now had sufficient money to establish themselves independently on the land. The same factors operated in the Puy-de-Dôme: in 1866, a landowner from Job, near Saint-Amant, testified that "one of the great evils of agriculture is the lack of laborers which is due to emigration: and upon returning, the emigrants demoralize those who remain."[25] Landowners claimed that it was more profitable to sell land than to farm it because: "the peasant buys at any price."[26] In many cases, peasants may have been willing to pay high prices in order to acquire adjacent land because such a rounding-off would make their property self-supporting.

Seen from the city, migrants' hopes of return were based on opportunities in agriculture. Seen from the country, however, these hopes were based on finding jobs in urban industry that would allow them to accumulate money. Hopes of accumulating sufficient money to return to the land were based on migrants' ability to find remunerative employment within the industrial city. Despite the growth of full-time industrial employment, the workings of the labor market alone could not ensure that relatively well-paying industrial jobs would be reliably obtained by any particular group of rural migrants. After all, industrial growth in the Stéphanois did not mean unlimited expansion in the number of jobs; as shown in chapter 2, the growth of full-time employment was counterbalanced by the contraction of seasonal employment, and there were many rural day laborers who might find industrial work attractive. In many cases, migrants who wished to return to the country needed to accumulate a relatively large sum of money in only a few years; long job searches or irregular industrial employment could frustrate their hopes.

Fortunately for the groups that actually did migrate to the industrial city, potential rural migrants were able to draw upon long-established contacts with the industrial cities, contacts established by their parents or between relatives and friends who had permanently migrated. As we have seen, in the years between 1840 and 1856 migrants were moving within a region, if not familiar to themselves, at least familiar to their parents, their kin, or their neighbors. Indeed, the marriage records frequently suggest the gradual, hesitant manner in which rural families migrated to the industrial city. The case of the Montagne family suggests the step by step, multi-stage character of migration. This family originated in the commune of Saint-Christo-en-Jarez (a commune to be shortly discussed). In 1867, André, a metalworker and a native of Saint-Christo-en-Jarez, was living with his older brother in Saint-Chamond and had been living there since he was nine years old. His brother, Jean, was twelve years older than André and was an established haberdasher in 1867. Jean may have brought his younger brother to the city to help him in his enterprise until André was old enough to get a job in the metal works. In any case, their father died in Saint-Christo in 1853, years after his sons had established themselves in Saint-Chamond. After her husband's death, their mother must have joined her sons in the industrial city for she was living with them in 1867.

The persistence of long-standing ties to a particular industrial city, such as those engendered by chain migration, facilitated access to remunerative employment for migrants from certain villages and regions. Young André's brother may have used his contacts in Saint-Chamond to find André his relatively remunerative job as a stoker. But, at least initially, the continuity of these urban–rural ties may also have encouraged migrants to believe that, although they were now spending several years in the city rather than just the agricultural off-season, they were still participating in the urban labor market on the same terms as their parents had, that is, as peasants residing temporarily in the city. While working in the Petin–Gaudet works, young André may have been putting aside money so that he could return to Saint-Christo, but the death of his father when André was only 16, the inability of his mother to survive on her own, and the well-paying positions of the two sons may have encouraged the family to establish themselves permanently in the industrial city.

The most striking feature of the villages and small towns that disproportionately sent their residents to the city in 1856 is the degree to which the migrants followed familiar and often short paths. Saint-Christo-en-Jarez, Saint-Romain-les-Atheux, Saint-Just-Malmont, and Saint-Symphorien-sur-Coise sent their residents to nearby industrial cities that were also local market centers or sites of fairs. Monistrol-sur-Loire and Saint-Just-Malmont were silkweaving centers that contributed their sons and daughters to Le Chambon-Feugerolles, a silk weaving center in the Stéphanois valley only a few kilometers distant, a short walk down well-traveled roads.[27] As we have shown, even more distant sending areas, communes such as Saint-Amant-Roche-Savine and Saint-Julien-Chapteuil, had long been connected both commercially and industrially with the Stéphanois.

By mid-century, and for many years afterward, the very means by which rural dwellers found jobs in the city facilitated their continued identification with the village and rural life. Over time, those villages and towns that sent a disproportionate number of migrants to the industrial city had developed a privileged relationship with the large and rapidly expanding local industries in the industrial city. Because most villages and communes did not send a large number of migrants that appear in the marriage records in any one year, a relatively long period is necessary to give a real overview of sending patterns. For both 1856 and 1876, the three communes that made the largest proportionate contribution of migrants to each industrial city were selected, and for the whole period 1856 to 1876, the marriage records of the industrial city were searched for migrants from these 18 communes.[28] Table 3.1 summarizes the findings for males in those industries where migrants were most concentrated;

Table 3.1   Origins of the male labor force in Le Chambon-Feugerolles, Rive-de-Gier, and Saint-Chamond

Industry	Natives: 1856 and 1876 combined		Non-natives from sending communes: 1856–1876, entire period		Other non-natives 1856 and 1876 combined	
	No.	*%*	*No.*	*%*	*No.*	*%*
Building trades	12	6.5	11	5.0	40	10.3
Day laborers	4	2.2	9	4.1	15	3.9
Machine-construction workers	57	31.0	79	36.2	114	19.3
Miners	26	14.1	38	17.4	42	10.8
Total in labor force	184		218		389	

it shows that those communes that sent large proportions of migrants to a particular industrial city were more liable to contribute workers to machine construction and to mining than were all other migrants or even the native population. (Tables 3.3 and 3.4 in appendix 3.2 contain a more complete breakdown of industries by nativity.)

The connection between village jobseekers and urban jobs helped to reconfirm and reassert a village regional identity. In 1856, a fellow villager who had become a permanent coal cutter, a roller, or a puddler, might easily find unskilled work for kin or acquaintances whose own stay in industry would be more transitory. In metalworking and coal mining, a strong and healthy male worker was suitable for many types of work, if a place could be found for him, and places were found for migrants from sending areas.

Compared with natives, migrants from the sending communities were at no disadvantage in gaining entry into the very top of the skill hierarchy in machine construction, as figure 3.3 shows. Most workers who made it into the highly skilled category probably were permanent residents; their pay was high, and the time spent acquiring their skill made a return to farming unlikely. Although migrants from the sending communities did not enter into the semi-skilled category in as great proportions as natives, and were far more likely to perform unskilled labor, they did have approximately equal representation among the most highly skilled workers. These highly skilled workers may have served to recommend their fellow countrymen to employers or even to hire them directly as aides or assistants. In machine construction, both natives and migrants from the sending communities were at a disadvantage compared to those migrants from established metalworking centers, from Saint-Etienne, Saint-Genis-Terrenoire, or Lyon, who brought their skills with them; a good many highly skilled metal workers were from Lyon or Saint-Etienne. Of course, the short stay of so many migrants from the sending communities in the Stéphanois probably also helps account for their relative absence among the semi-skilled and their disproportionate presence in the ranks of the unskilled.

NATIVES
1856 and 1876
combined

NON-NATIVES FROM
SENDING COMMUNES
1856–1876
entire period

OTHER NON-NATIVES
1856 and 1876
combined

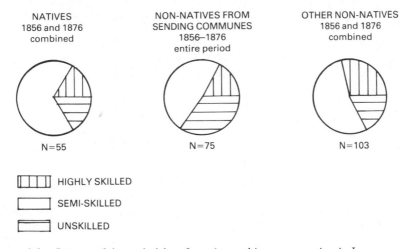

N=55

N=75

N=103

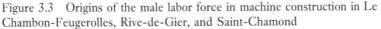

HIGHLY SKILLED

SEMI-SKILLED

UNSKILLED

Figure 3.3   Origins of the male labor force in machine construction in Le Chambon-Feugerolles, Rive-de-Gier, and Saint-Chamond

In the industrial city, the strength of the rural migrants' ties to their fellow countrymen, already consolidated by hiring practices, was further reinforced among those migrants who expected to return to the countryside. Young people who anticipated returning to the countryside looked for marriage partners familiar with the countryside and with rural skills. Such concerns further separated temporary migrants from native workers and permanent migrants. In fact, male temporary migrants were able to court and marry home-town women in the very heart of the industrial city. In 1856, in the three industrial cities, almost as many migrants from the Haute-Loire and the Puy-de-Dôme (26) married migrants from their native department as married natives of the department of the Loire (28).

Village recruitment networks and the expectation of returning to the countryside encouraged rural migrants to associate with one another in the industrial city. Marriage records suggest that migrants from the more important sending communities were surrounded by fellow villagers of their own age, perhaps the companions of their youth.[29] To cite one example, in 1856, Pierre Chennan, a day laborer at the Petin–Gaudet forge in Saint-Chamond and a native of Saint-Amant-Roche-Savine, married a young woman working in the textile mills of Saint-Chamond. His bride was a native of Fournols, a village in the Puy-de-Dôme, about six kilometers from Saint-Amant. The witnesses at Pierre's marriage were: his maternal uncle, a ragpicker, also living in Saint-Chamond; his brother-in-law, who was a day laborer at another forge and lived in Saint-Chamond; and his brother, who worked in the same forge as his brother-in-law. Pierre lived in a tenement building inhabited by another young man from the Puy-de-Dôme, who also married in 1856. This young man, Damiens Pagnal, was a forger at the Petin–Gaudet factory; he came from

Grandval, only three kilometers from Chennan's home town of Saint-Amant. Damiens' bride, a mill worker in Saint-Chamond, was a native of Saint-Amant. The witnesses at the wedding were: a German cousin of the groom, who was a machine operator at the forge; his brother-in-law, a nailer; and the bride's second cousin, a day laborer at the forge. All of them resided in Saint-Chamond.

Solidarity within specific rural migrants groups was further buttressed by the Occitan dialects spoken by the migrants. These dialects were different from those spoken in the Stéphanois, where Franco-Provençal dialects prevailed almost everywhere among the popular classes.[30] Although both migrant and native dialects were influenced by Oc and modern French, Occitan and Franco-Provençal differed considerably from each other. The varieties of patois spoken in the Stéphanois were labeled "*Gaga*" which was alleged to derive from the Latin *gagates*, or "inhabitant of a carbonaceous area."[31] In 1832, a military observer wrote that "The language of the inhabitants of the countryside and of the working class is a patois where one will remark certain traces of Latin. The workers understand French and speak it a little."[32] The Provençal dialects spoken in the Stéphanois were apparently closer to modern French than was the Occitan spoken by most migrants, but opinions about the degree to which French speakers could understand them differ.[33]

The persistence of the native dialect and the growing usage of French testify to the difficulties caused by linguistic differences in the cities. Over the decades between 1840 and 1860, while *Gaga* retained its hold on the native population, the increased numbers of migrants who did not speak the patois encouraged the use of French as the common tongue of the plebian classes. At least, both native and newcomer spoke it equally poorly. But as long as *Gaga* was used in local café culture, it undoubtedly reinforced and emphasized the differences between natives and non-*Gaga*-speaking migrants. In the 1840s, local songwriters composed their songs in *Gaga*, and some continued to compose patois songs into the 1860s and 1870s. The popular songwriter François Linossier, commander of the National Guard in Saint-Etienne in 1848, wrote most of his songs in patois until his death in 1871. But by the late 1850s, while most songwriters had authored a few native patois songs for special occasions, many composed mainly in French.[34] In the 1850s, Louis Napoleon's closing of many cafés, feared as centers of working-class opposition to the regime, certainly diminished employment opportunities for singers and may have encouraged professional singers to secure the widest possible audience by singing in French.

Traditional urban popular celebrations also were linked with native populations, and eventually, though gradually, declined along with the local patois. The large-scale entry of non-*Gaga*-speaking migrants and their clash with native culture is also shown by the relationship between the entry of migrants and the decline of customary urban celebrations; migrants do not seem to have participated in them with the enthusiasm of the natives. An 1853 police report from Rive-de-Gier lamented the lack of "variety" in Ripagérien celebrations that year.[35] In 1859 Leon Velle wrote a well-known lament for the decline of *Mer'luron*, the patois term for mardi gras, in Saint-Etienne:

An old *gagat* from the place Roanelle
  One day was crying
For the city that a new breed [*race*] was
  Regenerating.
It is no longer you, he was saying in his suffering.
  Not without reason!
Ah! give me back my old Saint-Etienne
  My *mer'luron*[36]

All through the 1860s and 1870s, newspaper reports from Stéphanois cities mourned the decline of customary celebrations such as carnival, so it is fair to say that these customs certainly took their time dying. Only in 1891 did a report from Rive-de-Gier finally proclaim that "carnival is dead in Rive-de-Gier."[37]

In 1856, the temporary duration of so much of the migration from rural areas, the persistence of close relations among rural migrants within the industrial city, and the presence of rural migrants in all leading industries and at every skill level often served to confound and alarm both outside observers and natives. The gap between migrants and natives seemed wide and insurmountable; a working class composed of such a large proportion of migrants seemed completely unwieldy and intractable to labor organization. In 1844, when the socialist leader Flora Tristan visited Saint-Etienne and Rive-de-Gier she was shocked by evidence of rural influence on the working class:

Beasts! Idiots! Each and every one, the appearance of peasants. – Indeed, the entire local population comes from the mountains adjacent to the town ... The dress of these people is that of the countryside "citified" [*envilisée*] ... Everyone speaks an abominable patois ... Between these people and those of Lyon there is forty years' difference.[38]

Basing her impressions on only a few days in Saint-Etienne and Rive-de-Gier, Flora Tristan may be excused for ignoring the existence of a native population in the Stéphanois, a population with long roots in urban industry. But Tristan's perceptions of the city were not so different of those of a long-time native. In 1844, a native of Rive-de-Gier lamented the changes occurring in his home town:

The population [of the city] has twice doubled in thirty years. With my own eyes I have seen the building of four-fifths of the local houses ... But, alas, the frank and happy poor of times past are now replaced, in great part, by a population born far from our city, ignoring its roman language, foreign to its joys and to its recollections.[39]

Despite exaggeration, such testimony captures at least one genuine aspect of the rapid population increase that was transforming Rive-de-Gier in these years. While the population that the author deplores was not born "far" from Rive-de-Gier and was not so "ignorant" of or "foreign" to its "joys" and "recollections" as suggested, still the enclaves of rural migrants, sometimes speaking their own patois and often keeping to themselves, provoked alarm among the settled working-class populations, whose wages they undercut and who considered them unorganizable. A similar alarm also spread among the native middle classes, whose clientele and familiar customers were drowned in a sea of new faces. Such nostalgia was based on the disappearance in the recent past of a relatively homogeneous and particularistic urban culture.

THE CULMINATION OF INDUSTRIAL TRANSFORMATION: 1860–1880

Around 1860, the nature of migration changed, and with it the extent of migrants' integration into local working-class culture. As will be shown in chapter 6, the increased integration of migrants into local popular culture indicated a changed relationship between migrants and the labor movement. In the first period of industrialization, many migrants who occupied proletarian industrial jobs were only temporarily proletarianized; they expected to return to peasant agriculture. As we will see, in the second period of Stéphanois industrial development, there was a substantial increase in the proportion of proletarian jobs filled by permanently proletarianized workers.[40] The growing importance of permanent proletarians in the migrant workforce facilitated migrants' assimilation into the established urban working class, and it helped to give existing migrant networks the same concerns as those of long-time proletarians.

Although the distribution of migrants among the industrial receiving cities changed somewhat between 1856 and 1876, the proportion of migrants in all the marriage records did not vary greatly over time: from 62.6 percent in 1856 to 60.7 percent in 1876. Figures 3.4 and 3.5 show the major sending areas for migrants in 1856 and 1876 and allow a comparison of changes over the two periods. The maps cover a space approximately 105 kilometers long and 110 kilometers wide; the crosses indicate the receiving cities and the circles are an indication of the proportionate number of migrants sent to receiving cities. The maps show that, in 1876, the recruitment region was smaller and nearer the receiving city than it had been in 1856. The combined contribution of the Haute-Loire and the Puy-de-Dôme declined from 16.1 percent of all non-natives to 13.3 percent, the slack being taken up by the Loire, which expanded its dominant contribution from 46 percent to 50.7 percent. The growth of Clermont-Ferrand and Grenoble drew away migrants on the periphery of the Stéphanois recruitment region.[41]

More important is the tendency of the sending areas to cluster around a line connecting the three cities. This area represents the industrialized portion of

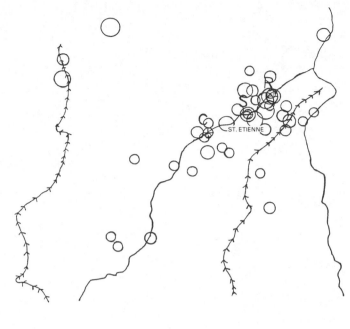

Receiving cities:

    C+ Le Chambon-Feugerolles

    R+ Rive-de-Gier

    S+ Saint-Chamond

    mountainous terrain

    rivers

    communes sending 2 migrants to receiving cities

    communes sending 3–6 migrants to receiving cities

    communes sending more than 6 migrants to receiving cities

Figure 3.4   Migration from sending areas to Stéphanois cities, 1856

the Stéphanois and the communes along the roads connecting this region to the outside world. The "C" on the maps identifies the location of Le Chambon-Feugerolles, the "S" Saint-Chamond, and the "R" Rive-de-Gier. Thus, the evidence of geographic origins reinforces the evidence from fathers' occupations and emphasizes the increasing tendency of growing cities to recruit from within the industrialized region.

While 1876 witnessed a falling away of the more distant portions of what, in 1856, had been the traditional area of labor recruitment, it also saw an increase

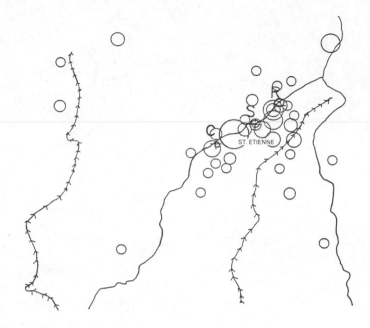

Receiving cities:

    C+ Le Chambon-Feugerolles

    R+ Rive-de-Gier

    S+ Saint-Chamond

    mountainous terrain

    rivers

    communes sending 2 migrants to receiving cities

    communes sending 3–6 migrants to receiving cities

    communes sending more than 6 migrants to receiving cities

Figure 3.5   Migration from sending areas to Stéphanois cities, 1876

in the proportion of migrants from beyond the region, a trend not shown in the maps. In the years between 1840 and 1860, a migratory network had linked mountain rural regions with valley industries; after 1860, this old network began to decline and, more and more, migratory networks grew up that linked neighboring industrial cities with one another and with more distant industrial regions. In 1876, the proportion of both brides and grooms born over 480 kilometers from the receiving cities increased, from 3.4 percent to 8.2 percent, and the contraction of regional recruitment networks coincided with an in-

Table 3.2   Occupations of surviving fathers of brides and grooms in the Stéphanois region: ·
1856 and 1876

	Agriculture	Machine construction and mining	N
1856			
All married	34%	23%	442
Migrant married	53%	18%	208
1876			
All married	18%	27%	310
Migrant married	37%	30%	196

crease in migration from beyond the region. In 1876, the largest component of this long-distance recruitment were young, unmarried, and unskilled Italians. But while the foothold gained by the Italians foretold developments in the late nineteenth and twentieth centuries, it was not yet the major factor in the migratory stream.[42]

While the regional boundaries of labor recruitment and the role of long-distance migrants in the labor force were slowly changing, more dramatic changes were occurring in the social background of the regional and native workers entering urban industry. The contribution of the small rural bourgs and villages that had long sent seasonal and temporary migrants to the city was declining, and the contribution of permanently proletarianized, regional working classes to the industrializing cities was increasing. Marriage records, which present only the occupation of all *surviving* fathers of brides and grooms, show the growing importance of the children of industrial proletarians in the migrant population. Table 3.2 summarizes the dramatic changes in occupational background for both the total and migrant populations that occurred between 1856 and 1876. Of those migrants with surviving fathers employed in machine construction or mining, a little under 70 percent of the fathers resided in the same industrial city as their child. In these cases, an entire family had probably moved to the industrial city. About 20 percent had fathers who resided in the *arrondissement* of Saint-Etienne; these migrant sons were only moving from one city to another within the Stéphanois industrial region.

Because a large minority of fathers (43.1 percent) died before their child's wedding, evidence from surviving fathers is not conclusive. But such indicators as commune size and industrial composition reinforce the evidence of growing internal recruitment within the industrial sector in the *arrondissement* of Saint-Etienne during the later period. Among the migrants from the *arrondissement*, the changing origins of local migrants can be seen from the size of the communities that sent migrants to the city. In 1856, 12 percent of all migrants came from communities with over 5,000 inhabitants; in 1876, it was 31 percent. Also, in 1856, 29 percent of all migrants came from one of the dozen small industrial communes that lined the railroad tracks between Givors and Firminy; by 1876, the percentage had risen to 44.[43]

Even among migrants from the countryside, from those communes with a population under 5,000, changes occurred that increased the proletarian component of the workforce. The two rural communes selected in 1876, Saint-Christo-en-Jarez and Pavezin, show that local agriculture was undergoing fundamental transformation (see figure 3.1). The commune of Saint-Christo-en-Jarez, the first selected commune in 1876, presents the case of a prosperous rural community that was well ahead of its neighbors in the shift from grain production to milk production. This commune's evolution foreshadowed that of the others; increasingly, the surrounding countryside abandoned rural industry and subsistence grain growing for a concentration in commercial dairying. In 1876, migration links had long existed between Saint-Christo-en-Jarez and Saint-Chamond. In 1876, the commune of Saint-Christo had about 1,200 inhabitants. Geographically, it is about eight kilometers from Saint-Chamond, but in some respects it is both further and nearer than eight kilometers. It is further because the eight kilometers are almost straight uphill, as Saint-Christo is perched on a mountain slope. It is nearer because from the square in front of the church in Saint-Christo one can still see the smokestacks and factories of Saint-Chamond (see figure 3.6). The inhabitants of Saint-Christo were confronted by the presence of Saint-Chamond every day of their lives.

When they looked down upon the industrial valley, the farmers of Saint-Christo saw not only a source of employment but also the major market for their products. Saint-Christo was thus a prosperous agricultural community, the agricultural census of 1875 showing that it had become one of the largest dairying and livestock-producing communes in the area adjacent to the Stéphanois valley.[44] In 1866, one of the few large landowners in the commune had reported before a government committee that "progress had been made in this area." He noted that "there is a tendency toward the increase in artificial meadows and cattle raising. The price of farm laborers had very much increased because they were attracted by the neighboring industrial cities."[45]

Within the region comprising the Puy-de-Dôme, the Haute-Loire, and the Loire, proximity to the Stéphanois industrial area accelerated the turn towards dairying. This proximity and a worldwide decline in grain prices ended the expansion of individual landholding. Between 1850 and 1880, the *arrondissement* of Yssingeaux, directly adjacent to the *arrondissement* of Saint-Etienne, witnessed a 12 percent decline in the number of resident landowners, while the more distant *arrondissement* of Le Puy saw only stagnation, an end to the era of rapid growth. The rise of dairying took place most rapidly in the *arrondissement* of Saint-Etienne itself.[46] In 1892 and 1893, Pierre du Maroussem collected evidence on this agricultural transformation in the commune of Saint-Genest-Malifaux, only a few kilometers from Le Chambon-Feugerolles. In this area, the first morning milk train was organized in 1857. Du Maroussem noted that, 35 years later, a "nearly completed revolution" had occurred in local agriculture. The

Figure 3.6 Saint-Christo-en-Jarez, late nineteenth century

entire surface of seven communes was covered with grazing land and grain crops nearly vanished.[47]

Dairying succeeded because it offered overwhelming advantages to the small group of farmers who had the sizeable sums of money required to buy cattle. The explosive urbanization of the Stéphanois created a large market nearby. Also, dairying did not require large amounts of seasonal labor; it needed year-round, constant effort but the work could be done with the help of a few extra hands. The reduction in the seasonal demand for labor was a very significant saving because farmers were no longer forced to compete with one another and with high-paying industry for laborers during the furious and danger-filled harvest season, when the crop was most at the mercy of the region's unstable climate; during the harvest season the wages of day laborers had routinely increased by 45 percent.

If Saint-Christo shows the effects of dairying progress, the case of Pavezin exhibits more clearly the collapse of the old grain-based agriculture. Pavezin was a commune of about 1,000 souls located eight kilometers from the city of Rive-de-Gier, where some of its migrants settled. Pavezin was a poor agricultural commune. In 1875, with only about 20 percent less area and 20 percent fewer inhabitants than Saint-Christo-en-Jarez, it had about half the number of cows and only about 60 percent of the total land area sown in grain crops.[48] Over 80 percent of the household head identified themselves as "farmers" (*cultivateurs*). In rural Pavezin, most farmers lacked the capital to shift quickly into dairying and remained trapped in rye growing.

In 1876, the rye-growing economy was on its last legs; the specific local plight of Stéphanois agriculturalists was only one manifestation of a nation-wide crisis for small farmers caused by falling prices and increased international competition. The extension of railways throughout France ended the transportation advantages that had accrued to local agriculture because of the early spread of railways in the region. The early 1870s witnessed the beginning of a fall in grain prices that was to continue unabated for 25 years, as the expansion of transportation networks in France and around the world brought increased competition. Between 1871 and 1875 and 1891 and 1895, the price of grain in France fell by more than a quarter; between 1856 and 1835 the price of rye in Saint-Etienne fell by more than one-third.[49] The urban demand for rye diminished to practically nothing. By 1870, workers in Saint-Etienne, Rive-de-Gier, and Saint-Chamond followed the example of the Parisian workers and demanded wheat bread.[50]

While Saint-Christo was more successful than Pavezin in adapting to the new agricultural climate that resulted from the crisis of grain growing, even successful adaptation led to out-migration. James Lehning's study of Marlhes, a commune near Le Chambon-Feugerolles, noted that one effect of the introduction of dairying was "deepening social divisions."[51] More than any of the sending communes under study, the census of Saint-Christo shows an agricultural population divided into a majority of landowners and a large minority, approximately one-third, of agricultural day laborers. Some of these agricultural day laborers were the sons of small landowners who were forced to work outside their parents' holdings, but there were also numerous households composed entirely of day laborers, men and women who owned little or no land.

The declining labor needs of a dairying economy severely undermined the position of these day-laboring families. The falling labor requirements of the dairying economy even persuaded some landholders to send their daughters to the textile mills developing in the nearby city. Thus in 1876 temporary migration continued to coexist with permanent migration among one section of the village population. Of the 25 migrants from Saint-Christo with living parents who listed an occupation, 19 parents identified themselves as "owner-farmers," (*propriétaires-cultivateurs*), three listed themselves as "tenants" (*fermiers*), and only one as a day laborer. While the defiant assertion by so many parents of their landowning status must be recognized, it is also likely that some of these "landowners" received most of their income working for more prosperous farmers.

In any case, the lessening need for labor in agriculture in Saint-Christo encouraged many young men and women to seek their fortune in the nearby city, many never to return. In 1862, twenty-one-year-old Etienne Coulon was already a highly skilled worker, an iron roller in the Petin–Gaudet works. A native of Saint-Christo, Etienne married a native Saint-Chamonnaise millworker. Etienne's fifty-five-year-old mother is listed as an "owner-farmer," resident in Saint-Christo. Ties of kinship connected the migrant from Saint-Christo with skilled workers in the industrial city; Etienne's uncle was one of the witnesses to the wedding. This uncle, with whom Etienne lived in Saint-Chamond, was a master puddler in the same shop as Etienne. Fourteen years later, Etienne's mother, Benoîte Montgrand, shows up in the 1876 census of Saint-Christo; this time she is living with her son Jean and his child. Jean is listed as a "day laborer" and also as "head of household."

Between 1862 and 1876, whatever pretension Benoîte Montgrand's household had to landholding was abandoned, and she probably became dependent on the income of her day-laboring son (and possibly on Etienne as well). Even if Etienne had given up any claims on the land, the ties of kinship may have helped the young man find his way in life. Perhaps with his uncle's help, he had found a relatively high-paying skilled job in machine construction. By 1876, it looked as if Etienne had got a better deal than his brother Jean, who remained in rural Saint-Christo.

Evidence from Pavezin suggests that migrants were leaving agriculture without looking back. Migrants from this commune had less reason than those from any of the other communes to maintain ties to communes where their parents still resided. Rural Pavezin had the highest percentage of parents of spouses who had left the commune; 47.4 percent of all parents of marrying migrants from this village either were living outside Pavezin or had died outside the commune.

By 1876, the changing nature of migration patterns had substantial influence on the integration of migrants into the workforce. The contraction of regional recruitment networks promoted the integration of migrants into the established urban working classes. At least in the case of migrants born in France, the distinction between native and migrant does not seem to have figured very prominently in working-class social life.

The manuscript census of Rive-de-Gier for 1876 contains information on the birthplace of the population. The census confirms the evidence of the marriage records concerning the extent to which migrants were recruited from other Stéphanois industrial towns and especially from villages neighboring Rive-de-Gier that spoke the Franco-Provençal dialect used there. Based on evidence in the marriage records, it seems likely that many more migrants came from areas that spoke the dialect of the receiving city in 1876 than in 1856. Moreover, in the case of Rive-de-Gier in 1876, the proximity of these villages suggests that there may have been a long-term overlapping between rural and urban society. Before these migrants moved to the city, many of them could have walked as many as four or five kilometers to work while continuing to reside in their village. The dairying revolution that cost many of these migrants their farms may have been only the very last stage in their involvement with industry rather than an abrupt break with an agricultural past.

In 1876, the characteristics of local migration are well illustrated by the process of recruitment into the work hierarchy in machine construction in Rive-de-Gier. In the machine construction industry in Rive-de-Gier, migrants were about as liable to gain access to skilled and semiskilled positions as natives (see figure 3.7), but a major reason for this was that the line between native and migrant was a blurry one. Figure 3.8 shows that recruits to machine construction came largely from rural communes only a few kilometers to the east and southeast of Rive-de-Gier, from villages such as Chateauneuf, Longes, Treves,

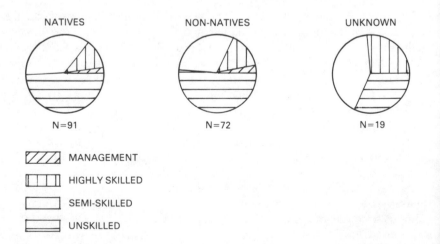

Figure 3.7   Origins of the male labor force in machine construction, 1876

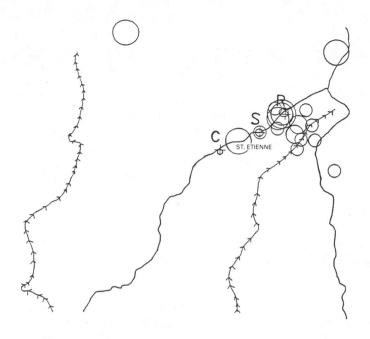

Receiving cities:

    C+ Le Chambon-Feugerolles

    R+ Rive-de-Gier

    S+ Saint-Chamond

    mountainous terrain

    rivers

    communes sending 2 migrants to receiving cities

    communes sending 3–6 migrants to receiving cities

    communes sending more than 6 migrants to receiving cities

Figure 3.8   Migration of machine construction workers from sending areas to Rive-de-Gier, 1876

Tartaras, and Condrieu, villages that were connected to the city by roads improved in the 1850s and 1860s.

New machine construction plants that opened in Rive-de-Gier in the 1860s established themselves on the southern and eastern outskirts of the city where cheap and plentiful land provided room for growth. The *Forges de Couzon,* founded by Lucien Arbel in 1869, was established opposite the train station on the southern outskirts of Rive-de-Gier; the new Morel works opened at Etaings

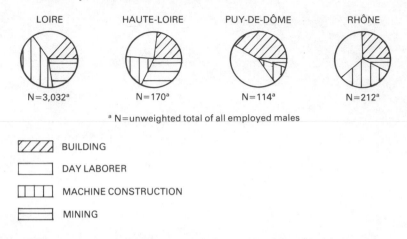

LOIRE   HAUTE-LOIRE   PUY-DE-DÔME   RHÔNE

N=3,032[a]   N=170[a]   N=114[a]   N=212[a]

[a] N=unweighted total of all employed males

▨ BUILDING

☐ DAY LABORER

▥ MACHINE CONSTRUCTION

☰ MINING

Figure 3.9   Origins of male industrial workers in Le Chambon-Feugerolles, Rive-de-Gier, and Saint-Chamond, 1876 (weighted manuscript census samples)

in 1868 next to the railway lines east of the city. Both these plants grew rapidly in the late 1860s and early 1870s, employing hundreds of workers, especially during the Franco-Prussian war. These workers not only may have participated in the local workforce while still resident of their native village, but they may have also participated very actively in popular society in Rive-de-Gier while still living at home. For instance, the village of Chateauneuf, 2½ kilometers from Rive-de-Gier, sent all its children to school in Rive-de-Gier. Recent migrants to the industrial city from Chateauneuf may well have known their new Ripagérien neighbors for the whole of their lives.[52]

The integration of migrants into the native labor force was encouraged by the contraction of the recruitment region, while other changes also encouraged the assimilation of the more distant migrants. Because the manuscript censuses for the industrial cities in 1876 contain information on department of birth, it is possible to examine more closely the relation between urban structure and migration.

Even if they no longer contributed the same proportion of migrants as formerly, however, the village and regional networks linking rural sending areas and receiving industrial cities retained their privileged links to urban industry. A look at figure 3.9, a weighted sample of the manuscript censuses for the three industrial communities in 1876, suggests the presence of specialized regional networks that channeled migrants into specific urban industries. Of course, these channels were partly based on bringing specialized skilled workers into particular skilled employments: the reason so many male migrants from the Puy-de-Dôme ended up in the building trades is because they came with construction skills. But the disproportionate number of migrants from the Haute-Loire in coal mining was more likely to have been due to the longstanding ties between this area and Le Chambon-Feugerolles, where coal mining was expanding, and to the presence of miners from the Haute-Loire in local mines, who helped to hire their own.

Although the village networks that brought workers to the city remained important, the diminishing prospects of returning to the countryside made village ties less central to urban migrants than formerly. In the industrial city, migrants such as those from Saint-Christo and Pavezin gradually realized the permanency of their condition. The early signs of this transition are the beginnings of change in patterns of intermarriage among migrants. For many migrants, their fate was now bound up with an urban world, and their more active participation in this world brought them new contacts and intimacies. In 1876, 16 migrants from the Puy-de-Dôme and the Haute-Loire married partners from the same department, while 29 married natives of the Loire. This ratio was almost two to one in 1876, compared with near equality in 1856.

The crisis of regional agriculture also led farm families to send their children into the city at a younger age than formerly. This resulted in an increased accumulation of young unmarried migrants in the city, but it also exposed these migrants to urban popular society at an earlier age and so probably encouraged their assimilation. The marriage records for Saint-Chamond contain information on the length of residence in the industrial city of marrying migrants. Although the median age at marriage of non-native grooms *declined* between 1856 and 1876, the average stay of non-native grooms in the city had *lengthened* by about two and a half years over the period.[53]

The growing size of the single, male population was a powerful force in shaping a new industrial working-class culture based on boarding houses, cafés, and voluntary social organizations. Single, non-native males were usually boarders. Among males, both native and non-native, the population of solitaries, heads of household living alone, and unrelated people living together was always quite small. In 1876, in each of the three industrial cities, there were more single male boarders in almost every age group than in 1856; the proportionate increase in single, male boarders was dramatic in Le Chambon-Feugerolles, though less so in Saint-Chamond and in Rive-de-Gier.[54] Nevertheless, in 1876, Rive-de-Gier even further increased its 1856 absolute lead over the other two cities as the city with the largest proportion of male boarders. In 1876, boarders in Rive-de-Gier were about 43 percent of the male workforce in the age group 20 to 24 and about 39 percent in the age group 25 to 29. In Saint-Chamond, male boarders were almost 32 percent of the male workforce in the age group 20 to 24 and 24 percent in the age group 25 to 29. In Le Chambon-Feugerolles, single, male boarders accounted for about 35 percent of the male labor force (age group 20 to 24) and 17 percent (age group 20 to 29). Between 1856 and 1876, there was no great change in the structure of boarding. In Le Chambon-Feugerolles and Saint-Chamond, roughly one-third of all boarders were the sole boarder residing in the household, and one-third of all boarders resided in large boarding houses (with four or more other boarders). In Rive-de-Gier, the large boarding house was more prevalent and held about 50 percent of all boarders, while the sole boarder residing with a household was rarer.

A look at large boarding houses in Rive-de-Gier in 1876 shows that they usually contained a mix of industrial occupations and migrants from different departments. Most large boarding houses comprised miners, metalworkers, and daylaborers who came from a variety of departments. Of the 19 boarding houses where most residents gave their department or country of birth, nine houses had 50 percent or more residents from the same department. Of these departmental majorities, four were composed of boarders from the Loire, three from the Rhône, one from the Creuse, and one from Italy; only three boarding houses were exclusively composed of boarders from identifiable areas, two from the Loire, and one from Turin, Italy.

Within the various industries, only workers in the construction trades tended strongly to board together. This concentration may have been a product of the *compagnonnage* tradition, which had been strong in the Stéphanois, but it was probably reinforced by the willingness of employers in the construction trades to board their workers. But among construction workers, boarding was an industrial matter much more than a regional one. In the three boarding houses dominated by the construction trades whose residents gave their department of birth, the department of the Creuse, legendary source of masons in France, was well-represented in each house. However, not one of the three boarding houses had 50 percent or more of all boarders from the same department. Two large boarding houses contained exclusively daylaborers, but unfortunately very few of these boarders listed their place of birth.

As the importance of the geographically diverse boarding house suggests, in the decades after 1860 the migrant population of single men was far better integrated into the developing urban industrial working-class culture than was the migrant population of a generation earlier. Less tightly knit together among themselves, rural migrants were no longer saving for a return to the farm and so were more likely to pay the money to patronize cafés on a considerable scale and so to participate fully in the working-class leisure culture that centered on the café. The presence of so many single migrants undoubtedly accounts for the astonishingly small ratio between the number of cafés in Stéphanois cities and the number of residents. In 1828 there was one café for every 879 residents of Rive-de-Gier; in 1895 the ratio was one to 55 inhabitants.[55]

While cafés had always been popular in the Stéphanois region, their golden period was the years after 1860 when Napoleonic repression eased considerably after the harsh repression of café life during the 1850s, a time when the number of cafés in Saint-Etienne decreased by 15 percent. Rural migration probably also caused the proliferation of cafés, as disabled, over-aged, or widowed migrants began serving drinks and food to their fellow migrants. Cafés spread through working-class neighborhoods and factory districts. The historian of the Stéphanois labor movement, Petrus Faure, himself a participant, discussing the cafés of the last quarter of the nineteenth century, records:

The cafés of the past were, before all else, meeting places for friends. One was a regular [*on y avait ses habitudes*]. There one read the newspaper and discussed the news. There one played cards or billiards . . . Sometimes one concluded business there or found a job. At the café one commemorated happy events, birthdays or retirement. One held meetings of social and political groups there. During strikes, the strike committee met there . . . The greater part [of the cafés] were small, the clientele coming from the *quartier* or the factory, and one was served by the owner himself or, most often, by his wife, if he worked elsewhere . . .[56]

In the café, migrants might also come into contact with native young men and, in the less boisterous cafés, with older working men and their families. Café culture thus further fostered the assimilation of migrants.

The expansion of the café helped to provide a culture for migrants in the large boarding house. Daniel Mandon, a student of working-class culture in Saint-Etienne, observes that "After 1864, the cabaret takes a more and more important place: numerous social or cultural activities gravitate around this place of privileged expression."[57] Mandon notes the rise of the *goguette*, cabarets specializing in topical songs. But many new forms of male leisure also clustered around the café. This was the age when voluntary leisure organizations began to spread among the working class; clubs of pigeon fanciers, *boules* enthusiasts, and blowgun players organized themselves. Other popular male leisure institutions that complemented the café culture were the male choruses and bands that began to assemble toward the end of the 1850s and throughout the 1860s and 1870s. The *Société musicale de Rive-de-Gier* was founded in 1858 and its choral society, *La Ripagérienne*, in 1879.[58] These choruses and bands entertained at every popular event, and in the decades after 1890, many of them would march in socialist and trade-union sponsored demonstrations. In the Stéphanois, a game played with blowguns was a favorite local sport. Although the numbers are small, the two blowgun clubs whose membership lists give place of birth, both in Saint-Chamond (one in 1865, the other in 1867), show percentages of migrants from the Haute-Loire and the Puy-de-Dôme somewhat larger than their proportions in the total population.[59]

An English artisan who in 1867 visited Paris and several other industrial cities, including Saint-Etienne, was struck by the importance of young males in the public recreational life of these cities. He noted that "the young French workman . . . is passionately fond of dancing and billiards, spending almost every evening at a café or a ball . . . there are numerous music halls . . . There are other amusements of a musical nature which are patronized by young French workmen. I allude to the numerous societies which exist for the practice of both vocal and instrumental music."[60]

As migrants married local residents, stayed longer in the city, and joined local social and political organizations, the fear and concern felt by the native working-classes 20 years earlier gave way to a growing recognition and acceptance of the rural contribution to the urban industrial population. A widely sung tune of 1865 written by one of Saint-Etienne's most popular local songwriters ran:

> When I was eight years old, I left my mountain home.
> Where happy lives the peasant,
> Always joyous, pocketing what he earns,
> In the present, sowing for the future.
> I made my way to the city
> Where one may be covered with gold through intrigue.[61]

The author of this song was himself a migrant, from Monistrol-sur-Loire in the Haute-Loire.[62]

By 1876, the decline of temporary migration contributed to the integration of migrants into an emerging urban working-class culture.[63] As we shall see, this did not mean that urban working-class culture was homogeneous or undivided. Yet the decline of temporary migration ended the internal division of the working classes between temporary and permanent proletarians that had provoked such bitter hostility in 1848. In 1876, in contrast to 1856, a very large and ever growing number of urban workers were permanent proletarians. An important step in the process of class formation had occurred.

NOTES

1 On "primitive capital accumulation," Karl Marx, *Capital* (New York, International Publishers, 1967), vol. 1, pp. 713–65. Also see Frederick Cooper, "Africa and the World Economy," *African Studies Review* 24, (2–3) (June–Sept., 1981), pp. 1–93; and John Saville, "Primitive Accumulation and Early Industrialization in Britain," in *Socialist Register: 1969* (New York, Monthly Review Press, 1969), pp. 247–71.

2 For a compelling vindication of Marx's position on enclosures, see K. D. M. Snell, *Annals of the Labouring Poor: Social Change and Agrarian England, 1660–1900* (Cambridge, Cambridge University Press, 1985). This latter also contains many other interesting, and well-documented, arguments.

3 The Crude Rate of Natural Increase, the Net Migration Rate and the Intercensal Growth Rate, a continuously compounded growth rate, are graphed for each community in my paper, "Nascent Proletarians: Migration and Class Formation in the Stéphanois Region," in *Migrants in Modern France: Population Mobility in the Nineteenth and Twentieth Centuries*, ed. P. E. Ogden and P. E. White (London, Allen and Unwin, forthcoming). On the intercensal growth rate see George Barclay, *Techniques of Population Analysis* (New York, NY, John Wiley, 1958), p. 32.

  In 1856 the population of Le Chambon-Feugerolles was 4,307, Rive-de-Gier's was 14,720, and Saint-Chamond's 10,472. Between 1856 and 1876 the population of Le Chambon-Feugerolles almost doubled, that of Saint-Chamond increased by almost 40 percent and that of Rive-de-Gier only by two percent.

4 In order to get some sense of the communities from which migrants came, six communes were selected that sent disproportionate numbers of migrants to the

industrial city. The means used was a simple gravity calculation. The gravity calculation technique was suggested by Leslie Moch, see her *Paths to the City: Regional Migration in Nineteenth-Century France* (Beverly Hills, Cal., Sage, 1983), pp. 30–1. The only claim made for this calculation is that it provides a systematic way of selecting communities that sent migrant workers. There is no one best way of making this calculation; the form of the calculation used, employing "D-squared" rather than "D," somewhat emphasizes the distance from which migrants came at the expense of the number of migrants who came. Since the number of migrants was small from any one community, the gravity formula was calculated only for those communes that sent three or more migrants to a receiving community. The properties of gravity calculations are discussed in Walter Isard, *Methods of Regional Analysis: An Introduction to Regional Science* (New York, NY, John Wiley, 1960) p. 515.

5　In 1856 the omitted commune was Monistrol-sur-Loire in the department of the Haute-Loire; in 1876 it was Jonzieux in the department of the Loire.

6　In 1856 the department of the Loire sent 46 percent of all migrants, and the department of the Rhône, 11.6 percent.

7　On rye cultivation in the region of the Massif Central, see Hugh Clout, *The Land of France, 1815–1914* (London, Allen and Unwin, 1983), pp. 19–20.

8　As an indicator of seasonal water power, I used the rate of flow of the Loire at Saint-Victor-sur-Loire, near Le Chambon-Feugerolles, as given in M. Devun, *Géographie du département de la Loire* (Grenoble, Les éditions françaises nouvelles, 1944), p. 21. The lowest months were the four from June to September, the lowest month of all was August. See also, M. Devun, "L'utilisation des rivières du Pilat par l'industrie," *Revue de géographie alpine* 32 (fasc. 2) (1944), pp. 241–305. The summer drought was a distinctive characteristic of southern France (and the southern Mediterranean generally); streams fed from the French Alps were the converse of those in the Stéphanois: Alpine streams were highest during the months when those of the Stéphanois were the lowest and vice versa. An area adjacent to the Stéphanois, the Basse Isère, benefited from its proximity to both watersheds and had abundant *year round* water power; see Maxime Perrin, *La région industrielle de Saint-Etienne* (Tours, Arrault, 1937), pp. 195–7.

9　In 1856, the cantons containing Le Chambon-Feugerolles, Rive-de-Gier, Saint-Chamond, and Saint-Etienne consumed three hectoliters of rye for every four of wheat, while producing four hectoliters of rye for every three of wheat. In neither grain were they self-sufficient, and they looked outside the individual canton for their food; in 1856 the four cantons imported a total of 214,889 hectoliters of rye and 339,212 of wheat. Some of these imports came from the four cantons in the *arrondissement* that contained no heavy industry, but the importance of domestic industry and, to a lesser extent, cattle raising in the rural cantons can be seen by the extent to which even these cantons depended on the import of grain for their survival; two of the four rural cantons also imported rye and three imported wheat. See Archives départementales de la Loire (ADL) 55/M/14.

10　Archives nationales (AN)-C/962

11　See Hugh Clout, *Agriculture in France on the Eve of the Railway Age* (London, Croom Helm, 1980), pp. 24–5; and AN-C/962 – "Saint-Amant-Roche-Savine."

12　Georges Mauco, *Les migrations ouvrières en France au début du XIXe siècle* (Paris, Lesot, 1932) pp. 56–7.

13 See Jean Merley, "Elements pour l'étude de la formation de la population stéphanoise à l'aube de la révolution industrielle," *Démographie urbaine XVe-XXe siècle, Bulletin,* Centre d'histoire économique et sociale de la région lyonnaise (8) (1977), pp. 261–75.

14 Ulysse Rouchon, *La vie paysanne dans la Haute-Loire,* 3 vols (Le Puy, Editions de la société des études locales, 1933–8), vol. 2, p. 125.

15 Jean Merley, *L'industrie en Haute-Loire de la fin de la monarchie aux débuts de la troisième république* (Lyon, Centre d'histoire économique et sociale de la région lyonnaise, 1972), table 28.

16 Ibid., p. 134.

17 P. Guillaume, "La situation économique et sociale du département de la Loire d'après l'enquête sur le travail agricole et industriel du 25 mai 1848," *Revue d'histoire moderne et contemporaine* 10 (Jan.–Mar., 1963), pp. 5–34, see p. 32.

18 Jean Merley, *La Haute-Loire: de la fin de l'ancien régime aux débuts de la troisième République* (Le Puy, Cahiers de la Haute-Loire, 1974), vol. 1, p. 588.

19 Ministère de l'agriculture, du commerce et des travaux publics, *L'Enquête agricole de 1866. 27e circonscription,* (Paris, Imprimerie impériale, 1867–72), vol. 9, p. 311.

20 Ibid., p. 320.

21 *Enquête agricole,* vol. 20, pp. 57–8; and Merley, *La Haute-Loire,* vol. 1, pp. 490–1.

22 In the department of the Haute-Loire, Merley concludes that, by 1881, "to a greatly increased extent, emigration, largely masculine in 1856, has henceforth conquered the female population . . . entire families left the country, taking their children, and . . . giving emigration a definitive character." See Merley, *La Haute-Loire,* vol. 1, p. 590.

23 Breaking down the category of "owner-cultivators," the proportion of the farming population that farmed only their own land in the *arrondissement* of Ambert was 35.4 percent, in the *arrondissement* of Yssingeaux, 39.7 percent, in the *arrondissement* of Saint-Etienne, 48.1 percent; of those who farmed their own land but also worked as day laborers the percentage of the total was 47 percent in Ambert, 20.7 percent in Yssingeaux, and 17 percent in Saint-Etienne. See Ministère de l'agriculture, *Statistique agricole, décennale de 1852,* 2nd series, (Paris, Imprimerie nationale, 1852).

24 *Enquête agricole,* vol. 20, pp. 10, 11.

25 Ibid., vol. 9, p. 315.

26 There are a good number of studies that touch on regional agriculture; two important ones are P. M. Jones, *Politics and Rural Society: The southern Massif Central, c.1750–1880* (Cambridge, Cambridge University Press, 1985), see p. 49; and Merley, *La Haute-Loire,* see pp. 358–9.

To put these regional changes in a larger perspective, see E. J. T. Collins, "Labour Supply and Demand in European Agriculture 1800–1880," in *Agrarian Change and Economic Development: The Historical Problems,* ed., E. L. Jones and S. J. Woolf (London, Methuen, 1969), pp. 61–94; George W. Grantham, "Scale and Organization in French Farming, 1840–1880," in *European Peasants and Their Markets: Essays in Agrarian Economic History,* ed. William N. Parker and Eric L. Jones, (Princeton, Princeton University Press, 1975), pp. 293–326; Paul Hohenberg, "Change in Rural France in the Period of Industrialization, 1830–1914," *Journal of Economic History,* 32 (1972), pp. 219–40, and "Migration et fluctuations démographiques dans la France rurale, 1836–1901," *Annales-ESC* 29 (2) (Mar.–April, 1974), pp. 461–97; William H. Newell, "The Agricultural Revolution in Nineteenth-Century France," *Journal of Economic History* 33 (4) (Dec., 1973), pp. 697–730; Roger Price, "The Onset of Labour Shortage in Nineteenth-Century French Agriculture," *Economic History Review*, 2nd series, 28 (2) (1975), pp. 260–79.

27 Distances given here between sending and receiving communes are listed in kilometers in the parentheses. For Le Chambon-Feugerolles the three selected communes in 1856 were: Monistrol-sur-Loire (16.5), Saint-Just-Malmont (6.0), and Saint-Romain-les-Atheux (5.0); for 1876: Jonzieux (10.0), Annonay (30.5), and Aurec-sur-Loire (10.5). For Rive-de-Gier in 1856: Saint-Julien-Chapteuil (61.0), Saint-Symphorien-sur-Coise (15.2), and Chuyer (8.9); in 1876: Pavezin (7.6), La Chapelle-sur-Coise (17.8), and Chateauneuf (2.5). For Saint-Chamond in 1856: Saint-Amant-Roche-Savine (68.6), Saint-Christo-en-Jarez (7.6), and Pelussin (15.2); for 1876: Saint-Christo-en-Jarez (7.6), Annonay (27.9), and Doizieu (7.6). There are some minor discrepancies between distances on the figure and distances listed in parentheses here. In most cases, these are because the figure is based on a map drawn up in the first half of the nineteenth century and the distances were calculated based on twentieth-century locations. Over the past hundred years, some communes annexed adjacent territory and, in the Stéphanois, many annexations followed the road, thus lengthening the commune by several kilometers and sometimes shifting the location of the town center by several kilometers.

28 Using the techniques described in n. 4, 18 communes were selected but, because a couple of the same communes appeared twice, only 16 different communes resulted. In 1876, Annonay was a selected sending area for both Le Chambon-Feugerolles and Saint-Chamond. Saint-Christo-en-Jarez was a selected sending area for Saint-Chamond in both 1856 and 1876.

29 To protect the anonymity of individual migrants, I have used fictional names.

30 See Pierre Gardette, "Situation linguistique de Forez," *Etudes foréziennes* 1 (1968), pp. 211–20.

31 M. Lappier de Gemeaux, "Mémoire militaire – sur le lever à vue de Saint-Etienne à la Loire," 1826, MdG MR/1266, p. 15. The lieutenant's conjecture as to the origin of the term "*Gaga*" is at least plausible. Andrews' Latin dictionary defines "gagates" as meaning "hard, black, asphaltum, jet." See E. A. Andrews, *A Latin Dictionary* (Oxford, Clarendon Press, 1980), p. 799.

32 "Mémoire sur la reconnaissance de la route de Saint-Etienne à Saint-Chamond," December 31, 1832, MdG MR/1266, pp. 40–1.

33 In 1839 in Rive-de-Gier, Michelet found it impossible to understand a conversation overheard among speakers of *Gaga*; in 1843, an observer pronounced the dialect merely a "bad French" and believed it was readily comprehensible to French speakers, "Mémoire sur les environs de Saint-Chamond," 1843, MdG MR/1266, p. 13.

34 See Jean-François Gonon, *Histoire de la chanson Stéphanoise et Forézienne* (Roanne, Horvath, 1906), pp. 151–5, 108–21. Some typical figures are Guillaume Roquille (1805–60), a Ripagérien *ferblantier* who wrote his early songs and poems in the patois of Rive-de-Gier and his later songs and poems in French, pp. 151–5. Remy Doutre (1845–85), metalworker and miner, wrote most of his songs in French, but wrote a few songs, under an assumed name, in patois.

35 Le commissaire de police de Rive-de Gier, February 16, 1853, ADL 10/M/60.

36 Gonon, *Histoire de la chanson Stéphanoise*, p. 84.

37 Bernard Plessy, *La vie quotidienne en Forez avant 1914* (Paris, Hachette, 1981), p. 325.

38 Flora Tristan, *Le tour de France, journal inédit 1843–1844* (Paris, François Maspero, 1980), vol. 1, p. 213.

39 J.-B. Chambeyron, *Recherches historiques sur la ville de Rive-de-Gier* (Rive-de-Gier, Antonin Sablière, 1844), pp. xvi–xvii.

40 On permanently proletarianized workers, see the essays in *Proletarians and Protest, The Roots of Class Formation in an Industrializing World*, ed. Michael Hanagan and Charles Stephenson (Westport, Conn., Greenwood Press, 1986).

41 The only expansion of the stream of migration into adjacent areas occurred in the south where the crisis of the metallurgical industry in the Ardèche in the early 1870s led a certain number of migrants to the Stéphanois. See Lequin, *Les ouvriers de la région lyonnaise*, vol. 1, p. 454.

42 Figures 3.4 and 3.5 are proportionate circle maps. The overlapping of circles is an indication that a sending commune was too close to the receiving commune for the mapping program to discriminate (within a second).

Italians represented 7.5 percent of the workforce in Rive-de-Gier in 1876, and were only a handful of the population of the other towns.

In Marseilles during the period 1820–70, Italians formed a disadvantaged section of the working class see William H. Sewell, Jr, *Structure and Mobility: The Men and Women of Marseilles, 1820–1870*, (Cambridge, Cambridge University Press, 1985). For a discussion of migration patterns in the Stéphanois in the later nineteenth century, see Jean-Charles Bonnet, "Les travailleurs étrangers dans la Loire sous la IIIe République," *Cahiers d'histoire*, 16 (1971), pp. 67–80.

43 In 1856, 31 percent of all migrants in the marriage records from the *arrondissement* of Saint-Etienne came from rural communities with populations less than 2,000; in 1876, it was 19 percent.

The "non-industrial" communes were all those communes in the *arrondissement* of Saint-Etienne not included as "industrial" communes. Following the rough classifications found in *Saint-Etienne et son agglomeration* (Paris, Documentation française, 1973), pp. 24–8, the 11 "industrial" communes in the *arrondissement* were: Le Chambon-Feugerolles, Firminy, Izieux, Lorette, La Ricamarie, Rive-de-Gier, Roche-la-Molière, Saint-Chamond, Saint-Etienne, Saint-Genis-Terrenoire, and Unieux.

44 ADL 55/M/17.

45 *Enquête agricole*, vol. 27, pp. 389–90.

46 Merley, *La Haute-Loire*, p. 358. From 1837 to 1875, the number of cows in the *arrondissement* of Saint-Etienne increased by more than one-half: for 1837, Ministère de l'agriculture et du commerce, *Statistique de la France. – Agriculture* (Paris, Imprimerie royale, 1840–1). vol. 2, p. 349; for 1875, ADL 55/M/17.

47 Pierre du Maroussem, "Fermiers montagnards du Haut-Forez (Loire-France)," *Les ouvriers des deux mondes*, vol. 4 (Paris, Firmin-Didot et cie., 1892) pp. 402–3.

48 ADL 55/M/17.

49 See Maurice Agulhon, Gabriel Desert, and Robert Specklin, *Apogée et crise de la civilisation paysanne, Histoire de la France rurale*, ed. Georges Duby and Armand Wallon (Paris, Seuil, 1976), vol. 3, p. 395; and L.-J. Gras, *Histoire du commerce local* (Saint-Etienne, Theolier, 1910).

50 Agulhon, Desert, and Specklin, *Apogée et crise*, pp. 395–8.

51 James R. Lehning, *The Peasants of Marlhes: Economic Development and Family Organization in Nineteenth-Century France* (Chapel Hill, University of North Carolina, 1980), pp. 40–4.
52 See C. Chomienne, *Histoire de la ville de Rive-de-Gier* (Saint-Etienne, 1912), pp. 156–8.
53 The marriage records record the duration of stay in Saint-Chamond at the time of marriage. In 1856, the average male non-native had spent 5.6 years in Saint-Chamond and the average female non-native, 7.1 years; in 1876 the duration of stay for males was 8.1 years, for females 7.4 years. But all these durations of stay are based on the length of stay *at the time of marriage*. Between 1856 and 1876 the median age of marriage for non-native males fell from 28 to 27 while that of females remained the same, 24. The small change in female duration of stay is undoubtedly due to the tremendous expansion of the textile dormitories in Saint-Chamond during this period; these dormitories housed young women and girls who worked in the textile mills.
54 In 1856, 18.6 percent of all young men between the ages of 20 and 24 in Le Chambon-Feugerolles were boarders or lodgers; in 1876, 32.6 percent. The comparable figures for Rive-de-Gier in 1856 were 45.3 percent; in 1876, 43.1 percent. For Saint-Chamond they were, in 1856, 26.2 percent; in 1876, 32 percent. In 1856, in Le Chambon-Feugerolles, 15.2 percent of all young men between the ages of 25 and 29 were boarders; in 1876, 17.3 percent. In Rive-de-Gier in 1856, 32 percent, in 1876, 39.3 percent. In Saint-Chamond in 1856, 29.7 percent; in 1876, 23.8 percent.

The overwhelming majority of non-related, non-servant residents of households identified themselves as "boarders" (*pensionnaires*), that is, people who habitually took their meals with the household. Only a very few identified themselves as "lodgers" or "roomers" (*locataires*), that is, people who do not habitually take their meals with the household. In this chapter and subsequent chapters, references to boarders include references to lodgers. Discussion of boarders does not include references to unrelated non-servants, who do not indicate themselves as either boarders or lodgers. This situation only occurs among a small population of generally older women in Saint-Chamond in 1856. The position of these women will be addressed in chapter 5. Discussion of boarding houses also omits bordellos, whose occupants generally were listed as "boarders."
55 Chomienne, *Histoire de la ville de Rive-de-Gier*, p. 63; and Gras, *Histoire du commerce locale*, pp. 406–7.
56 Petrus Faure, *Développement de la culture dans un département ouvrier: la Loire* (Saint-Etienne, Dumas, 1979), pp. 58–9.
57 Daniel Mandon, *Les Barbelés de la culture: Saint-Etienne, une ville ouvrière* (Saint-Etienne, FEDEROP, 1976) p. 227.
58 Chomienne, *Histoire de la ville de Rive-de-Gier*, pp. 142–4.
59 There were 41 members of the two dart clubs, 24 percent were born in Saint-Chamond; 56 percent in the *arrondissement* of Saint-Chamond; 15 percent in the departments of the Haute-Loire and Puy-de-Dôme; and 5 percent in the Rhône. Membership lists were found in ADL M/244 – tr. 427/6. In 1876, a 20 percent sample of the manuscript census (N=2,906) shows that 80 percent of the population of Saint-Chamond were born in the department of the Loire, 8 percent in the departments of the Haute-Loire and the Puy-de-Dôme, and 3 percent in the Rhône.

60 Robert Coningsby, "The Conditions and Habits of the French Working Classes," *Reports of Artisans Selected by a Committee Appointed by the Council of the Society of Arts to Visit the Paris Universal Exhibition, 1867* (London, Bell and Daldy, 1867), pp. 428–51, esp. 434 and 435.

61 Eugene Imbert, *Chants, chansons et poésies de Rémy Doutre* (Saint-Etienne, Menard, 1887), pp. 24–5.

62 Ibid., p. v.

63 Of course, the situation that I have described in the Stéphanois region and its hinterland involves only one type of rural–urban relationship. In cases where permanent proletarians retained ties to kin in the countryside or where irregularly employed proletarians were landowners, land might be a valuable resource in supporting worker resistance. As I will argue later in this book, this was probably the case for the miners of Le Chambon-Feugerolles in the years after 1860. Other instances of this are Rolande Trempé, *Les mineurs de Carmaux*, 2 vols (Paris, Les éditions ouvrières, 1971); James R. Greene, "The Brotherhood of Timber Workers, 1910–1917: A Radical Response to Industrial Capitalism in the Southern USA," in *Past and Present* 60 (Aug., 1973), pp. 161–200; and Herbert Gutman, "Black Coal Miners and the Greenback-Labor Party in Redeemer, Alabama, 1878–1879," *Labor History*, 10 (Summer, 1969), pp. 506–35.

APPENDIX 3.1   SOURCES OF MIGRATION: SENSITIVITY TESTS

To check whether the selected communes were, indeed, subject to large-scale migration, age pyramids for men and women were calculated for each sending community and, invariably in the case of men and frequently in the case of women, the distributions of these pyramids are *consistent* with the occurrence of large-scale out-migration. In the case of men, all sending communes show a deficit in the percentage population of males between the ages of 20 and 34, the ages most subject to migration. In France in 1856, 23.22 percent of the male population was aged between 20 and 34; in Saint-Amant, 19.62 percent; in Saint-Julien, 19.22 percent; in Monistrol, 18.54 percent. In the case of Saint-Amant, the male population aged between 20 and 34 includes those indicated as "seasonal migrants". In France in 1876, 22.71 percent of the male population was aged between 20 and 34; in Saint-Christo, 19.22 percent; in Pavezin, 17.63 percent, and in Jonzieux, 15.81 percent.

There are many difficulties with using marriage records as a source of information on migration. For an excellent summary of the problems involved, see Jean-Pierre Poussou, "Les mouvements migratoires en France et à partir de la France de la fin du XVe siècle au début du XIXe siècle," *Annales de Démographie Historique – 1970* (Paris, Mouton, 1970), pp. 11–79.

The 1876 census included information on department of birth and so provides a means of identifying marriage record biases; a comparison was made between the distribution of departments of birth in the male marrying population in 1876 and the distribution of departments of birth for the male population aged between 20 and 34 in a sample of the 1876 census and for the female marrying population in 1876 and the female population aged between 15 and

30 in the 1876 census sample. Since approximately 80 percent of all men in the marriage records of each of the three towns were between the ages of 20 and 34 and 80 percent of the women in each of the three towns were between 15 and 29, the effect of the comparison is a very rough age standardization.

Comparing the marriage records with a weighted sum of the men and women in the above age groups in the census samples for all three towns yields the following results: in 1876, the marriage records show 23.7 percent of *migrants* as coming from the Haute-Loire, 9.5 percent from the Puy-de-Dôme, 21.3 percent from the Rhône, and 5.9 percent from outside France. The weighted manuscript census populations show 14.6 percent from the Haute-Loire, 12.4 percent from the Puy-de-Dôme, 14.1 percent from the Rhône and 16.4 percent from outside France. Both lists agree that *within France* the most important sending regions were the Haute-Loire, the Puy-de-Dôme, and the Rhône; but in 1876, both migrants from the Puy-de-Dôme and non-French nationals were disproportionately absent from the marriage records. In 1876 migrants from the Puy-de-Dôme, as with migrants from Italy, may have been disproportionately composed of temporary migrants.

"Temporary" migration did not disappear from the Stéphanois region during the whole of the nineteenth century, although, as we have argued, it declined substantially. In 1895, in the mining community of La Ricamarie, temporary migrants from the Haute-Loire and the Ardèche were a recognized feature of community life. See Marius Chalendard, "Une enquête sur l'habitat ouvrier et la propriété du logement," *Economie et Humanisme* 4 (1945), pp. 657–63.

APPENDIX 3.2   NATIVES IN INDUSTRIAL LABOR FORCE

Table 3.3   Percentages of natives employed in the industrial labor force in Le Chambon-Feugerolles, Rive-de-Gier and Saint-Chamond (derived from marriage records), 1856

	Males		Females	
	% natives	Total of all employed	% natives	Total of all employed
Apparel	33.3	6	56.5	46
Building trades	21.4	28	—	0
Daylaborers	8.3	12	14.3	7
Machine construction	35.1	97	—	0
Ribbonweaving	35.7	14	38.9	18
Textiles	25.0	8	31.0	58
Mining	32.6	43	—	0
Domestic service	33.3	3	51.5	33
All natives in labor force[a]	31.9	298	37.2	199

[a]   Includes all employed (industrial and non-industrial). Figures derived from marriage records of the three cities in 1856.

Table 3.4   Percentages of natives employed in the industrial labor force in Le Chambon-Feugerolles, Rive-de-Gier and Saint-Chamond (derived from marriage records), 1876

	Males		Females	
	% natives	Total of all employed	% natives	Total of all employed
Apparel	100.0	2	45.5	44
Building trades	24.0	25	—	0
Daylaborers	33.3	9	—	0
Machine construction	28.8	80	100.0	1
Ribbonweaving	0.0	6	0.0	3
Textiles	0.0	7	21.6	51
Mining	30.8	39	—	0
Domestic service	0.0	1	50.0	34
All natives in labor force[a]	29.1	306	44.9	176

[a]   Includes all employed (industrial and non-industrial). Figures derived from marriage records of the three cities in 1876.

4

Patterns of Life-Cycle Employment in Industry: Miners and Metalworkers

Between 1840 and 1880, growing numbers of industrial workers in the Stéphanois region began to recognize that they had become permanent proletarians. The rural life that many of them had known was visibly collapsing and, for males, there existed genuine prospects of earning a life-long livelihood within the industrial city. Once they faced the prospects of spending their lives in the city, industrial workers confronted a whole series of problems for the first time. For temporary proletarians, forming families, raising children, providing against accident and old age were challenges to be resolved on the farm. Their basic strategy for survival depended on landownership and on teaching agricultural skills to their children. For permanent proletarians, however, raising and training children and providing against accident and old age were weighty new problems to be solved only in the context of a lifetime of wage labor and with reference to employers, who set the basic terms of industrial employment.

By setting educational requirements, providing social insurance, and establishing career opportunities, employers in heavy industry created an unprecedented framework for working-class life. The social stability permitted by the existence of long-term jobs in industry allowed workers to plan their future and to build their families on the basis of conditions pertaining in a particular industry. In establishing new work patterns, employers built on the character of productive activities in each industry. Because industrial conditions varied among local industries, so did the plans and expectations of workers and their families; to this extent, metalworkers and coal miners developed different career expectations and social identities. Yet although new differences arose, so did important new commonalities. Both miners and metalworkers labored in an interdependent industrial economy in which cheap coal and technically innovative metalworking supported one another: the fortunes of the local metal and coal industries were bound up with one another. Both miners and metalworkers confronted a proletarianization process that threatened to subordinate them hopelessly to their employers. As a result of the transformation of town and countryside alike, metalworkers and miners were entering into a new condition of lifetime proletarianization in which employers sought to gain greater control and authority over their workers by intervening in matters formerly considered the prerogative of families. The more metalworkers and miners realized the permanency of their condition, the more they viewed such employer intrusions as intolerable and searched for a remedy.

The common problems faced by all permanent semi-skilled workers need to be stressed because so much emphasis has been placed on their diversity. This is particularly true in regard to coal miners who have frequently been labeled "a race apart," in the words of an influential article by Clark Kerr and Abraham Siegel. Kerr and Siegel described miners as living in "separate communities" with their "own codes, myths, heroes, and social standards."[1] Even more anomalous is the portrait of French coal miners drawn by the demographer, Philippe Ariès. Ariès describes miners as islands of traditionalism in a world increasingly dominated by individualism. According to Ariès, mining in the Pas-de-Calais

succeeded in building up a significant concentration of people without resorting to immigration, thanks to its own natural development . . . a whole crowd of men, women and children commit themselves to the same tasks, the same schedules, the same joys and sorrows, the same climate . . . Then the collectivity behaves as an immovable block. Everyone accepts his condition resignedly without dreaming of leaving the area or the trade. Generations come one after another, resembling each other greatly, equally stable . . . equally fertile, unconscious of the opportunities available in the great outside world.[2]

While the differences between miners and metalworkers were real and substantial, we will see that these differences did not hinge on issues of social isolation versus social integration or traditionalism versus modernism. Indeed, the two groups were responding to a new and radical restructuring of the work situation in their respective industries. Both metalworkers and miners developed "modern" responses to changed industrial conditions – but different conditions engendered different responses. Because the importance of formal education, the rhythm of earnings over the course of the life-cycle, and the dangers of accident and death were not the same for metalworkers as for miners, it often happened that miners and metalworkers failed to understand one another. But a recurrent similarity of problems faced by miners and metalworkers also created bases for joint organization and action against industrial capitalism. The unifying elements of the industrialization process also became clear as the 1860s and 1870s witnessed a slowdown in the pace of industrial expansion, which had been explosive in the 1840s and 1850s. In the 1860s and 1870s, the Stéphanois region found itself to be an established industrial region beset by competition from newly industrializing regions in the north and east. Faced with aggressive outside rivals, Stéphanois industrialists responded by increasing productivity and with a new concern for profitability.

In this tougher climate, both metalworkers and miners battled to survive and to build and maintain their families against employer challenges to their autonomy.

Short of bankruptcy – a not impossible occurrence in the 1860s and 1870s – the need of large-scale employers to keep their machinery always at work usually guaranteed a minimum level of employment and thus of earnings for most experienced industrial workers. So, hours were shortened for all rather than lay-offs for some. Since, however, the financial needs of industrial workers were liable to change over the course of a lifetime, and at various points in their lives, the level of guaranteed minimum earnings was far less than was required. By providing a degree of coordination between the male worker's life-cycle and the structure of employment, employers in mining and metalworking helped to maintain and stabilize their workforce. Through taking into account life-cycle factors, employers gained another disciplinary tool for binding workers to their establishment; the use of this disciplinary tool was an especially serious consideration in the 1860s and 1870s when employers sought to keep the workers they had trained while, at the same time, keeping wages low enough to compete with serious outside competition. Such life-cycle employment structures were almost entirely a matter for males. Female workers' labor remained largely outside this new restructuring of work. They continued to be concentrated in seasonal, part-time, or temporary proletarian labor when many unskilled males were abandoning these traditional modes of employment. Because those aspects of industry that generated structured life-cycle employment patterns, forging and mining, were already dominated by males, the exclusion of females from this new type of employment was largely unremarked by contemporaries.

Life-cycle employment structures organized work so that male workers' earnings and responsibilities changed in very rough synchronization with the most important changes in the male worker's life course.[3] In both mine and mill, work was organized so that poorly remunerated job training was entirely concentrated at the beginning of a worker's entry into the workplace, when the young male worker did not have to earn wages to support a family. Growing out of adolescence, he was given access to better-paying jobs. In part, of course, this situation resulted from ability, but after a certain level of competence had been demonstrated, employers seem to have accepted age as a valid indicator of ability. Since the predominant form of payment in much of local metalworking and mining was some type of piecework, age simply served to put a worker in a position where his earnings were based on productivity. Against the eventuality that sickness or an industrial accident might interrupt the male worker's life cycle, most companies required, and sometimes partly subsidized, workers' insurance. For the workers' old age, companies usually provided some income for *loyal* workers whose physical capacities were reduced.

Life-cycle employment structures in metalworking and mining were different, and these differences affected many aspects of a worker's life. Imagine two young men born in the Stéphanois region in the heyday of the Industrial Revolution in the early 1840s: Etienne, the son of a miner in Le Chambon-

Feugerolles, and Martin, the son of a turner in a large factory in Rive-de-Gier. As was the case with most sons of industrial proletarians, they would likely follow their fathers' occupations, and this would lead them along paths that diverged ever more as they grew up, matured, and reached old age. Martin would go to school and learn to read, while Etienne would attend irregularly and remain a lifetime illiterate. Upon entering work at the mine or the factory, both would spend a number of years learning the ropes, until they began to earn adult wages. In the first decade of adult work, the miner's wages would be higher than the metalworker's wages but, after the first decade, the miner's pay would decline gradually below the metalworker's more stable earnings. As they grew older the miner would suffer the disabilities of age more obviously than the metalworker. Even if he was fortunate enough to avoid a mine accident, the last decades of Etienne's life would be spent as a semi-convalescent, while Martin's chances of avoiding both accident and prolonged semi-convalescence were better. This chapter will seek to explain and relate these aspects of workers' personal and family lives to their choice of a career, and it will show that differences in the pattern of earnings because of age and in the risk of morbidity and mortality are highly relevant for understanding the collective organization and actions of miners and metalworkers.

EDUCATION AND TRAINING OF SEMI-SKILLED WORKERS

Access to semi-skilled jobs differed dramatically between metalworking and mining. At a time when schooling was not generally required, metalworkers needed to send their male children to school to prepare them for the better-paying, semi-skilled jobs in the factory. Although the laws of 1841 and 1874 required a very minimum amount of education for factory children, it was not until 1882 that education was made compulsory for all children. But semi-skilled metalworking jobs such as turning, adjusting, and molding required some knowledge of drafting, geometry and mechanics. All the large employers in the area, Petin–Gaudet, the Jacksons, Gerian and Dorian, Claudinon, and the Holtzers, had their own schools. The services offered in these schools often exceeded legal requirements for the schooling of factory children because being able to read was a prerequisite for acquiring a skill.[4] Semi-skilled machinists were paid by the piece or by the job; the faster they could accomplish their task, the higher their individual pay. Learning new mechanical skills could bring real financial benefits. Metalworkers surely thus felt encouraged to enroll in the night courses offered by local schools to refresh the workers' reading ability. Metalworkers' incentives to educate their male children were doubtless intensified by the growth of opportunities in semi-skilled metalworking throughout much of the period. After 1860, the turn of Stéphanois metalworking away from mass steel production toward quality steel production and machine construction lessened the need for unskilled workers and increased the demand for semi-skilled workers.

In contrast with metalworkers, formal education was not necessary for any phase of mining. The work available for miners' children above ground, work such as sorting or washing coal, was unskilled manual labor and was essentially unrelated to below-ground work. Young migrants from outside who had no experience in mining were usually recruited directly to underground work. Here too, schooling was not required. Mine safety was taught on the job. Below ground, the young miner first worked as a hauler and picked up a few safety tips through informal conversations with his work mates. Next, the young miner worked as a filler, hauling rocks to fill mined-out shafts. Here the miner worked under an overman who made sure that the young man did not recklessly endanger his mates. The young man also learned to work underground in awkward physical conditions with a pick and shovel. Finally, after several years of hauling and filling, the miner got the opportunity to become first a timberman and, later, a coal hewer. These were jobs that were essentially unsupervised. The miner worked with a small number of other miners, and he was paid by the ton of coal that he produced. In its early days, the company paid workers collectively according to the productivity of the small team to which they belonged, but by the early 1850s an individual piecework system was prevalent; each hewer was paid according to the amount of coal he cut. The system encouraged miners to compete among themselves in the hard physical labor of hewing.[5]

Since their promotion in the mines did not demand schooling and because mining employment was easily available for most sons of coal miners over the whole period 1840 to 1880, mining families were free to use child labor in tasks that would bring more immediate benefit to the family. Although it does not show up in the manuscript censuses, probably the biggest employer of miners' children was seasonal agriculture. Where the permanent proletarians' fathers had come to the city seasonally, their sons went out to the countryside seasonally. Miners' children acted as cow herds and worked alongside other family members in the fields during the planting and harvesting periods, when wages in agriculture were high.[6] In addition, miners were more likely than metalworkers to possess their own bit of land that family members could tend. Analysis of census data shows that more miners than metalworkers lived in the countryside. Unlike Rive-de-Gier and Saint-Chamond, Le Chambon comprised a substantial portion of small hamlets, villages and isolated farms. Both mines and metalworks were built on the edge of the populated and urbanized portion of the commune; the mines especially were located in the countryside, an easy walk from both tenement and farm.[7]

Even when they did learn to read and write, the uselessness of these skills to coal mining often led to their neglect. An 1867 report on education by the Chamber of Commerce of Rive-de-Gier discussed this aspect of the problem: "The decrees on primary instruction are observed but it is necessary to recognize that the necessities of life, the absence of circumstances that will oblige them to read or to write often make children at a more advanced age forget that which they have learned in their youth."[8]

Almost every visitor to the region commented on the prevalence of miner illiteracy. In 1854, Audiganne estimated that "The coal miners are the most ignorant of the workers in this district. Out of twenty workers in this category chosen between the age of twenty-five and thirty, one would hardly meet two or three that would be able to write a few lines."[9] In 1876, the principal engineer of the Montrambert mines estimated the literacy of his workers in response to an inquiry of the justice of peace of Le Chambon-Feugerolles. In spite of the existence of local schools subsidized by the coal companies, he judged that 49 percent had never received any instruction, that 6 percent had learned to read, but could no longer do so, that 11 percent knew how to read but not to write, and that only 34 percent could both read and write.[10] As François Furet and Jacques Ozouf have shown, the discrepancy between the ability to read but not to write was often a legacy of the Counter Reformation tradition of Catholic education. Indeed, the department of the Loire and the two departments that sent so many migrants into local coal mining, the Haute-Loire and the Puy-de-Dôme, are all among the top ten departments that Furet and Ozouf cite with the highest incidence of "read only" literacy.[11]

A detailed study of local illiteracy, made in 1869, provides further insight into differences in literacy between occupations. In the department of the Loire, males were more literate than females. Due to seasonal employment in agriculture of both rural and urban children, the department had one of the highest rates of irregular school attendance of any department in France. Among the cantons of the *arrondissement* of Saint-Etienne, those cantons where coal mining largely predominated, the cantons in the west of the basin and the western and northern cantons of Saint-Etienne, produced the least literate conscripts for the army. Throughout the 1860s, the canton of Le Chambon-Feugerolles had one of the highest levels of illiterate conscripts of any in the department. In 1868, 39 percent of all conscripts from the canton of Le Chambon-Feugerolles could not read.[12]

Differences in literacy, themselves the result of prior family-decisions about whether to send male children to school, help to explain the self-perpetuating nature of participation in the two industries across generations. Unable to read, miners' sons had little opportunity to find semi-skilled employment in metalworking, and the sons of metalworkers seldom chose to work in the mines. For example, in 1856 and 1876, in Rive-de-Gier and Le Chambon-Feugerolles, employment opportunities existed in both mining and metalworking. A weighted average of sons resident in the same household as their father shows that roughly 60 percent of all employed sons of miners and machine-construction workers had the same industrial employment as their parent. Although inter-industrial mobility occurred in both towns, the sons of miners being particularly likely to enter machine construction, still the great majority of sons of miners and machine-construction workers followed their fathers' industrial employment.[13]

At least partially, job requirements help explain the value that metalworkers placed on education. Because education enabled their sons to follow their calling and also to increase their take-home pay, metalworkers often became involved in the educational process. A look at the membership of a voluntary society of alumni of a number of religious schools in Rive-de-Gier in 1895 shows an extraordinary difference in participation by industrial employment. Although the membership list does not give age, the presence of members who occupied relatively senior positions in mining and other local industries suggests that some members were middle-aged. Thus, the membership in this organization may provide some clue as to the occupations of those most actively involved in supporting education in the years before 1880.

The membership list gives occupation, and the manual working-class members of the association were overwhelmingly involved in metalwork. The "manual working class" includes both skilled and unskilled industrial workers but not those who identified themselves as clericals, engineers, or supervisors. Of the total membership, 46.2 percent were metalworkers employed in manual labor (N=143), mostly semi-skilled workers. Although miners still composed around 10 percent of the economically active population of Rive-de-Gier in 1891, only one person definitely involved in mining was a member of the association, and this was a "mining director." Several "day laborers" were members of the organization, and these could have been involved in mining, although the large number of day laborers in metalworking or glass manufacture in the 1880s and 1890s certainly makes it at least as likely that these members were employed in these industries. While the industry in which they were employed was not given, 18.2 percent of the membership represented clerks (*employés*) and accountants, who were not members of the manual working class.[14]

Schooling may also have been valued because it gave a few exceptionally talented individuals a way out of blue-collar work, but the number of white-collar workers in the region was so small that it could only have been a minor factor in workers' decisions about whether to send children to school. Even here, entry into the white-collar workforce was mediated through participation in company schools. An 1867 report from the Chamber of Commerce of Rive-de-Gier describes the company-run primary schools for child-workers as places "where moral ideas are inculcated as much as possible." From these schools, the "better students" were employed in offices and other "more important and better paid" jobs.[15] But the number of white-collar workers was so small in all three towns and the dominance of blue-collar workers so complete that education offered relatively little opportunity for ascension, at least within these working-class cities.[16] (See table 4.9, in appendix 4.1.)

But for most metalworkers, probably far more important than the possibility of social mobility was the value of education for preparing metalworkers for their jobs. In this area, the greater involvement of metalworkers in education brought them into conflict with company and religious teaching institutions. Employers' and clericals' conceptions of the purposes of popular education were not necessarily those of the workers. In 1848, just as company programs for educating their young workers were being established, representatives of the Petin–Gaudet company noted:

The state of instruction of our workers is nill, the spirit of our workers is good, but because of their lack of instruction they are easy to deceive, chiefly by the socialist theories that are preached to them. Thus we insistently demand that night courses be created for them and in a short time there will certainly be improvement.[17]

Because metalworkers were particularly interested in education, many were also alert to the dangers posed by employer education. Establishing vocational schools free of employer control was an idea that appealed to many metal workers. In 1883 at a national meeting of a metalworkers' trade union, a delegate from Saint-Etienne lectured his Parisian colleagues on this issue:

The delegate from Saint-Etienne recommended to his Parisian friends the example given by the trade union [*chambre*] that he represents. It has founded vocational [*professionnels*] courses for the use of apprentices. This is an excellent means for removing these [apprentices] from the employer's influence and exploitation.[18]

In 1912, a local historian suggested that the value of company apprenticeship programs had greatly diminished because they had become too specialized.[19] In any case, Stéphanois industry was no longer turning out the highly-skilled workers that it had produced in earlier decades. When they needed truly highly-skilled workers, local employers usually hired them from outside, particularly from nearby Lyon, as was shown in chapter 3. (see figure 3.7)

Employers turned to specialized training to meet the growing competition from metal producers in eastern France. Local industrialists often complained about recruiters from outside the region showing up in the Stéphanois. Responding to their ore-rich competitors, Stéphanois industrialists sought to take advantage of their large labor force and to maintain their reputation for quality production while keeping their prices stable. As the demand for semi-skilled workers increased in local metalworking, more specialized training enabled employers to prevent workers that they had schooled from taking better-paying jobs with their competitors. Many local factories possessed machines especially designed for the individual plant and detailed knowledge of the operation of such machines would not be easily transferable.

In addition, many local workers saw a connection between the dependence of local education on subsidies from employers and its reliance on poorly trained religious teachers. In the 1840s and 1850s, almost all the public schools as well as the private schools were staffed by religious teachers. Many of these received subsidies from companies, and indeed this must have seemed a good bargain since both religious and employers were as interested in instilling principles of order into the student as the rudiments of reading, writing, and arithmetic. In

1845, a school inspector reported that "the clergy tends to restrict teaching very narrowly, and it is of the opinion that too much instruction should not be given to the common child [*à l'enfant du peuple*]".[20] As late as the 1860s, teaching students to say their prayers was alleged to be the major goal of religious educators and their sole enduring achievement.[21]

The low cost of religious instruction made the use of nuns and lay brothers practically indispensible for the spread of popular education in a region populated by a large proportion of industrial workers; yet the low cost also generally kept the quality of instruction low. Clerical teachers in the public schools were less educated than lay or clerical teachers in the private schools. In the public schools, a smaller proportion of clerical teachers possessed an actual teaching license, certifying that they had been formally trained, than in the private schools. In the public schools, 90 percent of teachers possessed only a letter of obedience from their religious superiors, compared with about 70 percent in the private schools. Whatever the letters of obedience said about the character of the teacher they did not certify any knowledge about teaching whatsoever.[22] The insuperable advantage for local officials of having nuns and lay brothers teach was that they were paid very little. In 1853 an inspector noted: "For the arrondissement of Saint-Etienne . . . the misery of the teachers is such that one mayor gives them the aid destined for the poor. Discipline leaves a lot to be desired; the nuns are not always able to handle the boys. The child who is somewhat big or lax deserts the schools of the teaching nuns."[23]

Under such circumstances, the fight against an inferior educational system might easily turn into a struggle against clerical education. Because metalworkers were also more likely than miners to be affected by the abuses that flowed from the poverty and ill-training of clerical teachers, they were particularly vulnerable to such appeals. In 1869, an anti-clerical republican newspaper, *L'Eclaireur*, propagandized local workers:

The lay brother [*frère*] in charge of the second class in the school of the Quartier Saint-Pierre . . . practices: blows to the head with a pointer or a ruler, slaps, rabbit punches . . . the pinching and even the tearing of the ears . . . nothing lacks there . . . Fathers of families should not send their children to these schools; and if, as at Saint-Chamond, they have no other choice, they should watch and energetically bring charges. Justice will do its job.[24]

If for no other reason than their literacy, metalworkers were more likely to pay attention to the newspaper's charges than were miners.

In 1869, one of the major planks in the republican electoral program – a program that, as we shall see in chapter 6, won wide support among Stéphanois metalworkers – was a demand for the enactment of compulsory education and free public, secular, primary education, and the creation of vocational schools. The republican candidate who represented this program was César Bertholon, editor of *L'Eclaireur* and a close associate of the metal employer, Pierre-Frédéric Dorian.[25]

In common with some modern historians, Catholic paternalists such as Etienne Lamy were puzzled by the ability of bourgeois republicans to rally workers over such issues as secular education. Lamy believed that workers were responding to crude, anti-clerical prejudices that led them to ignore their true interests. According to Lamy:

The only thing that interested the workers was the social revolution. . . . Dorian, as the leading figure in the metallurgical industry, remained committed to traditional property arrangements, while as an aspiring politician he had to present the impression of being a passionate reformer. Under the Empire, his newspaper, the *Eclaireur*, distracted the workers from the true interests with red herrings, focused their hatred on the soldier and the priest, rather than the employer.[26]

But a paternalist such as Lamy was incapable of understanding why workers resented religious education and employer training programs, and why metalworkers rallied enthusiastically to the cause of secular education as represented by such as Bertholon. To put education in the hands of the municipality or the state was to take it from the direct control of employers and also from the hands of company-subsidized religious teachers, more intent on saving their students' souls than on educating them. State or municipally sponsored technical education promised to break the employers' control over job training and to free the worker from overspecialization. For metalworkers, to whom education was so vital, secular education was an important step in securing a modicum of independence from their employers. Men like Lamy could well understand and condemn employer oppression, but they could never understand or approve the desire for working-class autonomy and independence.

SEMI-SKILLED WORKERS AND THE FORMATION OF FAMILIES

Both metalworking and mining had their own distinctive patterns of life-cycle employment; the importance of life-cycle employment patterns for the working-class family is demonstrated by the degree to which these distinctions were to prove crucial in the shaping of metalworking and mining families. Over the course of the period 1840 to 1880, not only did the family patterns of metalworkers and miners become more divergent, but increased competition in local mining was to place great pressure on the family structure of the mining population.

One of the most important characteristics of life-cycle employment patterns in coal mining was the early peak in a coal miner's income.[27] Table 4.1, which shows an index of average increases in average wages by age and sector categories of mine employees in 1878 in the Montrambert mines on the outskirts of Le Chambon-Feugerolles, illustrates clearly the rapid mounting of

Table 4.1   Wage structure for men and boys in mining, by age and sector, in the Montrambert mines, 1878

Age categories	Average wage increase as % of average wage of preceeding wage group		% of male workforce employed in age group as % of all in sector	
	Below ground	Above ground	Below ground	Above ground
12–14			1.10	3.61
15–19	+36.26	+43.56	10.93	12.05
20–24	+33.87	+24.51	16.60	9.64
25–41	+12.65	+6.30	63.44	50.00
42–54	+2.67	−6.67	6.58	15.66
55 and older	−8.87	−6.40	1.37	9.04
N			1,882	332

miners' earnings in young manhood. These increases were particularly substantial for underground miners, whose wages were already more than a quarter larger than those of above ground employees in the beginning age category 12 to 14. For both categories of mine employees, the largest increases in salary had already occurred by age 25. After age 25, the increases were relatively small, and after age 55 (42 above ground), there was a decrease.[28] The early peak in the income of miners was because of the relative lack of skill involved in mining. Brawn (and hence youth) and not brain was rewarded more in mining, but unlike most jobs relying on physical strength, it was difficult to supervise many aspects of mining and so necessary to provide incentive pay. The major categories of underground mining, coal hewing, hauling, packing, and timbering required physically strong individuals, willing to take risks, and to work underground. Unlike hauling and packing, timbering and coal hewing, the best-paying mining occupations, were difficult to supervise. Employers thus used an incentive system, paying workers according to the distance timbered and the amount of coal produced.[29]

In comparison with the average wages of semi-skilled workers in machine construction, miners' average wages during their peak years were high. A survey for the period 1861 to 1865 in the *arrondissement* of Saint-Etienne, shows that the average wage of adult males was highest in mining: average adult males earned 3.65 francs in mining and 3.50 in forging and steelmaking.[30] A comparison of average daily wages of semi-skilled workers and the average wage of all miners working underground between 1857 and 1878 shows that underground miners usually earned more than semi-skilled metalworkers.[31] A direct comparison of wages by specific occupations in mining and metalworking is possible only for the late 1860s, when coal hewers' wages were declining. But in 1868 and 1869, the average wage of coal hewers was above the average wage of both forgers and boilermakers in 1867 and 1869.[32] A further breakdown of these wage figures is possible by treating maximum and minimum wage estimates as indicating positions in the skill hierarchies of metalworking and mining. A comparison of the two hierarchies shows that the lower positions in the mining hierarchy were better paid than in metalworking, while the higher positions in the hierarchies were more similar.[33]

Miners' high earnings early in their industrial life course were one powerful support for their maintenance of high fertility while fertility generally declined in the region. After 1850, fertility control within marriage began to spread in the region, but miners' did not employ it to the same extent as many other workers. At the age when miners were just establishing their household, they were making near their peak earnings, which were higher than those of metalworkers at a comparable stage in the life-cycle. In the early and most fertile years for females, miners could better afford the costs of raising children than could metalworkers. Over the 20-year period from 1856 to 1876, the fertility of metalworkers and miners became increasingly divergent. In 1856, the fertility of miners was already greater than that of metal workers; by 1876, high fertility had become a distinguishing characteristic of mining families.

Although the movement toward control of fertility within marriage had hardly begun in the department of the Loire as a whole at mid-century, Coale's index of marital fertility suggests the possibility that by 1856 its control had begun in the cities of Saint-Chamond and Rive-de-Gier. By 1876, it is practically certain that marital fertility was being controlled in Saint-Chamond and probable that fertility control had begun to occur in Rive-de-Gier and Le Chambon-Feugerolles as well.[34] A look at crude birth rates, the number of births per 1,000 in the population, gives a very rough idea of the evolution of fertility over the whole period 1836 to 1880.[35] Figure 4.1 shows substantial fluctuations in birth rates for all three cities. As measured by crude birth rates over the whole period, Le Chambon-Feugerolles stands out as a commune of relatively high fertility and Saint-Chamond as a commune of relatively low fertility. The single most noticeable characteristic of the evolution of crude birth rates is their long and sustained decline in Rive-de-Gier. Starting with extremely high crude birth rates in the 1830s, Rive-de-Gier exhibits fairly low rates in the 1870s.

If indeed marital fertility was being controlled in 1876, then miners, particularly those of Le Chambon-Feugerolles, stand out as exceptions to this trend. A comparison of differential fertility by town shows that miners had above-average fertility in both towns with large mining populations, while the fertility of machine-construction workers was average or below average in both towns (see table 4.2). For each town in 1856 and in 1876, the measures of fertility used are based on the number of children present in the household between 0 and 4 years old by five-year intervals of the age of the wife of the household head. These methods of measuring fertility from census records are frequently referred to as "own-child" techniques.[36] These "own-child" ratios are presented in two forms. The first ratios are based on the actual age distribution of the females married to the household head. The second set of ratios are standardized according to the model age distribution suggested by Tamara Hareven and Maris Vinovskis; these ratios compensate for the effect of differ-

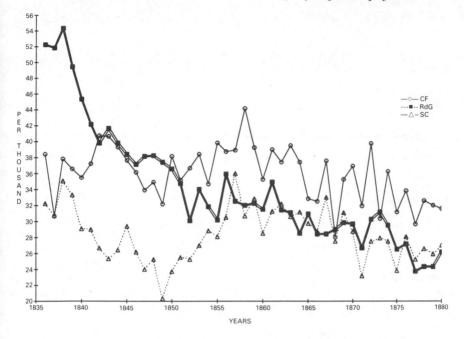

Figure 4.1   Annual crude birth rates in Le Chambon-Feugerolles,
Rive-de-Gier, and Saint-Chamond, 1836–1881

ences in the age distribution of women married to household heads in mining,
machine construction, and the total population.[37] These measures are best
interpreted for the present as getting at fertility differentials *within* towns, rather
than fertility differentials *among* towns, since infant or child mortality and a
number of other factors that varied from town to town will only be discussed in
the next chapter.[38] There was substantial variation in mortality among
Stéphanois towns, and the consideration of mortality strongly affects the
analysis of total fertility among towns.

That miners did not limit their fertility is further suggested by table 4.3 which
gives the results of a logistic regression analysis (with a polytomous dependent
variable) of own-child fertility including the following variables: the age of the
mother; the industrial employment of the household head; the presence of a
boarder; the department of birth of the parents (this is only available for 1876);
and residence in one of the three towns.[39] There are three separate models, one
for 1856, one for 1876, and one that combines both years. Logistic regression is
an extension of the general linear model. The models estimate the odds of
household heads and their spouses having zero to four children under five years
of age. The four, numbered "alphas" in the table are similar to intercept
estimates in multiple regression, each for different categories of the dependent
variable. The reduction in chi square associated with substituting the model for

Table 4.2 Child (0–4 years old) to woman (spouse of household head aged 20–49 years old) ratios, in machine-construction workers, miners, and total population, standardized to actual age distribution and to Hareven–Vinovskis age structure

	Le Chambon-Feugerolles 1856	Le Chambon-Feugerolles 1876	Rive-de-Gier 1856	Rive-de-Gier 1876	St-Chamond 1856	St-Chamond 1876
Machine construction: all						
Actual age structure	678.7	760.7	581.2	461.5	725.5	688.1
H–V standardized	636.5	695.1	559.6	415.2	696.2	698.9
N	103	99	69	63	91	76
Machine construction: semi-skilled						
Actual age structure	700.7	632.2	310.1	413.5[a]	—	615.0
H–V standardized	730.3	584.6	405.7	350.4[a]	—	671.1
N	77	73	48	22	—	41
Miners						
Actual age structure	944.2	1131.2	614.6	554.2[a]	—	—
H–V standardized	941.6	1006.0	561.5	580.8[a]	—	—
N	39	73	65	27	—	—
Total population						
Actual age structure	781.2	845.1	571.1	546.5	593.0	530.0
H–V standardized	734.3	832.9	539.0	566.8	584.8	527.1
N	294	344	429	362	398	390

[a] N = <30.

a baseline model that contains only the intercept is significant at the 0.001 level for all three models. The logistic regression shows that the fertility of miners was growing more distinctive over time. As fertility declined in the Stéphanois region, the fertility of miners and farmers became more anomalous.[40]

High miner fertility was facilitated by the early peak in miners' earnings, but there were probably other reasons for the fertility as well. For one, the cost of raising children was also lower for miners than for metalworkers. Certainly, coal miners who sent their male children to work in the mines – as most coal miners did – were able to benefit from the higher wages paid to younger workers in mining. Machine construction families sent most of their sons into the metalworks, where young workers earned less. Despite the frequent claims of observers that coal miners started work at an especially early age, there is no evidence, either in 1856 or in 1876, that miners in this study started work *in coal mining* earlier than workers in machine construction.[41] As mentioned earlier, the greater availability of *agricultural* work for miners' children in Le Chambon-Feugerolles reduced the cost of child rearing for mining families.[42] In the next section, when the course of miners' earnings in old age is discussed, it will be argued that high fertility may also have served an insurance function.

Table 4.3 Logistic regression equations with number of own children aged 0–4 of household head present as the dependent variable

Variables[a]	Combined	SE	1856	SE	1876	SE
ALPHA1	-3.411^d	0.66	-5.048^d	1.04	-2.320^d	0.87
ALPHA2	-5.040^d	0.67	-6.763^d	1.05	-3.881^d	0.88
ALPHA3	-7.436	0.68	-9.128	1.07	-6.314^d	0.90
ALPHA4	-10.482	0.92	-12.146^d	1.44	-9.392^d	1.33
WIFEAGE	0.299^c	0.04	0.412^d	0.07	0.226^d	0.05
WFAGESQ	-0.006	0.00	-0.007^d	0.00	-0.004^d	0.00
DAYLAB	0.184	0.18	0.095	0.32	0.243	0.22
RIBBON	-0.397	0.29	-0.880^c	0.38	0.189	0.47
MINER	0.398^d	0.14	0.287	0.20	0.498^c	0.20
FARMER	0.414^b	0.25	0.025	0.33	0.911^c	0.39
HARDWARE	0.015	0.22	-0.025	0.28	-0.021	0.37
GLASS	0.651^d	0.20	0.625^c	0.26	0.726^c	0.32
MCSKILL	0.187	0.18	0.270	0.26	0.052	0.27
MCSSKILL	-0.046	0.14	-0.068	0.20	-0.019	0.20
MCUNSKL	-0.014	0.18	-0.359^c	0.24	0.351	0.30
BOARDER	0.087	0.12	0.215	0.19	-0.028	0.17
ONENAT	0.054	0.17	—	—	0.068	0.19
BOTHNAT	0.031	0.18	—	—	-0.021	0.20
RIVE	-0.624^d	0.11	-0.624^d	0.16	-0.636^d	0.16
STCHAM	-0.481^d	0.11	-0.262	0.17	-0.634^d	0.16
Number of cases	2,894		1,467		1,427	

	Comparison with baseline model		
Reduction in chi square	865.03(16df)	487.55(14df)	400.86(16df)
Significance level	0.001	0.001	0.001

SE is Standard Error
[a] Variables:
WIFEAGE is age of spouse of household head
WFAGESQ is age of spouse of household head squared
DAYLAB is household head is daylaborer
RIBBON is household head is ribbonmaker
MINER is household head is coalminer
FARMER is household head is farmer
HARDWARE is household head is hardware maker
GLASS is household head is glassmaker
MCSKILL is household head is skilled worker in machine construction
MCSSKILL is household head is semi-skilled worker in machine construction
MCUNSKL is household head is unskilled worker in machine construction
ONENAT is one spouse is native of department of the Loire: 1876 only
BOTHNAT is both spouses are natives of department of the Loire; 1876 only
WIFEWORK is presence of employed spouse of household head
KIDWORK is proportion of children aged over 10 in household working
RIVE is inhabitant of Rive-de-Gier
STCHAM is inhabitant of Saint-Chamond
[b] $p<0.1$.
[c] $p<0.05$.
[d] $p<0.01$.

Miner illiteracy may have been a factor in high miner fertility. A republican newspaper editorial in 1869 claimed that "the younger generation [of miners] will be incontestably better instructed than the older generation," and suggested that illiteracy was one reason for the miners' ignorance of "Malthus's beautiful rule."[43] But in the 1870s, the miners of Le Chambon-Feugerolles disappointed the editorialist's expectations for, as they gradually became more literate, they also increased their fertility.

Whether rural migrants from high fertility regions exhibited higher fertility than migrants from low fertility regions remains elusive, though the possibility cannot be excluded. As indicated by department of birth in 1876, migrant fertility was not significantly higher than that of natives, and, as was shown in the last chapter, migrants entered mining and metalworking in almost equal proportions. The differences between the two occupations are not because of migration *per se*. For, in contrast with fertility studies of the United States where rural fertility seems generally to have been higher than urban fertility, the rural departments that sent migrants to the Stéphanois industrial area show wide variations in fertility behavior. In France as a whole, there is no reason to believe that rural origins indicate a high fertility background.[44]

Miners' higher earnings and their lower cost of child rearing encouraged high fertility, but their fertility made them especially vulnerable to fluctuations in earnings. Typically, there was more than a decade between birth and the time when a male child was old enough to earn wages; any decline in the head of household's income during these years would affect the more fertile miner much more strongly than the less fertile machine-construction worker. Machine construction was more heavily influenced by wage fluctuations than mining. During the Crimean War and other periods of military and naval expansion, semi-skilled workers could find remunerative work easily; at other times, only lesser paying piecework was available for semi-skilled workers. Faced with wage fluctuations, machine-construction workers made economies, such as giving up a few nights at the café or renting a small plot of land outside the town for a garden. Miners could respond to wage fluctuations by reducing the number of children they might have in the future but, in many instances, their options were limited by their previous high fertility. Although miners could send children aged eight or ten to the countryside to act as shepherds and cowherds, they could do little but share their own resources with their children who were too young to find a job.

In 1854, Armand Audiganne wrote patronizingly about Stéphanois miners' feelings but his conclusions about miners' concerns were not far wrong. He noted:

The miner considers his state as a job which in practically assuring him a fixed income, frees him from all cares. One might be inclined to pity him his hard lot; but the coal miner doesn't complain and, as long as the coal mine is not threatened by unemployment, or a reduction does not affect his wages, he descends into the pits a happy man.[45]

Audiganne's visit was close enough to 1848 that some of the miners could recall the shortened days that had been worked in the mines at that time. Toward the end of the 1850s there would also have been a brief slump in mining employment. But over the course of the period under discussion, unemployment was a relatively small-scale phenomenon in the Stéphanois, a phenomenon that employers easily solved by simply failing to hire back the many seasonal migrant workers who passed back and forth between town and countryside. Between 1830 and 1876, for the whole living memory of those employed not only in mining but also in metalworking, there had been a vast and practically continuous increase in employment in the Stéphanois.

Unfortunately for Stéphanois miners and their families, the late 1860s were to bring an unanticipated period of fluctuating earnings for those workers at the top of the mining hierarchy. By the mid-1860s, the first signs appeared that the golden years of regional expansion were over. Warnings of the end of Stéphanois industrial dominance appeared practically simultaneously in both coal mining and metalworking. As the Thomas–Gilchrist basic spread in French metalworking, it became possible to use the vast iron ore resources of eastern France in steelmaking. At the same time, the extension of the Siemens–Martin process produced large fuel economies in the mass production of steel. In consequence, the Stéphanois, too far from the ore fields, gradually abandoned mass steel production and specialized in quality steel. One result of this specialization was the further growth of the size of the semi-skilled workforce in metalworking. In coal mining, a sudden rise of competition from the expanding coal fields in northern France also brought new challenges to local coal mining. Stéphanois coal companies responded to this challenge by sinking new mines in the unexploited portions of the basin where cheap, good quality coal was still available.[46]

While they were in the process of opening new mines, the companies feared losing markets, particularly local markets, to northern coal. Thus, they desperately sought to find the quality coal their customers demanded in the old pits. They hired additional miners in an effort to continue to supply these markets. But as seams petered out and as the proportion of rocks to coal increased, it became impossible for miners in some pits to maintain production levels even as their numbers increased. The miners' pay, based on the amount of coal they produced, began to drop accordingly. In 1869, several months before the outbreak of the great strike of that year, a mine manager reporting to company executives in Paris lamented that

the examination of the table of sales shows the demonstrable differences of sales among our various pits. The Loire pits have sold only 28,745 tons; in the first trimester of 1868, it had sold 34,097 ... I'm afraid that we will not be able to accumulate the stocks indispensible for the winter.[47]

This manager, whose pits were to be hard hit by the strike, also noted that "the

Table 4.4   Wage differential indices (hewer's salary = 100) in the Compagnie des mines de la Loire

	1854	1868	1869	1883
Haulers and drawers	61.5	77.6	78.4	65.9
Packers	62.0	75.5	75.5	60.5
Timbermen	79.1	96.1	101.1	72.7
Hewers	100.0	100.0	100.0	100.0
Shaftmen[a]	86.4	105.1	103.4	75.5
Superintendents[b]	129.5	125.0	100.0	94.3
Above-ground mine employees	48.1	62.4	63.1	41.5

[a]   "Shaftmen" is a rough translation of the Stéphanois occupational designation "*mineurs*," defined as "ouvriers chargés d'ouvrir la mine à travers banc."
[b]   *Gouverneurs.*

Table 4.5   Wage changes in occupational categories in Stéphanois mining (1854 = 100)

	1868	1869
Haulers and drawers	118.6	122.1
Packers	114.5	116.7
Timbermen	114.2	122.5
Hewers	94.1	95.8
Shaftmen	114.5	114.8
Superintendents	90.8	84.0
Above-ground mine employees	121.9	125.6

scarcity of workers seems to put insurmountable obstacles in the face of production."[48]

In mining, unlike in metalworking, employers' attempts to modernize resulted in wildly fluctuating earnings that were felt particularly severely in those parts of the coal basin where miners with large families were concentrated. From the miners' perspective, the problem with modernizing the mines was that sinking pits and tunneling provided less opportunity for coal cutting (the most remunerative occupation in the mines), and much more opportunity for timbering and packing (the less remunerative occupations).

Tables 4.4 and 4.5 show this phenomenon in one local mine, owned by the Compagnie des mines de la Loire. They show the declining relative income of the coal hewer resulting from the difficulty of extracting coal in the old pits. They also reveal the rising income of timbermen and packers stemming from the increased demand for these categories of workers. As the old pits became less remunerative, some coal hewers were transferred from the old to the new pits; transfers usually involved the breakup of the existing mining team and an initial reduction in wages. Some coal hewers also were probably reduced to timbering and packing, a reduction that further reduced their salary.[49] Although the wages of some categories of workers were increased, these wage increases did not generally counterbalance the wage reductions. Overall, the real wages of coal miners declined between 1865 and 1869.

The combination of fluctuations in income, scarcity of work, and the family situation of miners was to prove explosive. In mid-1869, a great strike broke out in the Stéphanois. The great upheaval in Stéphanois mining occurred simultaneously with other strikes in heavy industry across France. Together, these strikes shook the Second Empire and revived the opposition to Napoleon III. Miners' willingness to strike, in 1844, in 1852, and in 1869, gave Stéphanois miners a lasting reputation as a combative and independent working-class population.

A look at the relationship between reproduction and production in the case of Stéphanois miners should give us some insight into the indignation that fueled this mass protest. The advantages of metalworkers during the crisis period of the 1870s only highlighted the miners' problems. Metalworkers who combined their wages with their smaller family size were as concerned as miners with issues of long-term family survival; secure in their own position, semi-skilled metalworkers sought to protect family interests by making sure that their position would be transmitted to their sons. During the same period, miners were threatened with a very real worsening of their own position.

Wage fluctuations among hewers caused enormous sacrifices for miners and their families by affecting the miners' ability to earn wages sufficient to form families and to raise children who could survive in the industrial world. The relatively high wages of hewers had made it possible for them to create a world of family ties separate from the world of the work place. Single male miners, able to leave the commune and to move to newly opened mines, were the most able to escape the wage cuts forced on workers by transfers and the increasing difficulties of extraction. If relatively high wages had encouraged workers to form families, then in times of increased competition, mining companies might use the very presence of their families to force workers to accept lower wages as an alternative to unemployment. Perhaps the miners' greatest fear was voiced in the 1880s by Michel Rondet, when he claimed "that the worker is under the employers' domination, because he has a family to feed."[50] By threatening the wage levels that made family stability possible, employers seemed to be challenging workers' sacred sphere of independence. In 1869, on the eve of the great strike, one of the miners' leaders launched a slogan that gives insight into the character of the miners' response. He demanded that miners raise the cry, "Long live the miners! Long live these brave and honest fathers of families . . ."[51]

The miners' cry raises some important questions about the relationship of gender to work, questions that will be examined in the next chapter. For now, it is important to note the common theme that ties together both metalworkers' enthusiasm for state-regulated secular education and miners' demand for a stable wage for coal hewers. Understanding the real thrust of their concerns rests on seeing the ways in which these issues were tied to life-cycle employment patterns and on realizing that both miners and metalworkers were intent upon removing those areas where work and family most closely intersected from the arbitrary regulation of their employers.

PROTECTION AGAINST OLD AGE

As workers began to settle in the city and build futures for themselves in urban industry, they also had to consider how to deal with the consequences of old age and of an ageing process that would cause their earnings to decline. By "ageing" not just chronological age is meant, but a whole biological process determined by a sum of genetic and environmental factors.[52] One aspect of ageing was association of chronological age with the decline of physiological processes and with the appearance of chronic diseases that incapacitated workers from their normal adult work.

It seems very likely that the miners of Rive-de-Gier and Saint-Etienne were right in 1848 when they singled out their profession as one where workers "still very young become incapable of working."[53] The theme of miner exhaustion at an early age was repeated often throughout the second half of the nineteenth century. In 1869, a middle-class resident of the Stéphanois declared "the population of the mines [is not] particularly weak or malingering; only it is necessary to have a robust constitution in order to resist so many causes of morbidity; the weak succumb and the strong age quickly."[54] In 1883, the Stéphanois miners' leader Michel Rondet claimed that, "the companies well know that at forty or forty-five, the worker is nearly worn out and that is why they try to get rid of him: he is no longer able to perform the same amount of work as at thirty five."[55] Zola described the miner's life-cycle in *Germinal*. In an early chapter, the newcomer, Etienne, meets old Vincent Maheu, nicknamed "Bonnemort," a lifelong miner who tells him:

began as a pit-boy, then haulage man when I was strong enough to push, then eighteen years as a collier. Then because of my perishing legs, they put me on ripping, then packing, then repairs, until in the end they had to bring me above ground because the doctor told them that if they didn't, I should stay down for good . . .[56]

Perhaps the most remarkable feature of old Maheu was his longevity as a collier.

Although the effects of mining and metalworking on the workers' life expectations and on their overall health need further investigation; the evidence strongly suggests that the effects of ageing on workers' incomes showed themselves much earlier among miners than among metalworkers. Miners' abilities depended more on physical strength and less on acquired skill than those of the worker in machine construction, and the miner could expect his income to fall gradually but continuously as he passed early middle age. While miners' earning peaked at a higher level than metalworkers', they also dropped off much more quickly.

Evidence indicates that for many miners the decline in income occurred early. Indeed, an 1885 national survey of the age of underground coal miners in France, suggests that ageing set in after age 40, when the proportion of workers employed underground began to decrease.[57] A comparison of the age distribution of males laboring underground and those above ground in the Montrambert mines in 1878 suggests the same phenomenon (see table 4.1). As miners aged, their participation in below-ground mining decreased dramatically, but their participation in above-ground mining increased at an even faster pace. Among underground male miners, 6.6 percent were aged between 42 and 55, and 1.4 percent were 55 or above; among males working above ground, 15.7 percent were between the ages of 42 and 55, and 9 percent aged 55 or above. These figures suggest that, at least after age 42, many underground miners shifted to above-ground jobs in mining. When they did so, their pay dropped dramatically; for age 55 and above, the wages of underground miners were 50 to 60 percent higher than those of above-ground workers. The same shift in the age distribution of above ground and below ground workers in mining is demonstrated in figure 4.2 which shows the age distribution of males by sector in the Compagnie des mines de la Loire.[58]

The miners' union acknowledged that companies often transferred incapacitated ageing miners, but it complained of the terms of such transfers. In 1883, Michel Rondet alleged to a government committee that in particularly dangerous mines where coal dust incapacitated workers at an early age, the "company employed these workers at light work; sometimes they have as mission to report on the behavior [*compte*] of their comrades."[59] Later in his testimony, Rondet added that incapacitated miners were transferred to work that was too demanding: "when a worker is no longer able to do the work of mining, they set him to day laboring, which is only able to be done by robust workers. He [the worker] must either take it or leave it."[60]

Their possession of manual skills enabled metalworkers to maintain their earnings steadily through middle age and to remain in their occupation even as their physical strength declined. In 1902, a visitor to Stéphanois metalworking plants marvelled at the occupational stability across age categories that prevailed there: "hardly ever [does it happen that] once attached to a workshop, one changes it . . . [until] the departure from the factory – that is to say often up to the departure from life."[61]

Stéphanois metal employers sought to reassure their workers that faithful employees would not be discharged due to age. The manager of one of the metalworking firms studied explained that "we have as a principle . . . not firing anyone when work lacks except for just cause. Under these circumstances [of labor surplus] we do not hire or replace those leaving."[62] The veracity of this claim is difficult to ascertain, but it certainly confirms the observation, frequently reiterated by employers and workers alike since 1840, that Stéphanois

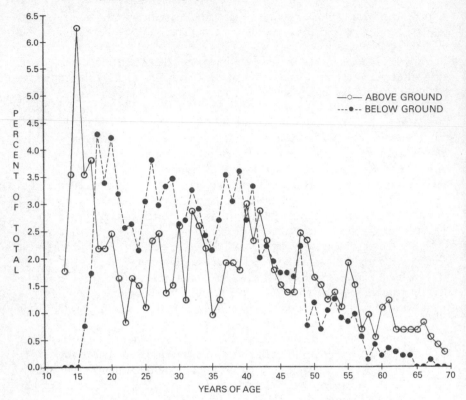

Figure 4.2   Age distribution of male miners in above-ground and below-ground workforce, 1885, from Société anonyme des mines de la Loire

employers in mining and metalworking tried to avoid firing workers possessing skills. A policy that promised to retain ageing workers was a powerful incentive for workers at any age to stay at their job. In 1869, a mining manager observed in private correspondence with his directors that the metalworks were working despite reduced demand, "in order to keep their personnel and to maintain their equipment."[63]

In the 1850s and 1860s, most of the larger coal companies began to institute retirement funds for miners who had either reached a certain age (usually 55 or 60), or worked in the mines for a certain duration (around 20 to 25 years).[64] Most retirement programs were adopted during periods of labor scarcity, and it is a bit difficult to distinguish between those aspects of company retirement policy that were adopted to induce workers to establish themselves in the mines and those aspects that were designed to coerce existing workers to remain.

From either view, the creation of retirement benefit programs by the individual companies had the effect of discouraging miner mobility, particularly in communities or towns such as Le Chambon-Feugerolles and Saint-Etienne where there were mines belonging to separate companies. In fact, the new individual programs probably placed more serious constraints on mobility than the central fund. Workers who left a job at one mine to take a job at a neighboring mine lost all right to retirement benefits. This proved particularly troublesome in the 1860s, when, as we have seen, miners' wages fluctuated. A worker with a large family who needed to maintain his income might find remunerative work in another mine, but the price paid for maintaining earnings was the loss of a pension in old age. In 1883, according to a miners' leader, over 90 percent of aged coal miners were ineligible for pensions because they had changed coal employers.[65] The coal monopoly had always refused workers permission to move independently from pit to pit in order to prevent the bidding up of miners' wages, and many miners had hoped that the break up of the monopoly would promote wage competition. The creation of retirement benefits were a powerful force to mitigate wage competition.

Metal companies were far behind mining companies in providing retirement benefits to their workers. In 1890, a government survey of employer benefits in the Stéphanois revealed that most metal employers did not possess a retirement fund. Of the handful of metal companies that did possess such a fund, one company noted:

The greater part of our old workers prefer, as long as possible, to stay at work in the factory that seeks to find for them work that takes account of their capacities [*force*]. Perhaps, they fear, to a certain extent, an idle life, to which they are not accustomed and which risks being for them a source of increased expenditure. It is also necessary to add that the salary maintained in our factory to the aged worker remain much superior to the continuing aid he might expect to receive upon retiring.[66]

The policy of this metal employer was not really so different from the over-whelming majority of metal employers, who reported that they "insure work to old workers in proportion to their capacity."[67]

The age structure of the day laboring workforce in all three towns in 1856 and in 1876 may have been a direct result of the policy of metal and mining employers towards their aged workers. In all three towns, the day laboring workforce was concentrated among the young and the old. It comprised children who had not yet found their way into the factory training programs and older workers, many probably workers who were physically unable to pursue better paying occupations in the mines and metalworks.[68]

The early decline in most miners' earnings was a powerful force in shaping miners' personal behavior as well as the goals of the miners' union, but struggles over these issues were of one piece with the struggle over sickness and accident policies. Before considering the workers' responses to the problems of ageing in the industrial city, let us first examine the problems raised by sickness and accident.

PROTECTION AGAINST SICKNESS AND ACCIDENT

Besides ageing, it was also necessary for permanent proletarians to consider the possibilities of having their work-life interrupted or ended in mid-life, either by temporary illness or by accidental death. Temporary migrants and permanent proletarians might have very different perspectives on the danger of industrial occupations. In 1884, arguing for compulsory deductions for health insurance for very short-term workers before a governmental committee, Michel Rondet distinguished between the attitudes of temporary migrants towards accidents and insurance protection and those of permanent miners:

There are . . . the mountain dwellers to whom one [the company] says, "the company has an insurance fund, it is not obligatory, I believe that you would do better to save your money yourself." And the mountain dweller accepts this situation. If he works fifteen days or a month and is injured during this time, he has miscalculated . . .
   The miners wish to assure their security [*prévoyance*]; it is difficult for a worker to save on his own.[69]

Sickness was an occupational hazard in both metalworking and mining. In 1848, doctors had noted in a governmental report that machinists were particularly susceptible to rheumatism and respiratory diseases. The report also noted that metalworkers' labor in a very hot environment weakened their resistance to disease.[70] Other studies of metalworkers had confirmed these conclusions. In 1866, a study of machine-construction workers in Prussia called attention to the high occupational mortality resulting from the strenuous nature of the job and workers' exposure to extremes of temperature and to dangerous fumes.[71]
   Yet most students of coal mining will agree with nineteenth-century observers in the Stéphanois that miners were more liable to occupational illnesses than metalworkers.[72] The incidence of illness among miners added an element of unpredictability to miners' life-cycle employment. As the medical report attached to the 1848 enquiry established, miners were especially subject to a variety of incapacitating diseases. The report noted that:

asthma and pulmonary catarrah [among miners] ravage more freely than in the other professions. We have noted that these two maladies are more tenacious and serious among miners . . . Rheumatism attacks some of them, but it is particularly severe among those . . . who hollow the galleries and the pits in the rock.[73]

The doctors' findings concerning miners' susceptibility to disease were accepted almost universally by contemporaries in the Stéphanois region. The asthma mentioned in the doctors' report is almost certainly silicosis, which was labeled "miners' asthma" in the nineteenth century. Although silicosis was one of those permanently incapacitating diseases that might finally end a miner's career and his life, it might also render him more liable to other respiratory diseases even in its early stages. Miners' susceptibility to respiratory diseases has also been confirmed by more recent studies of mining mortality.[74]

For both metalworkers and miners, there was also the possibility of accidents in addition to occupational illness; in regard to accidents especially, miners were subject to more risks than metalworkers. In 1855, a mutual aid society founded in Rive-de-Gier set special rates for miners; a society brochure explained that miners were "more exposed to accidents."[75] As late as 1930, a study of occupational mortality found that miners were more likely to die from accidents than any other single factor.[76] Every several years, a major explosion or cave-in occurred that took the lives of many miners. In 1855, an explosion killed 5 workers in the Charles pits at Firminy; a year later, an explosion in the same pit killed 14. In 1867, 37 miners were killed at the Vilars pits. In 1869 5 miners were killed at the Monteraud mines at Firminy and the next year, 2 separate explosions in the same pits killed 34 workers.[77]

In the Stéphanois, unlike in some northern fields, the accumulated minor cave-ins, explosions, and asphyxiations that took a steady toll of miners' lives were more murderous than the large explosions. Between 1860 and 1868, 444 miners were killed in mining accidents; the lowest mortality year for miners in this period witnessed 29 dead, the highest, 75.[78] Perhaps because of the increase in construction in newly opened pits, accidents were much more frequent in the newer western wing of the coal field. Systematic reports are not available for each year, but a series can be constructed for the eight years between 1865 and 1872. The base used is that of underground miners since the overwhelming proportion of accidents occurred underground. Between 1865 and 1872, 1.44 percent of all miners were killed or injured each year in the Ripagérien basin; 0.47 percent were killed and 0.97 percent were injured. For the same period, 2 percent of all miners were killed or injured each year in the Stéphanois basin; 0.8 percent were killed and 1.2 percent injured. Both deaths and injuries were more common in the western field where the new pits were located.[79]

In the process of assembling a labor force, the miners' employers too were forced to take into account miners' concerns about accidents and old age. To a degree, the mining companies' options were narrower than those of metal employers because of the considerable legal restrictions on French mines. As early as 1817, a French law had been passed providing for insurance and pension benefits for the miners of Rive-de-Gier to be paid for by the employer. But until the formation of the mining monopoly, the Compagnie des mines de la Loire in the late 1830s and early 1840s, this law had been almost completely ignored. The mining companies showed little signs of having been compelled by the law. Company medical and accident services surpassed the legal requirements, and, after mid-century, the mining companies began to provide for pensions on better terms than those provided by law.

The medical services offered by the Stéphanois coal mines were quite advanced for the time and easily equaled those available to nineteenth-century coal miners in the United States.[80] Between 1846 and 1848, the mining monopoly erected three hospitals, one in Saint-Etienne, and one each in the western and eastern extensions of the coal field. By 1853, these hospitals were staffed by 8 doctors and 34 nuns, who served as nurses. The hospitals provided medical care and free prescriptions to all miners employed by the company and to their families. Also in the 1840s, the mining companies created an insurance fund against accidents based on levies from workers; these levies were supplemented by a somewhat smaller company contribution. The insurance fund provided assistance to injured miners and long-term aid to the widows and children of miners killed in mining accidents. When the monopoly was dissolved by government intervention in 1854, the separate companies reconstituted their own insurance funds on a basis similar to that of the previous program.[81]

In the 1840s, the mining monopoly was erecting hospitals and creating insurance funds at the same time that it was lowering workers' wages. The creation of insurance protection combined with an attack on workers' living standards suggests that employers' insurance institutions involved more than employer beneficence. In the most immediate sense, better medical care also encouraged an early return to work. More generally though, company policies are probably best understood in the light of the difficulties in ensuring worker stability in a regional economy so subject to return migration. Just as in the case of retirement pensions, company insurance policies rewarded the worker who stayed continuously on the job and punished the worker who left. The insurance fund itself came partly from forced contributions from the workers; but these forced savings were only available to the worker for as long as he worked in the mines. There were mines in France, such as those in the Gard, that refunded all money contributed by a worker to an insurance policy when the worker quit or was discharged from his job, but Stéphanois employers adamantly refused to adopt such a policy.[82]

Miners were often described as unconcerned and barely recognizant of the dangers involved in their work; one observer labeled Stéphanois miners "insouciant."[83] But their behavior suggests that miners were deeply concerned about the dangers for themselves and for their families should they be seriously incapacitated or killed in the mines. The magnitude of dangers, from premature ageing to illness, injury and accidental death, was simply too great for miners to depend on their own resources. Very likely, as Dov Friedlander has argued in the case of English and Welsh coal miners, an additional reason for miners' high fertility was an attempt to provide against the high risks involved in the industry. He argues that "relatively early marriage and high marital fertility among the coal-mining population in England and Wales provided a kind of life insurance or a pension scheme particularly suited to their special occupational characteristics."[84] The high income of a miner early in the life-cycle enabled him to raise children, who might help support the miner and his family or his widow, when the miner's income declined or disappeared. The importance of children's wages for mining families was widely recognized. Zola evidently discovered the same conditions in his research on coal miners in the north of France. In *Germinal*, the old matriarch, Constance Maheu, argues against an early marriage for her son, Zacharie: "Shouldn't Zacharie show us some consideration? He has cost us money hasn't he? Well, he's got to pay some of it back, before saddling himself with a woman."[85] Zacharie's income was particularly important to Maheude because of the reduction of his grandfather's, Vincent Maheu, earnings due to weak legs and silicosis.

But high fertility was only one aspect of the miners' response to the uncertainties of their trade. They also organized collectively to bring to bear the strength of common organization. Miners' continuing concern with protecting themselves and their families against the dangers of accident, death, and ageing is one of the threads connecting the miners' movement over the whole of the nineteenth century and beyond.

In the 1850s and 1860s, a series of court rulings that favored employers helped to further workers' suspicion of employer dishonesty. For example, courts ruled that in job-related accidents where employer negligence was a factor, companies could not recompense the injured worker or his family out of company insurance funds. The courts ruled that because employers contributed to these insurances workers could not expect to collect money from the insurance funds at the same time as they collected money directly from the company.[86] This decision ignored the relatively large proportion of contributions coming directly from the workers; ironically, one consequence of proven employer negligence was the worker's loss of any claim to the money he himself had accumulated. An even more serious burden on injured workers and on the families of dead or wounded workers however was the extended litigation that resulted from the miners' need to establish company liability. As a result of an 1841 legal ruling, employers were required to take reasonable precautions against accidents.[87] But it was only through legal action that workers or their families could win compensation from their employers for having failed to take such precautions. While the court case was going on, the worker and his family could draw on the insurance fund but they might be expected to pay these sums back pending the outcome of the case. Many widows who were anxious to draw on the company charity that supplemented the insurance fund during the months, or years, in which their legal cases were settled felt pressured to drop their claims against the company.[88]

The administration of benefits programs was another source of worker grievance. Such programs were administered either solely by the company, or with the participation of workers' representatives. Some companies seem to have simply appointed the workers' representatives, others required that they had to come from those workers who had been in the company's employ for many years. The terms of the pension program itself meant that these workers were particularly under the companies' thumb because workers with many years of service had the most to lose if their own pensions disappeared through termination.[89]

As a result of such policies, miners had very little idea about the status of insurance funds. Ignorance about the size of the fund and the relative share contributed by workers and companies made it impossible for workers to bargain with the company about issues crucial to their lives. Companies invariably declared that the miners' contributions to the funds were too small to keep them going on the existing basis without consistent supplement by a generous company. Miners suspected that this was not the case but could not prove it. Also, the existence of the fund in company hands meant that company bankruptcy could destroy the fund. Workers had no privileged claim over other creditors to their pension fund, and in the several bankruptcies that occurred in the 1850s and 1860s, workers did lose almost the whole of their forced savings.[90]

One way in which miners got around their grievances against company benefit programs was by establishing their own insurance societies. Whenever the law allowed miners to set up their own mutual aid societies, they did so. For example, Antoine Prugnat, a miner delegate to the commission that conducted the official inquiry into labor conditions in 1848, established a mutual benefit fund for miners. Police reports alleged that this benefit association was a branch of the miners' union that grew up in 1848. Prugnat's benefit fund association included 363 members by 1851, but was abolished in the massacre of workers' organizations after the Napoleonic *coup d'état*.[91] In 1866, as the Second Empire liberalized, a new mutual aid association called *La Fraternelle*, was formed that provided benefits for miners throughout the coal basin. This association grew rapidly, and by 1868 it had 5,000 members, approximately one-third of the miners in the region.[92]

In the 1860s, just as in the early 1850s, powerful, miners' organizations became involved in politics. The leaders of *La Fraternelle* sought to win the legal right to participate in the administration of the coal companies' insurance funds. The associations' influence on the mining population brought it into conflict with the coal companies. *La Fraternelle* also became the *de facto* miners' representative to the Napoleonic administration, a role that in the troubled late 1860s was bound to lead to political confrontation.[93]

In contrast with the miners, metalworkers seem to have been less concerned about physical dangers that indeed threatened them less. The metal employers provided roughly the same sort of protection against accidents that the mining companies offered. Workers' wages were docked by a certain percentage and the company provided a matching contribution. In addition, the levying of fines for infringing work rules had become a fine art in Stéphanois metalworking, and these fines were also deposited in the mutual aid fund.[94] Workers were either appointed under similar conditions to those in mining or elected to represent the workers in the administration of the mutual aid fund. At no time during this period did metalworkers become involved in protests concerning the regulation of these funds.

Looking at employment patterns over the life-cycle among metalworkers and miners, it is instructive to examine the issues that separated these two working-class groups and those that united them. In one sense, the two industrial groups had very different interests. Metalworkers were deeply interested in educational issues, and miners were not. In contrast, miners were terribly concerned about accident and retirement issues and about wage fluctuations, issues evidently not of primary concern to metalworkers.

Yet, even their differences on individual issues reveal a remarkable unity of intent and concern. In many ways, the miners' desire to stabilize wages for those wage categories where fathers of families were concentrated and their interest in accident and retirement policies resemble the metalworkers' focus on educational issues. Neither working-class group was concerned primarily with its everyday standard of living or with the organization of work, but with those issues that went to the very heart of the concerns of newly proletarianizing workers in the cities. Those issues all revolved around the ability of workers and their families to survive in the industrial city. By choosing to involve themselves in these issues, miners and metalworkers were demonstrating their fundamental loyalties. Both groups were eager to stabilize the position of the working-class family as each group defined it. Both metalworkers and miners were preoccupied with the difficulties that arose from the area where the world of work and the world of the family intersected. If at the work place the employer had the right to order the worker to do whatever he willed, workers wanted to make sure that he did not have the right to decide about the education their children would receive, or their eligibility for retirement benefits, or their ability to feed their families.

Let us return for just a moment to those wholly fictitious creatures, Etienne and Martin, mentioned at the beginning of this chapter and intended to represent the typical life course of miners and metalworkers in the Stéphanois. By the late 1860s or the mid-1870s, they would be fathers of families, men with established occupational identities. The metalworker, Martin, earns a stable income and has little fear of unemployment; he might well reflect that with all their work's dangers, metalworkers were better off than miners. But Martin could well be concerned about his son's fate. In school, the nuns at best only succeeded in maintaining order, while at work, the boy received training that seemed excessively narrow, particularly in light of the well paying jobs available in local metalworking. In contrast with the metalworker, the coal miner's cares are heavier and more sorrowful. Changes in work assignments and decreased pay for hewers have unexpectedly disrupted many of his workmates' income, and he fears that the same thing might happen to him. This is a particularly grave concern because he has four children to feed and none to bring home income. Looking a few years forward, he can foresee a long-term decline in his own earnings and can only wonder about the future wages his sons will earn. With such fears, Etienne has been thinking about joining the newly formed miners' mutual aid society, *La Fraternelle*, which has won so many local adherents. Membership in such a society would allow him to insure himself against future dangers without any taint of company charity.

Such thoughts about their future and about their children's future must have occurred to many local proletarians as the era of rapid industrial expansion in the Stéphanois came to an end.

NOTES

1 Clark Kerr and Abraham Siegel, "The Interindustry Propensity to Strike – An International Comparison," in *Industrial Conflict*, ed. Arthur Kornhauser, Robert Dubin, and Arthur M. Ross (New York, McGraw-Hill, 1954), pp. 189–212, esp. pp. 191–2. For a review of the literature on mining, M. I. A. Bulmer, "Sociological Models of the Mining Community," *Sociological Review*, new series, 23 (1975), pp. 61–92.
2 Philippe Ariès, *Histoire des populations françaises* (Paris, Seuil, 1971), pp. 101–3.
3 On careers in organizations such as large corporations see James E. Rosenbaum, "Organizational Career Mobility: Promotion Chances in a Corporation during Periods of Growth and Contraction," *American Journal of Sociology* 85 (July, 1979), pp. 21–48.
4 Jacques Valserres, *Les industries de la Loire* (Saint-Etienne, Robin, 1862), pp. 235–6.
5 For a description of the different categories of miners and their tasks, see 1848 *enquête*, AN-F/14/3821–4195, "Le Procureur général à Monsieur le Garde de Sceaux" June 26, 1852; AN-BB/18/5506; and, for 1859–60, L.-J. Gras, *Histoire économique générale des mines de la Loire*, vol. 2, p. 748. Also, Pierre Guillaume, *La Compagnie des mines de la Loire 1846–1854* (Paris, Presses universitaires de France, 1966) pp. 144–5.
6 Petrus Faure mentions that children living in Le Chambon-Feugerolles and La Ricamerie were frequently employed in agriculture. Faure himself worked as a cowherd before going down into the mines. See *Un témoin raconte* (Saint-Etienne, Dumas, 1962). In the 1860s, the future socialist militant, Jean Colly, born in Unieux, not far from Le Chambon-Feugerolles, also worked in his youth watching cow and pigs; Colly's father died when he was 14 months old, and his mother abandoned him. Colly later worked in the mines and metalworks. See Maurice Dommanget, *La Chevalière du travail française 1893–1911* (Lausanne, Editions rencontre, 1967), pp. 240–1.
7 The manuscript census of 1856 divided the commune of Le Chambon-Feugerolles into densely and thinly populated areas. The 1856 census contained a detailed list of which areas belonged to each classification; such a list was lacking for the 1876 census. Using the 1856 geographic divisions for the 1876 census as well show that one can, in both years, miners were far more likely to live in the sparsely populated sections than were workers in machine construction. In 1856, 26.4 percent of all workers in machine construction lived in the rural areas of the commune; for miners the figure was 58.6 percent; in 1876, 43.9 percent of all machine-construction workers were rural dwellers, while 72.3 percent of all miners were. These estimates for 1876 are undoubtedly somewhat overstated since the urbanization of Le Chambon-Feugerolles did not proceed so much as a result of the expansion of an urban center outward as through the merging of urbanizing hamlets with the center. Still, the

decline of employment in the agricultural sector in Le Chambon-Feugerolles between 1856 and 1876 may have resulted in a greater ruralization of the industrial workforce.

8 AN-F/12 4723, July 9, 1867.

9 A. Audiganne, *Les populations ouvrières et les industries de la France*, 2 vols (Paris, Capelle Librairies, 1854), vol. 2, p. 103.

10 ADL 15/J/2659, Ingénieur principal.

11 François Furet and Jacques Ozouf, *Reading and Writing: Literacy in France from Calvin to Jules Ferry* (Cambridge, Cambridge University Press, 1982), p. 172. "Read only" literacy was a product of early educational theories, enshrined in Catholic educational practice after they had been banished elsewhere, and the church's primary concern with enabling its students to read prayer books.

12 F. Chapelle, "Etat de l'ignorance dans le département de la Loire en 1869," *Annales de la Société d'agriculture, industrie, sciences, arts et belles lettres du département de la Loire* 14 (1870), pp. 37–49.

13 In 1856, in Rive-de-Gier and Le Chambon-Feugerolles, a weighted average of sons of mining fathers shows 20.2 percent going into metalworking (N = 32); in 1876, the percentage was 16.7 percent (N=27). In 1856, a weighted average of sons of metalworking fathers shows none going into mining (N=84); in 1876, 13.7 percent (N=44).

14 ADL M/244/ tr. 427/6.

15 AN-F/12 4722.

16 For a breakdown of the economy of the individual towns by membership in social classes, see table 4.9 in appendix 4.1. I have roughly followed the classificatory scheme used by Ronald Aminzade, see "A Marxist Approach to Occupational Classification," Center for Research on Social Organization, working paper 132 (June, 1976). The extremely large size of the working-class population of all three towns in both 1856 and 1876 and the very small size of the middle classes makes the study of social mobility not a particularly fruitful topic in these towns.

17 AN-F/14 3821–4195.

18 Cited in *L'Echo des mines et de la métallurgie*, October 21, 1883.

19 "L'apprentissage à l'atelier est, d'ailleurs, loin d'être aussi bien fait que jadis; il l'est d'autant moins que le machinisme a prie une plus grande importance et que la tendance à spécialiser l'ouvrier s'accentue chaque jour," Chomienne, *Histoire de la ville de Rive-de-Gier*, p. 74.

20 MMe. G. Liogier, *Enseignement dans la Loire sous la Monarchie de Juillet et le Second Empire* (Saint-Etienne, Archives départementales de la Loire, n.d.).

21 *L'Eclaireur*, September 27, 1869.

22 Liogier, *Enseignement dans la Loire*, pp. 13–14. Table compiled in 1850.

23 Ibid.

24 *L'Eclaireur*, April 28, 1869.

25 According to *L'Eclaireur* of September 10, 1869, "M. Bertholon . . . réclaimait l'instruction gratuite et obligatoire, l'enseignement professionnel, industriel et agricole."

26 Lamy is quoted in Sanford Elwitt, *The Making of the Third Republic: Class and Politics in France, 1868–1884* (Baton Rouge, Louisiana State University Press, 1975), p. 85.

27 See Michael Haines, *Fertility and Occupation: Population Patterns in Industrialization* (New York, Academic Press, 1979) p. 57.

28 In Lowthian Bell, *Principles of the Manufacture of Iron and Steel with Some Notes on the Economic Conditions of their Production* (London, George Routledge and Sons, 1884) pp. 511–12.

29 See 1848 *enquête*, AN-F/14/3821–4195, "Le Procureur général à Monsieur le Garde de Sceaux" June 26, 1852; AN-BB/18/5506; and, for 1859–60, Gras, *Histoire économique générale des mines de la Loire*, vol. 2, p. 748.

30 Bureau de la statistique générale, *Statistique de la France – Résultats généraux de l'enquête effectuée dans les années 1861–1865* (Nancy, Berger-Levrault, 1873), pp. 318–23.

31 Wage estimates for *chaudronniers* and *forgeurs* were found in ADL 85/M/2; wages for Stéphanois coal miners in Francois Simiand, *Le Salaire des ouvriers des mines de charbon en France* (Paris, Cornely, 1907).

32 The wages for miners of the Compagnie des mines de la Loire in 1868 and 1869 were found in ADL 15/J/860, 1867–9.

33 A comparison of wages for haulers and drawers in the Stéphanois mines shows that, between 1845 and 1874, this lowest paid category of underground miners received higher wages than the day laborers in the Claudinon works. On the wages of day laborers at the Claudinon works, ADL 1/J/175.

The strength of the preceding piece of evidence is reinforced by evidence about the average mining wage. In the early 1860s (in 1860, 1863, 1863, and 1864), the *average* salary of all those working in the Stéphanois mines was higher than the "ordinary salary" of both *forgeurs* and *chaudronniers*. By the mid- and late 1860s (in 1866, 1867 and 1869), *forgeurs'* and *chaudronniers'* ordinary salaries were above that of the average miner but always by less than 10 percent. This difference remained for the rest of the 1870s. See Simiand, *Le Salaire des ouvriers des mines*, and ADL 85/M/2.

34 Coale's index of marital fertility, Ig, which expresses marital fertility as a proportion of Hutterite fertility, gives values of 0.577 for Rive-de-Gier, 0.541 for Saint-Chamond, and 0.652 for Le Chambon-Feugerolles: values of Ig below 0.600 indicate a probability that couples are using fertility control within marriage. In 1876, Rive-de-Gier had an Ig of 0.565, Saint-Chamond, 0.470, and Le Chambon-Feugerolles, 0.587. Igs below 0.55 indicate the near certainty of fertility control within marriage. See James Lehning, "The Decline of Marital Fertility: Evidence from a French Department," forthcoming in *Annales démographiques*.

35 Annual birth figures for each town were found in the Archives départementales de la Loire and at the Palais de Justice in Saint-Etienne.

36 On "own children" techniques, see Wilson H. Grabill and Lee-Jay Cho, "Methodology and the Measurement of Current Fertility from Population Data on Young Children," in *Demography* 2 (1965), pp. 50–73; and Lee-Jay Cho, "The Own-Children Approach to Fertility Estimation: An Elaboration," in *International Population Conference: Liège, 1973* (Liège, IUSSP, 1973), vol. 2, pp. 263–279.

37 For the Hareven–Vinovskis standard, see Tamara K. Hareven and Maris A. Vinovskis, "Patterns of Childbearing in Late-Nineteenth Century America: The Determinants of Marital Fertility in 1880," in Hareven and Vinovskis, *Female*

Population in Nineteenth Century America (Princeton, Princeton University Press, 1978), pp. 85–125; see p. 93 for standard distribution.

38 It is assumed that census undercounting, wetnursing, and infant and child mortality were the same for the different industries employing male household heads in each town; in fact, these assumptions seem most plausible when, as in the present case, fertility among the different industries employing male household heads are being compared rather than different social classes. Female employment patterns however are a complicating factor here. Mothers employed outside the home might well have left their infants with wetnurses, a factor that would have increased infant and child mortality. But this is only a real issue in Saint-Chamond in 1876 and does not affect the present intra-city comparisons.

39 The most important variables in the logistic regression were community of residence, wife's age, wife's age squared, household head in mining in 1876, head in ribbonweaving in 1856, head in farming in 1876, head in unskilled metalworking in 1856, and head in glassmaking in 1856 and 1876. Some of the factors that contributed to the community of residence variable, such as mortality and employment patterns, are discussed in the following chapter. The importance of wife's age is expected, although not very interesting. Similarly, wife's age squared was included because the relationship between wife's age and fertility is expected to be curvilinear. Farming and glassmaking were industries with unusually favorable opportunities for child labor; glassmaking was also greatly expanding in this period. Ribbonweaving was an industry in decline in these Stéphanois cities during the 1850s. The relationship between unskilled metalworking and own-child fertility is a bit surprising. Certainly between 1856 and 1876 the number of workers in unskilled metalworking declined dramatically and the occupation increasingly came to be dominated by the old and the young. Perhaps the occupation had already begun to decline in the 1850s, but this still remains puzzling.

40 On logistic regression, Stephen E. Fienberg, *The Analysis of Cross-Classified Categorical Data*, 2nd edn (Cambridge, Mass., MIT Press, 1981); and John H. Aldrich and Forrest D. Nelson, *Linear Probability, Logit, and Probit Models* (Beverly Hills, Sage, 1984). These logistic regressions were computed using the SAS program. For a description of their properties, Frank E. Harrell, Jr, "The Logist Procedure," in SAS Institute, *Supplementary Library Users Guide* (Cary, NC, SAS Institute, 1983), pp. 181–202.

41 Although contemporaries did not formally compare miners and metalworkers, they often explained miner fertility as due to the ability of children of miners to earn wages at an early age. Our census samples do not show any evidence that the miners went to work earlier than metalworkers. In 1856, in Le Chambon-Feugerolles, 12.9 percent of miners were under age 19, 21.7 percent of metalworkers; in 1876, 17 percent of miners, 12.5 percent of metalworkers. In 1856, in Rive-de-Gier, 9.2 percent of miners were under age 19, 12.2 percent of metalworkers; in 1876, 15.2 percent of miners, 13.8 percent of metalworkers. Did contemporaries get it wrong or might there be census undercounting of miners?

Most likely, contemporaries were not wrong but neither is there any evidence of census undercounting. It seems very likely that a major source of child employment in the mines was disappearing in 1847 when the underground hauling in the mines was mechanized; the 1848 *enquête* was not wrong when it found that many children worked underground as haulers, but hauling was rapidly disappearing. Even after 1848, *for the Stéphanois region as a whole*, miners did go to work at an earlier age than metalworkers but the difference was not that great. In 1867 an effort to estimate the number of children under 16 who were working in the *arrondissement* of Saint-Etienne gave it as 2.68 percent of the metal workforce and 4.54 percent of the mining workforce. Furthermore, it seems that child labor in the mines was particularly concentrated in a few mines that hired large numbers of children as sorters. Mines in Firminy and in the "environs" of Saint-Etienne are listed in that number. These mines may not have drawn on the child population in the cities in this study.

In 1890, an age distribution of the labor force was compiled for all the major basins of France. Interestingly, at this date, the Stéphanois mines were still distinguished by the small percentage of child laborers that they employed under ground and all together (see table 4.6). I have given the distribution for a selected number of the most important basins:

Table 4.6   Percentage of total labor force in sector aged 12–16

	% 12–16 underground	% 12–16 above ground
Valenciennes	10.01	21.5
Saint-Etienne	0.60	7.8
Alais	2.5	10.4
Creusot and Blanzy	6.5	16.3

See Rolande Trempé, *Les mineurs de Carmaux 1848–1914* (Paris, Les éditions ouvrières, 1971), p. 138.

42 On this point see Haines, *Fertility and Occupation*, p. 50.

43 "Lettres de Saint-Etienne," *L'Eclaireur*, September 27, 1869.

44 This point is illustrated by the example of two important rural sending areas in our study, the Puy-de-Dôme and the Haute-Loire. Marital fertility in the largely rural Puy-de-Dôme began at roughly the same level as that in the Loire and the two rates declined in tandem; on the other hand, marital fertility in the predominantly rural Haute-Loire was very high in the 1830s, and it only declined to the point that, by 1900, it was similar to that of the Loire in 1830. See Etienne van de Walle, *The Female Population of France in the Nineteenth Century: A Reconstruction of 82 Départements* (Princeton NJ, Princeton University Press, 1974).

45 Armand Audiganne, *Les populations ouvrières et les industries de la France*, vol. 2, p. 97.

46 Only in the decade 1860 to 1870 did coal production in the northern Valenciennes basin really overtake production in the Stéphanois. The relative pace of production in the two basins is shown in table 4.7, which uses coal production in the Stéphanois in 1850 as its base:

47 *Journal de la Compagnie des mines de la Loire*; company records are on deposit at the Archives départementales de la Loire; for 1867–9 see ADL, 15/J/860.

48 Ibid.

49 Wages for workers in mining in the Compagnie des mines de la Loire in 1854 and

Table 4.7   Relative pace of coal production in the Loire and Valenciennes (base = coal production in Stéphanois)

	Loire	Valenciennes
1850	1.00	0.64
1855	1.47	1.12
1860	1.52	1.40
1865	1.96	2.22
1870	2.16	2.78
1875	2.16	4.19
1880	2.31	5.52

Production figures were taken from *L'Echo des mines et de la métallurgie*, July 15, 1883.

1883 were found in Gras, *Histoire économique générale des mines*, vol. 2, p. 786. On the consequences of the break-up of the miner work team, see petition of miners from Rive-de-Gier, "A Monseigneur, le Prince Louis Napoleon, Président de la République," June 16, 1852, BB/18 1506.

50 Rapport A. Girard, Chambre des députés, n. 2760, Séance du 6 décembre, 1883, p. 704.

51 Jean-Claude Peyret, one of the "founders" of *La Fraternelle*, from a letter published in *L'Eclaireur*, June 4, 1869.

52 For the definition of "ageing," I have drawn on William Petersen, *Population* (New York, Macmillan, 1961), p. 579.

53 Cited in Rolande Trempé, "Travail à la mine et vieillissement des mineurs au XIXe siècle," *Le mouvement social* (124) (July–Sept. 1971), pp. 131–52, esp. p. 132.

54 *L'Eclaireur*, September 25, 1869.

55 Rapport Mazeron, Chambre des députés, JO, annexe no. 3965, Séance du 7 juillet, 1885, p. 1247.

In 1883, a mining engineer, after enumerating all the particular diseases to which miners were prone, declared, "the miner, when he is old is incapable of working," in Rapport A. Girard, Chambre des députés, p. 703.

56 Emile Zola, *Germinal* (New York, Penguin, 1954), p. 25.

57 This survey was based on mines in the Gard, Loire, Saône-et-Loire and Bouches-du-Rhône. See Rapport Mazeron, Chambre des députés, JO, annexe no. 3965, Séance du 7 juillet, 1885, p. 1263.

In 1887, a government report noted: "Mais il est incontestable que ces ouvriers qui ont atteint un age aussi avancé et sont généralement employés à la surface, ne peuvent rendre les mêmes services que lorsqu'ils etaient dans la force de l'age. Les salaires qui leur sont accordes sont, de reste, moins élévés que ceux payés aux ouvriers plus jeunes, et des lors, il est juste que la pension de retraite vienne leur apporter un complement de ressources." In Rapport Mazeron, Chambre des députés, JO, annexe Séance du 21 mars, 1887, pp. 1261–7.

58 Age distribution for the Société anonyme des mines de la Loire was found in Rapport Mazeron, Chambre des députés, p. 1265.

59 Rapport A. Girard, Chambre des députés, p. 703.

60 Ibid., p. 703.

61 Charles Benoist, "Le travail dans la grande industrie – II – La métallurgie," *Revue des Deux Mondes* 15 (June, 1903), pp. 637–71, p. 643.

62 Ibid., pp. 643–4, see footnote, p. 643.

63 "Rapport au conseil d'administration sur les operations du Ier semestre 1876," ADL 15/J/860 (176–9).

64 The mines d'Unieux et Fraisses offered a pension to workers age 60 or over with 25 years of service. The Compagnie de Montrambert offered one to workers over age 60 who were incapable of continuing to work. The Chazotte mines required age 60 and 30 years of service. Between 1867 and 1869 some of the largest mines in the region established a central mutual aid fund which provided pensions for workers age 55 and over with 30 years of service. See Gras, *Histoire économique générale des mines*, vol. 2, pp. 533–6.

65 Michel Rondet quoted in Gras, *Histoire économique générale des mines*, vol. 2, p. 538.

66 L.-J. Gras, *Histoire économique de la métallurgie de la Loire* (Saint-Etienne, Theolier, 1908), p. 100.

67 Ibid., p. 99.

68 The following table presents a comparison of the percentage of the population over age 55 among the unskilled and among the total population of those economically active:

Table 4.8　Percentage of distribution of unskilled and economically active population over 55

	Unskilled	Economically active
Le Chambon-Feugerolles, 1856	20.4	13.6
Le Chambon-Feugerolles, 1876	23.5	13.3
Rive-de-Gier, 1856	16.3	12.9
Rive-de-Gier, 1876	17.0	16.8[a]
Saint-Chamond, 1876	16.4	12.6

[a] Estimate derived from the complete portion of the manuscript census sample. See Appendix, pp. 213–14.

69 Rapport A. Girard, Chambre des députés, p. 692. As Alain Cottereau points out, workers dealt with many dangerous occupations by taking jobs in them for only a brief time. See Cottereau, "Usure au travail, destins masculins et destins féminins dans les cultures ouvrières en France, as XIXe siècle," *Le mouvement social* (124) (Mar.–April, 1983), pp. 70–109.

70 "Commission médicale adjointe à l'enquête industrielle et agricole des deux cantons de Saint-Etienne," AN-F/14/3821–4195.

71 M. le docteur Jordan, "Maladies des ouvriers dans les fabriques d'acier," *Annales d'hygiène publique*, 2nd series, 23 (1866), pp. 264–84.

72 In 1930, iron foundry workers came right after miners in number of deaths from influenza, and iron workers were those most likely to die from pneumonia. Metal-workers were also particularly liable to tuberculosis, though miners remained mysteriously free from the disease. See L. I. Dublin and R. J. Vane Jr, *Causes of Death by Occupation* (*Bulletin* of the United States Bureau of Labor Statistics, no. 507, Washington DC, GPO, 1930), pp. 46–51. Contemporary observers frequently

present statistics that purport to show that miners had higher rates of mortality than other workers. In 1848, Stéphanois doctors estimated that miners' average duration of life was 37 years while that of forgers was 48. A parliamentary committee reported that, in 1883, mutual aid societies throughout France provided sickness benefits to 24.9 percent of their members while the mining companies in the Loire provided sickness benefits to 35 percent of their workers. Frustratingly, because such reports do not take into account differences in the age structure of workers in the different industries, they cannot be considered reliable, although they cannot be entirely disregarded as representing the *opinions* of knowledgeable contemporaries. For estimates of differential mortality in 1848, "Commission médicale adjointe à l'enquête industrielle et agricole des deux cantons de Saint-Etienne," AN-F/14/3821–4195. On morbidity, Rapport Audiffred, Chambre des députés, JO, annexe séance du 21 mars, 1887, p. 559

Accurately capturing miner mortality and morbidity is difficult. As they became progressively incapacitated from diseases such as silicosis or as their lungs were weakened by bouts of pneumonia, miners were forced to quit their profession, and thus they appear in the death records as either unemployed or in some less physically demanding profession. Miners' susceptibility to death is probably better measured by looking at community mortality trends rather than occupational or industrial ones; although, here too, it is difficult to separate causes of mortality due to rapid growth from those due to occupation. Chapter 5 takes a look at patterns of community mortality in the Stéphanois.

73 "Commission médicale adjointe à l'enquête industrielle et agricole des deux cantons de Saint-Etienne," AN-F/14/3821–4195.

74 A study of occupational mortality made in 1930 showed that miners were more likely to die from influenza than were workers in any other occupation, and miners were also extraordinarily likely to die from pneumonia. See Dublin and Vane, *Causes of Death by Occupation*, pp. 46–51.

75 "Reglement de la société de secours mutuels de Saint-Joseph," Rive-de-Gier, 1855, pp. 9–10, ADL 27/M/1. The only other group required to pay special, higher rates were glassworkers who "have to fear being forced to quit work [at an early age]." On the effects of glassworking on Ripagérien workers, J.-F. Martinon and R. Riou, "Conditions de travail et de santé au XIXe siècle: les verriers de Rive-de-Gier," in *Cahiers d'histoire* 26 (31) (1981), pp. 27–39.

76 Dublin and Vane, *Causes of Death by Occupation*, pp. 32–5.

77 Gras, *Histoire économique générale des mines de la Loire*, vol. 2, p. 759.

78 Ibid. p. 752.

79 Ministère des travaux publics, *Statistique de l'industrie minérale* (Paris, Imprimerie nationale, 1865–72). On accidents in French mining, see Donald Reid, "The Role of Mine Safety in the Development of Working-Class Consciousness and Organization: The Case of the Aubin Coal Basin, 1867–1914," *French Historical Studies* 12 (1) (Spring, 1981), pp. 98–119.

80 See William Graebner, *Coal-Mining Safety in the Progressive Period: The Political Economy of Reform* (Lexington, Ken., University of Kentucky Press, 1976), pp. 61–2.

81 Gras, *Histoire économique générale des mines de la Loire*, vol. 2, p. 530.

82 On the Gard, Rapport A. Girard, Chambre des députés, p. 699.

On the policy of Stéphanois mining companies, a local journalist added "en effect quand la caisse est speciale à chaque exploitation, si l'ouvrier quitte la mine, s'il est congédie, il perd tout droit aux avantages que ses retenues *faites d'autorité* semblaient lui garantir, il ne peut répéter les qu'il à subier.

"C'est donc entre les mains du directeur un moyen d'aggraver la *peine du renvoi* en y ajoutant endirectement une amende pécuniare qui peut être considerable.

"C'est la un merveilleux instrument de domination réserve à la compagnie, qui tiendrait ainsi les ouvriers sous une despotique dépendance." From *L'Eclaireur*, February 5, 1870.

83 Audiganne, *Les populations ouvrières*, vol. 2, p. 97.
84 Dov Friedlander, "Demographic Patterns and Socioeconomic Characteristics of the Coal-mining Population in England and Wales in the Nineteenth Century," *Economic Development and Cultural Change* 22 (1) (Oct., 1973), pp. 39–51, esp. p. 51. For a similar argument, Eva Mueller, "The Economic Value of Children in Peasant Agriculture," in *Population and Development: The Search for Selective Intervention*, ed. Ronald G. Ridker, (Baltimore, Johns Hopkins University Press, 1976), pp. 98–153. For a recent review of the literature on this relationship and an articulate defense, see J. B. Nugent, "The Old-Age Security Motive for Fertility," *Population and Development Review* 11 (Mar., 1985), pp. 75–97.
85 Zola, *Germinal*, p. 107.
86 Gras, *Histoire économique générale des mines*, vol 2, p. 530.
87 François Ewald, *L'Etat providence* (Paris, Bernard Grasset, 1986), pp. 101–2.
88 See Forissier, *Séances de la 3ème session du Congrès ouvriers de France, Marseille 20–31, Octobre 1879* (Marseilles, J. Doucet, 1879), pp. 467–9.
89 The terms of worker participation in the mutual aid fund varied greatly from company to company. The Compagnie des mines de la Loire had six company representatives on the fund and nine workers' delegates who had 10 years of company service and were over 30. The Houillèries de Rive-de-Gier mentioned worker representation but did not specify how they were to be nominated. The Compagnie de Montrambert provided for the election of miners' representatives but the voters were confined to these workers over age 30 who had 10 years of company service. The mines of Roche-la-Molière et Firminy had no written rules; they claimed to follow the precedents built up over 30 years. Most other coal companies refused to divulge any information about the status of their welfare programs. Gras, *Histoire économique générale des mines*, vol. 2, pp. 532–7.
The extent of company contributions varied widely. The Compagnie des mines de la Loire declared that it alone would determine the extent of its contribution. The Houilleres de Rive-de-Gier levied 2 percent of the miners wages and supplemented the contribution by 1 percent. The Montrambert mines kept 2 percent of the worker's wages, a levy increased to 3 percent in 1861; the company's own contribution to the fund was discretionary. The company of Roche-la-Molière et Firminy levied 3 percent of the worker's wages and declared that its own contribution was "substantial." The central fund established between 1867 and 1869 was based on equal contributions of worker and company. Gras, *Histoire économique générale des mines*, vol. 2, pp. 532–6.
Workers were not wrong to fear company manipulation of the fund. The correspondence of the company director of the Compagnie des mines de la Loire, concerning the insurance fund (the *caisse particulière*) suggests as much: "Notre subvention à la caisse particulière à été comme precedemment de 12,000 fr, somme

suffisante puisque la caisse à continue à faire des économies. Sa réserve s'est accrue en 1876 de 19,893.59. Elle se montait au 31 décembre 144,219.29. L'importance de cette somme doit appeler l'attention car il pourrait devenir dangereux à un moment donné d'être obligé de s'en dessaisir. Il y à chercher une combinaison pour éviter cet écueil d'une organisation qui jusqu'à ce jour à donné de bons résultats." ADL 15/J/860 (1867–78).

90 Locally, a couple of coal mining companies went bankrupt in 1866. The collapse of the mining companies of Unieux et Fraisses and of Saint-Jean Bonnefonds entailed the loss of much of the pension fund. See *L'Eclaireur*, February 5, 1870.

91 Gras, *Histoire économique générale des mines*, vol. 2, p. 517. Police reports that deal with Prugnat and the mutual aid society, ADL 10/M/301, January 16, 1849, and ADL 1/J/440, February 20, 1853.

92 On membership in *La Fraternelle*, Gras, *Histoire économique générale des mines*, vol. 2, p. 532.

93 Bernard Delabre, "La grève de 1869 dans le département de la bassin minier Stéphanois," *Etudes Foréziennes* 4 (1971): 109–38.

94 The "Reglement de l'usine de Terrenoire en 1826." gives a comprehensive list of fines for metalworkers, see Gras, *Histoire économique de la métallurgie de la Loire*, pp. 482–512.

APPENDIX 4.1   SOCIAL CLASSES

Table 4.9   Social classes of the male and female economically active population and *propriétaires* in Le Chambon-Feugerolles, Rive-de-Gier and Saint-Chambon, 1856 and 1876 (by percentage)

	Le Chambon-Feugerolles 1856	Le Chambon-Feugerolles 1876	Rive-de-Gier 1856[b]	Rive-de-Gier 1876	Chambon 1856[c]	Chambon 1856
Upper middle class	2.3	3.4	3.9	8.1	2.8	3.1
Lower middle class	5.2	4.5	4.8	5.8	5.6	5.6
White-collar working class	2.6	4.9	5.7	6.1	6.2	7.0
Blue-collar working class	78.2	78.8	81.5	74.1	75.9	82.0
Lumpen-proletarian	0.0	0.0	0.4	1.9	0.6	0.3
Agricultural	9.2	5.9	1.5	2.5	2.3	0.9
Propriétaire	1.3	0.4	1.3	0.8	6.2	0.0
Unknown	1.2	2.1	0.9	0.7	0.4	1.1
Total[a]	100.0	100.0	100.0	100.0	100.0	100.0

[a] Rounded to total 100.0.
[b] Estimates for Rive-de-Gier 1856 are only from complete portion of the census. See Appendix The Manuscript Census Sample, pp. 213–14.
[c] Estimates for Saint-Chamond 1856 do not include the occupations of the wife and children of household heads. See Appendix The Manuscript Census Sample, p. 214.

5

The Working-Class Family Economy in the Industrial City

Even as it took root and grew, many contemporaries were skeptical about the viability of the industrial proletarian family as an enduring social institution. They questioned whether the proletarian family could sustain itself as its members underwent personal adversity or suffered the hardships of economic crisis. One of the most famous of nineteenth-century theorists of family life, and an acute student of working-class families, Frédéric Le Play, argued that the decline of church institutions and the distrust of government intervention in the economy put an increased burden on the family, a burden he feared the newly emerging nuclear proletarian family was unable to support.[1]

Le Play has been rightly accused of exaggerating the presence of multi-generational households and minimizing the diversity of inheritance patterns in the pre-industrial period, but the thrust of his argument has less to do with the presence of elders in the household or the prevalence of impartible inheritance than with parents' control over their children.[2] Deprived of those ties of property or skill that had attached earlier generations to their parents, working-class children would, he feared, "leave their parental firesides as soon as they gain any confidence in themselves."[3] Even in times of prosperity, Le Play believed, such conduct could not preserve either the individual's welfare or the moral order, faced as it would be with the "instability of engagements, social rivalry, wrongs leading to irritating disputations, diseases and premature deaths." But his crowning argument was that such selfish individualism had to turn to desperation and despair when faced with industrial downturns and the loss of employment that could produce only "destitution and misery".[4]

Over the past 20 years, the research of historians and sociologists has shown the centrality of the family to industrial proletarian life, but it has also revealed that Le Play's concerns were not ill-founded. Michael Anderson's classic work on family structure in mid-nineteenth-century Lancashire emphasized the benefits of family membership, but also stressed the importance of the economic environment to the working-class families' continued viability. Bad times and unemployment could lead younger families to leave the family and shift for themselves.[5]

Le Play was not wrong about the potentially disintegrating effects on family life of hard times, sickness, injury, and accident. Yet working-class families often were able to counterbalance uncertain economic conditions and murderous living conditions. Historical research has established the survival of the working-class family, but the question that remains to be answered is: how did it survive? Understanding how working-class families fought to overcome the difficulties of the urban and industrial environment and looking at the extent to which they were successful can provide insight into the necessary conditions for family survival. The working-class family did not simply adjust to its environment, rather workers were able to modify and change the urban and industrial environment and to fashion a world more conducive to the survival of the family.

For most workers in the Stéphanois, as for most other nineteenth-century workers, family life was an important resource for survival. Over the course of a lifetime, ties between husband and wife, between parent and child, could and very likely would be invoked to tide individuals over periods of temporary poverty or to sustain them in times of permanent incapacity. As we have seen, companies hoped to use their control of social welfare measures to gain control over their workers. Ultimately, however, it was the working-class families themselves who provided far more important social welfare services to their members than did employers. In this way, working-class families provided their members with a measure of independence from their employer.

If employers were willing to promote workers to better paying positions at the ages when they married and formed families, to keep aged workers on at the plant, or to enforce deductions for insurance programs, there were still some very big holes in company safety nets. An ailing miner in his forties would find it hard to support a family on the wages he earned in a surface job in mining. Retirement benefits and routine insurance fund awards to the permanently disabled were meager, less than a quarter of average take-home pay in the mines. Even the companies conceded that families of retired workers could not make do on retirement benefits alone.[6] As we have already seen, in metalworking, for the aged unable to work, company charity was the major recourse. Discharge, unemployment, or the prolongation of reduced hours would quickly reduce to desperation those families that depended only on the household head's income.

The instability of prices in the period 1840–80 made living on the margin a risky proposition. The overall trend for Stéphanois metalworkers and miners was one of increased real wages, but within this trend, annual real wages fluctuated in an extraordinary fashion, and not only Stéphanois workers but all French workers were subject to such fluctuations. In the years before the 1870s, the intercontinental grain trade was relatively undeveloped and the price of grain still depended on European markets. In addition, before 1869, French tariffs kept the price of grain artificially high. The result was that bread prices fluctuated dramatically between 1840 and 1870, far more dramatically than did nominal wages. Figure 5.1 presents a real wage index based on Stéphanois coal

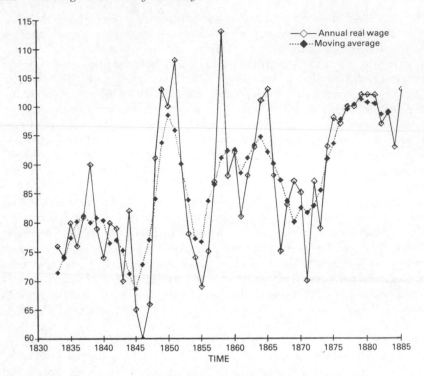

Figure 5.1   Annual real wages in Stéphanois mining compared to the five-year moving average, 1833–1883

miners' wages and reveals the clear influence of the fluctuations in bread prices.[7] While nominal wages were almost continually rising, they did not rise rapidly enough to counterbalance the dramatic low fluctuations in the price of commodities.

The large proportion of the real wage index determined by the cost of wheat bread undoubtedly exaggerates these fluctuations somewhat since it does not allow for the purchase of cheaper substitutes in times of high prices. But even if the fluctuations were not as dramatic as the graph suggests, variations in the price of wheat usually brought up the price of other grains and caused genuine hardship to working-class families. As we saw in chapter 1, in 1847, eyewitness accounts confirm that skyrocketing wheat prices did put many Stéphanois workers on the edge of starvation. From year to year, price instability made it nearly impossible for Stéphanois workers to have an accurate estimate of their real incomes.

If workers came up desperately short, they could appeal for religious charity or municipal aid. Religious charities were perhaps the most important source of support for the needy, but these rendered workers dependent on an institution with which they were coming into increased conflict. Moreover, even religious organizations had little institutional means for caring for the sick and the disabled. While religious groups maintained some large local orphanages, the only one of the three towns that possessed a charitable institution for the aged and permanently disabled was Saint-Chamond. In 1861, the hospice of that city, jointly administered by the clerical staff and the municipality, had space for a little under 60 persons. In that same year, the hospital in Rive-de-Gier, also staffed by nuns, took in charity patients, many of whom were probably old and distressed, but it too had space for only about 60 such patients.[8] Despite the paucity of local religious charities, in 1869 in Firminy, a commune adjacent to Le Chambon-Feugerolles, the charter of a "freethinkers" mutual aid society proclaimed that "the principal cause of the perpetuation of religious practices even when belief no longer exists among the religiously faithful is the organization of charity."[9] But despite the high public visibility of religious institutions, the overwhelming majority of sick and ill Stéphanois, poor or rich, were cared for at home.

In many workers' minds the distinction between municipal aid and that of the local Catholic charities must have seemed extremely vague. The priest usually present on the municipal welfare committee might also be the head of local religious charities. Nuns usually staffed hospitals, even municipally subsidized institutions. When religious morality conflicted with popular morality, tragedy could result. In 1870, an unwed pregnant woman was turned away from the public hospital at Saint-Chamond, by far the best of local hospitals, because the order of nuns staffing the hospital were not allowed to deliver illegitimate babies. The woman later died.[10]

Although the basic point is well known, it still bears underlining: the nineteenth-century state offered relatively little in the way of social welfare protection. On a routine basis, the local community welfare bureaus, the bureaux de bienfaisance, were the major official institutions for providing assistance for the needy. A bureau basically depended on municipal allotments and on donations; a local priest was usually a member *ex officio*.[11] Poor industrial working-class cities in the Stéphanois could ill-afford to provide generous aid. As late as 1885, the city of Le Chambon-Feugerolles contributed the incredibly meager sum of 200 francs in aid to its bureau over a whole year.[12]

Municipal administrations in Rive-de-Gier and Saint-Chamond contributed more than token grants. They provided 8,000 francs and 11,000 francs respectively in 1885, a year of deep depression in the Stéphanois, but these sums could only have supported 20 or 30 indigent families, and at least some of this money was scattered, going to supplement the income of families with inadequate incomes. Excluding funds that went to specified charitable purposes, this was the entire amount contributed directly by the municipality to the poor in an entire year. Except in the case of Le Chambon-Feugerolles, the special purpose funds that went directly to the poor were smaller than those given to the bureaus and, in this field too, the contribution from Le Chambon-Feugerolles, 800 francs, remained a token sum.[13]

Many needy local residents may have hesitated to apply for aid because there were frequent assertions that distribution decisions were based on political considerations. Patronage in the bureaus would not be particularly surprising since these organizations often sought generous donors to supplement municipal contributions. In Saint-Chamond, whose welfare institutions have been carefully analyzed by Elinor Accampo, it was claimed that rich, conservative Catholics controlled the bureau; indeed, it was alleged that this bureau had for generations been under the thumb of a single powerful family.[14]

Those unable or unwilling to obtain aid from miserly local welfare institutions or religious charities were forced to beg. Between 1840 and 1880, the boundaries between the world of the beggar and that of the industrial proletarian were still fluid. To get an accurate assessment of the background of beggars is difficult. Those beggars who were arrested in the *arrondissement* of Saint-Etienne were not necessarily representative; the police may have tolerated certain types of beggars and not others. However, in 1858, among those beggars who were arrested and who gave an occupation, about 3.6 percent listed mining and 4 percent a metalworking trade. However, 26.7 percent of all beggars listed their occupation as day laborer, and some of these may have been miners and metalworkers no longer physically able to work.[15] Beggars often claimed to be individuals deprived of familial support. It is hard to separate what beggars claimed in order to win public sympathy or judicial leniency from reality, but for one reason or another, three-quarters of all male beggars in 1858 were over 50 and claimed to be unaccompanied, and most female beggars claimed to be accompanied only by their children.[16]

Although the aid available from municipal and religious institutions was limited and could have been subject to criteria that were not based on need, most Stéphanois workers who had established themselves in the industrial city did not end up begging. Aside from life-cycle employment and employer welfare programs, the worker's major security against sickness, accident and a destitute old age was his family. The family was the major institution for sewing up the holes in the safety net left by employer policy. Whereas charity hospitals, orphanages, community welfare bureaus, and old folks homes could only provide aid to dozens or at best hundreds, thousands of people were provided for by their families in the three industrial towns. In one sense, the family was the only social institution in the region widespread enough to even comprehend the magnitude of the problem. For all three towns in both 1856 and 1876, more than three-quarters of all urban residents belonged to nuclear families where resident kin consisted only of parents who were household heads and children.[17]

While the working-class family routinely provided vital social resources for its members, like other resources they were not unlimited. The resources that working-class families could provide were influenced by demographic factors, household structure, and employment opportunities. All of these were subject to change and in fact did vary substantially over time and place. The Stéphanois working-class family was itself a historical product of the period in which it existed.

Viewing the family as a resource emphasizes aspects of family life often ignored by labor historians who have focused too exclusively on the work place. A summary of current labor historiography depicts the work place as a centrifugal force promoting class consciousness and the community as a centripetal force dissolving class ties.[18] A better understanding of the role of family in the working-class community challenges such a typology. Changes in family resources, generated outside the work place, could produce grievances and dissatisfactions that shaped work place demands. An understanding of family needs may yield important insights into the evolution of work place conflicts. If work places did not always produce conflict, community factors, such as threats to the working-class family economy, could sometimes radicalize workers.

The remainder of this chapter, first, examines the functioning of the working-class family and demonstrates how it tried to provide against the threat of the declining earnings of the household head and against the effects of old age, injury, and sickness. Secondly, the chapter looks at the urban environment of the industrial city and shows the importance of the particular type of urban environment to the operation of the family economy. Although their growth was extraordinarily rapid, the cities and villages in which the Stéphanois proletariat clustered all had their own histories. Alongside the course of modern economic development, housing patterns and employment opportunities inherited from the pre-industrial period exerted a significant influence on the welfare of proletarian families. While the working-class family economy exhibits many similarities in all three towns, differences in urban environment significantly affected the workings of the family economy in the individual towns. A look at the changes going on within the working-class family economy in the individual towns may provide new insights into the reasons behind the upsurge of worker militancy that occurred in the late 1860s (which will be discussed in the next chapter).

THE WORKING-CLASS FAMILY ECONOMY IN THE STÉPHANOIS

While the organization of work distinguished metalworkers from miners in the 1850s, households headed by metalworkers and miners shared family employment patterns common to the community in which they lived. For example, in 1856, in the small hamlet of La Malafolie that adjoined the built-up area of Le Chambon-Feugerolles on the west lived 50-year-old Louis Critaud, a miner, and his 50-year-old wife, Marguerite, a housewife. They had four children, one daughter and three sons. Their daughter, 18-year-old Antoinette, was a ribbonweaver, and their two oldest sons, sixteen-year-old Etienne and thirteen-year-old Antoine, worked in the mines like their father. Next door lived the machinist 45-year-old Pierre Raboulet and his 42-year-old wife, Claudine, a housewife. They had six children living with them, four daughters and two sons. The oldest daughter, 19-year-old Jeanne, was a dressmaker and her younger sister, 16-year-old Philomène, a ribbonweaver. The oldest son, 14-year-old Laurent, was a machinist like his father. Except for the fathers' trades which in turn dictated the employment of their sons, the patterns of family employment were the same in both households. Adolescents, both boys and girls worked in industry, married women generally did not.

Both in its structure and in its development, the working-class family economy in all three cities in the Stéphanois reveals some common features. First, in all three cities for which evidence exists, there was a broad similarity in the division of labor within the family and in the willingness of families to assume responsibility for older family members. Secondly, over time, the burdens assumed by the proletarian family economy increased. Finally, far from helping to relieve the pressures on the working-class family, the French state actually increased the strains on the operation of the family economy.

Let us begin by looking at the shared characteristics of the family economy. In all three cities, sex and age played fundamental roles in determining the family division of labor. The sexual division of labor within the working-class family economy reached its zenith among adults; while many married males participated in the pattern of life-cycle employment described in the previous chapter, most married women did not work in commodity production. Typically, as a report from Saint-Chamond in the 1870s noted, "women generally stop working in the factories at the time that they marry."[19] Table 5.1 shows the low rates of labor force participation by wives of the household head.

Although married women in the Stéphanois generally did not work in commodity production (except for the case of Saint-Chamond in 1856), they were pivotal to the operation of the family economy. In an economy where great importance was attached to nourishment, married women were in charge of preparing and distributing food. In metalworking, many male workers came home for dinner at noontime; in mining, women prepared the two meals per day that the miners took in the mines as well as the meal they took at home.[20] Not surprisingly, the preparation of food also involved enforcing a system of distribution that favored working males. In 1874, Louis Reybaud, a visitor to the area, noted that

It goes without saying that within the family distribution [of food] is done very unequally. Physical labor demands substantial nourishment; men must have meat and wine; women and children have only a reduced portion, dairy products, grain products, a little sausage on feast days.[21]

When several family members worked in metalworking and mining, the distribution of food could become a very complex chore. Shift-work prevailed generally in mining and in some portions of metalworking. Every two weeks, in

Table 5.1 Working women married to household head as a percentage of married women total in the Stéphanois region

	1856	N	1876	N
Le Chambon-Feugerolles	7.80	378	5.91	423
Rive-de-Gier	0.62	570	0.20	510
Saint-Chamond	–	–	8.21	499

order to distribute inconvenient night work among the whole workforce, the miner's shift alternated between day and night. Having two family members working in different shifts could create situations in which, morning, noon, and night, someone was leaving the household who required feeding and food to take with him.

Given the high mortality rate existing in the Stéphanois – a subject that will be discussed in greater detail – care of the sick was a crucial task, carried out mainly by married women.[22] Should a husband be injured in the mines, he would be carted to a company hospital, but, as soon as possible, his care would be transferred to the household. Caring for workers suffering from such serious illnesses as pneumonia and bronchitis, not considered work-related, was also left to the female relations. In addition, women were expected to nurse all the childhood illnesses. Given the profound state of medical ignorance prevailing between 1840 and 1880 and the wretched sanitary condition of the hospitals, patients with diseases such as pneumonia or typhoid were almost certainly far better off if they could obtain care at home than if they were forced to endure a hospital stay. The cholera epidemic of 1854 brought home with especial force the role of women in attending the sick. Cholera is a disease easily transmitted to those caring for patients; housewives were the largest single group to die in the epidemic.[23]

In addition to the services married women provided to family members, many married women contributed to family earnings by opening their homes to boarders. In aggregate, boarding was a major local industry, though most working-class homes took in only small numbers of boarders and the following figures on boarding are limited to households that had less than five boarders.[24] Leaving aside large boarding homes, a weighted average of all cities for 1856 and 1876 shows that 10.5 percent of all households headed by males took in boarders. Taking in boarders was of particular significance for widowed and single women; a weighted average of all towns reveals that 26.3 percent of all households that had under five boarders were headed by women. Households were able to take in boarders because they did not require a great deal of space. In 1869, it was noted that "Unmarried workers live as boarders [*en pension*]. They lodge and are fed by a host whom they pay on a monthly basis. The lodging consists of rooms filled with several beds, and often they sleep two to the bed."[25]

Married women were usually, although not invariably, identified in the census as "housekeepers." Particularly in the case where there were daughters engaged in domestic industry in the household, it is probable that married women engaged to some degree in domestic industry. In Saint-Chamond, a minority of married women did labor in the factory but both census records and contemporary witnesses agree that, given their many responsibilities, industrial work was not the primary task of many married women; they left the continuous industrial work to husbands and children.[26]

Age was an important factor in the family allocation of labor; child labor was widespread in the Stéphanois for both boys and girls. As was the case with married women's work, child labor was also missed by the census. Because it was only part-time work and usually neglected by the census takers, it is difficult to ascertain the typical age at which children began to work as coal sorters, cowherds, gardeners, or assistants in domestic industry. Much more can be said about children's entry into non-seasonal work, which is systematically recorded in the census. Young boys went to work sometime after their first communion, often the symbolic beginning of the entry to work. Half of all males were at work by the age of 13 or 14, and almost all working-class boys were at work by age 15 or 16, when apprenticeships began in metalworking and jobs opened up underground in the mines.[27]

Fewer young females worked than young males, but when female children did go to work, they usually began at an earlier age than males. Of all those women who would ever work, the age at which half of them had found work was a year or two younger than for males. In Le Chambon-Feugerolles in 1856, half the women who would ever work were doing so before they were 13; in the other cities, the age was 14 or 15.[28]

A logistic regression of the determinants of child labor in the Stéphanois towns for both 1856 and 1876 reveals a strong sexual division of labor within the family (see table 5.2). The model estimates the odds that a child would be working. Although separate analyses were carried out for each year, the results have been combined because the separate regressions for each year were similar.[29]

The logistic regression analysis shows the different childhood experiences of Stéphanois boys and girls. Girls were given chores connected with child-care and assisting their mother while boys were more liable to be sent out to work in industry. Daughters were less likely to be employed if there were younger brothers or sisters under the age of six in the household, or if there were boarders present in the household. None of these factors was a significant consideration in the industrial employment of males. The presence of an older brother in the household also discouraged female participation in industrial work; a working older brother probably encouraged a mother to keep her daughter at home to help her with the additional household work necessary to keep more than one family member working. In turn, the presence of younger siblings above the age of six in the household encouraged the employment of both males and females; the presence of younger children meant that there

Table 5.2   Determinants of child labor: logistic regression of male and female children over 10 years old in primary families with at least one parent present, 1856 and 1876

Variables[a]	Males	SE	Females	SE
		Parameter estimates		
Constant	−5.7657[d]	0.58	−4.2453[d]	0.54
AGE	0.1841[d]	0.02	0.0112	0.01
HEADAGE	0.0355[d]	0.01	0.0469[d]	0.01
OLDBRO	−0.0385	0.09	−0.2211[c]	0.11
OLDSIS	−0.1126	0.10	0.0195	0.10
YOUNGSIS	0.3846[d]	0.12	0.1088[d]	0.11
YOUNGBRO	0.4591[d]	0.12	0.3876[d]	0.11
MOTHPRES	−0.4489[c]	0.20	−0.4155[c]	0.21
BOARDER	0.2450	0.26	−0.8712[c]	0.40
FARMER	0.6768[c]	0.33	0.5526[b]	0.33
HARDWARE	1.2622[d]	0.38	0.8615[c]	0.36
GLASS	−0.5363	0.37	−0.4121	0.44
RIBBON	0.5814	0.51	1.2268[c]	0.57
MCSKILL	0.3881	0.33	0.0179	0.39
MCSSKILL	0.5242[c]	0.25	0.3803	0.25
MCUNSKILL	0.6226[b]	0.38	0.3318	0.41
MINER	0.5624	0.36	0.9474[d]	0.34
RIVE	1.4845[d]	0.23	−0.9118[d]	0.29
STCHAM	1.3712[d]	0.23	1.9604[d]	0.22
RIVEMINE	−0.6356	0.47	−0.0670	0.55
STCHMINE	−0.1752	0.93	6.7843	23.46
BOTHNAT	−0.1624	0.24	0.0279	0.26
ONENAT	0.1007	0.27	0.1184	0.29
YEAR	1.5563[d]	0.29	1.6070[d]	0.31
RIVEYR	−2.5510[d]	0.31	−0.8509[c]	0.38
KINPRES	0.0933	0.31	−0.3353	0.33
SIBUND6	0.0734	0.17	−0.3384[b]	0.20
Number of cases	1,505		1,345	
		Comparison with Baseline Model		
Reduction in chi square	618.25(26 df)		466.28(26df)	
Significance level	0.001		0.001	

SE is Standard Error.
[a] Variables:
AGE is age of child
HEADAGE is age of household head
OLDBRO is number of older brothers
OLDSIS is number of older sisters
YOUNGSIS is number of younger sisters over 10 years old
YOUNGBRO is number of younger brothers over 10 years old
MOTHPRES is presence of mother in household
BOARDER is presence of boarder in household
FARMER is household head is farmer
HARDWARE is household head is in hardware manufacture
GLASS is household head is glassmaker
RIBBON is household head is ribbonmaker
MCSKILL is household head is skilled machine-construction worker
MCSSKILL is household head is semi-skilled machine-construction worker
MCUNSKILL is household head is unskilled machine-construction worker

Table 5.2   continued

MINER is household head is coalminer
RIVE is inhabitant of Rive-de-Gier
STCHAM is inhabitant of Saint-Chamond
RIVEMINE is coalminer living in Rive-de-Gier
STCHMINE is coalminer living in Saint-Chamond
BOTHNAT is both spouses are natives of department of the Loire: 1876 only
ONENAT is one spouse is native of department of the Loire: 1876 only
YEAR is 1856
RIVEYR is inhabitant of Rive-de-Gier in 1856
KINPRES is the presence of a *non-working* kin of the household head or his spouse
SIBUND6 is the presence of a sibling aged between 0–6
[b] $p < 0.1$.
[c] $p < 0.05$.
[d] $p < 0.01$.

were more mouths to feed. Girls were also likely to be employed if their father was a ribbonweaver or a hardware worker; these trades were often practiced as domestic industries, and daughters worked in household workshops. In 1856, miners' daughters were particularly likely to be employed, but in 1876 this was no longer the case. Miners' daughters were disproportionately employed in ribbonweaving, an industry that declined over the period.

As long as they remained in the same city as their parents, most sons and daughters lived with their parents until marriage.[30] Marriage, however, marked the departure of children from their household of origin and the beginning of a new household. Although the median marriage age of both men and women tended to decline over the period 1856 and 1876, for the total population of all towns, the median age was high compared with that of workers in many countries of Europe and low compared with that of the French population as a whole. The average of the three median ages of grooms in the three towns in 1856 and 1876 was 26.9, the average of the median ages for brides was 23.2.[31] Typically, working males and females could be expected to contribute for well over a decade to the earnings of their family of origin. An 1872 survey from Saint-Chamond noted that children gave all their earnings to their parents until sometime between ages 16 and 18.[32] Although the survey did not elaborate, sooner or later, young men and women began to think about marriage or their dowry, and limited their contribution to a share of household expenses and rent. Of course, sharing rent and expenses could mean very significant savings for a working-class household. Moreover, in the event of an emergency, such as the sudden death or incapacitating illness of the household head, wage-earning children would surely be expected to contribute more to their family's needs.

Between 1856 and 1876, a growing number of working-class families incorporated working kin into the household, but they also assumed new and sometimes heavy responsibilities in regard to close relatives. In 1856, many workers had been part of the first generation of workers engaged in semi-skilled work in industry; by 1876, a second generation was growing up, with ties both to the city where their parents lived and to the country where other relatives lived. A look at the witnesses present at marriages in the three towns shows that kin witnesses were proportionately more numerous in 1876 than in 1856 in both Le Chambon-Feugerolles and Rive-de-Gier.[33] Many younger kin, specifically males under 40, came to the city in search of work, and they undoubtedly contributed some portion of their wages to the welfare of the family with which they resided.[34] In each of the Stéphanois towns, a proportionately greater number of kin was present within working-class households in 1876 than in 1856. In Rive-de-Gier and in Le Chambon-Feugerolles, the increase in kin presence was substantial. In 1856 in Le Chambon-Feugerolles, the proportion of kin to the number of nuclear families was 0.0848, in 1876 it was 0.1185; in 1856 in Rive-de-Gier, the proportion of kin was 0.0518, in 1876, it was 0.1348; and in Saint-Chamond the proportion was high in 1856, 0.1388, and stayed high in 1876, 0.1391. Women were the majority of resident kin in every period, indeed usually the overwhelming majority.[35]

Between 1856 and 1876, the proportion of kin over age 60 in the household increased rapidly in Le Chambon-Feugerolles and in Saint-Chamond; the increase in the number of kin aged over 60 in the sample resident with household heads was particularly dramatic in Saint-Chamond where the number increased from 14 to 37.[36] The growing proportion of aged kin and female kin present in Stéphanois households was particularly significant, because both groups had low rates of labor force participation. Although the proportion of male kin over 60 did increase in each of the Stéphanois towns between 1856 and 1876, the proportionate increase in female kin over 60 was the more dramatic, while the numbers increased from 35 in 1856 to 83 in 1876. In 1876, the labor force participation rate of these female kin was under 20 percent in all towns.

Many of these aged kin were the parents of the head of the household or his spouse. When it came to taking in an aged parent, it does not seem to have made any difference whether the parent was related to the head or his spouse: about 50 percent of parents were related to each spouse in all three of the towns. When it came to most other kin however, relationship to the head of the household did seem to matter, because more kin were related to the head than to his spouse.[37]

The rise in the proportion of kin in the household may be partly related to the decline in the proportion of solitary heads of household and households containing unrelated members. Between 1856 and 1876 the proportion of households consisting of solitaries and unrelateds in all three towns declined, and this was true for the proportion of solitaries and unrelated over 60 years old as well as below.[38] In the later period, 1876, it seems likely that many aged and single people were able to find relatives to live with while in the earlier period those in a similar predicament were forced to live alone. One reason for this increased kin presence was that, as a result of increased permanent proletarianization, there were more kin living in the industrial city in the later period than in the earlier.

For men over 60, withdrawal from the labor force meant giving up the position of household head, and, if they stayed in the industrial city, living with kin. Evidence for this shift is provided by the example of parents of the household head. Of the male population over 60, almost all male household heads worked; among male solitaries, somewhere between 87.5 percent and 96 percent of all males worked; but among male parents residing with the household head, almost none worked. In contrast to men, women were able to retain their headship even if they did not work. Women solitaries and unrelateds generally had higher rates of labor force participation than those of females living with kin, but the labor force participation rates of female household heads were generally only slightly higher than those of females living with kin.[39] Unlike men, women listed themselves as household heads though they did not participate in the labor force. These older women may have still provided valuable services for working children, and thus were able to preserve their status as household heads, while males who did not work may have been incapacitated and either unable or unwilling to assert claims to household headship.

Over the course of the period, the French state imposed new burdens on the working-class family economy. Conscription into the army prevented many young working-class men from fully contributing to their family's welfare and, as the extension of conscription that resulted from the reforms of 1866 and 1867 took effect, between 1868 and 1869 particularly, and then during the Franco-Prussian War, the loss of so many young men must have adversely affected family income overall. While French levies were low compared with those of Prussia and with those that would prevail in France at the end of the century, the size of the levies was increasing over the period, and the French army's preference for professional soldiers meant that the time served by most French conscripts was much longer than that served by most Prussian conscripts.

Throughout the period, the burden of conscription was undoubtedly magnified by the uncertainty of the lottery principle used to select young men for the service and by the length of military service. Before 1872, paid replacements or a very large sum of cash were accepted in lieu of the actual draftee. Workers sometimes formed insurance clubs to purchase replacements should their children lose the lottery. In January 1869, Stéphanois newspapers were filled with ads such as the following: "CLASS OF 1868 – A NOTICE TO FATHERS OF FAMILIES – M. Marcellin Abreal, landowner, for the present year will continue his operation of insuring against the lottery."[40] But replacements were expensive, and many workers could not afford insurance for all their sons.

The issue of insurance against the draft placed stress on working-class family life. The experience of some young proletarian men in the Stéphanois may have been similar to that of a share-cropper in the nearby Allier, Père Tiennon, as he recounted it to Emile Guillaumin. In the mid-1840s, although his two older brothers had been insured against the draft, Tiennon was told by his father that due to the costs of their recent move, the expenses occasioned by his grandmother's funeral and the burdens of a growing family, he would not be insured. The young man was fortunate in getting a lottery number that kept him out of the service, but shortly after he told his father that he was leaving his father's household and going to work on his own. As he explained to his father, who asked him to stay, "you were willing to let me leave as a soldier."[41] But the young Tiennon also explained to Guillaumin that he thought the family had become too large to live together in a single household.

Conscription into the regular army was an unmitigated catastrophe for working-class families. In 1867, an English artisan who toured Saint-Etienne and several other French industrial cities recorded witnessing the lottery:

Mothers and sweethearts stand round the doors of the bureau, wringing their hands and weeping, as now and again some young fellow steps out with a blank look on his face, which shows that he has drawn a low number; while a little further off, anxious-looking groups of men, who are no less interested in the fate of the lads within, stand smoking and chatting together, gloomily. The behaviour of the unfortunate youths themselves, who have got bad numbers, is just what may be expected of men of their age and nation. They bear their evil fortune bravely; some indeed look forward with real pleasure to a life of adventure; while others, who see in the piece of paper they hold in their hand, the death-warrant of all their hopes and expectations, hide their grief beneath a forced and manly smile, and accept their fate without a murmur.[42]

During the years between 1840 and 1880, although the duration of service in the regular army decreased, the effect of this was easily counterbalanced by the overall tendency for military service to become more generalized. After 1872, although mechanisms existed so that middle-class young men could avoid the full rigors of conscription, for most workers a lottery determined whether the worker would spend five years or six months in the service. Before 1866, recruitment into the army meant a seven-year stint and it deprived the family of a young male between the ages of 18 and 25. These were among the years when the child's contribution to the family economy would have been most valuable. After 1866, the term of service was reduced to five years, still a large portion of the time that young men might be contributing income to the household.[43]

In contrast to the conscription laws, which decreased the contribution of children to the family economy, the child labor laws in place during the period did little to influence Stéphanois child labor patterns. Although child labor laws were passed in 1841 and 1874, they had very limited impact for two reasons. First and most significantly, the child labor laws did not apply to some of the most important employers of child labor in the region; as a special concession to industries such as glassmaking, which employed a "continuous fire" on a twenty-four hour basis, the laws against night work by children between 13 and 16 were suspended in these industries. Glassmaking was a major local industrial employer of children. Neither law regulated domestic industry, the major employer of children, and both laws set age limits well below those in current practice in such important industries as mining and metalworking.

Where child labor laws and schooling laws did come into conflict with employment, as in the developing textile industry of Saint-Chamond and in glassmaking after 1874, they generally had minimal effect because the enforcement mechanisms were inadequate. In 1877, a commission reported that "in order to arrive at a proper application of this law, which concerns 50,000 families in the department, it will be necessary to create a departmental inspector."[44] In 1878, the divisional inspector reported that "the law is nearly unknown among the diverse categories that it concerns."[45] In 1881, the divisional inspector reported that "the Mayors charged with issuing the *livrets* for children employed in industry, for the most part ignore article 10 of the law."[46] (Article 10 required the mayors to maintain records open for inspection.)

Despite the weak enforcement of the child labor laws in the Loire, violation of the child labor laws was probably not very great among working-class families in Rive-de-Gier. Glassmaking did not employ a large proportion of the town's population, and many workers wanted their male children in school in order to increase their chances of getting jobs in the metalworks. When Ripagérien glassmaking expanded in the 1860s, there were rumors that many of the abused children were Italians brought from Italy especially for the purpose of working in the glassworks.[47]

Only in Saint-Chamond was there an industry that routinely employed child labor under circumstances that were regulated by the law. Time and again, Saint-Chamonnais braidmakers were accused of employing underage females and of forcing women to work longer than the legally prescribed limits. In 1878 the police chief in Saint-Chamond noted that in the largest braidmaking plant in the town, children under 16 were routinely working for twelve hours in both the day shift and the night shift. Both the duration of the work and night work were in violation of the law. When the police chief informed the owner of the works, the powerful local politician, Benoît Oriol, the owner stiffly responded that in his works the law was observed, and there the matter rested.[48] Many of these underage females were girls from the countryside sent by their parents to live in the textile dormitories, but if there is any city in which our census estimates may be low due to a desire to escape legal restrictions, it would surely be Saint-Chamond in 1876.

The very limited restrictions on child labor and the weak enforcement meant that the major area in which the French state intervened in the family economy was conscription, where the size of its levies, if not substantial by later standards, was none the less growing rapidly. Moreover, within the French army, time served by conscripts was long, and the criteria for exemption were arbitrary. The heavier exactions of the French state further increased the weight of the burden already accumulating on the working-class family. A second generation of industrial workers found itself with new and heavy responsibilities for aged and unemployed kin. The extension of conscription laws and the frequency of imperial wars deprived families of young males who might have contributed a share of their wages to the family welfare. But these changes were not the only changes occurring in the Stéphanois towns. The course of economic development differed greatly from town to town both in 1856 and 1876, depending on the economic background of the individual town and on the direction of its industrial expansion. The effect on the family economy in the three towns varied accordingly.

VARIATIONS IN PARTICIPATION IN THE FAMILY ECONOMY

By far the most important factor affecting the participation of children in the working-class family economy was mortality. A large minority of children were never able to contribute to the family economy because they died before reaching working age. Child mortality thus represented a ransom paid by the working-class family to the urban environment. In addition to the personal tragedy for a working-class family, the death of children could have long-term consequences for family welfare. Death could diminish the number of children participating in the family economy during the household head's declining years and the number of hands that could be called upon for aid in the event of a family catastrophe such as the death or injury of the household head.

In the case of infant deaths, the consequences for the number of children surviving to adulthood may not have been so severe. Families controlling their fertility might easily decide to have another child to replace the deceased infant. Among families not controlling their fertility, an infant death might still have little effect on the number of children reaching adulthood. Lactation inhibits conception through prolonging postpartum amenorrhea and would cease with the death of an infant.[49]

The death of children had greater bearing on the number of young adults who would finally participate in the family economy. In an economy of scarcity for the working-class, where contraception was beginning to spread, the death of a child meant that no portion of the substantial expense of raising the child would ever be recouped. Moreover, the family's financial ability to raise another child to replace the dead child might be compromised by the income spent on the dead youth. In addition, the death of children could easily occur after the female's reproductive period was past; even if a couple could afford to raise another child, it might be too late. Finally, overall decreases in child mortality meant that families were less likely to have had additional children in an effort to replace lost children and could devote additional income to other family needs.[50]

What makes these considerations especially significant is that the force of mortality varied considerably among three towns only a dozen kilometers distant. First, let us look at the overall patterns of mortality in the Stéphanois industrial cities. Expectation of life at birth has been calculated for the periods 1855–7 and 1875–7 for Rive-de-Gier and Saint-Chamond, for 1854–8 and 1874–8 for Le Chambon-Feugerolles, and for 1856 and 1876 for the *arrondissement* of Saint-Etienne and is shown in tables 5.3 and 5.4.[51] National life tables for comparable periods for all of France are also included. Each town also

Table 5.3   Male life expectation at birth (still births in parentheses)

	1855–7	1875–7
Le Chambon-Feugerolles[a]	36.44 (31.50)	37.26 (35.83)
Rive-de-Gier	29.18 (28.00)	33.49 (31.49)
Saint-Chamond	27.28 (23.51)	34.60 (31.03)
Arrondissement of Saint-Etienne[b]	33.19	40.16
France	38.33 (in 1851)	41.33 (in 1874–8)

[a]   For Le Chambon-Feugerolles life tables were calculated on the basis of averages of five years' mortality, so these life tables cover the periods 1854–8 and 1874–8.
[b]   For the *Arrondissement* of Saint-Etienne tables were calculated for 1856 and 1876.

Table 5.4   Female life expectation at birth (still births in parentheses)

	1855–7	1875–7
Le Chambon-Feugerolles[a]	39.65 (36.00)	41.70 (40.13)
Rive-de-Gier	31.45 (29.01)	39.57 (37.62)
Saint-Chamond	30.84 (28.58)	42.02 (37.63)
Arrondissement of Saint-Etienne[b]	35.56	40.82
France	39.67 (in 1851)	43.72 (in 1874–8)

[a]   For Le Chambon-Feugerolles life tables were calculated on the basis of averages of five years' mortality, so these life tables cover the periods 1854–8 and 1874–8.
[b]   For the *Arrondissement* of Saint-Etienne tables were calculated for 1856 and 1876.

reported a category labeled "still births" and it is possible that some infant deaths were reported as still births either because parents were ignorant of legal and medical terminology or because parents' reports were misunderstood by the authorities. In any case, the parentheses in tables 5.3 and 5.4 show life expectations at birth recalculated to include the "still births" as if they were infant deaths.

The tables show that everywhere in the Stéphanois, expectation of life at birth was lower than that in France as a whole. But in both 1856 and 1876, children in Le Chambon-Feugerolles had a substantially higher life expectation than children in the other two towns and a higher expectation than children in the *arrondissement* of Saint-Etienne. The difference between child mortality in Le Chambon-Feugerolles and the other towns is attenuated somewhat if still births are counted as infant deaths, but it still remains considerable. Also, life expectation improved substantially over time, increasing fastest in the industrial towns, slower in the *arrondissement* of Saint-Etienne, and slowest in France as a whole.

The major improvements in life expectancy over the period and the chief differences between the three towns in 1856 were in the life expectancy of children aged between one and 14. In 1856, Le Chambon-Feugerolles had far lower child mortality than the other two towns, but by 1876 child mortality was about the same in all three towns. Given the levels of mortality prevailing in individual towns in 1856, of those male children surviving to age one, 68.3 percent could expect to reach age 25 in Le Chambon-Feugerolles, 58.6 percent in Rive-de-Gier, and 52.6 percent in Saint-Chamond. In 1876, the figures were 74.7 percent in Le Chambon-Feugerolles, 73.4 percent in Rive-de-Gier, 77.6 percent in Saint-Chamond. Between 1856 and 1876, there was a dramatic improvement in the survival possibilities of those aged one to four, and usually for those between five and nine. In Saint-Chamond, there was a steep decrease in mortality among men and women aged 15 to 25 but, in 1856, mortality in this age group was mysteriously high. Between 1856 and 1876, infant mortality varied little among the three towns, and it did not consistently decrease; also, there was only a small improvement in life expectation above age 35.[52]

In the years between 1855 and 1857, the most dramatic improvements occurred in life expectation in Saint-Chamond and Rive-de-Gier, though they started from very low levels; in the early period, towns such as Rive-de-Gier and Saint-Chamond were truly perilous places. Even for cities of the Industrial Revolution, these towns had low life expectancies. Male life expectations of 27.28 years put Saint-Chamond at the level of the poorest English industrial cities, such as ill-famed inner-city Liverpool in 1861, where male infants had a life expectation of 26 years.[53] The dangers of coal mining were discussed in the preceding chapter, but it was far more dangerous to be child in Rive-de-Gier or in Saint-Chamond in 1856, than a local miner.

The foregoing tables of life expectations at birth focus on the mortality conditions of the industrial community. The risks of dying in infancy or young childhood were further intensified if children were put out to nurse in the countryside. The heightened mortality due to rural wetnursing escapes the tables of life expectations based on *urban* conditions of mortality prevalent in the industrial community. Fortunately, wetnursing seems to have been little employed by workers in Rive-de-Gier and Le Chambon-Feugerolles where the lack of employment opportunities in factories or in family workshops obviated the conditions that promoted wetnursing. In Saint-Chamond, married women's work in family workshops and outside the home was more prevalent and the presence of wetnursing among a minority of married women is suggested in both 1856 and 1876 (see appendix 5.2).

While many aspects of mortality in the industrial cities still need investigation, some general causes of the prevalence of high mortality among children in the 1850s and 1860s are reasonably clear. Geography and the pre-existing urban structure encouraged a population density that promoted ill health. Rive-de-Gier and Saint-Chamond are located along a narrow river valley interrupted by a few valley passes. Space was lacking in these towns, and the existing stock of housing consisted of old tenements previously inhabited by the glassworkers and ribbonweavers, who had for a century concentrated in the center of the two cities. In 1856, there were 70.8 persons per hectare in Saint-Chamond, and 20.28 in Rive-de-Gier; in 1876, there were 97.4 persons in Saint-Chamond, and 20.67 in Rive-de-Gier. By themselves, these densities were not particularly alarming. In 1861, the population per hectare of Paris was 217 and that of the rapidly growing working-class *quartier* of Belleville, 152. But in the Stéphanois this growing population was packed into ageing housing that it more than filled. Industrial workers generally got the housing that more skilled workers did not want. In 1848, a medical report had noted that "married miners generally reside in one room, [that is] very dirty, and as they seek above all cheap rents, they occupy the poorly lighted floors or the humid ground-level floors [*rez-de-chaussée*]." The miners themselves complained about the draftiness of their dwellings.[54] The canal system flowing through the center of Rive-de-Gier was another important vehicle for the dissemination of disease.

Although systematic compilations of the causes of death are unavailable for this period, a look at the seasonality of death can provide some clues about the causes of mortality. An analysis of seasonal mortality of the urban population of the *arrondissement* of Saint-Etienne in 1856 and 1876 shows that, as local doctors observed, August and September were unusually deadly months, matched only by another peak in January, February, and March. In 1856, 19.8 percent of all urban mortality occurred in August and September and 27.5 percent in January, February, and March; in 1876, mortality for the same periods was 19.1 percent and 29.6 percent. To judge from the case of Saint-Etienne in 1887, winter peak mortality was dominated by pneumonia and acute and chronic bronchitis. The summer peak of mortality in Saint-Etienne was associated with diarrhea and gastro-enteritic disorders. In 1887, in Rive-de-Gier and Saint-Chamond, the leading killers were influenza, acute and chronic bronchitis, and tuberculosis – these were the chief causes of death in most of Western Europe in the late nineteenth century.[55]

Between 1840 and 1880, the summer diseases and the connection between water supply, sewers, and public health dominated local public discussion of health issues. In 1870, a petition signed by 1,500 residents of Firminy, near Le Chambon-Feugerolles, underlined the urgency of increasing the water supply:

In the present condition of our fountains, we suffer each summer not only from the lack of water, but also from its purity; the public health is often compromised by the unhealthy water distributed so sparingly by our fountains ... The quantity of worms [*vermicules*] and filth there is such that it is not prudent to use it without first filtering it ... With a dam ... our wives will no longer be forced to walk four or five kilometers down the road in order to do the wash ...[56]

Perhaps the citizens of Firminy were too sanguine about what a dam could accomplish. A report from Saint-Chamond in June 1870 noted that "the general public has believed until today that it sufficed to have a large quantity of water in reserve in order that it would be good ... for the last eight days, we have had water which resembles mud."[57] In 1870, Doctor Hervier launched a campaign for water sanitation in Rive-de-Gier with the slogan, "cleaning the Augean stables."[58]

But polluted drinking water was not the only culprit. In 1870 a female correspondent to a local newspaper noted:

I see in the arms of their mothers, lovable infants. At two years of age, they possess flourishing health, then . . . one sees them die . . . I believe that the most important cause is the bad condition of the streets . . . children in these *quartiers* have from morning to night, their feet in water. They play in the midst of all the impurities, liquid or solid, wastes, household water, etc. . . .[59]

In general, the life tables shown in tables 5.3 and 5.4 are not based on years of epidemic mortality.[60] Still, in addition to the normally high mortality of the Stéphanois industrial towns, there were years when mortality shot upward due to epidemic diseases. In Rive-de-Gier and Saint-Chamond, in the years before 1860 the population seems to have been especially prone to dramatic increases in disease. A number of high mortality years can be located between 1833 and 1881 when annual crude mortality shot up more than 10 percent above a trend line consisting of a five-year moving average. In the two industrial cities, 11 of the 12 high mortality years fell before 1860.

The inadequacies of the sewer and water systems that contributed to summer peak diseases also facilitated the spread of those water-borne epidemic diseases so common in the nineteenth century: cholera and typhoid. Epidemic diseases can be especially revealing because they often set contemporaries ruminating about the causes of disease. After the disasterous cholera epidemic of 1854, a doctor noted that the epidemic had begun in the small hamlet of Bachafson:

Entirely inhabited by unfortunate day laborers whose low salaries condemn to all kinds of deprivations . . . situated on the great road that ties Saint-Chamond to Rive-de-Gier, it is a dangerous foyer, where the least spark may kindle a terrible fire. The agglomeration has a large number of individuals whose lodgings are narrow, badly aired where husband, wife, children and domestic animals live as friends: . . . the confined air, the bad quality of food and water, the presence of stored manure and puddles of fetid water surrounded by dirty housing, the misery, the accumulation finally of all the deleterious agents which weigh on the inferior classes of society, all must attract the storm of cholera.[61]

Beginning in August 1854, the epidemic killed at least 258 people in the canton of Rive-de-Gier, 98 in Rive-de-Gier alone, before it disappeared in November.[62] Patrice Bourdelais and Jean-Yves Raulot have argued that two important agents for the transmission of the epidemic were seasonal migrants returning from large cities and soldiers returning from the Crimean War.[63]

In 1870 in Rive-de-Gier, there was a large audience interested in the discussion of sanitary measures. A year before, a terrible typhoid epidemic had hit the town. In October 1869, Doctor Hervier had reported to the local community:

The epidemic of gastric fever, bilious typoid, that has grown more severe at Rive-de-Gier since the last days of the month of August, is due to the contagious miasmas developed along the Givors canal . . . the pestilential influence of the drying up of the lateral basin of the canal [Bief] must be the predisposing and determining cause of this intoxication. . . . Actually four hundred people, among them infants and adults, have been stricken during the course of the epidemic. What is particularly bizarre, is that the plague has chosen its victims mainly among the better-off class and in a street, two kilometers long, parallel to a canal . . . the canal is presently dry and filled with filth . . . never has one seen eighty-six people dead in one month, ten in the same day. The same month of the cholera epidemic [1854] had only witnessed seventy-five.[64]

While the doctor accepted the prevalent miasmatic theory that disease was caused by the noxious vapors exuded by filth, he was most likely right to link the pollution of the canal to the typhoid epidemic.[65] In any case, his practical conclusion that there was a need to do something about the canal and the water supply was undoubtedly correct.

Rive-de-Gier and Saint-Chamond were densely inhabited urban areas at mid-century, but Le Chambon-Feugerolles still remained in good part a rural area. At least some of the reasons for the overall lower mortality in Le Chambon-Feugerolles probably have to do with the dispersal of housing throughout the commune. Scattered habitation meant less pressure on water and drainage systems and less close contact for the spread of disease. It also meant that the income of the inhabitants of Le Chambon-Feugerolles could be increased by agricultural labor and their diet improved by garden vegetables.

As in Rive-de-Gier and Saint-Chamond, the pattern of settlement in Le Chambon-Feugerolles was partly the result of geography and partly the result of antecedent economic developments. Like the other two industrial cities, Le Chambon-Feugerolles is strung along a little stream, the Ondaine; but unlike the other two cities, a sloping plain exists along the southern edge of Le Chambon-Feugerolles that left plenty of room for outward expansion. The combination of domestic industry and agriculture which had previously characterized the economy of the town, had encouraged the dispersal of settlements across the plain and along the Ondaine. The town's residents were spread over a score of hamlets as well as in the built-up area. In 1856, the number of persons per hectare was only 2.48, ten times less than in Rive-de-Gier in the same year, and 30 times less dense than in Saint-Chamond; in 1876, the number of persons per hectare in Le Chambon-Feugerolles was still only 4.78.[66] This dispersed character, nearer to that of the surrounding agricultural villages than the other two industrial cities, helps explain why life expectancy in industrial Le Chambon-Feugerolles (36.4 years for men in 1855–7, and 39.7 years for women) was more similar to that of the nearby peasant village of Marlhes, (40 years for both men and women in 1851).[67]

But as the coalmines expanded in Le Chambon-Feugerolles in the 1860s and 1870s, there is some evidence of a housing shortage that might have caused a sanitary decline. Between 1856 and 1876, the number of houses in the town was practically stationary, but the number of inhabitants per house increased from 7.69 to 14.48. This was the highest ratio of inhabitants per house of any of the three cities.[68] Such conditions may have increased the liability of Le Chambon-Feugerolles to epidemic in the later period. A look at periods when annual mortality shot up more than 10 percent above the trend between 1833 and 1881 shows that this occurred eight times, five of them after 1860.

However the reasons for the overall decline of high mortality conditions are harder to understand than the reasons for its earlier prevalence. To pinpoint one major cause for the decline of mortality is difficult. The most obvious source of change, sanitation improvements, seems to have been a factor, but not the only one. Had sanitation improvements been the only cause of better health, their effect should have been clearly visible in the distribution of seasonal mortality. Improvements in the water supply or the sewer system should have had a special effect on the August–September mortality peak by diminishing the water-borne diseases so characteristic of that season. The seasonal pattern of *urban* mortality in the *arrondissement* of Saint-Etienne between 1856 and 1876 does suggest some decline in the August–September mortality peak, from 19.8 percent of all deaths occurring in these two months, there was a drop to 19.1 percent, but the summer peak remained important.[69]

Improvements in water systems may well account for a considerable portion of the improvement in life expectation in Saint-Chamond. Between 1866 and 1872, a major dam was constructed to provide water for drinking and for industrial purposes.[70] Although, as noted above, the dam did not guarantee the purity of the water, it may have substantially improved the situation.

In the case of Rive-de-Gier, improvements in the water system seem a much less plausible explanation for the dramatic increase in life expectancy that occurred in that town. Between 1850 and 1880, the citizens of Rive-de-Gier talked a lot about providing a healthier water supply. But no major changes were made in the existing system, which dated back to 1845. In that year, an engineering company had been hired to dig and maintain three wells in the city. The wells were completed in 1847, but one of the wells drew on the water table of the Gier, which served as a major channel for sewage. Since the well water appeared clear, unlike the "black" contaminated water of the stream, it was assumed to be drinkable. Another of the wells ran dry in the summer, and it was alleged that the company maintained the well by secretly supplementing it with water from the dam intended to maintain the canal. Because plans to draw on distant streams were judged too expensive, no major reforms were carried out until the 1880s.[71]

The decline in mortality between 1856 and 1876 may have been because of a host of reasons associated with an increase in the local standard of living. Between 1840 and 1850, average *per capita* municipal spending in Rive-de-Gier increased by two and a half times and continued to grow rapidly. Some of this money may have been used for relatively minor urban improvements that had a cumulative effect on popular health. During this period, although most public money went to building churches and a new bridge, there was work on the river quays and the road system; the latter two improvements could have affected local sanitation.[72]

Other changes were going on whose contribution to local health should not be neglected. A look back at the transformation of the Stéphanois countryside as described in chapter 3 should remind us of the important dietary changes which were occurring. The decline of rye consumption meant that the local population no longer relied on a particularly dangerous grain product. Rye was subject to contamination that produced a mold poison nearly undetectable in the nineteenth century. Ergotic diseases from rye consumption could have been an important cause of epidemic death, particularly for children, who consumed more food per unit of body weight than adults.[73] Far more important, the shift of Stéphanois agricultural production toward dairying meant fresher and more abundant milk for young children. As Dorothy Hollingworth has noted, "no country without an adequate milk supply has wholly solved the problem of assuring the consumption of adequate amounts of good quality protein by young children after they are weaned from the breast."[74] At the very least, the routinization and cheapening of milk supplies provided an alternative drink for children during the summer months when contaminated water was such a serious local problem. Increased real wages also made it possible for workers and their families to buy warmer clothes and to protect themselves better against the elements.

A factor in the decline of epidemic mortality may have been the fact of permanent proletarianization itself. Epidemics were particularly severe in rapidly growing cities such as those of the Stéphanois because rural dwellers were now thrust together in densely packed communities where they were exposed for the first time to contagious diseases transmitted by migrants from a wide variety of different regions. The initial mortality caused by exposure to the "crowd diseases" – small pox, measles, and certain respiratory diseases – was often quite high but the survivors of such diseases acquired an immunity that protected them from subsequent outbreaks. As the urban populations stabilized and the numbers of permanent urban dwellers increased, infection often became endemic, keeping urban mortality high, but because of the presence of many immune individuals, the opportunity for epidemics diseases to break out suddenly, killing large numbers of urban dwellers, declined.[75]

In sum, despite improvements toward the end of the period, it is clear that in the Stéphanois region between 1840 and 1880, many of the classic conditions for epidemics and general ill health flourished. In order to get some grasp of the consequences of this regime of mortality for working-class families in the Stéphanois, estimates have been prepared of the total fertility rate, the net reproduction rate and the gross reproduction rate for the wives of household heads in the three Stéphanois cities in 1856 and in 1876 (see table 5.5).

These rates show how changing mortality affected the fertility trends discussed in the previous chapter. In that chapter, it was seen that the control of marital fertility was spreading, particularly in Rive-de-Gier and in Saint-Chamond. But without discussing mortality, it cannot be known whether the

Table 5.5   Total fertility rate and gross and net reproduction rates of women married to head of household in all three Stéphanois towns, 1856 and 1876

	Total fertility rate	Gross reproduction rate	Net reproduction rate	N
Le Chambon-Feugerolles, 1856	5.317	2.570	1.431	296
Le Chambon-Feugerolles, 1876	5.355	2.586	1.605	350
Rive-de-Gier, 1856	4.511	2.215	1.031	440
Rive-de-Gier, 1876	4.116	2.018	1.195	369
Saint-Chamond, 1856	4.340	2.170	1.012	401
Saint-Chamond, 1876	3.768	1.933	1.246	394

number of children reaching adulthood actually declined or rose. The total fertility rate for the wives of household heads is a summation of the age specific birth rates at a given point in time. It tells how many births a women married to a household head would be expected to have over the course of her child-bearing years given the schedules of fertility prevailing at a given point in time if there was no mortality among either children or married women. The net reproduction rate for the wives of household heads is a summation of age-specific birth rates for *female* babies, adjusted for maternal mortality. It is a measure of the extent to which a cohort of newly born girls will replace themselves given the fertility *and mortality* schedules prevailing at a certain point in time. Net reproduction rates less than 1.0 mean the married population is not reproducing itself. These estimates have been prepared using reverse survival rates for the population aged five to nine in the census and using vital statistics survival rates for the births recorded in the birth registers for the preceding five-year period.[76] (See appendix 5.2 on fertility rate estimation.)

Very rough confirmation for these trends in fertility decline is found in the work of Elinor Accampo, whose own estimates of marital fertility in Saint-Chamond are based on family reconstitution of that city's population. Despite our differences of opinion as to the extent of married women's labor-force participation and the prevalence of wetnursing in Saint-Chamond, Accampo finds a total fertility rate for married women in reconstituted families of 4.93 in 1861–6, while my own estimate from the census sample for 1856 is 4.34.[77]

The major conclusion to be drawn from these rates is that, despite the fall in fertility in Rive-de-Gier and in Saint-Chamond, there were more children reaching adulthood in 1876 than in 1856. These rates show that, in 1856 in Rive-de-Gier and in Saint-Chamond, married women were only barely repro-ducing themselves, though the situation was somewhat better than this in Le Chambon-Feugerolles. In 1876, although fertility had declined in Rive-de-Gier and Saint-Chamond, the net reproduction rate for women married to household heads had increased because mortality declined even faster. In Le Chambon-Feugerolles, where fertility increased, the net reproduction rate for women married to household heads also increased. Interestingly, despite their declining fertility, the percentage increase in the net reproduction rate from 1856 to 1876 was higher in Saint-Chamond and in Rive-de-Gier than in Le Chambon-Feugerolles. With more children surviving to adulthood, working-class families in Saint-Chamond and in Rive-de-Gier may have felt freer to have fewer children.

The survival of children benefited working-class families most directly when children remained in the household contributing wages for a long period of time. The sad conditions of local boarding houses and the low wages of female workers must have greatly discouraged young men and women from setting up their separate residence; marriage was their major opportunity for independence. Between 1856 and 1876 in Le Chambon-Feugerolles and Rive-de-Gier, a growing number of children were deciding to marry and leave their parents' household at an earlier age. Coal miners were the group most responsible for the declining age of marriage. Expanding opportunities encouraged miners to marry and form families. More completely than most other industrial occupations, mining is a boom or bust industry. As the English geographer, Arthur Smailes, reminds us, "Mining is a form of destructive exploitation of the earth's resources, a fact which is reflected by the population cycle of colliery settlements."[78] Typically, nineteenth-century coal mining dramatically enlarged the population of communities as coal production increased. Communities declined just as rapidly when the coal veins were exhausted and when mining then moved to adjacent communities to follow the coal deposits.

During the Second Empire, Rive-de-Gier, the pre-eminent Stéphanois coalmining community of the first half of the nineteenth century, gradually lost this position to the communities in the western coal basin. In 1856, 17.2 percent of all employed males in Rive-de-Gier were miners; in 1876, the figure was 9.1 percent. Straining heavily to reach its peak production in 1857, Ripagérien mining deteriorated rapidly. In that year, citing its precarious financial position, the Société des houillères de Rive-de-Gier cancelled its half-day holiday for the celebration of the feast of Sainte-Barbe, the miners' saint, which was commemorated in the area by vacations and an annual dinner. The feast was not to be resumed for at least the next 12 years.[79] In contrast, mining in Le Chambon-Feugerolles continually expanded. In 1856, 9.2 percent of all employed males were miners, in 1876, 22.3 percent. The coal resources of the western wing were still considerable, and the major mines were all concentrated there.

Between 1870 and 1875, the natural cycle of mining growth and decline was offset by a coal shortage that affected all of Western Europe. A spurt of railroad-building in the United States put pressure on the British metallurgical industry that increased the domestic demand for coal.[80] France found itself forced to rely on its own resources, and the price of coal skyrocketed. Particularly between 1871 and 1873, French producers found that they could sell coal at almost double the usual price. This situation enabled companies to mine coal that was too costly to mine at normal prices. Changes in the mean age of marriage in Rive-de-Gier and Le Chambon-Feugerolles reflect this boom climate. In 1856, the mean age of marriage of Ripagérien miners was 31.3 (N=34); in 1876, the mean age of marriage fell to 28.5 (N=18). In Le Chambon-Feugerolles, the increased demand for coal also encouraged miners to marry early. In 1876, the mean age of marriage of Chambonnaire miners was 26.0 (N=21), below that of the town's population and equal to that of metalworkers. In Le Chambon-Feugerolles, increased coal production had resulted in more promotions to coal hewer and in higher wages.

There is no evidence about how miners' parents viewed their children's tendency towards earlier marriage. In so far as male parents were active underground miners themselves, they would have shared in local prosperity. But the loss of so many male wage earners whose earnings were at their peak must have strained many households. Of course, as mentioned earlier, the formation of a family did not always mean the end of the previous family economy. While young married couples seldom lived in a household headed by a parent, parents sometimes lived in households headed by their children. But in so far as men and women attempted to remain household heads, sons' marriages meant the departure of a valued contributor to the family economy.

VARIATIONS IN CONTRIBUTIONS TO THE FAMILY ECONOMY

Between 1840 and 1880 the growing financial burden on the working-class family led Stéphanois families to put a high priority on income. Except in the case of married women and in the case when there were special needs for child labor in the household, such as boarders or young children, families generally valued wage earnings over the performance of domestic tasks within the household. Many families tried to achieve a balance between home and wage labor, but frequently this was not possible. In particular, there was not always available wage work for daughters. Much recent literature has focused on the underenumeration of female labor in the census as an important distortion of women's economic role; while, as has been seen, census underenumeration was real, a too exclusive focus on underenumeration can obscure the important current of industrial evolution that produced a systematic structural unemployment for women after the mid-nineteenth century.[81] In the early period, the presence of domestic industry in cities like Le Chambon-Feugerolles and Saint-Chamond enabled daughters to supplement family income with earnings. But between 1856 and 1876, leading domestic industries such as silkweaving *à la basse lisse* collapsed. Without a rise in industries that employed young females, the disappearance of traditional industries could seriously affect the situation of proletarian families whose heads were employed in metalworking or mining. In towns such as Rive-de-Gier, where traditional industries had not employed women, the family economy of industrial workers might be particularly precarious, especially at mid-century when wages were lowest. Between 1840 and

Table 5.6   Refined activity rate: men

	Standardized by actual age structure	Standardized by Stéphanois standard age structure
Le Chambon-Feugerolles, 1856	0.8675	0.7957
Le Chambon-Feugerolles, 1876	0.7676	0.7756
Rive-de-Gier, 1856[a]	0.7744	0.7715
Rive-de-Gier, 1876	0.8734	0.8553
Saint-Chamond, 1856	–	–
Saint-Chamond, 1876	0.8434	0.8396

[a] Refined activity rates for Rive-de-Gier in 1856 are based on estimates.

Table 5.7   Refined activity rate: women

	Standardized by actual age structure	Standardized by Stéphanois standard age structure
Le Chambon-Feugerolles, 1856	0.3454	0.3355
Le Chambon-Feugerolles, 1876	0.1856	0.1878
Rive-de-Gier, 1856[a]	0.1484	0.1519
Rive-de-Gier, 1876	0.1592	0.1583
Saint-Chamond, 1856	–	–
Saint-Chamond, 1876	0.4432	0.4230

[a] Refined activity rates for Rive-de-Gier in 1856 are based on estimates.

1880, new employment opportunities appeared for daughters in Saint-Chamond, but employment opportunities for daughters declined dramatically in Le Chambon-Feugerolles.

At mid-century, the most important determinant of employment opportunities for the daughters of families headed by industrial workers was the pre-industrial background of the community in which they lived. Comparing rates of female participation in wage earning with rates of male participation gives an idea of the extent of differences in female participation among the three towns and over time. Tables 5.6 and 5.7 show unstandardized and age-standardized refined activity rates for males and females in Le Chambon-Feugerolles and Rive-de-Gier in 1856 and for all three towns in 1876.[82] Refined activity rates are the number of employed males and females over 10 years of age divided by the number of males and females over 10 in the population.

As a rule, married women did not commonly engage in wage labor in the Stéphanois. However there may be a significant exception with married women in Saint-Chamond in 1856. The decline of artisanal ribbonweaving in Saint-Chamond led many males to abandon the trade, and married women seem to have taken over these family workshops. Ribbonweaving in Saint-Chamond was a highly skilled trade, and it was probably remunerative enough to induce married women to engage in industry. Unfortunately, the census of 1856 provides no information on family employment for members of the household other than the head, and the extent of married female participation in this industry is unknown. The domestic workshop in ribbonweaving declined after mid-century, and by the 1870s, it had completely vanished from Saint-Chamond.[83]

While the extent of married women's work in Saint-Chamond in 1856 cannot be documented, elsewhere the biggest difference in family employment opportunities concerned male and female children. In Le Chambon-Feugerolles, 31.78 percent of all household heads had a working child living in the household in 1856, while in 1876 this figure dropped to 19.70 percent. In Rive-de-Gier there were 14.76 percent of households with employed children in 1856, while the figure had risen to 22.27 percent in 1876. In 1876 in Saint-Chamond, 26.88 percent of all household heads had a working child. To a large extent, differences in the refined activity rates reflect differences in employment of young children, and not simply that unmarried, unemployed older children were staying longer in households.

A look at employment opportunities in the three cities helps to explain the varying participation of daughters. A community such as Le Chambon-Feugerolles participated fully in the economy of domestic ribbonweaving, which dominated the rural economy for many miles east and south of the Stéphanois. In 1856 in Le Chambon-Feugerolles, many daughters worked in ribbonweaving. These daughters were relatively less-skilled workers using looms *à la basse lisse* to weave unpatterned ribbons of blended silks. In 1856, 24.1 percent of Chambonnaire females between the ages of 10 and 14 were employed and 67.1 percent of all females between the ages of 15 and 19; 60.6 percent of ribbonweavers were daughters of household heads, 7.9 percent were wives of the head, and 11.8 percent were female kin. Unlike domestic work in hardware manufacture in Le Chambon-Feugerolles, which remained confined to natives, ribbonweaving at mid-century was an occupation that included many migrants as well.

The ease of entry into ribbonweaving *à la basse lisse* meant that the number of ribbonweavers was large and their wages low. The 1848 *enquête* for the canton of Le Chambon-Feugerolles estimated that the average female ribbonweaver earned 60 centimes a day, and this for a workday that lasted between twelve and fourteen hours during the busy season.[84] In 1859, Louis Reybaud observed of these ribbonweavers: "Wages in this category are the most modest. They reach 1.50 for the best paid workers, and in order to earn this kind of pay, no other domestic work can be pursued. In the winter season it is by prolonging the *veilles* that the work is finished and then they must deduct the cost of light and heating."[85]

After 1857, the decline of rural ribbonweaving must have caused a falling off of family income as most ribbonweaving was consolidated into the Stéphanois capital of Saint-Etienne.[86] With ribbonweaving vanished the opportunities of many females in Le Chambon-Feugerolles to earn wages. By 1876 the percentage of young females employed was down by almost half; only 9.5 percent of females between 10 and 14 were employed, and 36.1 percent of those between 15 and 19. In Le Chambon-Feugerolles, seasonal domestic employment was declining in both ribbonweaving and metalworking with a loss of job opportunities for both men and women. What created a specific crisis for women's employment was that in Le Chambon-Feugerolles, as throughout the whole region, new jobs were being created for less-skilled males, but new job opportunities for less-skilled women were not being created on a comparable scale.

While employment opportunities for daughters declined in Le Chambon-Feugerolles, they were flourishing in Saint-Chamond. By 1876, factory textile production had displaced the domestic workshops in Saint-Chamond. In 1876, 37.93 percent of female braidworkers in Saint-Chamond were daughters of the household head, 5.41 percent were wives of the head, and 4.19 percent were his kin; 41.68 percent of the female workforce resided in dormitories, and an additional 3.2 percent boarded in private homes. In 1856, many widows and older women had been employed in textiles; by 1876 these older workers had been replaced by young women who either lived in dormitories or who were the children of urban workers. In 1876, 37.3 percent of all females between the ages of 10 and 14 were employed and 74 percent of those between 15 and 19.

Factory braidmaking was tedious work which might usefully supplement a family income, but which allowed little leeway for an independent existence. Except for a handful of skilled machinists who were employed in each factory to repair the machines, the textile workforce was completely feminine. Factory workers spent 12 hours in the factory, and they earned for their sum a meager 1.30 francs. In 1862, an observer noted that "the work does not require very much strength [*force*] but it is very fatiguing over the long haul [*à la longue*], for the workers must stand continuously and the workshops are poorly ventilated."[87]

In contrast with Le Chambon-Feugerolles and Saint-Chamond, there were almost no wage-earning jobs for women throughout the period in Rive-de-Gier. In the half-century before 1848, Rive-de-Gier had been a mining and glassmaking center. Women were never employed underground in Stéphanois mining, and glassmaking was a highly skilled industry that was carried out by men and young male children in factories. Women were excluded from the skilled aspects of glassmaking by both employers and artisans. In addition, the high wages and shift work that dominated in glassworking probably did not encourage women to participate in ribbonweaving which never developed there. In Rive-de-Gier, glassmaking had expanded rapidly by 1876, and the glassworks employed larger numbers of male children than in 1856. As the mines expanded, creating the new category of semi-skilled workers, many Ripagérien daughters doubtless sought employment as did their counterparts in Le Chambon-Feugerolles and Saint-Chamond. But the lack of established industries open to women however made work for women unusually difficult to find.

Thus, between 1856 and 1876, there were dramatic differences among the three towns in female labor participation. In Le Chambon-Feugerolles, there had been plentiful jobs for daughters in 1856, but these had declined dramatically by 1876. In Saint-Chamond, there were abundant jobs for women in 1876, and probably in 1856 as well. In Rive-de-Gier, there were few jobs for women either in 1856 or in 1876. Even when the incomes of metalworkers and miners in the three towns were identical, differences in female labor force participation substantially affected the prosperity of the working-class family in the three towns.

Over the period between 1856 and 1876, there was little tendency for the variations within the family economy to cancel one another out; indeed, they seem to have had a cumulative effect. In 1856, the interaction of the economic and demographic factors that molded the family economy had served to benefit working families in Le Chambon-Feugerolles compared with those in Rive-de-Gier and Saint-Chamond. By 1876, the same forces seem to have conspired to weaken and destabilize the family economy in Le Chambon-Feugerolles while strengthening that in the other towns.

The accumulation of changes hit hardest miners' families in Le Chambon-Feugerolles. A particularly stark example of the impact of economic and demographic change can be seen in 1876 in the small hamlet of Cotatay, an old industrialized community on the eastern edge of Le Chambon-Feugerolles. In a two or three story soot-encrusted building, lived the 45-year-old widow Elisabeth Truvet and her six children, four boys and two girls, aged from 19 to three. The three oldest sons worked in the mines, doubtless performing the relatively low-paying jobs assigned teenagers in the mines. Neither of the girls had an occupation. If the widow's husband had died in a mining accident, the family would have received a small sum from the company, but death, high fertility, and the lack of female employment opportunities all must have made family survival a terribly difficult proposition.

Some of the effects of changing family employment patterns and demographic trends are revealed by the worker/consumer ratios within nuclear families and households for each of the three cities in 1856 and in 1876. The "worker/consumer ratio" is the number of workers in the nuclear family or the household divided by the weighted number of consumers in the nuclear family or the household. The ratio measures the balance of wage earners to consumers within families and within households. In this study, the worker/consumer ratio is used as a measure of wage dependency. A single family of two or more people in which everyone worked would have a ratio of 1. A single family with a working head, a non-working spouse, and a non-working fifteen year-old child would have a ratio of .3333. If the child was below 15, say 14, the ratio for the above family would be .3636 because children below 15 are assumed to consume less than an adult and are assigned different weights to account for their lesser consumption. The following ratios only include workers who were

Table 5.8   Worker/consumer ratios, Le Chambon-Feugerolles

	1856		1876	
	Ratio	N	Ratio	N
	Members of nuclear family			
Daylaborers	0.3722	18	0.4421	38
Machine construction	0.4472	127	0.3312	125
Hardware	0.4696	46	0.4568	37
Mining	0.4043	46	0.3352	91
Total population	0.4541	440	0.3680	525
	All members of household			
Daylaborers	0.3500	18	0.4158	38
Machine construction	0.4331	127	0.3408	125
Hardware	0.4457	46	0.4027	37
Mining	0.3891	46	0.2956	91
Total population	0.4143	440	0.3206	525

Table 5.9   Worker/consumer ratios, Rive-de-Gier

	1856		1876	
	Ratio[a]	N	Ratio	N
	Members of nuclear family			
Daylaborers	0.4583	48	0.4298	78
Machine construction	0.3603	73	0.3694	85
Glassworkers	0.3000	29	0.3711	45
Mining	0.3621	95	0.3775	40
Total population	0.3587	527	0.3913	623
	All members of household			
Daylaborers	0.4208	48	0.3962	78
Machine construction	0.3425	73	0.3318	85
Glassworkers	0.2862	29	0.3200	45
Mining	0.3347	95	0.3350	40
Total population	0.3218	527	0.3391	623

[a] Incomplete portion of Rive-de-Gier 1856 census removed.

heads of nuclear families, workers living alone or with unrelated fellows were excluded.[88] In tables 5.8, 5.9 and 5.10 these ratios are given for nuclear families and for households in each town, and they are broken down by the industrial classification of the household head.

Stress is placed on the interpretation of the worker/consumer ratio as a measure of wage dependency rather than as a straightforward measure of family welfare.[89] Although there are a number of problems with the measure, the principal difficulty of using it as a measure of family welfare is that it does not take into account unpaid domestic labor. One of the important reasons for

Table 5.10 Worker/consumer ratios, Saint-Chamond, 1876

	Ratio	N
	Members of nuclear family	
Daylaborers	0.5164	55
Machine construction	0.4827	104
Textiles	0.7148	27
Total population	0.4623	686
	All members of household	
Daylaborers	0.4964	55
Machine construction	0.4558	104
Textiles	0.6778	27
Total population	0.4020	686

variation in the ratio is the changes in employment patterns among daughters of the household head. Non-working teenage daughters are counted only as consumers, but in most cases they performed important but unpaid housekeeping services. The logistic regression on child labor (table 5.2) suggested that the presence of boarders or young children encouraged parents to keep older daughters at home rather than sending them to the factory. Still, the regularity with which daughters worked when work was available indicates that, in most circumstances, Stéphanois working-class families preferred their female children to work for wages and believed that wage earning best served family welfare. In the context of a Stéphanois economy where wage-earning opportunities declined or became increasingly precarious and where families sought unavailingly to put daughters to work, the ratio probably does get at some real differences in family welfare, but only with an element of exaggeration.

Over time, the most dramatic changes in the worker/consumer ratios occurred in Le Chambon-Feugerolles. This ratio graphically illustrates the effects of some factors that have been discussed separately. It shows the effects of the declining rates of labor force participation in Le Chambon-Feugerolles and the effects of the increased effective fertility of city families. Considering only nuclear families, the declines are most dramatic among machine-construction workers, −25.9 percent, and miners, −17.1 percent. Given the already low worker/consumer ratio in mining, these indices show the increasing dependency of coalminers' families on the labor of the household head, a consequence of the movement of young family men into this sector of the economy. The ratio in mining also shows the declining employment of females and the increase in miners' effective fertility. The declining ratios for machine-construction workers and miners that obtained for the nuclear family reappear when all household members are considered. However, the rate of decline for miners' households, −24 percent, then becomes greater than for machine-construction workers' households, −21.3 percent. Mining families may have taken in disproportionate numbers of non-working kin during this period.

In contrast, the case of Saint-Chamond in 1876 exhibits a family economy whose members contributed more earnings than that of Le Chambon-Feugerolles in 1876. The worker/consumer ratios for both nuclear families and household are much higher in Saint-Chamond for almost all categories of workers. The biggest single factor in explaining the high Saint-Chamonnais ratios was probably the high rate of female labor participation in Saint-Chamond, though the lower number of children at non-working ages must also have been a factor. Job opportunities for females in Saint-Chamonnais textiles had an important spillover effect on almost every category of industrial-worker family. Working-class families' preference for wage work over housekeeping for daughters is suggested in these findings. Worker/consumer ratios for household are much higher than the ratios for the other towns, but still lower than the ratios for nuclear families. This indicates that working-class families increased their proportion of non-working kin just as in other towns.

The example of Saint-Chamond should drive home the importance of family work patterns. In 1876 the family income of most working-class families in Saint-Chamond was probably higher than that of most working-class families in Rive-de-Gier and Le Chambon-Feugerolles in the same year. This was true even when the household head in Saint-Chamond was employed in the same industry at the same wage rate as his counterparts in the other two cities.

The combined effect of demographic and labor force factors is further illustrated by the effect of changing labor force participation and family size on family welfare through the life-cycle of the family head (see figure 5.2). The effect of changes in labor participation and demographic patterns is further shown by contrasting the percentage of the nuclear family in the labor force by the age of the household head in Le Chambon-Feugerolles in 1856 and in 1876. The dramatic decline in the period between 30 and 45 is most likely a result of the presence of young non-working children in the household. As the age of the household head increases, the presence of working children in the household grows and the percent of working members increases. The result of declining labor force participation among women and children in 1876 affected Chambonnaire household heads at every age, but it had its greatest effect on older household heads, those between 40 and 65. As figure 5.2 shows, the combination of demographic and labor force factors produced much greater hardship for families headed by middle-aged persons in 1876 in Le Chambon-Feugerolles than in 1856.

But Stéphanois workers were by no means simply passive victims of changing configurations of family earnings. While there was little they could do to restore earnings lost due to the decline of domestic industry, they could attempt to stabilize their family situation by making new demands on employers and on the state. It was not coincidental that the miners of Le Chambon-Feugerolles played a leading role in the wave of industrial militancy that swept the Stéphanois in the late 1860s. Their own dispersed and thus relatively healthy urban environment meant that they had not shared as fully in the improvements of life expectation as the other towns, but the expansion of coalmining in the

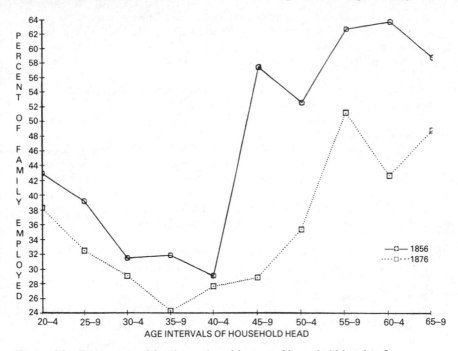

Figure 5.2 Percentage of family employed by age of household head in Le Chambon-Feugerolles in 1856 and 1876

western basin had taken many young men out of existing households and encouraged them to form their own families. Although demands for the stabilization of wages figured prominently in their strike demands, their militancy must also be seen as influenced by the declining income of other family members in the western region and the early departure of children from the family. In the late 1860s, as conditions changed both in mining and in the family economy in the western coal fields, miners took collective action to remedy their situation.

NOTES

1 On Le Play, see Carle C. Zimmerman and Merle E. Frampton, *Family and Society: A Study of the Sociology of Reconstruction* (New York, Van Norstrand Company, 1935).
2 See Frédéric Le Play, *The Organization of Labor in Accordance with Custom and the Law of the Decalogue* (Philadelphia, Claxton, Remsen and Haffelfinger, 1872).
3 Ibid., p. 41.
4 Ibid., pp. 58–167.
5 Michael Anderson, *Family Structure in Nineteenth-Century Lancashire* (Cambridge, Cambridge University Press, 1971).

6　As the administrator of the société des mines de Saint-Etienne testified: "la pension de retraite qu'ils obtiennent à l'age de 55 ans n'est que de 300 fr.; mais elle peut s'élever plus haut, s'ils ne quittent pas la mine." Documents parlementaires, Rapport Audiffred, Chambres des députés, JO, annexe PV, séance du juin 1886, no. 777, p. 1853.

7　In Service éducatif, *La Mine et les Mineurs* (Saint-Etienne, CDDP, 1981). For a different view of changes in standard of living, see Elinor Accampo, *Industrialization, The Working-Class Family and Class Relations: Saint-Chamond, 1815–1914* (Berkeley, University of California Press, forthcoming)

8　For 1861, Statistique de la France, *Statistique de l'Assistance publique, Hopitaux et Hospices, Enfants assistés, Bureau de Bienfaisance* (Strasbourg, Imprimerie administrative de Veuve Berger-Levrault, 1866), 2nd series, vol. 15. A report for 1853 shows pretty much the same situation in that year; see Direction de l'assistance et de l'hygiène publique, *Statistique de l'Assistance Publique de 1842 à 1855* (Strasbourg, Imprimerie administrative de Veuve Berger-Levrault, 1858).

9　*L'Eclaireur*, October 24, 1869.

10　*L'Eclaireur*, June 12, 1870. In 1861, the *Statistique de l'Assistance Publique* noted concerning the hospice at Saint-Chamond and the hospital at Rive-de-Gier: "Cet etablissement n'accept pas les filles-mère, les femmes en couches, les syphlitiques, les teigneux, et les galeux."

11　See John H. Weiss, "Origins of the French Welfare State: Poor Relief in the Third Republic, 1871–1914," *French Historical Studies*, 13(1) (Spring, 1983), pp. 47–78.

12　Direction de l'assistance et de l'hygiène publique, *Statistiques des dépenses publiques d'assistance faites en France pendant l'année 1885* (Paris, Imprimerie nouvelle, 1889). On the functioning of a large bureau de bienfaisance during the Second Empire, see Pierre Pierrard, *La vie ouvrière à Lille sous le Second Empire* (Paris, Bloud and Gay, 1965), pp. 232–48. By the end of the Second Empire, despite generous endowments, the municipal administration of Lille contribution was almost 300,000 francs to the bureau. This was roughly 1.9 francs per inhabitant in 1872. In contrast, the municipal administrations at Rive-de-Gier and Saint-Chamond were contributing 0.56 francs and 0.76 francs per inhabitant in 1887, and the 1880s were exceptionally difficult years in the Stéphanois.

13　Ibid.

14　See *L'Eclaireur*, February 7, 1870, and Accampo, *Industrialization, The Working-Class Family, and Class Relations*, chap. 5.

15　Claude Chatelard, *Crime et Criminalité dans l'arrondisement de Saint-Etienne au XIXe siècle* (Saint-Etienne, Centre d'etudes Foréziennes, 1981) p. 115.

16　Ibid., p. 114; this ratio held in 1859 and 1872. The portion of the Stéphanois working class that engaged in seasonal work contained a large portion of the beggar population; seasonal migration and begging were practically synonymous. Arrests for begging followed a seasonal pattern; they rose in March and April and then again in August and September; many beggars were seasonal workers, relying on handouts as they passed on their way to and from their sending villages. But local people too made use of the rituals of the seasons of passage to leave their own home commune and go begging in nearby communes. In 1872, the Mayor of Saint-Martin-la-Plaine complained that his village was frequented by twenty beggars "mostly" from Rive-de-Gier; see Chatelard, *Crime et criminalité*, p. 119.

17 The percentage of the total population of each town that belonged to the nuclear family of the head is in 1856, Le Chambon Feugerolles, 85.3 percent, Rive-de-Gier, 82.6 percent, Saint-Chamond, 75.9 percent and in 1876 Le Chambon-Feugerolles, 84.2 percent, Rive-de-Gier, 75.9 percent, Saint-Chamond, 76.1 percent.

18 John Laslett, "Challenging American Exceptionalism: 'Overlapping Diasporas' as a Model for Studying American Working Class Formation," *Newberry Library Papers in Family and Community History*, paper 87–1, pp. 16–17.

19 Chambre consultative de Saint-Chamond, enquête de 1871–1875, AN-C/3022.

20 On meals, "Enquête de 1848 – mineurs de Rive-de-Gier," AN-C/956, and *L'Eclaireur*, September 25, 1869.

21 Louis Reybaud, *Le Fer et la houille* (Paris, Michel Levy, 1874), p. 150.

22 On importance of female care for the sick within the household, talk by Ruth Schwartz Cowan at Vassar College, February, 1987.

23 See Patrice Bourdelais and Jean-Yves Raulot, "La marche du choléra en France: 1832–1854," in *Annales: ESC*, 33(1) (Jan.–Feb., 1978), pp. 125–42, esp. p. 137.

24 The overwhelming majority of non-related, non-servant, residents of households identified themselves as "boarders" (*pensionnaires*), people who habitually take their meals with the household. Only a very few identified themselves as "lodgers" or "roomers" (*locataires*), that is, people who do not habitually take their meals with the household. In this chapter, references to boarders include references to lodgers. However, discussion of boarders does not include references to unrelated, non-servants, who do not indicate themselves as either boarders or lodgers. This situation only occurs among a small population of generally aged women in Saint-Chamond in 1856. It is probable that these were female textile workers who set up households in which they shared the expenses.

25 *L'Eclaireur* September 25, 1869.

26 Unfortunately, few reliable estimates of female employment are available outside the census. A frequently cited report of 1885 which breaks down the number of women workers by rough age categories is for the "region de Saint-Chamond." This region would probably include the adjoining textile town of Izieux and St-Martin-en Coailleux and St-Julien en Jarez as well as many rural mills in the near countryside. See L.-J. Gras, *Histoire de la rubanerie*, p. 735.

27 The idea of computing deciles based on the prevalency of work was derived from John Model, Frank F. Furstenberg, Jr, and Theodore Hershberg, "Social Change and Transitions to Adulthood in Historical Perspective," *Journal of Family History* 1 (Autumn, 1976), pp. 7–32.

28 In the case of women, if only the proportion of the population that would ever enter the work force by age 55 is considered, the median age of entry into the workforce was typically even younger than for males. In Le Chambon-Feugerolles in 1856 the median age was 12.9: in 1876, it was 14.3. In Rive-de-Gier in 1856 the median age of entry was 15.7. In Saint-Chamond in 1876, the median age was 16.5.

29 The case of Saint-Chamond in 1856 has been omitted from the analysis because the census did not contain information on the employment of household members other than the head, and an incomplete portion of the census of Rive-de-Gier was also omitted.

30 The evidence that young workers stayed with their families in the city is most complete and most persuasive in the case of the single town which had the most

important population of migrants during the year when the boarding population was exceptionally large, the case of Rive-de-Gier in 1876. A look at birth records indicates that boarders tended to be men who came from some distance from Rive-de-Gier, while most residents of Rive-de-Gier were natives or short-distance migrants. It seems almost certain that boarders could not have been the sons of native parents who moved out of the family home, and it seems probable that they were not the children of the many men and women who migrated to the city from the nearby countryside. For the year 1876 for all three towns, the department of birth was recorded for everyone in the census, but for Rive-de-Gier the census enumerators also recorded the commune of birth of everyone in the census. The example of Rive-de-Gier shows that more than two-thirds (67.31 percent) of all boarders were born outside the department of the Loire; of those boarders who were natives of the department of the Loire almost one-third (32.77 percent) were born outside of Rive-de-Gier. Almost 80 percent (78.02 percent) of all boarders then were not native Ripagériens. In contrast, almost two-thirds of the inhabitants of Rive-de-Gier were born in the Loire (68.5 percent) and of these almost half were natives of Rive-de-Gier.

For a moment let us focus on those boarders who were natives of Rive-de-Gier. Among that 20 percent of boarders who were Ripagériens, only a handful could have been men and women who voluntarily left Ripagérien households. Almost 40 percent (38.75) of native boarders were over 50 years' old. The modal age of male native boarders was 33.5, exactly 6 years above that of the total boarding population (27.5). Over half of all female boarders were natives, and their modal age was 57.5. Clearly, the majority of female boarders who were natives of Rive-de-Gier, and many of the male boarders, were simply too old to have surviving parents with whom they could live. For Rive-de-Gier it is unlikely that many young native workers moved away from their families into the boarding house. If few native Ripagériens left their families to enter boarding houses, it seems unlikely that other Ripagériens who had family present in the city would have behaved differently.

Evidence from the other communes for 1876 where only department of birth was recorded is less complete. In 1876 in Saint-Chamond, 55.68 percent of all boarders were born outside the department of the Loire; in this same year 36.71 percent of all boarders in Le Chambon-Feugerolles were from other departments. But in these cities boarders were a smaller percent of the labor force than in Rive-de-Gier. Moreover, Rive-de-Gier was located on the edge of the department of the Loire, and short-distance migrants from three sides of the city would have been from other departments, while both Le Chambon-Feugerolles and Saint-Chamond were more centrally located within the department and short-distance migrants were more likely to be residents of the Loire. In any case, the smaller proportion of migrants makes it unlikely that boarding represented a serious alternative to remaining within the family household.

Boarding was much less common for women than for men. Only Rive-de-Gier in 1876 shows any appreciable number of female lodgers and their proportion in the workforce is never more than 8 percent of the total number of females in the age group. Employment as a servant is often accounted as the female equivalent of male lodging. But even if it was equivalent, there was much less job opportunity for female servants in all three cities than for males in heavy industry. In the beginning of the period, in cities like Saint-Chamond and Rive-de-Gier around 10 percent of the employed population were domestic servants, but 20 years later the percentage had dropped anywhere from one-third to one-half. In the two decades between 1856 and 1876 there was a strong trend towards the feminization of servants, but the number of female servants never compared with that of male boarders, the number of male boarders was many times greater at every period. Between 1856 and 1876 the proportion of the male workforce employed as servants declined while that of females changed relatively little; most female servants in both periods were between the ages of 15 and 30.

31 In 1856, median age of marriage for men in Le Chambon-Feugerolles was 27.5, in 1876, 26; in Rive-de-Gier in 1876, 28, in 1856, 26; in Saint-Chamond in 1856 27, in 1876, 27. In 1856, the median age of marriage for women in Le Chambon-Feugerolles was 24, in 1876, 22; in Rive-de-Gier in 1876, 23, in 1856, 22; in Saint-Chamond in 1876, 24, in 1856, 24.

Marriage was the major path to family formation in the Stéphanois

Table 5.11 The percentages of all births that were illegitimate in the three cities in 1856 and 1876

	1856	1876
Le Chambon-Feugerolles	3.01	1.78
Rive-de-Gier	3.80	4.89
Saint-Chamond	5.67	7.27

Sources: ADL 48/M/58 and Statistique de la France, *Mouvement de la population pendant les années 1855 & 1856 & 1857*, 2nd series, vol. 10 (Strasbourg, Berger-Levrault, 1861).

32 Chambre consultative de Saint-Chamond, enquête de 1871–1875, AN-C/3022.

33 Each marriage was required to have four witnesses and it was required that kin of either the bride or the groom be identified. In 1856 in Le Chambon-Feugerolles less than 1.5% of all witnesses were kin; in 1876 the figure was 17.2%. In 1856 in Rive-de-Gier, less than 0.2% of all witnesses were kin, in 1876 9.1%. In 1856 in Saint-Chamond 20.3% of all witnesses were kin and, in 1876, this decreased to 16.8%.

34 In Le Chambon-Feugerolles in 1856 84.2% of kin of the head or the spouse were employed, in 1876, 48.4%; in Rive-de-Gier in 1856, 31.0%, in 1876, 78.9%; in 1856 in Saint-Chamond, 20.8%, in 1876, 70.0%.

35 The following proportions of all kin to the head of household or his spouse were women, in 1856 in Le Chambon-Feugerolles, 66.1%(N=56), in Rive-de-Gier 51.5%(N=66), in Saint-Chamond 61.0%(N=146); in 1876 in Le Chambon-Feugerolles, 62.0%(N=100), in Rive-de-Gier, 56.0%(N=150), in Saint-Chamond 61.9%(N=147).

36 In 1856 in Le Chambon-Feugerolles 12.5% of all kin were over 60, in 1876 38.0%; in 1856 in Rive-de-Gier 30.3% of all kin were over 60, in 1876, 24.0%; in 1856 in Saint-Chamond 9.6%, in 1876 25.2%.

37 In 1856 in Le Chambon-Feugerolles there were two parents of the household head and three of the spouse living with their children; in 1876 there were 18 parents of

the head and 15 of his spouse. In 1856 in Rive-de-Gier there were 15 parents of the head and 8 of his spouse; in 1876 14 of the head and 16 of his spouse. In 1856 in Saint-Chamond there were 6 of the head and 4 of his spouse, in 1876 14 of the head and 19 of his spouse.

38 The proportion of households headed by solitaries or unrelateds among all households was in Le Chambon-Feugerolles in 1856, 7.5%, in 1876, 5.2%; in Rive-de-Gier in 1856, 8.0%, in 1876, 7.7%; in Saint-Chamond in 1856, 13.5%, in 1876, 8.6%.

39 For male heads of nuclear families, solitaries and unrelateds, and kin, the labor force participation rates in 1856 in Le Chambon-Feugerolles was, respectively, 98.8%, 93.9% and 84.2%, in 1876, 97.5%, 87.5%, and 48.4%; in Rive-de-Gier in 1856, 96.8%, 89.1%, and 31.0%, in 1876, 97.7%, 100%, and 78.9%; in Saint-Chamond in 1856, 98.9%, 98.8%, and 20.8%, in 1876 97.6%, 96.0%, and 70.0%. For female heads of nuclear families, solitaries and unrelateds, and kin, the labor force participation rate in 1856 in Le Chambon-Feugerolles was respectively, 62.1%, 66.7%, 59.4%, in 1876, 66.1%, 75% and 79.6%; in 1856 in Rive-de-Gier it was, 23.2%, 44.2%, and 20.6%, in 1876, 22.6%, 54.0%, 23.9%; in 1856 in Saint-Chamond, 80.5%, 91.2% and 15.6%, in 1876, 32.0%, 65.0%, and 38.3%.

40 *L'Eclaireur,* January, 1869.

41 Emile Guillaumin, *La vie d'un simple: mémoires d'un métayer* (Boston, Ginn and Company, 1926), pp. 108–9.

42 See Robert Coningsby, "The Conditions and Habits of the French Working Classes," in *Reports of Artisans: Paris Universal Exhibition, 1867* (London, Bell and Daldy, 1867), p. 436. Besides Paris, Coningsby visited Lyons, Saint-Etienne, Chalons-sur-Saône and Le Creusot.

43 On the evolution of French conscription laws, Richard D. Challener, *The French Theory of the Nation in Arms, 1866–1939* (New York, Russell and Russell, 1965); and chap. 1, section 4 of Michael Howard, *The Franco-Prussian War: The German Invasion of France, 1870–1871* (London, Rupert Hart-Davis, 1968).

44 Liogier, *Le travail des enfants,* p. 11. The basic law concerning child labor and schooling in effect for most of the period was the law of 1841. This law provided that in factories children could not be employed below the age of 8, and that between 12 and 16 years of age children could not be employed for more than 12 hours out of 24. The law forbade night work, alleged to have a baneful effect on children's morals, by requiring that children between 8 and 16 could only be employed between the hours of 5 in the morning and 9 at night. Children were expected to be in school until age 12 unless the mayor of the parents' commune provided a letter that the child had received a basic education or, alternatively, unless factory owners provided schools within the factory.

While this law did affect a substantial number of child laborers in the departments of the Nord and in Alsace-Lorraine where young children were employed in very large numbers in textiles, it had little effect in the Stéphanois. Provisions of the law specifically excluded the largest employers of child labor in the *arrondissement.* First of all the law only applied to employers who employed more than 20 workers. This meant that it did not limit employment for children within domestic industry. But the law also specifically noted that: "Night work by children over thirteen . . . will be tolerated if it is recognized as indispensable in establishments employing a continuous fire whose operation cannot be suspended during a twenty-four hour day." In the Stéphanois, the continuous-fire provision was taken to mean that the Ripagérien glass industry was dispensed from most of the applications of the law; the glass industry was one of the largest employers of children in the area.

The same piece of legislation might well have been applied to metalworking which also required continuous fire in some operations. But this interpretation of the law was seldom invoked. As the Chamber of Commerce of Saint-Etienne noted, in 1867, "as for metalworking, this genre of production demands such strength that most of the time it is fortunately impossible to use children."

In 1874 the law on child labor was extended. The 1874 law forbade children to be employed before age 12 in factories, shops or yards and decreed that children employed before age 12 could not be employed for more than 6 hours. In addition the prohibition against night work was extended to include women between the ages of 16 and 21. Also underground work in the mines was forbidden to children under 12. The 1874 law did not affect the children employed in mining since in 1856, as, as discussed in the last chapter, the great majority of them were over 12.

45 Ibid, p. 13.
46 Ibid.
47 Léon Bonneff and Maurice Bonneff, *La vie tragique des travailleurs* (Paris, Marcel Rivière, 1914).
48 G. Liogier, *Le travail des enfants dans la seconde moitié du XIXe siècle* (Saint-Etienne, CDDP, 1970), p. 13.
49 See the well-known articles by John Knodel and Etienne van de Walle, "Breast-feeding, Fertility, and Infant Mortality: An Analysis of Some Early German Data," *Population Studies* 21 (1967), pp. 109–31 and John Knodel, "Infant Mortality and Fertility in three Bavarian Villages: An Analysis of Family Histories from the Nineteenth Century," *Population Studies* 22 (1968), pp. 297–318.
50 See Samuel H. Preston, "Introduction," in *The Effects of Infant and Child Mortality on Fertility*, ed. Samuel H. Preston (New York, Academic, 1978).
51 For an explanation of the methodology of these life tables' construction see appendix 5.1.
52 A diversity of measures of infant mortality are used by demographers. Presented in table 5.12 are averages of conventional infantile mortality rates, averages over the years 1855–7 for Rive-de-Gier and Saint-Chamond and over the years 1854–8 for Le Chambon-Feugerolles and 1875–7 for Rive-de-Gier and 1874–8 for Le Chambon-Feugerolles. Conventional infantile mortality rates are the number of infants dying under age 1 during the year divided by the number of infants born during the year. Rates including stillbirths are presented in parentheses.

Declining mortality among children aged 1 to 4 and 5 to 9 was typical of French

Table 5.12   Conventional infant mortality rates

	1855–1857 or 1854–1858		1875–1877 or 1874–1878	
Le Chambon-Feugerolles	145.83	(222.22)	204.72	(257.99)
Rive-de-Gier	176.56	(244.80)	167.27	(229.58)
Saint-Chamond	149.67	(235.63)	140.92	(210.93)

Table 5.13   Age-specific mortality rates (per 1,000)

| | 1855–1857 or 1854–1858 | | 1875–1877 or 1874–1878 | |
	Males	Females	Males	Females
Le Chambon-Feugerolles 1–4	49.37	35.90	38.07	39.40
Le Chambon-Feugerolles 5–9	12.21	8.15	8.41	12.32
Rive-de-Gier 1–4	72.57	75.43	45.26	38.66
Rive-de-Gier 5–9	11.95	17.57	7.09	7.90
Saint-Chamond 1–4	64.83	57.19	27.97	20.41
Saint-Chamond 5–9	18.74	8.58	5.94	4.80

mortality decline in the second half of the nineteenth century; see Odin W. Anderson, "Age-Specific Mortality in Selected Western European Countries with Particular Emphasis on the Nineteenth Century," *Bulletin of the History of Medicine* 29 (3) (May–June 1955), pp. 239–54, esp. p. 244.

Table 5.13 shows the age-specific mortality rates for the population aged 1–4 and 5–9 in Rive-de-Gier and Saint-Chamond for 1855–7 and 1875–7, and for Le Chambon-Feugerolles for 1854–8 and 1874–8:

53 See Robert Woods and John Woodward, "Mortality, Poverty and the Environment," in *Urban Disease and Mortality in Nineteenth-Century England*, ed. Robert Woods and John Woodward (New York, St Martin's Press, 1984), pp. 19–36, p. 40.

54 "Commission médicale adjointe à l'enquête industrielle et agricole des deux cantons de Saint-Etienne," AN-C/956.

55 Direction de l'assistance et de l'hygiène publique, *Statistique sanitaire des villes de France et d'Algérie pour l'année 1887* (Paris, Imprimerie nationale, 1889).

56 *L'Eclaireur*, February 26, 1870.

57 *L'Eclaireur*, June 1, 1870.

58 *L'Eclaireur*, February 26, 1870.

59 *L'Eclaireur*, February 26, 1870.

60 1875 was a high mortality year in Le Chambon-Feugerolles, but above average mortality was entirely concentrated in the population above age 50.

61 "Docteur Vial à Monsieur le Préfet," ADL 37/M/6.

62 Ibid.

63 Bourdelais and Raulot, "La marche du choléra en France: 1832 et 1854," pp. 125–42.

64 *L'Eclaireur*, October 8, 1869.

65 On typhoid in industrial cities, F. B. Smith, *The People's Health: 1830–1910* (London, Croom Helm, 1979) pp. 244–8. On medical theories concerning epidemic disease in France between 1840 and 1880, William Coleman, *Death is a Social Disease, Public Health and Political Economy in Early Industrial France* (Madison, University of Wisconsin Press, 1982).

66 Information on number of people and household size in the three cities was found in the manuscript census for the three cities, consulted at the Archives départementales de la Loire.

67 James R. Lehning, *The Peasants of Marlhes: Economic Development and Family Organization in Nineteenth-Century France* (Chapel Hill, University of North Carolina Press, 1980), p. 56.

68 Information on the number of houses is contained in the manuscript census.
69 Seasonal mortality for urban areas in the *arrondissement* of Saint-Etienne were found in ADL 48/M/38 and ADL 47/M/10.
70 Condamin, *Histoire de Saint-Chamond*, p. 572–3.
71 Chomienne, *Histoire de la ville de Rive-de-Gier*, pp. 99–106.
72 In 1858, the canal quays were walled in and in 1870 a good deal of road work was done on the newly developing portions of the town. In both 1860 and 1870 a round of road building occurred. See Chomienne, *Histoire de la ville de Rive-de-Gier*, pp. 211–13.
73 On mold poisoning, Mary Kilbourne Matossian, "Mold Poisoning and Population Growth in England and France, 1750–1850," *Journal of Economic History* 44 (3) (Sept. 1984), pp. 669–86.
74 Quoted in M. W. Beaver, "Population, Infant Mortality, and Milk," *Population Studies*, 27 (2) (1973), pp. 243–54. Milk would have been a valuable source of vitamin D for growing children, and it would have prevented "rickets" which is mentioned as a cause of death among Stéphanois children; see *L'Eclaireur*, February 26, 1870. In England, rickets was a major cause of childhood death in industrial cities in the late eighteenth century. Although it had already declined as an important cause of childhood mortality, only in the 1840s was the effectiveness of cod liver oil discovered in providing the missing vitamin, but cows' milk would have been equally effective; see J. C. Drummond and Anne Wilbraham, *The Englishman's Food: A History of Five Centuries of English Diet* (London, Jonathan Cape, 1939), pp. 169–92 and 321–5. But increased consumption of milk, some of which was probably contaminated, may have been a mixed health blessing. See Anthony S. Wohl, *Endangered Lives; Public Health in Victorian Britain* (Cambridge, Mass., Harvard University Press, 1983), pp. 21–2.
75 See J. Landers, "Mortality and Metropolis: The Case of London, 1675–1825," *Population Studies* 41 (1987), pp. 59–76.
76 On computing total fertility rate, gross reproduction rate, and net reproduction rate from own-child ratios, see Wilson H. Grabill and Lee-Jay Cho, "Methodology for the Measurement of Current Fertility from Population Data on Young Children," *Demography* 2 (1965), pp. 50–73; and Lee-Jay Cho, "The Own-Children Approach to Fertility Estimation: An Elaboration," in *International Population Conference – Liège 1973* (Liège, IUSSP, 1973), vol. 2, pp. 263–79.
77 On the issue of mortality, it is not necessary the case that Accampo's findings conflict with my own as that we measure two different populations. Family reconstitution most accurately captures the experience of relatively stable populations. Census calculations capture a snap-shot picture (sometimes a cloudy picture) of a population at one point in time. Family reconstitution allows the calculation of some extremely valuable fertility indicators, such as birth intervals, but it does not estimate the total population as well as census estimates. This is particularly the case for a town such as Saint-Chamond the population turnover of which was the most considerable of any of the towns in this study. As Accampo shows, many ribbonweavers left the city as the trade declined.
78 Arthur E. Smailes, "Population Changes in the Colliery Districts of Northumberland and Durham," *Geographical Journal* 91 (Jan.–June, 1938), pp. 220–32, esp. p. 220. On this point see also, T. H. Bainbridge, "Population Changes over the West Cumberland Coalfield," in *English Rural Communities: The Impact of a Specialized*

Economy, ed. Dennis R. Mills (London, Macmillan, 1973), pp. 137–44.

79 On 1857 peak, see Gras, *Histoire économique générale des mines*, p. 731. On cancellation of Sainte-Barbe, *L'Eclaireur*, November 26, 1869.

80 On the coal shortage, see Lamb, "Coal Mining in France," pp. 76–7.

81 See Edward Higgs, "Women, Occupations and Work in the Nineteenth Century Censuses," *History Workshop* 23 (Spring, 1987), pp. 58–80; and the important article by Ellen Jordan, "Female Unemployment in England and Wales 1851–1911: an examination of the census figures for 15–19 year olds," *Social History* 13 (May, 1988), pp. 175–90.

82 The population used as the "standard" is a weighted sum of the population of all three cities in both 1856 and 1876.

83 On the reasons for the decline of ribbonweaving in Saint-Chamond, see Henri de Boissieu, "La rubanerie Stéphanois," in *Le mouvement économique et sociale dans la région lyonnaise*, ed. Paul Pic and Justin Godart (Lyon, A. Storck et cie., 1902), vol. 1, pp. 69–126, esp. pp. 71–5.

84 "Canton du Chambon-Feugerolles," AN-C/956.

85 Louis Reybaud, *Etudes sur le régime des manufactures* (Paris, Michel Levy, 1859), pp. 215–33.

86 Silkweaving decline was triggered by the American depression of 1857; a large share of Stéphanois ribbons went to the US. Gras, *Histoire de la rubanerie*, p. 610.

87 J. Valserres, *Les industries de la Loire* (Saint-Etienne, Robin, 1862), p. 322.

88 The application of the worker/consumer ratio was suggested to me by Louise Tilly. The weights come from Peter Lindert's work, found in Karen Oppenheim Mason, Maris Vinovskis and Tamara Hareven, "Women's Work and the Life Course in Essex County, Massachusetts, 1880," in Tamara K. Hareven (ed.), *Transitions: The Family and the Life Course in Historical Perspective* (New York, Academic Press, 1978), pp. 187–216; see also Louise A. Tilly and Steven J. Dubnoff, "Families and Wage Earning in Amiens and Roubaix, 1906: Measures of Income Adequacy and Household Response in Two French Cities," paper presented to the Annual Meeting of the Social Science History Association, 1978.

89 Nancy Folbre pointed this problem out to me.

APPENDIX 5.1 METHODOLOGY OF LIFE TABLE CONSTRUCTION

The mortality rates on which these abridged life tables were based were taken from an average of the mortality figures given in the vital statistics recorded by each commune. The base population was the total census population; whereas most of the analyses in this study were carried out with a sample population, the life tables were calculated from the age distribution of the total population; a separate handcount of the population age structure was done for this purpose. For Rive-de-Gier and Saint-Chamond, average mortality, nMx, was based on the age-specific mortality of the years 1855–7 and 1875–7. Because Le Chambon-Feugerolles was smaller than the other two towns, and the number of deaths in any one year less, it was decided to widen the period on which the Chambonnaire life table was based in order to lessen the influence of relatively minor yearly fluctuations. For Le Chambon-Feugerolles nMx was based on the age specific mortality for the years 1854–8 and 1874–8.

The life tables were calculated using Chiang techniques to convert nMx to nQx. Estimates of nAx, the person years lived in the interval by those dying in the interval, were taken from Keyfitz and Flieger tables for France in 1851 and for France in 1874–8, except that nAx for 0 to 1 and 1 to 4 were taken from Coale-Demeny relations for populations with 1M0 greater than 107. Life tables were rounded off at age 75 using the formula L75 = 175/M75.

Model tables were not used to smooth the mortality curve. As discussed in this chapter, the age structure of mortality changed during the period. Using Coale–Demeny tables, the best fitting mortality estimates for the 1856 period were model South tables; fitting nQx from the life tables with that of the Coale–Demeny tables, model South tables fit best with 5 of the 6 life tables. But the model South were only best fitting for 2 out of the 6 1876 life tables; a variety of models were better fitting, particularly North models for males in all three towns: I am intrigued by this apparent sex division in mortality, but cannot explain it. Given the variety of models that might apply it seemed best not to use any for the discussion of age-specific mortality. The use of different models would make comparison between towns and over time difficult while the use of the same models would suppress important differences between periods. Model tables were used for the estimation of fertility rates discussed in appendix 5.2.

The list of applicable life tables makes some of the same points already made in the body of this chapter. The model South life tables have very high rates of mortality between 1 and 4 and these mortality rates are often associated with diarrheal diseases. It has been argued that death in the second year of life, when the child often first comes into contact with contaminated and inadequate food and water, is the best single indicator of sanitary and nutritional standards. (See Preston and van de Walle, "Urban French Mortality in the Nineteenth Century".) Model North life tables which apply to men in 1876 often suggest the presence of tuberculosis; in 1886, tuberculosis was less a scourge of the Stéphanois than influenza and pneumonia, but information on causes of death in the period under study is still lacking.

A problem in estimating mortality was the number of still births recorded in the local vital statistics. The ratio of still births to live births that ended in death in the first year fluctuated dramatically from commune to commune. The largest fluctuations in reported still births occurred in Le Chambon-Feugerolles in 1856 and in Saint-Chamond in 1856 where still births were approximately 65 percent of live births that ended in death in the first year. In order to estimate the effects of these still births, the still births were included as live births that ended in death in the first year. The results for Le Chambon-Feugerolles in 1856 were a life expectancy 31.5 for males and 36 for females; for Saint-Chamond in 1856 the results were 23.51 for males and 28.58 for females. The results would strongly affect the life table, lowering life expectations anywhere from 2 to 5 years. In Le Chambon-Feugerolles, the result would be to show a very dramatic improvement in life expectation between 1856 and 1876 while the already extraordinarily high mortality in Saint-Chamond in 1856 would be even further reinforced. In two towns, there is an uncomfortably wide margin of error in infant mortality but, for reasons stated in this chapter, child mortality was very likely of more significant influence on the family economy than infant mortality. To give a bottom limit on the influence of still births on expectation of life at birth, life tables have been computed that include still births for all the towns; these are in parentheses in tables 5.3 and 5.4.

Results of estimates of the population between 0 and 4 presented later in this chapter suggest that a portion of the population may be missing due to underenumeration or absence from the city due to wetnursing. Let us assume the worst and imagine that all missing children under 5 were underenumerated and that all these infants were between 0 and 2 and distributed in the same proportion as in the enumerated population. For males in a typical city with underenumeration, Rive-de-Gier in 1875–7, life expectation would be 35.52; a real improvement, but not challenging the broad findings.

APPENDIX 5.2   DERIVING AGE-SPECIFIC FERTILITY RATES FROM CHILD–WOMAN
RATIOS

1   Here I have computed the total fertility rate (TFR), gross reproduction rate (GRR), and net reproduction rate (NRR) for women married to the household head. The more common indices are the TFR, GRR and NRR for all women between 15 and 49 in the total population. But, given the large, unmarried female population of textile workers in Saint-Chamond, this would make it very difficult to compare marital fertility among the three towns. In most calculations of fertility rates it is assumed that proportions of marriage are roughly similar or that differences in fertility rates will lead us to differences in the proportions of married. But in Saint-Chamond the existence of a very large unmarried female population is already well-known and nothing is to be gained by using fertility rates to rediscover it.

2   First, it is necessary to discuss the estimation of the population aged 0 to 4. Most studies of French fertility focus on the issue of wetnursing as an important complicating force. In Paris and Lyon, large numbers of children were sent out to wet nurses and the mortality of these infants was extraordinarily high. George D. Sussman's important study of nineteenth-century wetnursing indicates that industrial workers were less likely than other sectors of the population to have recourse to wetnursing, and this would argue against its use among metalworkers and miners in most of the Stéphanois valley towns. Wetnursing was an industry practiced in the Stéphanois countryside; James Lehning's study of wetnursing in the commune of Marlhes supports Sussman's contention that it was relatively little used by metalworkers or miners in the Stéphanois industrial towns. (See James R. Lehning, "Les nourrissons de Marlhes: Mercenary Wetnursing in a French village, 1841–1900," unpublished paper.) Following this argument however, the prevalence of wetnursing cannot be rejected for Saint-Chamond in 1856 or 1876; in that town, we know that there were mothers who ran small domestic work shops in 1856 and who worked in factory industry in 1876, and these were the situations that particularly promoted wetnursing; worst of all, the census's failure to record married women's work in Saint-Chamond in 1856 does not even permit an estimation of the extent of wetnursing for this commune. In addition to wetnursing, there are other sources of underestimation of the number of children aged between 0 and 4. Infants are often ignored by census-takers, and there is evidence of age heaping and sex imbalance among infants that suggests that census officials were not too careful in their recording of the very young.

Given all these problems, I decided to estimate the population between 0 and 4. The techniques of estimation employed are found in Henry S. Shryock, Jacob S. Siegel et al., *The Methods and Materials of Demography*, (Washington, D.C., US Department of Commerce, 1975), vol. 2, pp. 742–4. Using model life tables, reverse survival techniques

Table 5.14

	Discrepancy	Average
Le Chambon-Feugerolles, 1856	5.53	−0.77
Le Chambon-Feugerolles, 1876	0.54	+9.94
Rive-de-Gier, 1856	2.85	−10.59
Rive-de-Gier, 1876	5.78	−10.52
Saint-Chamond, 1856	11.46	−9.68
Saint-Chamond, 1876	6.25	−18.27

were employed on the population aged 5 to 9 in the existing census. Next, using the same life tables, the children whose births were recorded in the vital statistics were "forward survived" for the previous five-year period. The two estimates were then averaged to get the estimate of the children aged 0 to 4. The largest discrepancy between the census figures and the two estimates was for Saint-Chamond in 1856, most estimates show smaller discrepancies between the two estimates; these estimates do reveal systematic underenumeration in Saint-Chamond and Rive-de-Gier, although not in Le Chambon-Feugerolles, but whether or not these discrepancies are due to wetnursing, undercounting, or migration is impossible to prove. Table 5.14 presents the absolute value of the discrepancies between the two estimates, the estimate by forward survival from vital statistics and the estimate by backward survival from the population 5–9. It also presents the average of the two estimates. This is the percentage by which the actual census population would have been inflated to arrive at the estimate. The two estimates provide an opportunity to get some handle on the presence of rural wetnursing. If infants were forward survived using lower mortality urban life tables and some infants were subject to higher rural wetnursing mortality, then the vital statistics method should provide a higher estimate than the reverse survival method. This is indeed the case for Saint-Chamond in 1876 and for Rive-de-Gier in 1876, but the extent of underestimation is much greater in Saint-Chamond than Rive-de-Gier. A look at the population distribution by single years also suggests the presence of wetnursing in Saint-Chamond in 1876. While several censuses tended to place children under 1 year in the category of 1 year, if the proportion of children under 2 is compared with the population under 5, then there are a disproportionate number of children under 2 missing from Saint-Chamond in 1876 compared with the other communities. These estimates support Elinor Accampo's contention that wetnursing increased in Saint-Chamond as the nineteenth century wore on but, even if there were no undercounting, these estimates do not suggest that surplus mortality due to rural wetnursing was as prevalent as she finds in the case of her stable families.

3   Using reverse/forward survival rates, it was possible to obtain a better estimate of the actual child–woman ratios. In going from child–woman ratios to fertility rates, the following things need to be done:

(a)   Corrections for mortality need to be made. These were done using model life tables. The estimation of these life tables is discussed elsewhere.

(b)   Corrections need to be made for children who did not live with their mothers. There were two kinds of non-own-children. The first were those non-own-children whose mother was either not identified or not present in the census enumeration of the

Table 5.15

	Percentage own-children (*nourrissons* excluded)	Percentage own-children (*nourrissons* included)
Le Chambon-Feugerolles, 1856	99.62	93.26
Le Chambon-Feugerolles, 1876	96.22	93.90
Rive-de-Gier, 1856	97.82	97.45
Rive-de-Gier, 1876	97.83	96.97
Saint-Chamond, 1856	96.31	95.57
Saint-Chamond, 1876	98.74	98.74

household. This was a relatively negligible group. The second group of non-own-children were "*nourrissons*" – children who were residing with nurses. The first group of children must unambiguously be treated as residents of the city in which they are recorded. I have also included *nourrissons* as residents of the city. In Le Chambon-Feugerolles, particularly in 1856, the number of *nourrissons* is not large, but still not negligible. The status of *nourrissons* depends on whether they were the children of Chambonnaire parents or of parents residing elsewhere; there was involvement in domestic hardware production in Le Chambon-Feugerolles in 1856, and this was performed in family workshops, a situation that might have encouraged wetnursing. I have included *nourrissons* as inhabitants of the industrial city and have distributed them among all households with children; the same has been done for *nourrissons* for all the towns, but outside Le Chambon-Feugerolles the differences are negligible. Table 5.15 gives the percentage of the population under 5 that were identified as own children. It also shows the importance of *nourrissons* in the total population of children aged 0 to 4. The first column gives the percentage if the *nourrissons* are excluded from the denominator and labeled as non-residents, the second column gives the percentage of own children identified if the *nourrissons* are included in the denominator.

Excluding the *nourrissons*, non-own-children were distributed according to the proportion of own-children resident with male household heads, female household heads, kin and boarders. Since the proportion of own-children resident with mothers with a male household head present was very large, in every case around 90 percent, the great majority of non-own-children were apportioned to families with male household heads present.

(c)   Corrections may be made for underenumeration of the female population. In his study of the female population of France, Etienne van de Walle suggests that the female population of France, was underenumerated by about 1 percent in 1856 and by 1.1 percent in 1876. This correction factor is not large for our purposes, and the difference between the two periods is only one-tenth of one percent. Van de Walle also suggests corrections for the Loire, although he compensates for the effect of migration as well as underenumeration. For 1856 he suggests that the female population should be decreased by 1.7 percent and for 1876 it should be decreased by 2 percent; presumably the effect of the migration of females to the Loire is the reason for this decrese. But for our purposes the fertility of migrants from other departments is as important as that of those from other departments. Also in the case of both national and departmental corrections,

corrections would not effect the comparisons between cities. *No attempt to compensate for underenumeration of the female population above age 4 has been made.*

(d) In considering marital fertility, it is necessary to take into account the continuing accession to the married population. Few women in the Stéphanois married before age 20, but by age 30 most of those women who would ever marry had married. For the ages between 15 and 29 it is necessary to compensate for the fact that many women were not exposed to marriage for the full five-year age interval. It is also necessary to compensate for the mortality of married women who, especially in the five-year intervals between 15 and 30, were not exposed to the possibility of mortality over the full five-year period.

4 The methodology of the "own-children" transformations was found in Lee-Jay Cho, Wilson H. Grabill, and Donald J. Bogue, *Differential Current Fertility in the United States* (Chicago, Community and Family Study Center, University of Chicago, 1970), in chap. 7, "Methodology," pp. 303–53.

6

Proletarians and Protest in the Stéphanois: the Origins of the Modern Labor Movement

In mid-September 1872, Léon Gambetta, the great republican tribune, began his most famous whirlwind speaking tour in the Stéphanois town of Firminy, only a few kilometers from Le Chambon-Feugerolles. There, he was the guest of Pierre-Frédéric Dorian, a local metal employer and an old political acquaintance. For five days, Gambetta toured some of the most important factories in the region with Dorian by his side. On his last day, he gave a brief series of talks to working-class crowds that always included a large contingent of metalworkers. His final talk centered on a favorite topic that would have interested the metalworkers in his audience, the topic of education. The task of republicans, he explained, was to establish a new government:

a government of justice, of justice for all, and of equality . . . which recognizes no other distinctions among men than those of character, of probity, of intelligence, and of active involvement in life's struggles, on the condition, however, that at the beginning the state or society had done its duty, the duty of assuring to the child, at his entry into life, of the first and most indispensable capital, education.[1]

The factories he visited in the Stéphanois and his warm reception from the workers must have made a strong impression on Gambetta, for two weeks later he mentioned them in a more historically significant context. On September 26, in Grenoble, Gambetta made his celebrated speech in which he foresaw the entry of the "working world," a "new social stratum," into French politics. As examples of this newly emerging working class, Gambetta cited groups of workers in Marseilles, Paris, Lyon, Le Havre, and Saint-Etienne.[2]

Seven years later, at a workers' congress in Marseilles, a delegate from Saint-Etienne demonstrated Gambetta's prescience while also addressing the topic of education. According to the delegate, Charles Ava-Cottin, "We have therefore the conviction that one renders service to the child, to his family, to society, in founding everywhere, in the city as well as in the country, professional schools." For Ava-Cottin as for Gambetta, the schools, especially technical schools, were a necessary first step in a larger restructuring of working-class life. Yet the restructuring he had in mind was not only political, but also economic:

We agree with a numerous group of socialists, that an educational period is necessary to the proletariat before demanding vigorously and in a revolutionary manner our social emancipation by the suppression of wage earning, that is to say, the substitution of a new right – the collectivity – to the old right – individuality.[3]

By 1879, some notable leaders of the Stéphanois working classes had indeed begun to make their entry into the world of politics, but in a more militant and vigorous manner than even Gambetta had foreseen.

This chapter explores the relationship between the growth of republicanism and socialism in the Stéphanois and shows how workers used local political battles to gain more control over their lives and to fight for a greater degree of social security. As we will see, the forces behind the political evolution of Stéphanois working-class political leaders were dependent on a variety of factors, some contingent and conjunctural. But at almost every step the field of class action was defined and demarcated by the growing recognition of the semi-skilled workers of the permanency of their proletarian condition and by their effort to free themselves and their families from the dependent status imposed on them by large employers. The issues that drew Stéphanois workers into politics, their receptivity to various political doctrines, and the birth of a collective consciousness were based both on work place issues and on family interests; class solidarities and family ties frequently intersected and overlapped.

REPUBLICANS AND IMPERIALISTS: THE ELECTIONS OF MAY–JUNE 1869

The militant republicanism that Gambetta found in the Stéphanois region in 1872 was itself a product of the events of the late 1860s. As the Napoleonic Empire liberalized and political debate reappeared in France, the dissatisfaction of permanent semi-skilled workers with their situation emerged as it had among the miners of Rive-de-Gier during the Second Republic. As a new proletarian working class settled down in the industrial city and began to establish families, the terms of existing industrial organization became less palatable. Manipulation of job-training programs and social insurance plans by employers were only some of the more flagrant techniques used to dominate their employees. The vital importance to workers of family life made these issues explosive.

But while dissatisfaction with the terms of industrialization served to politicize workers generally, their decisions in local politics were crucially influenced by the terms of pre-existing political debates and by issues where embattled workers could find allies. In the 1860s and 1870s in the Stéphanois, the battle between republicans and Bonapartists grew increasingly bitter. Since all the elections between 1851 and 1870 were on the basis of universal manhood suffrage, several attempts were made to involve proletarians in politics. Following time-honored political practice, both parties tried to win support by developing programs that they knew would appeal to workers. But the efforts of Bonapartists and republicans to build support depended not simply on *ad hoc* programs, but also on larger issues of political outlook and philosophy. As the party with the closest ties to power, the Bonapartists could almost always outbid the republicans in obtaining real benefits, but, uncompromised by the trappings of power, republicans were free to appeal to principle.

The opening shot in a political battle that would intensify in the last years of the Second Empire was the election in 1863 of Pierre-Frédéric Dorian as deputy in the circonscription that included Rive-de-Gier, Saint-Chamond, and Le Chambon-Feugerolles. Dorian owned a small factory, and his father-in-law, Jacob Holtzer, was one of the more important middle-sized metal employers in the region. In some respects, the election of Dorian was a legacy of the Second Republic. As shown in chapter 1, republican sympathies had spread among coal miners in Rive-de-Gier as far back as 1848; republican ideas had spread even more widely among ribbonweavers and other artisans in most Stéphanois cities. During the 1850s and early 1860s, although an organized republican movement hardly existed in the Stéphanois, the industrial cities regularly turned out a large minority of votes against the Empire.[4]

In the 1860s, new opponents of the Second Empire appeared among the metal employers. The Anglo-French trade agreements of 1860 antagonized many metal employers who feared the competition of English metal producers. As government orders to industry had risen in the 1850s with rearmament and the expansion of the railroads, conflicts among employers also arose. Some metal producers, mostly smaller scale metal producers, believed that the government unfairly favored companies in which Napoleonic associates had a stake. The republican resurgence in 1863 that swept so many other areas of France as well enabled popular and elite hostility to coalesce and to elect a republican deputy in the Stéphanois.[5]

In 1864, republicans moved to consolidate their growing political influence in the region. Appeals for compulsory, universal, and secular education and vocational training were probably an important factor in explaining the especially strong support for republicanism in those towns and cities where metalworkers predominated. By the mid-1860s, a reaction against inferior clerical education was gathering momentum in the region. In the mid-1860s, the city council of Saint-Etienne decided that all new schools would by staffed by lay teachers. The unwillingness of the state to fund primary education, even after the appointment in 1863 of Victor Duruy as the first Minister of Public Education, gave imperial candidates nothing to boast about in this regard.[6]

As well as promoting the schooling issue, republicans also found it necessary to develop a program that would appeal to miners, many of whom did not send their children to school. In addition, republicans appealed to miners' well-known hostility toward the system of accident pensions that dominated in Stéphanois mining. As discussed in chapter 4, these funds came partly from the wages of miners, but workers who left an individual employer had no claim on these accrued funds. The diversity of insurance systems in Stéphanois mining and the importance of voluntary employer grants enabled companies to use these funds to discourage workers from leaving individual companies to take jobs elsewhere. The lawyer and deputy, Jules Favre, one of the best known republicans in late-imperial France, opened a legal attack against the accident funds of two local mining companies in which he questioned the legality of the lack of Stéphanois miners' control over the administration of the fund. Even though they did not win the case, at least the republicans had put the imperial justice system on record as supporting an unpopular company policy; judicial support for the coal companies would prove useful in winning miners' support at election time.[7]

Alarmed by the revival of republicanism in the Stéphanois, the empire acted to build popular support and to counteract the effects of the court case. Its response followed lines already familiar to imperial politics. In the 1850s, when the empire struck down all but a favored few producers' and consumers' associations, it generally spared workers' mutual aid societies. Clearly republican societies, such as that of the miners of Rive-de-Gier, were dissolved. But religious mutual aid societies, formed to replace the republican societies in Rive-de-Gier and in Saint-Chamond in the 1850s, were encouraged by special financial favors and tax exemptions for contributors.[8] However the empire's break with the church, which originated with Louis Napoleon's Italian policies and his on-going conflicts with the papacy, removed the workers in church-sponsored clubs from the orbit of imperial influence.

In 1866, to recover its lost influence, the government decided to take advantage of an application by miners in the Stéphanois to organize a new mutual aid society that would encompass the entire basin and gradually would be enlarged to provide retirement benefits as well as accident insurance. Thus, the empire (for its own reasons) would loosen the chains with which the mining companies had tried to bind the miners and provide social benefits that the republicans were not yet in a position to deliver. While the empire respected private property and would not intervene in the sphere of production to set wages, it would intervene in the sphere of family reproduction to benefit workers and to increase its own political influence. In 1866, a new Prefect, Castaing, was brought in with experience with such societies; he had already organized mutual aid associations among miners in the Nord.[9]

To build a new miners' mutual aid society, which would soon take the name *La Fraternelle*, the Prefect relied on men whose reputation was established among workers. A hardware artisan who had been active in Saint-Etienne in 1848 was authorized to set up the society under his leadership. He was promised that the society would be given all the necessary liberties so long as it remained outside of politics.[10] Only political neutrality could have insured the successful launching of a large mutual aid society, because many miners were republicans who looked with suspicion on imperial initiatives. As in many other instances of imperial dealings with workers, the leaders administering the society were not well-known supporters of the empire. In fact, some of its officials, such as the young Michel Rondet, had supported Dorian's efforts in 1863.[11] From its origins the formation of the mutual aid society represented an imperially supported political protest against coal company policy. Looking back on the organization's beginning, its founder reflected in 1869 that "Because the discussion that occurred on the topic of the accident insurance irritated the men, they supported *La Fraternelle*. It was in their opinion a protest which would prove the necessity of a general fund."[12]

The new mutual aid society proved a great success; in a few years, 5,000 miners were members, over one-third of all the miners in the basin. A look at the officials of the new mutual aid society shows that it was most firmly rooted in the western basin, which included the commune of Le Chambon-Feugerolles, and less rooted in the eastern basin which included Rive-de-Gier.[13] Previous chapters have provided a basis for understanding why this might be the case. The greater percentage of accidents in the western basin made workers there more concerned with insurance issues. In addition, new and relatively secure employment opportunities in the western basin encouraged workers to form families there, and family formation gave workers a greater interest in such long-term investments as insurance funds. Declining family income among miners in western basin communities, communities which also depended on the faltering ribbonweaving industry, such as Le Chambon-Feugerolles, meant that even the most temporary incapacity put an intolerable strain on family resources. The greater role of migrants in the mining workforce in towns such as Rive-de-Gier and the inherent instability in mining in the declining eastern portion of the basin made workers less concerned with such issues.

However, as could be expected, the great success of *La Fraternelle* and the growing imperial tolerance of trade unionism only encouraged leaders to raise their expectations. First, they sought to gain control over company-controlled insurance funds and to establish a basin-wide insurance program with unified rules that would enable miners to move from one company to another without having to worry about insurance issues. Insurance funds remained a dominant issue to which miners' organizations returned again and again. It is also possible that the society's interest in these funds was kindled by the links to 1848 of miners' leaders such as the society's president. If a workers' society gained the right to participate in the company insurance funds, might this not be a first step in carrying out the great dream of so many artisans and of Ripagérie miners, of sharing in the operation of industry?

Secondly, at about the same time, the leaders of the society began to consider wage demands. The growing fluctuations in miners' wages in the Stéphanois in the 1860s have already been discussed. To maintain their income in declining pits, miners had to work longer and harder in mines that now contained the least valuable kinds of coal. In new and expanding pits, miners often found their income threatened when they were transferred from hewing to jobs in excavation and timbering as part of the process of mine-development. In January 1869, the society began to discuss demanding a regulation of working hours and a minimum wage: a regulation of working hours would limit the time that miners would be forced to work, while the minimum wage would guarantee their take-home pay. A minimum wage might also appeal to those miners in the western basin who were transferred from hewing to other, less remunerative occupations. Miners' concern for wage stability also reflected a long-term investment in a particular occupation; in most cases, able-bodied migrants could find work that exceeded the lowest pay in mining in other industries.[14]

The issue of whether to turn their mutual aid society into a trade union and the demand to participate in the company insurance funds were being considered when the election campaign of 1869 heightened political debate throughout the basin.

THE EVOLUTION OF STÉPHANOIS REPUBLICANISM

Like the Bonapartists, republicans in the Stéphanois also sought to appeal to workers. In order to understand the appeal of republicanism to workers – both metalworkers and miners – it is necessary to look beyond the success with which republicans exploited any single issue, such as accident insurance or vocational education. Stéphanois republicanism contained a distinctive political perspective that would contribute greatly to the development of a working-class political outlook. Although the events of 1848 and the Second Republic had attracted many workers in the first generation of proletarians to the cause of republicanism, the failure of workers' attempts to cooperate with employers in the administration of production had led also to disillusionment. Years later, Michel Rondet labeled utopian the attempts of Ripagérien miners in 1848 to elect their supervisors.[15] In the late 1860s, new republican doctrines would provide a coherent perspective on French politics that partly replaced the doctrines that had been prevalent 20 years before. But these new republican doctrines, like those of 1848, found a response in local workers not simply because they were locally current, but also because their emphasis on equality and concern for family welfare spoke to some of workers' deepest concerns.

Although Stéphanois republican leaders in the 1860s never hesitated to draw on the legacy of 1848 in their political rhetoric, they enunciated very different political principles from those of the middle-class republicans that had allied with local workers in 1848. The decline of highly skilled ribbonweaving had weakened an important component of traditional, 1848-style, republicanism in the Stéphanois region, while opposition to imperial policies had helped to forge a new basis for republicanism. The principal leaders of Stéphanois republicanism in the 1860s were successful industrialists who were much more forthright champions of a market economy than the artisans and small businessmen of the earlier period. On some issues, they could be quite conservative. In its first month of publication, *L'Eclaireur*, the newspaper founded by Pierre-Frédéric Dorian to rally the republican party, condemned the presence of beggars in Saint-Etienne and advocated the establishment of a local *dépôt de mendicité* to incarcerate them. The paper pointed out that if the small children who ran after pedestrians crying "I haven't had anything to eat since this morning" were really starving, they wouldn't have had the energy to run so fast. Local republicans argued that those who would send children out to beg did not deserve to have children, and it was up to society to take such children in hand and teach them the elements of morality.[16]

Dorian was himself a left republican who, like many of those republicans of the 1860s, paid public homage to the men of 1848 but charted a new political course. The experience of both the Second Republic and the Second Empire had rendered these new republicans suspicious of government efforts to intervene in the economy. But, in addition, the need to win working-class support encouraged them to develop more consistently those aspects of the republican doctrine that could appeal to proletarians. Far more than the republicans of 1848, they feared state intervention, but they also realized that the state was not the only threat to individual rights. While they saw the empire's support of *La Fraternelle* as an example of state manipulation, they also believed that the large companies' control over their workers could be a threat to individual rights.[17] Furthermore they began to draw an increasingly important distinction between able-bodied adult male workmen whose independent wage-earning status was to be preserved at all cost, and children too young to work or poorly paid who were dependants. In either the case of young beggars or in the case of miners' families, intervention to protect children was regarded as legitimate if it was done to help them become independent wage earners when they grew up.

Occasionally, *L'Eclaireur* made a favorable reference to the application of associationist principles in the distant future. But the major political project of these republicans was really the establishment of the principles of what Harold Perkin has labeled, in the case of mid-Victorian England, a "viable class society." Dorian and the majority of editorialists for *L'Eclaireur* shared and constantly reiterated their belief that, in Perkin's terms, "class conflict is not a war to the death but a limited contest for power and income between opponents who recognize each other's right to exist."[18] If employers and workers could only realize that they both needed one another and resolve their antagonisms in the market arena, then state intervention and the loss of individual rights could be avoided. Unlike the men of 1848, whose ideal was social harmony, these men believed that a certain amount of conflict between workers and employers was inherent in modern society and should be allowed to surface.

Local republicans charged that the two obstacles to the establishment of a democratic and stable society in the Stéphanois were the lack of adequate education available to workers of all categories and the coalition of the mining companies, tacitly supported by the central government, that used the benefit system to prevent the operation of a free labor market in mining. Inadequate education and company manipulation were the real causes of the recurring cycle of repression, exploitation, and resistance so characteristic of industrial relations in mining.

Within limits, republicans were willing to support miners who went on strike against the coal company. In a long series of letters published in *L'Eclaireur* that surveyed conditions in Stéphanois mining, Louis Jezierski condemned the coal companies for the forced contributions that they levied on the miners and claimed that it was contrary, "if not to the law, at least to the most elementary principles of justice."[19] The company should admit, he argued, that these contributions were really deferred wages and belonged to the worker. Jezierski also alleged that the low wages paid to workers in this hazardous occupation precluded their putting any savings aside and that, as a result, "a secure future, the acquisition of property, dignity and independence is scarcely possible."[20]

Crucial to Jezierski's argument was the distinction between good republican capitalists and bad imperial monopolists. For example, he noted that some glassworkers and metalworkers also engaged in hazardous occupations but that at least such workers earned very high wages: "In the Dorian factory, puddlers and rollers earned 10 to 15 francs a day. In the glassworks of M. Richarme at Rive-de-Gier, one worker out of three earns 10 francs."[21] He did not add, however, that such workers earned these high wages because of worker-controlled apprenticeships in glassmaking and puddling and not because of the generosity of the noted republican leaders, Dorian and Richarme. Neither did Jezierski make the more appropriate comparison between the wages of the mass of semi-skilled metalworkers employed by Dorian and those of the miners.

The republicans tended to attribute low wages to governmental restrictions on workers' ability to organize into trade unions. For many republicans of the 1860s, such as those gathered around Gambetta, the trade union replaced the producers' association as the fundamental agency for representing workers' interests.[22] Many republicans of the 1860s rejected associationism because it preserved workers' illusions about the impermanency of proletarian labor, illusions that, as had been shown in 1848, could be dangerous. Unlike producers' associations which suggested the possibility of turning the worker into a part-owner, trade unionism at least involved the recognition that the workers' interests were bound up with the wage-earning condition. Workers organized into trade unions could formally bargain with employers. According to the editor César Bertholon:

What is involved here? A negotiation between employers and workers on the issue of wages. . . . The workers are therefore legitimately authorized to use this liberty to discuss with their employers their wage rate; and, as they would never have the chance of representing their demands if they tried to deal with them in an isolated fashion, they have no other recourse but to coalesce and consequently, if they are not heard, of going on strike.

The employers enjoy the same right, each of the parties obeys the same motive, to the same calculation, from his particular point of view. It is necessary that there exist between them a morally valuable contract that there may be free consent on the part of one and of the other.[23]

However, Bertholon felt sure that in most cases strikes would be avoided, if only employers and workers had more opportunity to bargain and negotiate on a more equal basis, because, on account of their participation in a common productive endeavor, "employers and workers are tied by the most narrow solidarity."[24]

With higher wages and adequate insurance, miners would cease to be a "mass of wage earners equally indigent and ignorant, whose intelligence is still raw and whose consciousness [is] insufficiently enlightened, undefended against unhealthy utopias, against brutal instinct and misery."[25] Once a certain level of family income was achieved, miners could then send their children to school, where the real social transformation would occur. Stéphanois republicans shared Emile Zola's conviction that drink was the real curse of the workingman. *L'Eclaireur* assured its readers that, "the cabaret for the miner is the wife abandoned or given over to drunkenness alongside her husband, it is children abandoned to vagabondage, the lodgings badly maintained, health and savings ruined." But there was hope in the rival of the cabaret, the school, which would prepare him for labor and train him in civic virtue. "It represents a moral perfection that fortifies the spirit of order and of the family and makes workers more able and productive, that gives the man a conception of his rights and duties as a worker and a citizen."[26] With education, miners could also be expected to better their condition by limiting their family size to two children; at present "this beautiful rule of Malthus is unknown to them."[27]

While some workers may have been provoked by the condescending tone of these abstemious bourgeois republicans, others realized a need for greater self-discipline among workers. In any case, there was much else in the republican political outlook that elicited workers' support. The republican view of the family was one that must have elicited particular sympathy. As was the case with many other reform-minded nineteenth-century liberals, republican individualism stopped when dealing with the situation of children within the family unit. For republicans, the family was the institution that educated all children and prepared male children for individual achievement in the public world; as the cradle of "individualism," the family was entitled to special state protection. Republicans condemned the large metalworks that monopolized technical education and the large mining companies that restricted the mobility of their labor force. Both republicans and workers could agree that company control over family life must be resisted because of its unfortunate consequences for child-rearing, and they were willing to turn to the state or to support social conflict to find a remedy. Republican support for increased wages for miners and for the legitimation of trade unions further increased the miners' attraction to republicanism.

The election of 1869 brought the competition between imperialists and republicans to a head. Because of the last-minute withdrawal of the republican candidate, Pierre-Frédéric Dorian agreed to run in the circonscription of Saint-Etienne to save the republicans' electoral chances in this key area.[28] In his place, César Bertholon, an old middle-class republican, well-known in the whole Lyonnais area during the 1830s and 1840s, was recalled from his residence in Algeria, where he had been exiled after the 1851 *coup*, and asked to run for Dorian's seat.[29] This circonscription included Le Chambon-Feugerolles, Rive-de-Gier, and Saint-Chamond. Against Bertholon was the imperial candidate, the Comte de Charpin-Feugerolles, a well-known Catholic leader whom Dorian had ousted in 1863.[30]

From the point of view of imperial officials, anxious to win back the circonscription containing the three industrial cities, the candidacy of a republican from outside the area presented a real opportunity. The success of the officially sponsored *La Fraternelle* and its leaders' desire to share some measure of control over the company insurance funds gave the administration the means with which to remake the political situation. The Prefect met with 18 leaders of *La Fraternelle* and promised them that after the election he would intervene with the coal companies in support of their demands for participation in the companies' pension program and their requests for a minimum wage and a limitation of hours. In turn, he expected them to support the imperial candidate, the Comte de Charpin-Feugerolles.[31] Although a significant minority, including Michel Rondet, opposed such an arrangement, the majority of the society's leaders agreed to support the imperial candidate.

As might be expected, the election was a heated contest. Bertholon's appeals to workers adopted the political principles elaborated in Jezierski's articles, and Bertholon's policy positions were a toned-down version of Gambetta's famed Belleville program.[32] To attract workers, Bertholon emphasized the need for compulsory secular education for both sexes and for publicly supported technical training. He advocated the legalization of meetings and trade unions. He demanded the creation of a national militia. He also called for the lowering of taxes and the reduction of administrative salaries.[33] In contrast, his opponent, de Charpin-Feugerolles, extolled the virtues of imperial support for the workers' cause.

As the election approached, at the end of May 1869, tension in towns which contained both metalworking and mining populations grew. The first-round elections on 24–25 May elected Dorian in Saint-Etienne and two imperial candidates in Roanne and Montbrison, but necessitated a run-off between Bertholon and de Charpin-Feugerolles. The run-off brought popular interest to a peak. A republican song entitled "Advice to the Miners" reminded the miners of de Charpin-Feugerolles's noble title and underplayed Bertholon's own status as a landholder in the Isère. The song counseled:

They tell you that all your demands
Will be granted, due to Charpin;

These are only large Chimeras
It is more butter than bread.
Papist, friend of the monopoly,
The count will betray you
A plebian keeps his word.
Miners, vote for Bertholon.[34]

Conservative metal employers who depended on government contracts, such as the management of the Petin–Gaudet plant, posted their usual proclamation on the factory door, telling their employees that only the election of de Charpin-Feugerolles and the party of order could "assure the work they had needed in order to support their families."[35]

Correspondingly, republican metal employers rallied their workers behind Bertholon. At Firminy, a mining director reported:

The elections always impassion this area . . . relations are very sensitive between the miners and the workers at the steelworks. These last [the steelworkers are] partisans of M. Bertholon . . . the miners have voted together for M. le Charpin. They have done so with so much unanimity that one [a steelworker] has cried "down with the miners," which has deeply offended them. We will do our best to restore calm . . . if not [there will be] the fights and stabbings to which they are naturally inclined . . .[36]

In fact, shortly after the shouting match, and before the second balloting, one of the leaders of *La Fraternelle*, Jean-Claude Peyret, issued his own statement on the events at Firminy. The statement showed that many miners must have been tempted by the republican appeal but that loyalty to *La Fraternelle* must also have been high because this was the core of the argument for supporting de Charpin. Without extolling general imperial politics, Peyret pointed out that opposing imperial candidates could lead to the society's dissolution. Furthermore, he pointed out that supporting imperial politicians might result in the extension of the society's powers:

Please tell all your friends that if we do not vote for M. de Charpin-Feugerolles, it will have the effect of preventing the transformation of the existing society [*La Fraternelle*] into a great institution that will forever insure our future.

Even if we are abandoned, combatted by those men who claim to belong to the democracy, we must all naturally support the candidate who will help us to definitively constitute [our society] . . . long live the miners!, long live these brave and honest fathers of families who, in peril of their lives, painfully tear each day from the bowels of the earth, the daily bread of industry . . . LONG LIVE LIBERTY WITH THE EMPEROR.[37]

The support of the leaders of *La Fraternelle* does seem to have been a significant fact in the imperial candidate's victory in the election of 7 June. Although the republican candidate swept Saint-Chamond by a two-to-one margin and won with a smaller margin in Rive-de-Gier, the combination of lukewarm support in the western wing of the coal field plus rural voters, support for the imperial candidate led de Charpin-Feugerolles to a narrow victory. The imperial candidate carried the commune of Le Chambon-Feugerolles, a stronghold of *La Fraternelle*, by two-to-one.[38]

THE MINERS' STRIKE OF 1869

The election of de Charpin-Feugerolles on June 6, 1869 seemed to augur the appearance of two new political coalitions in the Stéphanois. On one side the coalition would include the imperial administration, conservative metal employers, prosperous farmers, and the majority of coal miners. Opposing it would be a republican coalition comprising republican metal employers, the majority of metalworkers, a minority of miners, and the artisans of Saint-Etienne. But the new political alignment was shattered, before it could establish a firm foundation, by the force of events after only ten days. Imperial efforts to use *La Fraternelle* to enlist support among permanently proletarianized miners by improving their long-term condition proved too successful. Workers responded so enthusiastically to these efforts that the organization developed a momentum of its own that would bring the organization into conflict with the empire. The miners' strike of June 1869 and its tragic outcome would definitively unify the working classes under the republican banner and prepare the way for the development of a more politicized working-class movement.

Unfortunately, for the future of the imperial coalition, the government administration proved unable or unwilling to reward miners for providing their crucial votes. As we have seen, the election of de Charpin-Feugerolles had split the miners' movement. Militants such as Michel Rondet, who had resigned from *La Fraternelle* months before, now began openly to attack its leadership. As the days went by and no sign of concessions from the mining companies appeared, workers began to wonder if they had not been betrayed. The Prefect also found the coal companies unwilling to make concessions. Some of *La Fraternelle*'s highest leadership considered that only a strike could pressure the imperial administration into extracting concessions from the coal companies.

The exact circumstances for the outbreak of the strike remain unclear. Neither the society nor the major republican dissidents called for a strike on the day that it actually occurred and the call was probably issued by a fringe group of republican miners. The degree of mystery surrounding the outbreak of the strike could be explained by the ambiguity of the laws regulating strikes. While strikes had been legalized in 1864 and public meetings partially legalized in 1868, there was no official recognition of trade unions and rare legal recognition of meetings that might be called to discuss strike actions. The chances that officials would give permission for a meeting to take a strike vote were negligible. Applying for such a meeting was liable only to identify the leaders and to alert the officials to the likelihood of a forbidden meeting. Thus, most strikes were launched in a clandestine fashion, as was certainly the case here. On 11 June, a number of miners launched the strike movement as they stood on billiard tables in cafés in Firminy and addressed packed crowds of miners. From Firminy, the orators moved on to cafés in Le Chambon-Feugerolles and La Ricamarie.[39] Local miners who had heard that the Prefect had pledged to intercede for them and who were debating whether to strike had no way of knowing that the bands that called them out of the pits were not authorized to do so by the leadership of their mutual aid society.

Within a few hours of the Firminy assemblies, several bands of workers spread the strike through the western and central coal basins, with drums beating; some carried long sticks with silk ribbons streaming from them as they sang the *Marseillaise* and chanted "Down with Charpin! Long Live Bertholon! Long Live the Republic!"[40] As each band came to a mining pit, they demanded to be allowed to descend to call the miners out on strike. The strike betrayed no trace of the division between temporary migrants and permanent proletarians that had loomed so large in 1848. One incident suggests that migrants, at least migrants from the nearby Haute-Loire, participated enthusiastically in the strike. A band of strikers seeking to spread the strike informed a supervisor that if there were really fewer than three miners underground, as he was assuring them, they would cut the cable on the elevator to prevent further miners from descending. Evidently, the supervisor possessed a sense of humor and was able to identify these leaders' native origins by their accents. He informed them that if they touched the cable, he would see that the Haute-Loire was burned down.[41]

However uncertain its origins, the widespread support of the strike stimulated all factions of the mutual aid society to support it and provide leadership. On 15 June, miners throughout the region elected representatives to formulate demands and represent their interests to the employers. With these elections, the mutual aid society took control of the strike. Most pits and most mines elected representatives from the society, while some pits of one mining company elected a dissident, republican slate led by Michel Rondet. At the moment of decision in the midst of one of the most important strikes of the Second Empire, Stéphanois miners again revealed their concern with issues of primary interest to proletarians who expected to spend a long time on the job. Although the demands of the two groups differed somewhat, their major focus were the issues raised in early June when the Prefect had allegedly promised his mediation, workers' participation in the company insurance program, and a minimum wage – now a wage increase was added to these earlier demands. Once again, workers' participation in a centralized accident insurance program and a minimum wage emerged as the miners' greatest preoccupations. The prominence of issues of social security in social conflicts, issues such as those of accident insurance, clearly indicate the presence of a permanent proletariat.[42]

Unfortunately for the Prefect, who was still unable to extract concessions from the coal employers, the Minister of the Interior, Jean de Forcade-

Laroquette, responded vehemently to the outbreak of the strike. Perhaps the strike's outbreak, which nearly coincided with recent riots in Paris, suggested the presence of a conspiracy to the minister. On June 14, he ordered the Prefect to arrest the strike leaders, and on June 15, this counsel was reinforced with the order "be firm for the maintenance of order."[43]

The Prefect of the Loire was hardly so keen to repress the strike as was Forcade-Laroquette. He refused the Minister's offer of a large contingent of troops from Montbrison to reinforce the regular troops at his disposal.[44] Attempting to intimidate the strikers without displaying overwhelming force was a mistake. In the next few days after June 11, large bands of strikers roamed through the area trying to prevent the export of the coal that had already accumulated before the strike.[45] The Prefect was forced to disperse the troops at his disposal in tiny outposts stationed at every pit. With increasing frequency, small detachments of troops found themselves confronted by large crowds, in one case a crowd of over 2,000, chanting "To the guillotine" and "The captain to the chopper."[46]

The firmness of the central government response resulted in the loss of a first-class political opportunity to widen the gap between the miners and the republican camp. Dorian, the leader of the republican opposition, was among the first to violate the strike. Republican leaders, normally well-informed about developments in the labor movement, were completely caught off-guard, a fact that clearly indicates the unexpected character of the strike. Dorian had been expecting a strike but not so soon, and his metal company found itself with large orders to fill and a shortage of coal. Although the miners had made clear their opposition to the filling of orders for manufacturers, Dorian sent a crew of metalworkers to mines in Firminy to pick up coal. Just as they were starting to gather the coal, bands of miners appeared, and the metalworkers withdrew.[47] Dorian's embarrassment, in his case at having his men found breaking the strike, was shared by Captain Gausserand, commander of the soldiers protecting the metalworkers. The troops guarding the Montrambert mines might be accused of failing to protect Dorian's metalworkers, even though the metalworkers had withdrawn at the first sight of the miners. Consequently, a reinforced squadron marched out several hours later and managed to capture about 40 members of the band.[48]

To avoid making a public spectacle of the captured, who were being taken back to Saint-Etienne, the captain decided to take one of the few side roads that traversed the coal basin. He and his troops found themselves approaching the northern edge of the inhabited area between the commune of Le Chambon-Feugerolles and the commune of La Ricamarie. In fact, the decision to take a side route was a tactical mistake. Word had quickly spread about the arrests and about the route of the prison convoy; given the small number of roads that followed the valley, concealment was impossible. The narrow road was bounded on both sides by hills at the point where it met the built-up area on the outskirts of Le Chambon-Feugerolles. The troops conveying the prisoners thus quickly found themselves surrounded by a crowd of 800 men, women, and children, many of them relatives of the prisoners. Not only were they facing a large crowd, but on both sides there were small groups of spectators commanding the heights of the valley in which they marched.[49]

Despite differing accounts, in most important particulars the variations are those of perspective rather than of fact. According to the strikers, the women and children of the prisoners began to beg the troops to release their relatives; a local strike leader actually went to formally request the Captain to do so.[50] To the soldiers, it seemed that they were surrounded by a troop of women whose "frenzied cries and violent gestures augmented the exaltation of the crowd."[51] In desperation, rocks were thrown, and some in the crowd began to rush into the band of prisoners in an effort to free them. Without orders, but with the admitted concurrence of their superior, the troops charged and fired on the crowd.[52] Fourteen people were killed, including two women, one of them pregnant, a young girl, and a 15-month-old child. Dozens more were injured, some seriously.[53]

After this episode – the "massacre of La Ricamarie" as it would be called – all effort at reconciliation between the empire and the miners ended. In the plebiscite of 1870 following Napoleon III's liberal reforms, when all of France seemed to rally around the empire, Le Chambon-Feugerolles rejected it with a resounding 60 percent vote against.[54] While the brutal massacre undoubtedly played the key role in miners' rejection of the empire, perhaps ultimately more significant are the issues that sparked the miners' politicization and crystalized the strike movement in the first place. These issues arose both from the long-term context in which workers now viewed their jobs and from their new determination to reshape this context in a manner more favorable to themselves. As a result both of their efforts to better their long-term condition and of the events of La Ricamarie, the Stéphanois proletariat found itself unified within the republican party.

THE RISE OF THE MODERN LABOR MOVEMENT

The rise of the modern labor movement in the Stéphanois in the decade after 1869 was built on foundations laid in earlier periods. The socialist movement of the 1870s was a direct descendant of the working-class republicanism of the 1860s. Bourgeois republicans of the 1860s had helped to unify politically the Stéphanois working classes, albeit to accomplish their own political ends. Through their joint political battles with the bourgeois republicans, workers acquired a schooling in republican doctrine that helped them to articulate some of their most important concerns in a politically effective manner. But by the 1870s, this political alliance had begun to fracture. Increasingly, Stéphanois workers found themselves thrown into conflict with bourgeois republicans on issues of wages and industrial reform. Yet on many issues, especially family issues, conflict arose when workers built on the republican program that had been elaborated in the late 1860s.

Despite the fact that the conflict between working-class republicans and bourgeois republicans was intensifying, what was distinctive about the 1870s was the triumph of the political coalition of republicans and workers that had been formed in 1869. The brief outbreak of an uprising in Saint-Etienne in support of the Paris Commune led to a spate of repression that somewhat slowed down the development of a labor movement in the Stéphanois. The arrest or flight of many of radical working-class republicans, many of them republicans in the 1848 tradition, allowed men like Dorian to further consolidate their hold over the local republican party. But neither the uprising in Saint-Etienne nor the events of the Paris Commune fundamentally disrupted the course of development of the labor movement from the last days of the Second Empire. In the elections of 1876, the Loire became solidly republican.[55] Although Dorian died unexpectedly in 1873, the tradition of bourgeois leadership of the republican movement remained strong. The republican deputies from the Loire included Petrus Richarme, the glass magnate from Rive-de-Gier, and Emile Crozet-Fourneyron, who owned a metal plant in Le Chambon-Feugerolles. In 1876, César Bertholon finally won election as deputy. The republic took shape alongside working-class institutions. Although their legal situation was unsettled and their existence precarious, trade unions began to spring up after 1874 throughout the Stéphanois, particularly in Rive-de-Gier, Saint-Chamond and Saint-Etienne. In 1876, a miners' union was once again organized in Saint-Etienne and Rive-de-Gier.[56]

The best indicator of the development of class consciousness among working-class leaders in the Stéphanois is the records of national labor congresses. In 1877, after the initial republican electoral victory of February, republican workers throughout the country began to organize and to discuss the development of working-class politics and action. The first congress, held in 1877, declared: "From the moment that the republican form of government was assured, it was indispensable for the working class, which had marched until then together with the republican bourgeoisie, to affirm its own interests and to seek the means by which it could transform its economic condition."[57] Delegates from Saint-Chamond and Saint-Etienne were among the 37 provincial towns represented at the first working-man's congress in Paris in 1877.[58]

The Stéphanois was better represented in the 1878 congress held in Lyon, where its delegates actively participated in the exciting debates of that year. An English observer at the Lyonnais congress caught the spirit very well:

My first impression conveyed is this, that Communism, or indeed any systematic Socialism, is entirely extinct in France. The difference is conspicuous between the language now used and that of some thirty years ago ... Throughout the whole proceedings ... the names of Fourier, Cabet, L. Blanc did not once occur. Proudhon is quoted, not as a systematic socialist, but for incidental reflections. I do not think that the doctrines of any school, much less the schemes of any practical socialism, are advocated by any single delegate.[59]

Despite the absence of organized socialism at Lyon, the observer also noted that "the assembly is altogether socialist in one sense."

It is socialist in the sense that every man of them insists that the economic relations of society are not in a healthy state, that they must be transformed in the future of civilization is to advance. They cry out that the condition of labor is radically wrong somewhere, that it is not in a permanent shape at all, and that its condition is often heartrending.[60]

If the Lyonnais congress of 1878 testified that French workers were grappling with new problems, the Congress of Marseilles in 1879 saw the appearance of a new solution: collectivist socialism. This congress was one of the two or three turning points in the history of the French labor movement – such as the trade union congress of Amiens in 1906 or the Socialist party congress of Tours in 1920 – when a new and enduring strategy was adopted by the assembled representatives of the working classes. The nearly two-year period between the Congress of Lyon and the Congress of Marseilles witnessed a dramatic change in the orientation of labor leaders both in the Stéphanois and throughout France. At Marseilles, French Marxists made their first appearance and, with their aid, the congress announced its support for socialism. Among the vanguard of supporters for nationalization was the delegation from the Stéphanois. Yet their support for collectivism did not indicate unquestioning adherence to Marxism; the roots of Stéphanois socialism can be found within the working-class critique of republican doctrines that evolved from the social struggles of permanent proletarians.

Important changes were occurring in the Stéphanois in the late 1870s. For one, the economic depression that began toward the end of 1876 was particularly severe in the Stéphanois.[61] Although its larger significance escaped the notice of contemporaries, the depression of the 1870s effectively ended the leadership role of the Stéphanois in France's industrial transformation. After the mid-1870s, the Stéphanois would struggle to adapt and to preserve itself against steelmakers in the east of France and coal producers in the north. The particular severity of the depression in the Stéphanois was the sign of the beginning of real restructuring of political alignment.[62] The growing precariousness of the Stéphanois economy in the 1870s served to push workers to the left, but in a direction already anticipated by the political developments of the 1860s.

The increase of strikes in the 1870s also brought increased conflict between republicans industrialists and Stéphanois workers. The attempt of industrialists to avoid large strikes through the invocation of republican loyalty reflected poorly on the republican cause. In March 1878, a month after the Lyonnais Congress, female textile workers in Saint-Chamond joined male dyers on strike. The republican municipality posted the following proclamation through-out the city:

> We invite the striking workingmen and workingwomen to return as soon as possible to the workshop.
>
> The miners' strike in the Nord, following the failure of the Bonapartist candidate, served the interests of our political adversaries.
>
> We very much fear that they will profit from this situation in view of the coming senatorial elections.
>
> In the name of the republic which we all love: we will serve as intermediaries among the patrons to improve your lot as soon as commercial circumstances will permit.[63]

At the same time, a republican newspaper, *Le Petit Lyonnais*, hinted that the republican administration was suspicious that "clericals and Bonapartists" had provoked the strike.[64] The resignation of MacMahon from the Presidency in January of 1879 also removed an immediate threat to the republic's existence and left workers freer to criticize fellow republicans.

The economic depression, the conservatism of local republicans, and the presence of Marxist socialists at the next working-class congress all served to stimulate and radicalize Stéphanois working-class leaders. But by themselves, neither the business downturn nor the internal division within the republican camp will sufficiently explain the origin of socialism in the Stéphanois. Only in the context of a permanent proletariat with a long history of conflict and a well-developed political consciousness do these factors prove politically signifi-cant. At the Congress of Marseilles in 1879, Stéphanois militants were at the forefront in promoting the adhesion of that body to socialism. All five delegates from the Stéphanois were on the list of 63 delegates who formally proposed that the congress reject the old-style associationism. They believed in the "absolute sterility of repurchases, of cooperation, of the alliance of capital and labor."[65] They wanted the congress to declare "that the collective appropriation of all the instruments of work and the forces of production, must be pursued by all possible means."[66]

The socialism that Stéphanois workers embraced at Marseilles grew from the republican convictions forged under the Second Empire. Despite what seems a dramatic turnabout in position between the Congress of Lyon and the Congress of Marseilles, the arguments advanced by Stéphanois delegates to the congress reveal that their adherence to socialism remained within the context of their previous experience, aims, and political beliefs. At Marseilles, Louis Goudefer, a mechanic from Saint-Etienne and delegate of the city's workers' societies, simply took up the argument that republicans had used to rally workers against the vestiges of coal monopoly and applied it to attack capitalism generally. Goudefer's basic criticism of capitalism sounds Marxian, but it is more likely only another application of the argument that Stéphanois republicans had used in 1869 to defend the position of the coal miners' families and to condemn the mining monopoly:

The worker, having nothing of his own to work with, is forced to rent his labor, without always being able to discuss freely the conditions [of its rental], this renders wages insufficient and paralyzes saving, without which old age became an expiation for a life completely sacrificed to work.[67]

While his argument appealed to those raised in the school of Stéphanois republicanism, it also made concessions to the associationist tradition. Goudefer attempted to reconcile those committed to associationism by incorporating this doctrine into a larger strategy. Speaking of producers' and consumers' associations, he explained that "if we favor these associations presently, it is because of the difficulty of leading the indifferent masses to our trade unions." Associations could be valuable in "easing proletarian life" and in inculcating the "necessity of social evolution." But along with the bourgeois republicans, Goudefer saw the trade union as the major vehicle for representing workers under capitalism.[68]

Like Goudefer, other Stéphanois workers used republican doctrines to express their own deeply felt needs and beliefs. Republicanism provided a way of articulating the new sense of working-class unity that the republicans had helped to create, and it enabled workers to convey family concerns that stemmed from the demographic and economic processes of class formation. The republican socialist doctrines defined by local workers allowed them to demarcate themselves from the industrialists, while still defining a common territory where they could work together. Socialists appealed to workers' grievances and frustrations, but by the 1870s these grievances were those of workers long experienced with the ways of industrial capitalism. Workers were less concerned about the means of forming democratic associations to run production, as they had been in 1848, than they were about advocating a form of socialism that provided equal education and compassion for the sick and injured. Although local socialists were bitterly critical of industrial capitalism, their own critique was shaped in important ways by the dominance of the new industrial order.

Perhaps the most dramatic statement of class issues and of the continuity of working-class concerns was that of the Stéphanois miner, Antoine Forissier, from Le Chambon-Feugerolles. No other speaker reveals so clearly how membership in a permanent proletariat, family solidarity, and violated personal rights could merge together effectively into class consciousness. In several addresses, Forissier called the attention of the congress to the ways in which the coal companies policies on accident insurance exploited miners by manipulating family loyalty. He cited the example of the adolescent miner pushed by greedy supervisors, who would none the less "kill his body in order to keep his place" in the mines, in order to "work and contribute to provide bread for his younger brothers."[69] He denounced the intimidation used by the mining companies to force miners to perjure themselves about company liability for accidents. He claimed that a worker "finds himself father of a family, [and] in order to provide bread for his children, he lies to his conscience."[70]

Forissier's discussion of pension benefits reveals that his conception of the role of the working-class family, at least under capitalism, differed little from that of the republicans of 1869. The republican argument was well-suited to Stéphanois miners; it asserted that in a market society the working-class family deserved special consideration in order to protect the growing child. This meant that miners must be paid sufficient money to send their children to school while worker control of accident and sickness insurance would permit education even in family adversity. Family concerns were the major justification for the miners' continuing demand, voiced by Forissier again in 1879, that the companies' control over insurance programs be legally limited. For Forissier, as for the republicans of the 1860s, the family was the social institution *par excellence* for the instillation of morality into the child. He argued:

If the widow's pension was brought to 1 franc, and that of the orphan to fifty centimes per day, one would see fewer prostitutes among the widows, and the children would be able to learn a little morality; in place of becoming vagabonds, they would be honest citizens who would be able to serve the republic with honor and fidelity, instead of peopling the prisons . . .[71]

As his speech proceeded, with examples of miners' widows and orphans deprived of adequate support, Forissier virtually transformed the miners' struggle into a battle between employers and their families and workers and their families. He argued:

Ah yes! messieurs of the monopoly, we are the yokels and the financial tools from which you profit every day by providing you the means to support yourselves generously and your families, and you have only to pass your claw-like fingers . . . to collect our sweat and blood which escapes from our mutilated bodies and you will find enough gold in order to make a dowry for your daughters and to provide enough of a fortune to your sons that they may come to steal our children.[72]

The day before, in a speech to the congress, Forissier had recalled the roots of Stéphanois republicanism in 1848 and concluded:

we miners and sons of miners . . . we aspire to be one day the worthy children of the democratic and social Republic.[73]

While Forissier's pride in being a miner's son reveals an outlook different from that of his father's generation, his reference to the "democratic and social republic," suggests that the tradition that had perhaps inspired the father remained alive alongside the socialist theories advocated by the son. While agreeing with most republican demands, Forissier saw them only as preparatory steps towards a socialist republic. Forissier no longer believed that the whole solution would be found in the republicanism of the Dorian's and Bertholon's. Like them, he placed his faith in "freedom of association and of conscience, equality before the law," but he believed that these republican goals could only be obtained by "fraternity among the workers," and the expropriation of industry by them.[74] The "democratic and social Republic" advocated by the son was different from that which rallied the miners in 1848. Unlike both bourgeois republicans and the associationists of 1848, Forissier believed that the democratic and social republic necessitated the abolition of the bourgeoisie and the collectivization of property by the state and the formation of a separate workers' party.

The Congress of Marseilles of 1879 began the construction of a socialist party in France and in the Stéphanois, and a branch of the *Parti ouvrier français* was founded in Saint-Etienne in 1880.[75] This early socialist party marks only the beginnings of the modern French labor movement. It would take several decades and a series of other battles before a strong and independent socialist movement was constructed in the Stéphanois. The very ease with which local working-class republicans had made the transition to socialist politics also made it easy for them to return to the republican fold in times of reduced social conflict. But the socialist breakthrough at Marseilles was not to be reversed, and socialist parties had gained a significant foothold in the Stéphanois, one which they were not to lose.

The growth of socialism among semi-skilled workers in the Stéphanois was greatly facilitated by those republicans who united the working classes on a common political platform and inculcated in workers a critique of paternalistic capitalism that could be extended to the entire capitalist system. But the appeal of republicanism, its ability to mobilize proletarianized workers, in turn depended on the presence of a permanent proletariat already engaged in a bitter struggle to defend itself and its family members from complete subservience to industrial capital.

NOTES

1 *Discours et plaidoyers politiques de M. Gambetta*, ed. Joseph Reinach, (Paris, Charpentier, 1881), vol. 3, p. 8. On the relationship between Gambetta, Dorian, and *La Gauche Républicaine* of 1870–1, see Frank Herbert Brabant, *The Beginning of the Third Republic* (London, Macmillan, 1940), pp. 402–3. According to E. A. Vizetelly, Dorian "was the only man of the ruling band that emerged from the trials of the Siege of Paris with an enhanced reputation," *Republican France, 1870–1912* (London, Holden & Hardingham, 1912) p. 14. After the end of the Franco-Prussian War, Dorian and Gambetta were reconciled, see J. P. T. Bury, *Gambetta and the Making of the Third Republic* (London, Longman, 1973), pp. 114–15.
2 Ibid., pp. 101–2.
3 *Séances de la 3eme session du Congrès ouvrier de France, Marseilles 20–31, octobre 1879* (Marseilles, J. Doucet, 1879), p. 387.
4 In the legislative elections of 1852, 25.4 percent of all voters in the *arrondissement* of Saint-Etienne went to the left opposition; in 1857, 31.9 percent; and in 1863, 48.7

percent. See Jean Merley, "Les élections de 1869 dans le département de la Loire," *Cahiers d'Histoire* 6 (1) (1961), pp. 59–93, esp. p. 73.

5 David M. Gordon, *Merchants and Capitalists: Industrialization and Provincial Politics in Mid-Nineteenth Century France* (Alabama, University of Alabama Press, 1985), pp. 84–5.

6 For a survey of French education in the period, see R. D. Anderson, *Education in France, 1848–1870* (Oxford, Clarendon Press, 1975). On education in Saint-Etienne, Joseph N. Moody, *French Education since Napoleon* (Syracuse, Syracuse University Press, 1978), p. 76.

7 Gras, *Histoire économique générale des mines de la Loire*, p. 531.

8 Albert Thomas, *Le Second Empire (1852–1870)*, (Paris, Jules Rouff et cie., 1904), p. 68.

9 Gordon, *Merchants and Capitalists*, p. 108.

10 Testimony at the Tribunal correctionnel de Saint-Etienne, Audience de 3 août; reprinted in *L'Eclaireur*, August 4, 1869.

11 Gras, *Histoire économique générale*, p. 532.

12 Testimony at the Tribunal correctionnel de Saint-Etienne, Audience de 3 août; reprinted in *L'Eclaireur*, August 4, 1869.

13 Comparison of the members of *La Fraternelle* identified in the competing strike committees of 1869 shows that the overwhelming number were concentrated in Saint-Etienne and the western basin; only a handful came from the eastern basin which joined the strike a day after it had begun.

14 Testimony at the Tribunal correctionnel de Saint-Etienne, Audience de 2 août; reprinted in *L'Eclaireur*, August 3, 1869.

15 "On a dit qu'en 1848 les ouvriers avaient déjà nommé des délégués, et que le résultat obtenu etait mauvais: ce n'etait plus la même chose: les ouvriers nommaient leurs maîtres mineurs; mais l'ouvrier d'aujourd'hui n'est plus l'ouvrier de 1848; cet réclame aujourd'hui c'est en vue de la securité de l'ouvrier et de la bonne exploitation des mines." Michel Rondet, Rapport A. Girard, Chambre des députés, séance du 3 avril 1884, annexe no. 2760, pp. 704–5.

16 *L'Eclaireur*, January 31, 1869.

17 *L'Eclaireur*, June 13, 1869.

18 Harold Perkin, *The Origins of Modern English Society* (London, Routledge and Kegan Paul, 1969), p. 375.

19 *L'Eclaireur*, September 27, 1869.

20 *L'Eclaireur*, September 25, 1869.

21 Ibid.

22 On the changed attitude of the republicans of the 1860s towards associationism and trade unionism, see the very interesting article by Jeanne Gaillard, "Les associations de production et la pensée politique en France (1852–1870)," *Le mouvement social* 52 (1965), pp. 59–84.

23 *L'Eclaireur*, October 19, 1869.

24 Ibid.

25 *L'Eclaireur*, September 27, 1869.

26 *L'Eclaireur*, October 8, 1869.

27 *L'Eclaireur*, September 27, 1869.

28 According to Sanford Elwitt, "Dorian had originally intended for one of his lieutenants, Martin Bernard, to contest Saint-Etienne's seat for the Legislative

Body. But rather than run the risk of a weak candidate being eclipsed by a socialist, Dorian himself stood for election" (Banford Elwitt, *The Making of the Third Republic: Class and Politics in France: 1868–1884* (Baton Rouge, Louisiana State University Press, 1975), p. 84). There may be something to this, but it is not entirely plausible. First of all, far from being one of Dorian's "lieutenants," Martin Bernard was a very well-known and widely beloved veteran of 1839 and 1848 who was exiled in 1851, who had more credibility among workers than either Dorian or Martin in 1869. As far as I know there is no reason to doubt Martin Bernard's published explanation that he withdrew because ultimately, as a veteran of 1848, he could not take the oath to the empire required of all those elected (*L'Eclaireur*, April 12, 1869). If there were other reasons, they are neither cited in the evidence in Elwitt's notes or discussed in Latta's biography of Bernard (Claude Latta, *Un républicain méconnu: Martin Bernard 1808–1883* (Saint-Etienne, Centre d'études Foréziennes, 1980).)

The reliability of Elwitt's treatment of this incident is not strengthened by his misunderstandings of events. He claims that in 1869 Dorian, "coordinated the employers' anti-strike action" (p. 84). Actually, Dorian and Dorian's newspaper supported the strike. According to Elwitt, "Martin's campaign speeches inflamed class hatred and . . . recalled Dorian's role as strikebreaker" (p. 84). The problem here is that the election came *before* the strike, in which Dorian did, in the terms described in the chapter, play the role of strikebreaker. On 6 December 1869, *L'Eclaireur* answered a charge printed in *La Réforme* that Dorian had broken the strike. It claimed that he didn't know that the miners were opposing the hauling from the mines of coal that had already been dug and that he was out of town when his men went to take delivery. In view of the fact that the miners had already prevented several efforts to take delivery of coal at other mines, this first reason does not seem very credible and, even if he was not personally responsible, the charge of strikebreaking against Dorian seems well-founded.

29 For a brief sketch of César Bertholon's life, see *L'Eclaireur*, March 23, 1869.

30 See Merley, "Les élections de 1869 dans le département de la Loire," p. 77.

31 Testimony of Chapelardot to the Tribunal correctionnel de Saint-Etienne, Audience de 2 août, reprinted in *L'Eclaireur*, August 3, 1869. Taking the government position, he stressed: "Non, il [the Prefect] nous a seulement promis d'être notre intermédiaire, mais n'a rien promis *absolument*" (italics in original).

32 The similarity between the two programs was probably more than coincidental. Both Gambetta and Bertholon likely drew on Jules Simon, see J. P. T. Bury, *Gambetta and the National Defence: A Republican Dictatorship in France* (New York, Howard Fertig, 1936), p. 17. Letters from Jules Simon appeared in *L'Eclaireur*, Simon was a firm advocate of the need to defend individual rights. On Simon, see Claude Nicolet, *L'Idée républicaine en France (1789–1924)* (Paris, Gallimard, 1982), pp. 154–5. Positivist republicanism so current at the end of the Second Empire hardly seems to have penetrated the Stéphanois.

In a sense, the attitude of Stéphanois republicans toward the "social question" was embodied in Gambetta's celebrated speech at Le Havre on 18 April 1872. Gambetta declared that: "Believe me there is no social remedy because there is not a social question. There is a series of problems to be resolved, of difficulties to be overcome, which vary according to localities, climates, customs and sanitary conditions, economic problems which change within the interior of a single country;

well, these problems must be resolved one by one and not by a single formula . . .":
see Bury, *Gambetta and the Making of the Third Republic,* pp. 98–99. Stéphanois
republicans saw the remnants of the coal monopoly as one of a "series of problems,"
"difficulties to be overcome." The transformation of Stéphanois republicanism into
republican socialism occurred as workers began to see the exception as the rule.

33 *L'Eclaireur,* September 10, 1869.

34 *L'Eclaireur,* June 5, 1869.

35 *L'Eclaireur,* May 24, 1869.

36 The director of the mines of Roche-la-Molière et Firminy, June 1, 1869, ADL
15/J/2655.

37 *L'Eclaireur,* June 4, 1869.

38 In Le Chambon-Feugerolles, the Comte de Charpin-Feugerolles received 932
votes, Bertholon 480; in Firminy, 1,013 for Charpin, 1,414 for Bertholon; in
Rive-de-Gier, 836 for Charpin, 1,486 for Bertholon; and in Saint-Chamond, 677
for Charpin, 1,360 for Bertholon. See *L'Eclaireur,* June 13, 1869.

39 Testimony to the Tribunal correctionnel de Saint-Etienne, Audience de 2 août,
reprinted in *L'Eclaireur,* August 3, 1869. There is a possibility that the International
was involved in the outbreak of the strike. In this regard, attention has been focused
on the character of "red Micol," the violent agitator who played an important role in
the days preceding the strike, but who disappeared shortly after its commencement.
On Micol and his associates, see the statement of the *procureur impérial* at the
Tribunal correctionnel de Saint-Etienne, Audience de 5 août, reprinted in *L'Eclaireur,* August 6, 1869. At the miners' trial the government tried to suggest that the
strike was really political, provoked by the republicans at *L'Eclaireur;* see testimony at
the Tribunal correctionnel de Saint-Etienne, Audience de 5 août, reprinted in
L'Eclaireur, August 6, 1869. Probably as valid a point as any was made by the
reactionary industrialist, Euverte, who declared, "La politique se mêlait à la question
des salaires," see testimony to the Tribunal correctionnel de Saint-Etienne, Audience de 4 août, reprinted in *L'Eclaireur,* August 5, 1869. The mining director at
Roche-la-Molière et Firminy believed that, "In the beginning, we had to deal with a
political uprising, today the uprising becomes a strike," see June 14, ADL 15/J/
2655. On the first day of the strike, one leader announced that they were "not
striking but making the revolution," testimony to the Tribunal correctionnel de
Saint-Etienne, Audience de 2 août, reprinted in *L'Eclaireur,* August 3, 1869.

40 Testimony to the Tribunal correctionnel de Saint-Etienne, Audience de 3 et 4 août,
reprinted in *L'Eclaireur,* August 4 and 5, 1869.

41 *L'Eclaireur,* August 6, 1869.

42 On the election of workers' representatives and the strike demands, see Bernard
Delabre, "La grève de 1869 dans le bassin minier Stéphanois," *Etudes Foréziennes* 4
(1971), pp. 109–38, esp. pp. 121–3.

43 Thomas, *Le Second Empire,* p. 350; and Fernand L'Huillier, *La lutte ouvrière à la fin
du Second Empire* (Paris, Armand Colin, 1957), pp. 24–7.

44 Ibid., p. 47.

45 Testimony to the Tribunal correctionnel de Saint-Etienne, Audience de 3 août,
reprinted in *L'Eclaireur,* August 4, 1869. One of the miners who was mistreated
emphasized the role of women: "Les femmes nous insultaient. La femme Largeron
nous tirait les oreilles. On a voulu me faire boire de l'eau ou on avait lavé du linge."

46 "Au couperet le capitain." Testimony at the Tribunal correctionnel de Saint-Etienne, Audience de 3 août, reprinted in *L'Eclaireur*, August 4, 1869.
47 Gausserand's June 17 report to his commandant, reported in *L'Eclaireur*, June 18, 1869.
48 Ibid.
49 Described in the celebrated "massacre" issue of *L'Eclaireur*, of June 17, in the article by Emile Critot, "Le massacre du puits Saint-Quentin." Later, the paper was fined the heavy sum of 3,491.65 francs for "fausses nouvelles, excitation de haine et au mépris du governement et au mépris des citoyens les uns contre les autres," see *L'Eclaireur*, July 10, 1869.
50 Testimony of Durand to the Tribunal correctionnel de Saint-Etienne, Audience de 3 août, reprinted in *L'Eclaireur*, August 4, 1869.
51 Gausserand's June 17 report to his commandant, reported in *L'Eclaireur*, June 18, 1869.
52 Ibid.
53 On the victims see the report on "enterrement des victimes" from the *Moniteur universel*, reprinted in *L'Eclaireur*, June 25, 1869.
54 ADL 2/M/4.
55 On the commune in Saint-Etienne, see the records of the "Cour d'assises du Puy-de-Dôme," published in *L'Eclaireur* between 17–20 November 1871. The best indicators of the coal miners' attitudes are the reports of the company supervisors. In a letter of March 27, 1871 to his superiors, the director of the mines of Roche-la-Molière et Firminy reported that "up to the present order has not been troubled here, although the entire population went to the city yesterday [this was a Sunday] to see what was going on." In a letter dated March 28, he added that the workers had been "perfectly calm" Saturday, March 25, and concluded that "for the moment" the troubles at Saint-Etienne were over. See ADL 15/J/2655.
   On the elections of 1876, see Latta, *Un républicain méconnu*, pp. 247–57. On the continuity of the labor movement between the Second Empire and the early Third Republic, see Aimée Moutet, "Le mouvement ouvrier à Paris au lendemain de la Commune au premier congrès syndical en 1876," *Le mouvement social* 58 (Jan.–March 1967), pp. 3–39.
56 On strikes and trade unions in the Stéphanois in the 1870s, see ADL 92/M/15. L.-J. Gras also gives a list of the founding dates of some important local trade unions in his *Histoire du commerce local* (Saint-Etienne, Theolier, 1910), pp. 382–3.
57 Quoted from Bernard H. Moss, *The Origins of the French Labor Movement, 1830–1914: The Socialism of Skilled Workers* (Berkeley, Cal., University of California Press, 1976), p. 66.
58 *Séances de la 2eme session du Congrès ouvrier de France, Lyon, 28 janvier–8 février 1878* (Lyon, J. Trichot, 1878).
59 Frederic Harrison, "The French Workmen's Congress," *The Fortnightly Review*, new series, 23 (May 1878), pp. 662–77, esp. pp. 662–3.
   Of all major figures on the French left, Pierre-Joseph Proudhon was the least influential among Stéphanois militants. In his *Systeme des contradictions économiques, ou philosophie de la misère*, published in 1846, Proudhon had condemned the miners' strike in Rive-de-Gier and even approved the fusillade that had helped bring the strike to a close with the deaths of two young men. In his *De la capacité politique des*

classes ouvrières, published after his death, Proudhon approvingly quoted his whole discussion of the Ripagérien strike. Commenting on the military repression at La Grand-Croix on April 5, 1844, Proudhon wrote: "le fait à relever ici, par le juriste et l'économiste, n'est pas le nombre des morts et des blessés: cela regarde l'hôpital: c'est le principe meme de la repression. Les ouvriers etiaent-ils dans leur droit . . .", *De la Capacité politique* (Paris, Marcel Rivière, 1924), p. 377. Such sentiments were hardly likely to win the hearts of local miners.

60 Ibid., p. 663.

61 According to Willard Long Thorp's *Business Annals* (New York, NBER, 1926), p. 190, 1876 in France began a "gradual recession" when "industry slowly relapses into dullness." 1877 saw a mild depression and 1878 a deepened depression; the revival began in 1879. For the Stéphanois, however, the quarterly prefectoral reports record a fairly satisfactory year with an pick-up in the last quarter of 1876; the depression seems to have begun in the Stéphanois in the first quarter of 1877. See AN-F12/4511B.

62 Yves Lequin, *Les ouvriers de la région lyonnaise (1848–1914)* 2 vols (Lyon, Presses Universitaires de Lyon, 1977), vol. 1, p. 76.

63 Archives de la préfecture de police, Ba 171.

64 *Le Petit Lyonnais*, July 25, 1878.

65 *Séances de la 3eme session du Congrès ouvrier de France, Marseille 20–31, octobre 1879* (Marseilles, J. Doucet, 1879), p. 717.

66 Ibid.

67 Ibid., p. 235.

68 Ibid., p. 236.

69 Ibid., p. 69.

70 Ibid., p. 468.

71 Ibid., p. 468.

72 Ibid., p. 467.

73 Ibid., p. 72.

74 Ibid., p. 472.

75 In Saint-Etienne, after 1882, Brousse's "Parti Ouvrier Socialiste Révolutionnaire Français" (POSR) organized most local trade unions. A list of its supporters is found on pp. 197–8 of the Congress Report. The miners however did not participate as a group; initially they asked for a block vote and then they withdrew altogether. The declarations passed at this congress show a substantial degree of Marxist influence, although the POSR was the major opponent of the Guesdist Marxists in France. See Parti ouvrier Socialiste Révolutionnaire Français, *Compte rendu du sixième congrès national tenu à Saint-Etienne du 25 au 31 septembre 1882* (Paris, aux bureaux du Prolétaire, 1882).

Conclusion

A new type of worker appeared in the Stéphanois region of France in the years between 1840 and 1880, the male semi-skilled industrial worker. A special attention to industrial workers does not imply that they were the only contributors to the labor movement or to local social protest; the ribbonweavers of Saint-Etienne and the glassworkers of Rive-de-Gier certainly contributed their share. The concentration on the male semi-skilled industrial worker and his family stems from their newness. Whereas the history of artisanal protest in the Stéphanois can be traced back beyond the French Revolution to the Wars of Religion, the history of the semi-skilled industrial proletariat begins in the 1840s. Focusing on the male semi-skilled worker provides an opportunity to look at the birth of a new social group and at the origins of social and political consciousness. It draws attention to how economic and social conditions interact with political circumstances to create collective identities.

Looking at class formation calls attention to men's and women's experiences before they became workers or members of working-class families and to the processes which led to their entering the working class. In many European countries, the formation of a proletariat in agriculture preceded and supplied the labor force for the development of the urban industrial proletariat. In the Stéphanois, urban industrial development occurred first, and only later did a permanent industrial proletariat really develop. The timing of proletarianization is important because it can provide insight into the historical background to working-class development. Despite the beginnings of the French Industrial Revolution in the Stéphanois in the 1820s, the Stéphanois proletariat was born during the turbulent years of the 1840s and of the Second Empire. These years provided the context in which proletarian culture and the political attitudes it reinforced would first grow and develop. An emphasis on the origins of an enduring working-class also draws attention to issues of reproduction as well as production; nineteenth-century social classes were reproduced by means of families. Family formation is concomitant with class formation. In order to constitute an enduring social class, proletarian men and women had to successfully raise children in a murderous industrial environment and to prepare them for industrial employment. In an age when neither state nor church was very forthcoming with aid, men and women had to provide against the decline in earnings caused by accident, illness, and old age.

What made it possible for men and women to attempt to maintain proletarian families in the city was the changing nature of male industrial employment. The creation of long-term employment patterns in heavy industry enabled male workers to identify themselves with specific industries and to plan their lives and the lives of their male children based on the demands and opportunities available in the industry in which they worked. `

The changing character of adult male employment for non-artisanal workers in the Stéphanois had immediate and important implications for their families. The male head's occupation influenced his proneness to accident and illness, his life-time pattern of earnings, how many children he and his wife would have, and whether the children would be sent regularly to school. Even as the world of work and the world of family became increasingly separate, the world of work continued to exert considerable influence over the world of family.

But the relationship between work and family was too complicated to be unilaterally determined by the conditions of adult male employment. A look at the long-term evolution of less-skilled work, shows that transient, seasonal employment for men and women was being replaced by permanent long-term employment for adult males. But at the same time as males followed a life course dictated by the newer and slower rhythm of an industrial career, children continued to follow the older, more erratic and rapidly changing rhythms of seasonal and transient work. The rhythm of seasonal and transient employment was harder to follow after 1840 than before, because formerly men and women had been free to move to where the work was. With the family's geographic location fixed by the head's permanent employment, adolescent children were less able to respond to employment opportunities. If work was available for them in the neighborhood, adolescent children usually took it; but if it was not, they were left unemployed. As a result, even when male household heads were involved in the same occupation and received the same wages, household earnings could vary considerably from community to community, depending on the availability of work for women and children. In hard times, when adult male earnings dropped, the ability of children to earn wages might be the difference between cutting corners and genuine hunger.

To fully understand the relationship between work and family in the Stéphanois, the employers' behavior must also be considered. Intrinsic to semi-skilled work was the employer's investment in his worker. The employer trained him, or at least kept him employed until he learned the job from his workmates. Employers in an old industrial area such as the Stéphanois were conscious that their supply of proletarians put them at an advantage compared with the newly developing industrial regions of France. Perhaps declining fertility was a factor here, and French employers may have been more acutely conscious of the problems of labor scarcity here than elsewhere. But in any case, employers wanted to preserve their labor force in place even during times of temporary downturn.

The strategies employers used to maintain their workforce often sparked protest. The semi-skilled workers in the Stéphanois received higher wages than the casual and temporary workforce that surrounded them. But at the same time, employers' efforts to maintain their workforce by manipulation of accident and pension plans and by narrowing workers' training were bound to provoke workers' anger. All the more because such schemes directly affected workers' families and the welfare of wives and children. To many workers, it seemed that employers were holding workers' families hostage against their own faithful behavior. Workers' efforts to maintain a family life distinct from their work were only partially successful but, under the conditions of heavy industrial employment, it became a goal fought for by industrial workers and their families. In those communities where employment opportunities for children were limited, the task of preserving family independence from employers was especially difficult and demanding.

In such circumstances, hostility was bound to develop among miners and metalworkers in the Stéphanois. Employers' manipulation of their labor force inevitably provoked hostility and the decline in income from adolescent employment, where it occurred, was sure to provide hardship. But these developments were not certain to produce class antagonism. Bitter hostility was generated most frequently in the mines, where employer manipulation was routine and consequential, where concern about illness and accident was greatest and where, in communities such as La Chambon-Feugerolles, female workers watched employment opportunities decline. The miners' high fertility also made them especially sensitive to economic down-turns. But miners might have vented their anger in many ways. The Napoleonic state made a valiant effort to make the miners loyal clients of the state machine, and for a brief moment succeeded. That the various groups of semi-skilled workers might join together among themselves and alongside other workers was only one possibility inherent in the social and economic situation of the 1860s.

Political coalitions were crucial in taking advantage of workers' concerns and in bringing workers together politically. The struggle for the republic and the revolts against the established order provide an indispensable context for understanding the development of class identity. In the 1860s, republican employers served as a bridge for the creation of working-class unity. The men who dominated local republican politics in the 1860s were very different from those of 1848. In 1848, small shopkeepers, artisans, and professional men had led the republican cause and encouraged workers to consider alternatives to large-scale capitalism, even though these bourgeois republicans recoiled as soon as workers took them seriously. By the 1860s however, the local republican cause was led by industrialists who took for granted the existence of capitalism and of social classes. The republican industrialists' commitment to competitive individualism limited their ability to appeal to workers, but family issues constituted an area where republicans could win workers' support. Even vigorous individualists conceded that, if an adult's situation should be considered of his own making, the child's situation should not. The demand for the expansion of educational opportunities for working-class children, with its criticism of a manifestly inadequate clerical education, was a handy stick with which republicans could beat the empire. Republicans also charged that workers' forced contributions to insurance and retirement funds over which they had no control limited workers' individual decision-making in unacceptable ways.

Despite their hesitation, workers finally banded together behind the republican banner, and it was from the republican ranks that working-class socialism tentatively emerged in the 1870s. This socialism retained many links to its middle-class origins. It remained suspicious of the state while at the same time focusing its attention on education and on providing workers' security against accident, illness, and old age. Class struggle would wring these victories from employers and pave the way for a vaguely defined cooperative commonwealth. Disappearing from the factory and mine were those traditions of 1848 that attempted to join together workers' immediate grievances with plans for democratizing the work place. They disappeared as capitalism consolidated its hold over the workforce and as a new generation of workers grew up who had known only the regime of industrial capitalism. Less aware than their predecessors of alternatives to industrial capitalism, workers in the 1870s were most sensitive to the daily grievances inflicted on them and their families by industrial capitalism.

By 1880, Stéphanois semi-skilled workers had taken some important steps in the direction of constituting themselves as part of a class. Some of the most prominent leaders of the local labor movement had identified themselves as socialists and socialism was beginning to make progress among the electorate. Still, it would be misleading to speak about the Stéphanois industrial working class as having been "formed" by 1880. First of all, socialist ideas were still far from firmly implanted in the working classes. For several decades to come, left-republicans, reformist socialists, orthodox socialists, and revolutionary syndicalists would alternately win and lose the support of the mass of workers. The bitter mass struggles of the years between 1890 and 1914 were required to root socialist and syndicalist ideas tenaciously among the mass of workers.

More importantly, the very language of "class formation" is misleading if it suggests that class formation is an irreversible process like that of concrete hardening. Class is a far more pliable relationship; once formed, class relationships are almost continually reforming. No one series of events in the development of the Stéphanois labor movement fatally and forever determined the growth of class consciousness. But over decades, an accumulation of social developments and social actions served to institutionalize class consciousness within the organized labor movement and to spread it widely within the working classes.

As we have seen, the development of class in the Stéphanois was a product of economic and social forces common to many industrial proletariats and a series of economic and political developments specific to France. Class formation among the Stéphanois workers reveals only one pattern of class development but an important one. It suggests that in the case of class formation among industrial workers, the work of both labor historians and family historians is required. But the development of class in the Stéphanois should be seen as important not because it foreshadows or predicts similar developments in other countries of the world, but because it sheds light on *French* class formation. To understand one significant portion of French class formation is to gain some insight into the development of class consciousness in France and in the modern world. Through its influence on intellectuals, on European politicians and workers, and on observers from the developing world, surely the French working class has been among the principal class actors in European and in world history.

Appendix   The Manuscript Census Sample: Measurement Problems

In the course of working with the manuscript censuses for the three industrial cities in 1856 and in 1876, a number of deficiencies in individual manuscript censuses were uncovered. In this appendix the problems of the various censuses are discussed and, where relevant, a description of the derivation of estimates to correct these deficiencies is given.

The following were the chief problems with the manuscript censuses: first, for Rive-de-Gier in 1856 there was incomplete information on patterns of household employment for family members other than the household head. Secondly, for Saint-Chamond in 1856 there was no information on family employment other than the household head and for boarders. Thirdly, for Saint-Chamond in 1876 there were difficulties in deciphering the handwriting of one of the census registrars. Fourthly, for Le Chambon-Feugerolles in 1856, there was incomplete information on the occupation and employment status of some boarders. Fifthly, there is evidence of undercounting of children aged between 0 and 4 but, this problem is discussed in appendix 5.2 of chapter 5. Except for this final issue, which is treated elsewhere, these problems will be discussed in order.

Child employment patterns for roughly 25 percent of the Rive-de-Gier census of 1856 had to be estimated because this information was unaccountably missing from the manuscript census records. The process of estimation proceeded in two stages. Occupations of household heads, which are intact even in the incomplete portion of the census, were used as a basis for estimating the employment of male children of the household head, details of which are missing from a portion of the census. First of all, children of those household heads who belonged to occupational groups that were disproportionately represented in the missing material were estimated on the basis of the child employment patterns of children of household heads belonging to those occupational groups in the complete census. Secondly, children of those household heads belonging to other occupational groups were estimated on the basis of the child employment patterns of the children of household heads belonging to all the remaining occupations once the larger groups were ignored.

Miners and metalworkers were disproportionately absent from the missing portion, and no possible values could be assigned to the miner employment patterns that would change the results of worker/consumer ratios or estimates of overall employment substantially. In the incomplete portion miners were head of 6.1 percent of households, in the completed portion of 17.1 percent: in the incomplete portion, metalworkers were heads of 10.8 percent of families, in the completed portion, 13.8 percent. The incomplete portion was disproportionately composed of glassworkers (28.4 percent) and of daylaborers (18.2 percent) who probably worked in the glassworks. Of all the glassworker household heads in Rive-de-Gier 58.3 percent lived in the incomplete portion. Perhaps the difficulty of obtaining estimates of child labor in glassworking accounts for the incompleteness of the census in this area. If this is true, then there may be some underestimation of overall worker/consumers' ratios and activity rates for the town, although the small number of glassworkers' male children would not make this underestimation very significant.

In comparing rates for the complete portion of the populations with rates for the total population that includes the complete portion plus the estimated portion, the relative absence of children in the missing portion results in only a small change in the refined activity rate for men. The refined activity rates for men in 1856 were 0.8145 for the complete portion and 0.7715 for the total population. All figures for aggregate employment in Rive-de-Gier in 1856 are estimates.

Secondly, information on family employment other than for the head of household for Saint-Chamond was completely missing in 1856. This was particularly unfortunate because literary sources suggest that there may have been substantial female employment in this city. In this case no estimate was possible, and all aggregate information on Saint-Chamond for 1856 is based on household heads or on household heads and boarders.

Thirdly, in order to compile life tables, the total population of the censuses was handcounted from the manuscript census. This information provided a breakdown by age and sex of the total population with which it was possible to check on the reliability of our census samples. A series of chi-square tests were applied to the samples for such dimensions as age and sex distributions. Except in the case of males in Saint-Chamond in 1876, the tests revealed insignificant differences between the sample and the actual distributions. An examination of the Saint-Chamond census revealed that one of the census registrars had a particularly illegible handwriting; this registrar recorded the ages of approximately 20 percent of all the inhabitants of the city. Essentially, the portion of the census with which this registrar was involved – about half of the census contains portions of his handwriting – was subjected to very close scrutiny. All cases of dubious age classification were identified, many of these were copied and their interpretation was carefully scrutinized by a highly reliable reader, an advanced graduate student in French history, and by myself. The resulting age distribution was close to that of the first student who had made the handcount (but not to that of a second). For the calculation of the life tables for men and women in Saint-Chamond in 1876, our most carefully and intensively prepared age distribution was used. The correlation between the most carefully prepared handcounted distribution and the inflated sample was 0.949.

Finally, in Le Chambon-Feugerolles in 1876, about one-third of boarding houses did not return any information on the occupation of boarders. Since in all other cases, male boarders over 10 years of age were almost invariably listed as having an occupation (98 percent), the male boarders over 10 years of age in Le Chambon-Feugerolles were classified as occupied members of the labor force; female boarders over 10 years of age, who were not numerous, were classified as occupied in the same proportion as female boarders in Le Chambon-Feugerolles in 1856, 56 percent.

Select Bibliography

PRIMARY SOURCES

Archives
Selected newspapers and periodicals
French government publications
Congresses
Books and articles

ARCHIVES

Archives administratives de la Guerre, Service Historique de l'Armée de terre (MdG)
Archives de la préfecture de police, Paris
Archives départementales de la Loire (ADL)
Archives départementales de la Haute-Loire (AHL)
Archives départementales du Puy-de-Dôme
Archives départementales du Rhône
Archives nationales (AN)
Palais de Justice de Saint-Etienne

SELECTED NEWSPAPERS AND PERIODICALS

La Démocratie Pacifique, 1844–8
L'Eclaireur, 1869–71, 1874–6
Journal de Saint-Etienne, 1861–3, 1870, 1872, 1875–83
La Loire, 1868–9
Le Mercure ségusien, 1844–8
La Sentinelle populaire, 1848
Le Stéphanois, 1875–6

FRENCH GOVERNMENT PUBLICATIONS

Direction de l'assistance et de l'hygiène publique, *Statistique de l'assistance publique, hôpitaux et hospices, enfants assistés, bureaux de bienfaisance*, 2nd series (Strasbourg,

Imprimerie Administrative de Veuve Berger-Levrault, 1866), vol. 15.

—— *Statistique de l'Assistance Publique de 1842 à 1855*, 2nd series (Strasbourg, Imprimerie Administrative de Veuve Berger-Levrault, 1858), vol. 6.

—— *Statistique des dépenses publiques d'assistance faites en France pendant l'année 1885* (Paris, Imprimerie nouvelle, 1889).

—— *Statistique sanitaire des villes de France: Année 1890 et période quinquennale 1886–1890* (Melun, Imprimerie administrative, 1891).

—— *Statistique sanitaire des villes de France et d'Algerie pour l'année 1887* (Paris, Imprimerie nationale, 1889).

Documents Parlementaires, Rapport Audiffred, Chambre des députés, JO, annexe PV, séance du juin 1886, no. 777.

—— Rapport Audiffred, Chambre des députés, JO, annexe, séance 21 mars 1887, no. 1665.

—— Rapport A. Girard, Chambre des députés, séance du 3 avril 1884, annexe no. 2760.

—— Rapport Lanessan, Chambre des députés, JO, annexe, séance du 26 décembre 1884, no. 3446.

—— Rapport Mazeron, Chambre des députés, JO, séance du 7 juillet 1885, no. 3965.

Ministère de l'agriculture et du commerce et des travaux publics, *L'Enquête agricole de 1866. 27e circonscription: Jura, Loire, Rhône, Ain* (Paris, Imprimerie impériale, 1867–72), vol. 9.

—— *Résultats généraux de l'enquête décennale de 1862* (Nancy, Berger Levrault, 1870).

—— *Statistique agricole décennale de 1852*, 2nd series (Paris, Imprimerie impériale, 1852), part 1, vol. 7.

—— *Statistique de la France. – Agriculture* (Paris, Imprimerie royale, 1840–1), vol. 2.

—— *Territoire et population*, 2nd series (Paris, Imprimerie impériale, 1855), vol. 2.

Ministère du commerce, de l'industrie, des postes et des télégraphes, *Les Caisses patronales de retraites des établissements industriels* (Paris, Imprimerie nationale, 1898).

Ministère des travaux publics, *Statistique de l'industrie minérale* (Paris, Imprimerie impériale et Imprimerie nationale, 1851–78).

Statistique générale de la France, Ministère du travail et de la prévoyance sociale, *Répertoire technologique d'industrie et de professions* (Paris, Berger-Levrault, 1909).

CONGRESSES

Séances du Congrès ouvrier de France, Paris, 2–10 octobre, 1876 (Paris, Sandoz, 1877).

Séances de la 2eme session du congrès ouvrier de France, Lyon, 28 janvier–8 février, 1878 (Lyon, J. Trichot, 1878).

Séances de la 3eme session du Congrès ouvrier de France, Marseille, 20–31 octobre, 1879 (Marseille, J. Doucet, 1879).

Congrès Socialist Ouvrier de Marseille 1879 (Paris, I. Dauther, 1880).

Congrès du Havre (quatrième session), septembre, 1880 (manuscrit au Musée social).

Ve Congrès national ouvrier socialiste, tenu à Paris du 27 novembre–5 décembre, 1881 (manuscrit au Musée social).

VIe Congrès socialiste national ouvrier de Bordeaux, septembre, 1881 (manuscrit au Musée social).

Parti Ouvrier Socialist Français, *Compte rendu du 5e congrès national tenu à Reims, du 30 octobre–6 novembre, 1881* (Paris, aux bureaux du Prolétaire, 1882).

Parti Ouvrier Socialiste Revolutionnaire Français, *Compte rendu du sixième congrès national tenu à Saint-Etienne du 25 au 31 septembre, 1882* (Paris, aux bureaux du Prolétaire, 1882).

Sixième Congrès national ouvrier de Saint-Etienne, *Compte rendu de la séance de nuit du 25, septembre* (Paris, bureaux du Prolétaire, 1882).

BOOKS AND ARTICLES

Babu, M. L., "L'industrie métallurgique dans la région de Saint-Etienne," *Annales des Mines*, 9th series, 15 (1899), pp. 357–462.

Beaunier, L. A., "Mémoire sur les mines du département de la Loire," *Annales des Mines*, 1st series, 1 (1836).

Bell, Lowthian, *Principles of the Manufacture of Iron and Steel with Some Notes on the Economic Conditions of their Production* (London, George Routledge and Sons, 1884).

Blanqui, J. A., "Des classes ouvrières en France pendant l'année 1848," in *Petits traités publiés par l'Academie des sciences morales et politiques* (Paris, Firmin-Didot, 1849).

Brion de la Tour, M., *Tableau de la population de la France avec les citations des auteurs* (Paris, chez l'auteur, 1789).

Cabet, Etienne, *Voyage en Icarie* (Paris, Populaire, 1848).

Chambeyron, J.-B., *Recherches historiques sur la ville de Rive-de-Gier* (Rive-de-Gier, Antonin Sablière, 1844).

Chapelle, F., "Etat de l'ignorance dans le département de la Loire en 1869," *Annales de la société d'agriculture, industrie, sciences, arts et belles lettres du département de la Loire* 14 (1870), pp. 37–49.

Combes, M., "Notes sur le travail des hommes et des chevaux employés à l'exploitation des mines", *Annales des mines* 3rd series, 8, pp. 425–60.

Council of the Society of Arts, *Reports of Artisans Selected by a Committee Appointed by the Council of the Society of Arts to Visit the Paris Universal Exhibition, 1867* (London, Bell and Daldy, 1867).

Delseries, M., "Notices sur les accidents arrivés dans les mines de houille du département de la Loire depuis 1817 jusqu'en 1831," *Annales des mines*, 3rd series, 2, pp. 496–8.

D'esterno, H. P. F., *De la misère, de ses causes, de ses effets, de ses remèdes* (Paris, Chez Guillaumin, 1842).

Du Lac de la Tour d'Aurec, *Précis historique et statistique du département de la Loire* (Le Puy, J. B. La Combe, 1807), vol. 2.

Dumay, Jean-Baptiste, *Mémoire d'un militant ouvrier du Creusot (1841–1905)* (Paris, Maspero, 1976).

Dupuynode, Gustave, *Des lois du travail et des classes ouvrières* (Paris, Joubet, 1845).

Euverte, J., "De l'organisation de la main d'oeuvre dans la grande industrie," *Journal des économistes* 19–20 (Sept. 1870), pp. 340–89.

Exposition universelle de 1851, "Nouveaux progrès accomplis dans la construction des machines et lames et forger le fer," *Exposition universelle de 1851: travaux de la commission français IIe groupe* (Paris, Imprimerie impériale, 1852), vol. 3, part 1, section 1.

Feugueray, H., "L'association ouvrière industrielle et agricole" (Paris, Gustave Havard, 1851).

Fonteret, A. L., *Hygiène physique et morale de l'ouvrier dans les grandes villes et dans la ville de Lyon en particulier* (Paris, Victor Masson, 1858).

Fourier, Charles, *Le nouveau monde industriel et sociétaire* (Paris, à la librairie sociétaire, 1845).

Fournier, M., *Le roman d'un petit verrier* (Paris, Libraire Gedalge, 1925).

Granger, Auguste, "Rapport de la commission chargée de rechercher les causes de la décadence de la quincaillerie et les moyens de la régénérer," Société agricole et industrielle de l'arrondissement de Saint-Etienne, *Bulletin* 23 (1852), pp. 97–122.

Gras, L.-J., *Histoire de la chambre de commerce de Saint-Etienne* (Saint-Etienne, Theolier, 1913).

—— *Histoire des premiers chemins de fer français et du premier tramway de France* (Saint-Etienne, Theolier, 1924).

Guillaumin, Emile, *La vie d'un simple: mémoires d'un métayer* (Boston, Ginn and Company, 1926).

Hedde, Philippe, *Revue industrielle de l'arrondissement de Saint-Etienne* (Saint-Etienne, chez Janin, 1836).

Hennequin, Victor, *Féodalité ou association, types d'organisation du travail pour les grands établissements industriels à propos des houillères du bassin de la Loire* (Paris, Libraire Sociétaire, 1846).

Huret, Jules, *Les grèves* (Paris, éditions de la revue blanche, 1902), pp. 93–104.

Jackson, W. F., *James Jackson et ses fils* (Paris, chez l'auteur, 1893).

Janin, Jules, "La ville de Saint-Etienne (Loire)," in *Mélanges et variétés*, Jules Janin (Paris, Librairie des Bibliophiles, 1876), pp. 75–96.

Jordan, M., "Maladies des ouvriers dans les fabriques d'acier," *Annales d'hygiène publique*, 2nd series 23 (1866), pp. 264–84.

Lallemand, C., "Les industries du bassin de la Loire: la vallée de Gier," *L'illustration, Journal Universel* 33 (1000) (1862), pp. 263–6.

—— "Les industries du bassin de la Loire: usine de Saint-Chamond," *L'illustration, Journal Universel* 33 (1002) (1862), pp. 299–302.

—— "Les industries du bassin de la Loire: Usine de Rive-de-Gier," *L'illustration, Journal Universel* 33 (1003) (1863), pp. 317–19.

Lamy, Etienne, "Le gouvernement de la defense nationale – la conquête de la France par le parti républicain," *Revue des deux mondes*, 5th period, 22 (22 août, 1904), pp. 768–807.

Lavallée, C., "Sur l'organisation des caisses de secours et de participation aux bénéfices établies dans certaines usines en faveur des ouvriers," *Bulletin de la société d'encouragement pour l'industrie nationale*, 2nd series, 19 (Paris, 1872), pp. 684–90.

Legentil, M., "Rapport . . . sur le livre de M. Tallon," *Bulletin de la société d'encouragement pour l'industrie nationale*, 3rd series, 4 (1877).

Lepine, Louis, *Mes souvenirs* (Paris, Payot, 1929).

Malon, Benoît, *Le nouveau parti* (Paris, Derveaux, 1881).

Messance, M., *Nouvelles recherches sur la population de la France* (Lyon, Frères Perisse, 1788).

—— *Recherches sur la population des généralités d'Auvergne, de Lyon, de Rouen et de quelques provinces et villes du royaume* (Paris, chez Durand, 1765).

Meugy, M., "Historique des mines de Rive-de-Gier," *Annales des mines*, 4th series, 12 (1847), pp. 177–86.

Michelet, Jules, *Journal 1828–1848*, 4th edn (Paris, Gallimard, 1959), vol. 1.

—— *Révolution française – origines des Bonapartes* (Paris, Calmann-Levy, 1925), vol. 8.

—— *Spiritual Direction and Auricular Confession: Their History, Theory, and Consequences* (Philadelphia, James A. Campbell, 1845).

Ministère de l'intérieur, *Circulaire – Dénombrement de la population en 1891* (Paris, Imprimerie nationale, 1891).

Montegut, Emile, *En Bourbonnais et en Forez* (Paris, Hachette, 1881).

Mullots, Abbé, *Livre des classes ouvrières et des classes souffrantes* (Paris, Frères Perisse, 1854).

Nadaud, Martin, *Leonard maçon de la Creuse* (Paris, Maspero, 1976 (1895)).

Ordonnance du Roi, "Caisse de prévoyance – Ordonnance du Roi, en date du 25 juin 1817, portant établissement d'une caisse de prévoyance en faveur des ouvriers mineurs de Rive-de-Gier, département de la Loire," *Annales des Mines*, 1st series, 2, pp. 503–9.

Palikao, Le général de, *Papiers secrets et correspondance du Second Empire*, A. Poulet-Malassis, 11th edn (Paris, Auguste Ghio, 1878).

Peyret, Alphonse, *Statistique industrielle du département de la Loire* (Saint-Etienne, Chez Delavie, 1835).

Pinjon, M. le Docteur, "Recherches sur la durée moyenne de la vie dans l'arrondissement du Saint-Etienne," *Bulletin*, Société industrielle et agricole de l'arrondissement de Saint-Etienne, 20 (1845–7) pp. 89–103.

P-L, "Du paupérisme et de la mendicité," *Bulletin*, Société industrielle et agricole de l'arrondissement de Saint-Etienne, 18 (1841), pp. 121–34.

Poulot, Denis, *Le sublime: ou le travailleur comme il est en 1870, et ce qu'il peut être* (Paris, Maspero, 1980 (1872)).

Proudhon, P. -J., *Carnets* (Paris, Marcel Rivière, 1960), vols 1 and 2.

—— *De la capacité politique des classes ouvrières* (Paris, Marcel Rivière, 1924).

Reybaud, Louis, *Etudes sur le régime des manufactures* (Paris, Frères Michel Levy, 1859).

Roland de la Platière, Jean-Marie, *Lettres écrites de Suisse, d'Italie, de Sicile et de Malthe en 1776, 1777, et 1778* (Amsterdam, 1780), vol. 6.

Roquille, Guillaume, *Poèmes français et patois, oeuvres complètes de Guillaume Roquille de Rive-de-Gier* (Saint-Etienne, Imprimerie du Républicain de la Loire, 1883).

Simonin, L., *La vie souterraine: les mines et les mineurs*, 2nd edn (Paris, Libraire de L. Hachette et cie., 1867).

Smith, Victor, "Chants du pauvre en Forez et en Velay," *Romania*, 2 (1873), pp. 455–76.

—— "Chants de quêtes – noël du premier de l'an – chants de mai," *Romania*, 2 (1873), pp. 59–71.

—— "Chants du Velay et du Forez – chants de saints et de damnés," *Romania*, 4 (1875), pp. 437–52.

Straku, Georges, *Poèmes du XVIIIe siècle en dialecte de Saint-Etienne (Loire)* (Paris, Société d'édition "Les Belles Lettres", 1964), 2 vols.

Sylvère, Antoine, *Toinou: Le cri d'un enfant auvergnat* (Paris, Plon, 1980).

Tallon, Eugene, *La vie morale et intellectuelles des ouvriers* (Paris, E. Plan et cie., 1877).

Tristan, Flora, *The Workers' Union* (Urbana, Ill., University of Illinois Press, 1983).

Valles, Jules, *L'enfant* (Paris, Bibliotheque Charpentier, 1937 (1881)).

Valserres, J., *Les industries de la Loire* (Saint-Etienne, Robin, 1862).

Varilles, Mathieu, "Legendes des montagnardes du Forez," *Revue de Folklore* 6 (Nov. –Dec., 1936), pp. 251–63.

Villerme, M., "Notes sur quelques monopoles usurpés par les ouvriers de certaines industries suivie de quelques observations sur la situation actuelle des ouvriers dans les bassins houillers de la Loire et du Centre," *Journal des économistes* 17 (1847), pp. 157–68.

—— *Tableau de l'état physique et moral des ouvriers* (Paris, Jules Renouard, 1840), vol. 1.

Voisin, Marcel, *C'était le temps de la "Belle Epoque"* (Paris, La pensée sauvage, 1978).

SECONDARY SOURCES

Books
Articles and essays
Unpublished dissertations

BOOKS

Agulhon, M., Désert, G., and Specklin, R., *Apogée et crise de la civilisation paysanne: 1789–1914* (Paris, Seuil, 1976), vol. 3, *Histoire de la France rurale*, ed. Georges Duby and Armand Wallon.

Alter, George, *Family and the Female Life Course: The Women of Verviers, Belgium, 1849–1880* (Madison, University of Wisconsin Press, 1988).

Anderson, Michael, *Family Structure in Nineteenth-Century Lancashire* (Cambridge, Cambridge University Press, 1971).

Anderson, R. D., *Education in France, 1848–1870* (Oxford, Clarendon Press, 1975).

Ariès, Philippe, *Histoire des populations françaises* (Paris, Seuil, 1971).

Barker, Theo, and Drake, Michael (eds), *Population and Society in Britain, 1850–1980* (New York, New York University Press, 1982).

Beaubernard, R., *Montceau-les-Mines: Un "laboratoire social" au XIXe siècle* (Avallon, Civry, 1981).

Berg, Maxine, *The Age of Manufactures, 1700–1820* (Totowa, New Jersey, Barnes and Noble, 1985).

Berg, M., Hudson, P., and Sonenscher, M., *Manufacture in Town and Country before the Factory* (Cambridge, Cambridge University Press, 1983).

Berlanstein, Lenard R., *The Working Poor of Paris, 1871–1919* (Baltimore, Johns Hopkins, 1984).

Bezucha, Robert J., *The Lyon Uprising of 1834: Social and Political Conflict in the Early July Monarchy* (Cambridge, Mass., Harvard University Press, 1974).

Bodnar, J., Simon, R., and Weber, M. P., *Lives of Their Own: Blacks, Italians and Poles in Pittsburgh, 1900–1960* (Urbana, University of Illinois Press, 1982).

Bonnet, Serge, *L'homme du fer: mineurs de fer et ouvriers sidérurgistes lorrains 1889–1930* (Nancy, Centre Lorrain d'Etudes Sociologiques, 1976), vol. 1.

Brunet, Jean-Paul, *Saint-Denis: la ville rouge, 1890–1939* (Paris, Hachette, 1980).

Buriez, M.-P. et al., *L'homme, la vie et la mort dans le nord au 19e siècle* (Lille, Université de Lille-III, 1972).

Burnet, Macfarlane, *Natural History of Infectious Disease* (Cambridge, Cambridge University Press, 1953).

Bury, J. P. T., *Gambetta and the Making of the Third Republic* (London, Longmans, 1973).

—— *Gambetta's Final Years: The Era of Difficulties, 1877–1882* (London, Longmans, 1982).

Caldwell, John C., *Theory of Fertility Decline* (New York, Academic Press, 1982).

Camp, Wesley D., *Marriage and the Family in France since the Revolution* (New York, Bookman Associates, 1961).

Caron, François, *An Economic History of Modern France* (New York, Columbia University Press, 1979).

Carré, J.-J., Dubois, P., and Malinvaud, E., *French Economic Growth* (Stanford, Stanford University Press, 1975).

Castells, Manuel, *The Urban Question: A Marxist Approach* (Cambridge, Mass., MIT Press, 1979).

Cayez, Pierre, *Crises et croissance de l'industrie lyonnaise 1850–1900* (Paris, Editions du CNRS, 1977).

—— *Métiers jacquard et hauts fourneaux aux origines de l'industrie lyonnaise* (Lyon, Presses universitaires de Lyon, 1978).

Chalot, Michel, *L'Escarbille: histoire d'Eugene Saulnier, ouvrier verrier* (Paris, Presses de la Renaissance, 1978).

Chandler, Alfred D. Jr, *The Visible Hand: The Managerial Revolution in American Business* (Cambridge, Mass., Belknap, 1977).

Chatelain, Abel, *Les migrants temporaires en France de 1800 à 1914*, 2 vols (Villeneuve-d'Ascq, l'Université de Lille-III, 1976).

Chatelard, Claude, *Crime et criminalité dans l'arrondissement de Saint-Etienne au XIXe siècle* (Saint-Etienne, Centre d'études Foréziennes, 1981).

Chomienne, C., *Historie de la ville de Rive-de-Gier du canton et de ses principales industries* (Saint-Etienne, 1912).

Clout, Hugh D., *Agriculture in France on the Eve of the Railway Age* (London, Croom Helm, 1980).

—— *The Land of France, 1815–1914* (London, Allen and Unwin, 1983).

Coleman, William, *Death is a Social Disease: Public Health and Political Economy in Early Industrial France* (Madison, University of Wisconsin Press, 1982).

Condamin, J., *Histoire de Saint-Chamond* (Paris, Alphonse Picard, 1890).

Cooper, Frederick, *On the African Waterfront: Urban Disorder and the Transformation of Work in Colonial Mombasa* (New Haven, Yale University Press, 1987).

Crew, David F., *Town in the Ruhr: A Social History of Bochum, 1860–1914* (New York, Columbia University Press, 1979).

Dennis, Richard, *English Industrial Cities of the Nineteenth Century: A Social Geography* (Cambridge, Cambridge University Press, 1984).

Devillers, Christian, and Huet, Bernard, *Le Creusot: Naissance et développement d'une ville industrielle, 1782–1914* (Seyssel, Champ Vallon, 1981).

Devun, M. *Géographie du département de la Loire* (Grenoble, Les éditions françaises, 1944).

Dommanget, Maurice, *Victor Considerant: Sa vie son oeuvre* (Paris, Editions sociales internationales, 1929).

Dublin, Louis I. *Length of Life: A Study of the Life Table* (New York, Ronald Press Company, 1936).

Dublin, Louis I., and Vane Jr, Robert J., *Causes of Death by Occupation*, Bulletin of the United States Bureau of Labor Statistics, 507 (Washington D.C., GPO, 1930).

Dublin, Thomas, *Women and Work: The Transformation of Work and Community in Lowell,*

Massachusetts, 1826–1860 (New York, Columbia University, 1979).

Duveau, Georges, *La vie ouvrière en France sous le Second Empire* (Paris, Gallimard, 1946).

Elwitt, Sanford, *The Third Republic Defended: Bourgeois Reform in France, 1880–1914* (Baton Rouge, Louisiana State University Press, 1986).

—— *The Making of the Third Republic: Class and Politics in France, 1868–1884* (Baton Rouge, Louisiana State University Press, 1975).

Evans, David Owen, *Social Romanticism in France* (Oxford, Clarendon Press, 1951).

Evans, Richard J., *Death in Hamburg: Society and Politics in the Cholera Years 1830–1910* (Oxford, Oxford University Press, 1987).

Ewald, François, *L'Etat providence* (Paris, Bernard Grasset, 1986).

Faure, Petrus, *Développement de la culture dans un département ouvrier: la Loire* (Saint-Etienne, Dumas, 1979).

—— *Histoire de mouvement ouvrier de la Loire* (Saint-Etienne, Dumas, 1956).

Fienberg, Stephen E., *The Analysis of Cross-Classified Categorical Data*, 2nd edn (Cambridge, Mass., MIT Press, 1981).

Flinn, Michael W., *The European Demographic System 1500–1820* (Baltimore, Md., Johns Hopkins University Press, 1981).

Forrest, Alan, *The French Revolution and the Poor* (New York, St Martin's Press, 1981).

Fox, Bonnie (ed.), *Hidden in the Household: Women's Domestic Labour under Capitalism* (Oshawa, Ontario, Women's Press, 1980).

Furet, François, and Ozouf, Jacques, *Reading and Writing: Literacy in France from Calvin to Jules Ferry* (Cambridge, Cambridge University Press, 1982).

Gaillard, Jeanne, *Paris, La ville 1852–1870* (Paris, Honoré Champion, 1977).

Garrier, Gilbert, *Paysans du Beaujolais et du Lyonnais 1800–1970*, 2 vols (Grenoble, Presses universitaires de Grenoble, 1973).

Gonon, Jean-François, *Histoire de la chanson Stéphanoise et Forézienne* (Roanne, Horvath, 1906).

Gordon, David M., *Merchants and Capitalists: Industrialization and Provincial Politics in Mid-Nineteenth-Century France* (Alabama, University of Alabama Press, 1985).

Goubert, Jean-Pierre, *La conquête de l'eau: l'avènement de la santé à l'age industriel* (Paris, Robert Laffont, 1986).

Griffen, Clyde, and Griffen, Sally, *Natives and Newcomers: The Ordering of Opportunity in Mid-Nineteenth-Century Poughkeepsie* (Cambridge, Mass., Harvard University Press, 1978).

Guillaume, Pierre, *La compagnie des mines de la Loire 1846–1854: Essai sur l'apparition de la grande industrie capitaliste en France* (Paris, Presses universitaires de France, 1966).

—— *La population de Bordeaux au XIXe siècle* (Paris, Armand Colin, 1972).

Gutton, Jean-Pierre, *La société et les pauvres, l'exemple de la généralité de Lyon 1534–1789* (Paris, Société d'édition "Les Belles Lettres", 1969).

Haines, Michael, *Fertility and Occupation: Population Patterns in Industrialization* (New York, Academic Press, 1979).

Hanagan, Michael, *The Logic of Solidarity: Artisans and Industrial Workers in Three French Towns, 1871–1914* (Urbana, University of Illinois Press, 1980).

Hareven, Tamara K., *Family Time and Industrial Time* (Cambridge, Cambridge University Press, 1982).

—— (ed.), *Transitions: The Family and the Life Course in Historical Perspective* (New York, Academic Press, 1978).

Harris, Marvin, and Ross, Eric B., *Death, Sex, and Fertility: Population Regulation in Preindustrial and Developing Societies* (New York, Columbia University Press, 1987).

Harvey, David, *The Limits to Capital* (Chicago, University of Chicago Press, 1982).

—— *Social Justice and the City* (Baltimore, Johns Hopkins University Press, 1977).

Heritier, P., et al., *150 ans de luttes ouvrières dans le bassin Stéphanois* (Saint-Etienne, Editions le champ du possible, 1979).

Hershberg, Theodore (ed.), *Philadelphia: Work, Space, Family, and Group Experience in the 19th-Century City* (Oxford, Oxford University Press, 1981).

Howard, Michael, *The Franco-Prussian War: The German Invasion of France, 1870–1871* (London, Rupert Hart-Davis, 1968).

Hudson, Pat, *The Genesis of Industrial Capital: A Study of the West Riding Wool Textile Industry, c.1750–1850* (Cambridge, Cambridge University Press, 1986).

Hufton, Olwen, *The Poor of Eighteenth-Century France 1750–1789* (Oxford, Clarendon Press, 1974).

Hunt, H. J., *Le socialisme et le romantisme en France* (Oxford, Clarendon Press, 1935).

Hvidt, Kristian, *Flight to America: The Social Background of 300,000 Danish Emigrants* (New York, Academic Press, 1975).

Jacquemet, Gerard, *Belleville au XIXe siècle: du faubourg à la ville* (Paris, Editions de l'école des hautes études en sciences sociales, 1984).

Johnson, Christopher H., *Utopian Communism in France: Cabet and the Icarians, 1839–1851* (Ithaca, Cornell University Press, 1974).

Jones, P. M., *Politics and Rural Society: The southern Massif Central c.1750–1880* (Cambridge, Cambridge University Press, 1985).

Katz, Michael B., *The People of Hamilton, Canada West: Family and Class in a Mid-Nineteenth Century City* (Cambridge, Mass., Harvard University Press, 1975).

Katz, Michael B., Doucet, Michael J., and Stern, Mark J., *The Social Organization of Early Industrial Capitalism* (Cambridge, Mass., Harvard University Press, 1983).

Katznelson, Ira, and Zolberg, Aristide R. (eds), *Working-Class Formation: Nineteenth-Century Patterns in Western Europe and the United States* (Princeton, Princeton University Press, 1986).

Kriedte, P., Medick, H., and Schlumbohm, J., *Industrialization before Industrialization* (Cambridge, Cambridge University Press, 1981 (1977)).

Kulstein, David I., *Napoleon III and the Working Class: A Study of Government Propaganda under the Second Empire* (Los Angeles, Cal., California State Colleges Press, 1969).

Latta, Claude, *Un républicain méconnu: Martin Bernard 1808–1883* (Saint-Etienne, Centre d'études Foréziennes, 1980).

Le Bras, Herve, and Todd, Emmanuel, *L'invention de la France: atlas anthropologique et politique* (Paris, Librairie générale française, 1981).

Lefort, J., *Les caisses de retraites ouvrières*, 2 vols (Paris, Albert Fontemoing, 1906).

Lehning, James R., *The Peasants of Marlhes: Economic Development and Family Organization in Nineteenth Century France* (Chapel Hill, University of North Carolina Press, 1980).

Léon, Pierre, *La naissance de la grande industrie en Dauphiné (fin du XVIIe siècle–1869)*, 2 vols (Paris, Presses universitaires de France, 1954).

Lequin, Yves, *Les ouvriers de la région lyonnaise (1848–1914)*. 2 vols. Lyons, Presses Universitaires de Lyons, 1977.

Levasseur, E., *Histoire des classes ouvrières et de l'industrie en France de 1789 à 1870*, 2nd edn (Paris, Arthur Rousseau, 1904), vol. 2.

—— *La Population française*, 3 vols (Paris, A. Rousseau, 1888–92).

Levine, David, *Family Formation in an Age of Nascent Capitalism* (New York, Academic Press, 1977).

—— *Reproducing Families: The Political Economy of English Population History* (Cambridge, Cambridge University Press, 1987).

L'Huillier, Fernand, *La lutte ouvrière à la fin du Second Empire* (Paris, Armand Colin, 1957).

Lis, Catharina, *Social Change and the Labouring Poor: Antwerp, 1770–1860* (New Haven, Yale University Press, 1986).

Lis, Catharina, and Soly, Hugo, *Poverty and Capitalism in Pre-Industrial Europe* (Atlantic Highlands, New Jersey, Humanities Press, 1979).

Mandon, Daniel, *Les Barbelés de la culture: Saint-Etienne, une ville ouvrière* (Saint-Etienne, FEDEROP, 1976).

Manuel, Frank E., *The New World of Henri St Simon* (Notre Dame, Indiana, University of Notre Dame Press, 1963).

Meillassoux, Claude, *Femmes, greniers, et capitaux* (Paris, Maspero, 1979).

Merley, Jean, *La Haute-Loire: de la fin de l'ancien régime aux débuts de la troisième République (1776–1886)*, 2 vols (Le Puy, Cahiers de la Haute-Loire, 1974).

Merriman, John, *The Agony of the Republic: The Repression of the Left in Revolutionary France: 1848–1851* (New Haven, Yale University Press, 1978).

—— *The Red City: Limoges and the French Nineteenth Century* (New York, Oxford University Press, 1985).

Milkman, Ruth. *Gender at Work: The Dynamics of Job Segregation during World War II* (Urbana, Ill., University of Illinois Press, 1987).

Mitterauer, Michael, and Sieder, Reinhard, *The European Family* (Chicago, University of Chicago Press, 1982 (1977)).

Moch, Leslie Page, *Paths to the City: Regional Migration in Nineteenth-Century France* (Beverly Hills, Cal., Sage, 1983).

Monteilhet, J., *Les institutions militaires de la France: 1814–1932* (Paris, Félix Alcan, 1932).

Moody, Joseph N., *French Education since Napoleon* (Syracuse, Syracuse University Press, 1978).

Moore, Jr., Barrington, *Injustice: The Social Bases of Obedience and Revolt* (White Plains, NY, M. E. Sharpe, 1978).

More, Charles, *Skill and the English Working Class, 1870–1914* (New York, St Martin's Press, 1980).

Morris, R. J., *Cholera 1832: The Social Response to an Epidemic* (New York, Holmes and Meier, 1976).

—— *Class and Class Consciousness in the Industrial Revolution, 1780–1850* (London, Macmillan, 1979).

Moss, Bernard H., *The Origins of the French Labor Movement 1830–1914: The Socialism of Skilled Workers* (Berkeley, Cal., University of California Press, 1976).

Mougin, Henri, *Pierre Leroux* (Paris, Editions sociales internationales, 1938).

Noirel, Gérard, *Longwy: Immigrés et prolétaires, 1880–1980* (Paris, Presses universitaires de France, 1984).

Perkin, Harold, *The Origins of Modern English Society, 1780–1880* (London, Routledge and Kegan Paul, 1969).

Perrot, Michelle, *Les ouvriers en grève: France 1871–1890*, 2 vols (Paris, Mouton, 1974).

—— (ed.), *Histoire de la vie privée* (Paris, Seuil, 1987), vol. 4, "De la révolution à la grande guerre."

Peuvergne, René, *De l'organisation par l'état des caisses de retraite pour les ouvriers* (Paris, Larose and Forcel, 1892).

Pierrard, Pierre, *La vie ouvrière à Lille sous le Second Empire* (Paris, Bloud et Gay, 1965).

Pinot, Robert, *Les oeuvres sociales des industries métallurgiques* (Paris, Armand Colin, 1924).

Piore, Michael J., *Birds of Passage: Migrant Labor and Industrial Societies* (Cambridge, Cambridge University Press, 1979).

Poitrineau, Abel, *La vie rurale en Basse Auvergne au XVIIIe siècle*, 2 vols (Paris, Presses universitaires de France, 1965).

Pounds, N. J. G., *An Historical Geography of Europe 1500–1840* (Cambridge, Cambridge University Press, 1979).

Pourrat, Henri, *Gaspard des Montagnes* (Lyon, H. Lardanchet, 1924).

Preston, Samuel H. (ed.), *The Effects of Infant and Child Mortality on Fertility* (New York, Academic Press, 1978).

Rancière, Jacques, *La nuit des prolétaires* (Paris, Fayard, 1981).

Reddy, William M., *The Rise of Market Culture: The Textile Trade and French Society, 1820–1870* (Cambridge, Cambridge University Press, 1985).

Reid, Donald., *The Miners of Decazeville: A Genealogy of Deindustrialization* (Cambridge, Mass., Harvard University Press, 1985).

Riasanovsky, Nicholas V., *The Teaching of Charles Fourier* (Berkeley, Cal., University of California Press, 1969).

Rouchon, Ulysse, *La vie paysanne dans la Haute-Loire*, 3 vols (Le Puy, Editions de la société des études locales, 1933–8).

Rowlands, Marie B., *Men and Masters in the West Midland Metalware Trades before the Industrial Revolution* (Manchester, Manchester University Press, 1975).

Rowntree, B. Seebohm., *Poverty: A Study of Town Life* (London, Macmillan, 1901).

Schnetzler, J., *Les industries et les hommes dans la région Stéphanoise* (Saint-Etienne, Imprimerie "Le Feuillet Blanc," 1975).

Segalen, Martine, *Love and Power in the Peasant Family* (Chicago, University of Chicago Press, 1983 (1980)).

Sewell, Jr, William H., *Structure and Mobility: The Men and Women of Marseilles, 1820–1870* (Cambridge, Cambridge University Press, 1985).

—— *Work and Revolution in France: The Language of Labor from the Old Regime to 1848* (Cambridge, Cambridge University Press, 1980).

Shapiro, Ann-Louise, *Housing the Poor of Paris, 1850–1920* (Madison, University of Wisconsin Press, 1985).

Sheridan, Jr, George J., *The Social and Economic Foundations of Association among the Silk Weavers of Lyon 1852–1870*, 2 vols (New York, Arno Press, 1981).

Shorter, Edward, and Tilly, Charles, *Strikes in France 1830–1968* (Cambridge, Cambridge University Press, 1974).

Smith, F. B., *The People's Health: 1830–1910* (London, Croom-Helm, 1979).

Smith, Richard M. (ed.), *Land, Kinship and Life-Cycle* (Cambridge, Cambridge University Press, 1984).

Snell, K. D. M., *Annals of the Labouring Poor: Social Change and Agrarian England, 1660–1900* (Cambridge, Cambridge University Press, 1985).

Spree, Reinhard, *Health and Social Class in Imperial Germany* (Oxford, Berg, 1988).

Stearns, Peter N., *Old Age in European Society: The Case of France* (New York, Holmes and Meier, 1976).

Stedman Jones, Gareth, *Outcast London: A Study in the Relationship between Classes in Victorian Society* (Oxford, Oxford University Press, 1971).

Stern, Mark J., *Society and Family Strategy: Erie County, New York 1850–1920* (Albany, State University of New York Press, 1987).

Stewart-McDougall, Mary Lynn, *The Artisan Republic: Revolution, Reaction and Resistance in Lyon 1848–1851* (Kingston and Montreal, McGill–Queen's University Press, 1984).

Sussman, George D., *Selling Mothers' Milk, The Wet-Nursing Business in France 1715–1914* (Urbana, Ill., University of Illinois Press, 1982).

Sutet, Marcel, *Montceau les mines: essor d'une mine – naissance d'une ville* (Roanne, Horvath, 1981).

Taylor, Barbara, *Eve and the New Jerusalem: Socialism and Feminism in the Nineteenth Century* (New York, Pantheon Press, 1983).

Tchernoff, I., *Le parti républicain au coup d'état et sous le second empire* (Paris, A. Pedone, 1906).

Thomas, Albert, *Le Second Empire (1852–1870)* (Paris, Jules Rouff et cie., 1904) vol. 10 "Histoire socialiste," ed. Jean Jaures.

Thomas, P.-Félix, *Pierre Leroux: Sa vie, son oeuvre, sa doctrine* (Paris, Félix Alcan, 1904).

Tilly, Charles, *The Contentious French: Four Centuries of Popular Struggle* (Cambridge, Mass., Belknap Press, 1986).

—— *From Mobilization to Revolution* (Reading, Mass., Addison-Wesley, 1978).

Tilly, Louise, and Scott, Joan, *Women, Work and Family* (New York, Holt, Rinehart and Winston, 1978).

Trempé, Rolande, *Les mineurs de Carmaux:1848–1914*, 2 vols (Paris, Les éditions ouvrières, 1971).

Tunzelman, G. N. von, *Steam Power and British Industrialization* (Oxford, Clarendon Press, 1978).

Viard, Jacques, *Pierre Leroux et les socialistes Européens* (Avignon, Actes Sud, 1982).

Vincent, K. Steven, *Pierre-Joseph Proudhon and the Rise of French Republican Socialism* (Oxford, Oxford University Press, 1984).

Willard, Claude, *Les guesdistes: le mouvement socialiste en France 1893–1905* (Paris, Editions sociales, 1965).

Wohl, Anthony S., *Endangered Lives: Public Health in Victorian Britain* (Cambridge, Mass., Harvard University Press, 1983).

Wright, Erik Olin, *Class, Crisis and the State* (London, New Left Books, 1978).

—— *Class Structure and Income Determination* (New York, Academic Press, 1979).

Wrigley, E. A., *Industrial Growth and Population Change: A Regional Study of the Coalfield Areas of North-West Europe in the Late Nineteenth Century* (Cambridge, Cambridge University Press, 1961).

Wrigley, E. A. and Schofield, R. S., *The Population History of England, 1541–1871: A Reconstruction* (Cambridge, Mass., Harvard University Press, 1981).

Wrightson, Keith, and Levine, David, *Poverty and Piety in an English Village, Terling 1525–«1700* (New York, Academic Press, 1979).

Zeldin, Theodore, *The Political System of Napoleon III* (London, Macmillan, 1958).

ARTICLES AND ESSAYS

Accampo, Elinor, "Entre la classe sociale et la cité: identité et intégration chez les ouvriers de Saint-Chamond, 1815–1880," *Le mouvement social* 118 (1982), pp. 39–59.

Aminzade, Ron, "A Marxist Approach to Occupational Classification," CRSO working paper, 132 (June, 1976).

Armengaud, A., "L'attitude de la société à l'égard de l'enfant au XIXe siècle," *Annales de la démographie historique* (Paris, Mouton, 1973), pp. 303–12.

Bainbridge, T. H., "Population Changes over the West Cumberland Coalfield," in *English Rural Communities: The Impact of a Specialized Economy*, ed. Dennis R. Mills (London, Macmillan, 1973), pp. 137–44.

Beaver, M. W., "Population, Infant Mortality, and Milk," *Population Studies* 27 (2) (1973), pp. 243–54.

Benenson, Harold, "Victorian Sexual Ideology and Marx's Theory of the Working Class," *International labor and Working Class History* 25 (Spring, 1984), pp. 1–23.

Berlanstein, Lenard R., "Illegitimacy, Concubinage, and Proletarianization in a French Town, 1760–1914," *Journal of Family History* (Winter, 1980), pp. 360–74.

Biraben, Jean-Noël, "Sur l'évolution de la fécondité en Europe occidentale," in *European Population Conference, Strasbourg, 1966*, vol. 1 (Strasbourg, Council of Europe, 1966), pp. 1–29.

Bodnar, John, "Immigration, Kinship, and the Rise of Working-Class Realism in Industrial America," *Journal of Social History* 14 (1) (Fall, 1980), pp. 45–65.

Bonnet, Jean-Charles, "Les travailleurs étrangers dans la Loire sous la IIIe République," *Cahiers d'histoire* 16 (1971), pp. 67–80.

Booth, Douglas, "Karl Marx on State Regulation of the Labor Process: The English Factory Acts," *Review of Social Economy* 36 (Oct. 1978), pp. 137–57.

Bouchard, Gérard, "L'utilisation des données socio-professionnelles en histoire: le problème de la diachronie," *Histoire sociale–Social History* 16 (32) (November, 1983), pp. 429–42.

Bourdelais, Patrice, and Raulot, Jean-Yves, "La marche du choléra en France: 1832–1854," *Annales-ESC* 33 (1) (Jan.–Feb. 1978), pp. 125–42.

Bourgeois-Pichat, J., "The General Development of the Population of France since the Eighteenth Century," in *Population in History: Essays in Historical Demography*, ed. D. V. Glass and D. E. C. Eversley (London, Edward Arnold, 1965), pp. 474–506.

Braun, Rudolf, "The Rise of a Rural Class of Industrial Entrepreneurs," *Cahiers d'histoire mondiale* 10 (3) (1967), pp. 551–66.

Bulmer, M. I. A., "Sociological Models of the Mining Community," *Sociological Review*, new series, 23 (1975), pp. 61–92.

Burawoy, Michael, "Karl Marx and the Satanic Mills: Factory Politics under Early Capitalism in England, the United States, and Russia," *American Journal of Sociology* 90 (2) (Sept., 1984), pp. 247–82.

Cameron, Rondo, and Freedeman, Charles E., "French Economic Growth: A Radical Revision," *Social Science History* 7 (1) (Winter, 1983), pp. 3–30.

Campbell, Alan, "Honourable Men and Degraded Slaves: A Comparative Study of Trade Unionism in Two Lanarkshire Mining Communities, c.1830–1874," in *Independent Collier*, ed. R. Harrison (New York, St Martin's, 1978), pp. 75–113.

Carlsson, Gosta, "The Decline in Fertility: Innovation or Adjustment Process," *Population Studies* 20 (1966), pp. 149–74.

—— "Nineteenth-Century Fertility Oscillation," *Population Studies* 24 (1970), pp. 413–22.

Chalendard, Marius, "Une enquête sur l'habitat ouvrier et la propriété du logement," *Economie et Humanisme* 4 (1945), pp. 657–63.

Chatelain, Abel, "L'attraction des trois plus grandes agglomérations françaises: Paris – Lyon – Marseille en 1891," *Annales de démographie historique* (1971), pp. 27–41.

—— "Les usines-internats et les migrations féminines dans la région Lyonnaise: seconde moitié du XIXe siècle et début XXe siècle," *Revue d'histoire économique et sociale.* 48 (3) (1970), pp. 373–94.

Chiang, Chin Long, "The Life Table and Its Construction," in Chin Long Chiang, *Introduction to Stochastic Processes in Biostatistics* (New York, John Wiley and Sons, 1968), pp. 189–208.

Cho, Lee-Jay, "The Own-Children Approach to Fertility Estimation: An Elaboration," in *International Population Conference – Liège 1973* (International Union for the Scientific Study of Population, Liège, 1973), vol. 2, pp. 263–79.

Christofferson, Thomas R., "The French National Workshops of 1848: The View from the Provinces," *French Historical Studies* 11 (4) (Fall, 1980), pp. 505–20.

Chudacoff, Howard, and Hareven, Tamara K., "Family Transitions and Household Structure in the Later Years of Life," in *Transitions: The Family Life Course and the Life Cycle in Historical Perspective*, ed. Tamara K. Hareven (New York, Academic Press, 1978), pp. 217–44.

Claeson, Claes-Fredrik, and Egero, Bertil, "Migration and the Urban Population – A Demographic Analysis of Population Census Data for Tanzania," *Geografiska Annales*, series B, "Human Geography," vol. 54B (1972), pp. 1–15.

Coale, Ansley J., "Age Patterns of Marriage," *Population Studies*, part 2, 25 (July, 1971), pp. 193–214.

Coleman, D. C., "Proto-Industrialization: A Concept Too Many," *Economic History Review*, 2nd series, 36 (3) (Aug., 1983), pp. 435–48.

Collins, E. J. T., "Labour Supply and Demand in European Agriculture 1800–1800," in *Agrarian Change and Economic Development: The Historical Problems*, ed. E. L. Jones and S. J. Woolf (London, Meuthen, 1969), pp. 61–94.

Cottereau, Alain, "La tuberculose: maladie urbaine ou maladie de l'usure au travail," *Sociologie du travail* (June, 1978), pp. 193–224.

—— "Usure au travail, destins masculins et destins féminins dans les cultures ouvrières en France, au XIXe siècle," *Le mouvement social* (124) (Mar.–April, 1983), pp. 70–109.

Curtis, Bruce, "Capital, the State and the Origins of the Working-Class Household," in *Hidden in the Household: Women's Domestic Labor under Capitalism* ed. Bonnie Fox (Oshawa, Ontario, Women's Press, 1980), pp. 101–34.

Daly, Herman E., "A Marxian–Malthusian View of Poverty and Development," *Population Studies* 25 (Mar., 1971), part 1, pp. 25–37.

Davis, Kingsley, "The Theory of Change and Response in Modern Demographic History," *Population Index* 29 (4) (Oct., 1963), pp. 345–66.

Davis, Kingsley, and Blake, Judith, "Social Structure and Fertility: An Analytic Framework," *Economic Development and Cultural Change* 4 (April, 1956), pp. 211–35.

230 *Select Bibliography*

Delabre, Bernard, "La grève de 1869 dans le département de la bassin minier Stéphanois," *Etudes Foréziennes* 4 (1971), pp. 109–38.

Devun, M., "L'utilisation des rivières du Pilat par l'industrie," *Revue de géographie alpine* 32 (fasc. 2) (1944), pp. 241–305.

Dupaquier, Jacques, "Sur la population française au XVIIe et au XVIIIe siècle," *Revue historique* 239 (Jan.–Mar., 1968), pp. 43–79.

Dyhouse, Carol, "Working-Class Mothers and Infant Mortality in England, 1895–1914," *Journal of Social History* 12 (1978–9), pp. 217–67.

Easterlin, Richard A., "Does Human Fertility Adjust to the Environment?" *American Economic Review* 61 (2) (1971), pp. 399–407.

—— "Influences in European Emigration before World War I," *Economic Development and Cultural Change* 9 (pt 2) (April, 1961), pp. 331–51.

Erikson, Ingrid, and Rogers, John, "Mobility in an Agrarian Community: Practical and Methodological Considerations," *Aristocrats, Farmers, Proletarians: Essays in Swedish Demographic History* (Uppsala, Almquist and Wiksel, 1973), pp. 60–87.

Estienne, P., "Un demi-siècle de dépeuplement dans le Massif Central," *Revue de géographie alpine* 44 (fasc. 3) (1956), pp. 463–72.

Farraq, Abdelmegial M., "The Occupational Structure of the Labor Force: Patterns and Trends in Selected Countries," *Population Studies* 18 (pt 1) (July, 1964), pp. 17–34.

Fitzpatrick, Maria, "Proudhon and the French Labor Movement: The Problem of Proudhon's Prominence," *European Historical Quarterly* 15 (4) (Oct., 1985), pp. 406–30.

Friedlander, Dov, "Demographic Patterns and Socioeconomic Characteristics of the Coal-mining Population in England and Wales in the Nineteenth Century" *Economic Development and Cultural Change*, 22 (1) (Oct., 1973), pp. 39–51.

Friedmann, Harriet, "World Market, State, and Family Farm: Social Basis of Household Production in the Era of Wage Labor," *Comparative Studies in Society and History* 20 (1978), pp. 545–86.

Gaillard, Jeanne, "Les associations de production et la pensée politique en France (1852–1870)," *Le mouvement social* (52) (1965), pp. 59–84.

Garrier, Gilbert, "La formation d'un complexe économique-sociale de type 'rhodanien', Chaponost (1730–1822)," in *Structures économique et problèmes sociaux du monde rural dans la France du sud-est (fin du XVIIe siècle 1835)*, ed. Pierre Leon (Paris, Société d'édition "Les Belles Lettres", 1966), pp. 317–70:

Gibert, Andre, "La vie industrielle Stéphanoise à la veille de la guerre," *Les études rhodaniennes* 19 (1–2) (1944), pp. 210–14.

Gille, Bertrand, "La formation de prolétarian ouvrier dans l'industrie sidérurgique française," *Revue d'histoire de la Sidérurgie* 4 (4) (1973), pp. 244–51.

Goldin, Claudia, "Family Strategies and the Family Economy in the Late Nineteenth Century: The Role of Secondary Workers," in *Philadelphia: Work, Space, Family, and Group Experience in the 19th Century*, ed. Theodore Hershberg (Oxford, Oxford University Press, 1981), pp. 277–310.

Goubert, Pierre, "L'ancienne société d'ordres: verbiage ou réalité?" *Colloque franco-suisse d'histoire économique et sociale Genève 5–6 mai 1967* (Genève, Georg et cie., 1969), pp. 35–40.

Grabill, Wilson H., and Cho, Lee-Jay, "Methodology for the Measurement of Current

Fertility from Population Data on Young Children," *Demography* 2 (1965), pp. 50–73

Granovetter, Mark, and Tilly, Charles, "Inequality and Labor Processes," Research paper 939 (Graduate School of Business, Stanford University, 1987).

Grantham, George W., "Scale and Organization in French Farming, 1840–1880," in *European Peasants and Their Markets: Essays in Agrarian Economic History*, ed. William N. Parker and Eric L. Jones (Princeton, Princeton University Press, 1975), pp. 293–326.

Greene, James R., "The Brotherhood of Timber Workers, 1910–1917: A Radical Response to Industrial Capitalism in the Southern USA," *Past and Present* 60 (Aug., 1973), pp. 161–200.

Grew, R., Harrigan, P., and Whitney, J., "The Availability of Schooling," *Journal of Interdisciplinary History* 14 (1) (Summer, 1983), pp. 25–63.

Griffen, Clyde, "Occupational Mobility in Nineteenth-Century America, Problems and Possibilities," *Journal of Social History* 15 (Spring, 1972), pp. 310–30.

Grmek, Mirko D., "Préliminaires d'une étude historique des maladies," *Annales – ESC* 24 (6) (Nov.–Dec., 1969), pp. 1473–83.

Guillaume, Pierre, "Les débuts de la grande industrie houillère dans la Loire: les mines de Roche-la-Molière et de Firminy sous la restauration," *Cahiers d'histoire* 4 (2) (1959), pp. 147–66.

—— "Grèves et organisation ouvrière chez les mineurs de la Loire au milieu du XIXe siècle," *Le mouvement social*, 11 (April-June, 1963), pp. 5–18.

—— "La situation économique et sociale du département de la Loire d'après l'enquête sur le travail agricole et industriel du 25 mai 1848," *Revue d'histoire moderne et contemporaine* 10 (Jan.–Mar., 1963), pp. 5–34.

Gullickson, Gay L., "Agriculture and Cottage Industry in the Pays de Caux, 1750–1850," unpublished paper delivered to the SSHA, 1980 annual meeting.

Gutman, Herbert G., "Black Coal Miners and the Greenback–Labor Party in Redeemer, Alabama, 1878–1879," *Labor History* 10 (Summer, 1969), pp. 506–35.

Gutman, Myron P., and Leboutte, René, "Rethinking Proletarianization and the Family," *Journal of Interdisciplinary History* 14 (Winter, 1984), pp. 587–607.

Habakkuk, H. J., "English Population in the Eighteenth Century," *Economic History Review*, 2nd series, 6 (2) (1953), pp. 117–33.

Hanagan, Michael P., "Agriculture and Industry in the Nineteenth-Century Stéphanois: Household Employment Patterns and the Rise of a Permanent Proletariat," in *Proletarians and Protest: The Roots of Class Formation in an Industrializing World*, ed. Michael P. Hanagan and Charles Stephenson (Westport, Conn., Greenwood Press, 1986), pp. 77–106.

—— "Nascent Proletarians: Migration and Class Formation in the Stéphanois Region: 1840–1880," in *Migrants in Modern France: Population Mobility in the Nineteenth and Twentieth Centuries*, ed. P. E. Ogden and P. E. White (London, Allen and Unwin, forthcoming).

—— "Proletarian Families and Social Protest: Production and Reproduction as Issues of Social Conflict in Nineteenth-Century France," in *Work in France: Representations, Meaning, Organization, and Practice*, ed. Steven Laurence Kaplan and Cynthia J. Koepp (Ithaca, Cornell University Press, 1986), pp. 418–56.

Hareven, Tamara K., "Cycles, Courses, and Cohorts: Reflections on the Theoretical and Methodological Approaches to the Historical Study of Family Development,"

Journal of Social History 12 (Sept., 1978), pp. 97–109.

Hartmann, Heidi, "Capitalism, Patriarchy, and Job Segregation by Sex," *Signs* 1 (3) (pt 2) (Spring, 1976), pp. 137–69.

Hartmann, Heidi, and Markusen, Ann R., "Contemporary Marxist Theory and Practice: A Feminist Critique," *Review of Radical Political Economics* 12 (2) (Summer, 1980), pp. 87–94.

Hershberg, Theodore, and Dockhord, Robert, "Occupational Classification," *Historical Methods Newsletter* 9 (2–3) (Mar.–June, 1976), pp. 59–98.

Higgs, Edward, "Women, Occupations and Work in the Nineteenth Century Censuses," *History Workshop* 23 (Spring, 1987), pp. 58–80.

Hohenberg, Paul, "Change in Rural France in the Period of Industrialization, 1830–1914," *Journal of Economic History* 32 (1972), pp. 219–40.

Hudson, Pat, "From Manor to Mill: The West Riding in Transition," in *Manufacture in Town and Country before the Factory*, ed. Maxine Berg, Pat Hudson, and Michael Sonenscher (Cambridge, Cambridge University Press, 1983), pp. 124–46.

Hughes, J. R. T., "Industrialization – Economic Aspects," *International Encyclopedia of the Social Sciences* (New York, Macmillan, 1968), vol. 7, pp. 252–63.

Humphries, Jane, "Class Struggle and the Persistence of the Working-Class Family," *Cambridge Journal of Economics* 1 (1977), pp. 241–58.

—— "The Working-Class Family, Women's Liberation and the Class Struggle: The Case of Nineteenth-Century British History," *Review of Radical Political Economics* 9 (3) (Fall, 1977), pp. 25–41.

Hunt, Lynn, and Sheridan, George, "Corporatism, Association, and the Language of Labor in France, 1750–1850," *Journal of Modern History* 58 (Dec. 1986), pp. 813–44.

Jackson, R. T., "Mining Settlements in Western Europe: The Landscape and the Community," in *Urbanization and its Problems: Essays in Honour of E. W. Gilbert*, ed. R. P. Breckinsale and J. M. Houston (New York, Barnes and Noble, 1968), pp. 143–70.

Jeannin, Pierre, "La proto-industrialization: développement ou impasse?" *Annales–ESC* 25 (1980), pp. 52–65.

Jones, E. L., "The Seasons and Economic Affairs," in Jones, *Seasons and Prices, The Role of the Weather in English Agricultural History* (London, George Allen and Unwin, 1964).

Jordan, Ellen, "Female Unemployment in England and Wales 1851–1911: An Examination of the Census Figures for 15–19 year olds," *Social History* 13 (May, 1988), pp. 175–90.

Katznelson, Ira, "Working-Class Formation: Constructing Cases and Comparisons," in *Working-Class Formation: Nineteenth-Century Patterns in Western Europe and the United States*, ed. Ira Katznelson and Aristide R. Zolberg (Princeton, Princeton University Press, 1986), pp. 3–44.

Kerr, Clark, and Siegel, Abraham, "The Interindustry Propensity to Strike – An International Comparison," in *Industrial Conflict*, ed. Arthur Kornhauser, Robert Dubin, and Arthur M. Ross (New York, McGraw-Hill, 1954), pp. 189–212.

Knodel, John, "Family Limitation and the Fertility Transition: Evidence from the Age Patterns of Fertility in Europe and Asia," *Population Studies* 31 (1977), pp. 219–49.

—— "Infant Mortality and Fertility in three Bavarian Villages: An Analysis of Family Histories from the 19th century," *Population Studies* 22 (1968), pp. 297–318.

Knodel, John, and van de Walle, E., "Breastfeeding, Fertility, and Infant Mortality: An Analysis of Some Early German Data," *Population Studies* 21 (1967), pp. 109–31.

Landers, J., "Mortality and Metropolis: The Case of London 1675–1825," *Population Studies* 41 (1987), pp. 59–76.

Laurie, Bruce, and Schmitz, Mark, "Manufacture and Productivity: The Making of an Industrial Base: Philadelphia, 1850–1880," in *Philadelphia: Work, Space, Family, and Group Experience in the 19th Century*, ed. Theodore Hershberg (Oxford, Oxford University Press, 1981), pp. 43–92.

Lazonick, William, "The Subjection of Labour to Capital: The Rise of the Capitalist System," *Review of Radical Political Economy* 10 (1) (Spring, 1978), pp. 1–27.

Lee, Evrett S., "A Theory of Migration," *Demography* 3 (1) (1966), pp. 47–57.

Legendre, Bernard, "La vie d'un prolétariat: les ouvriers de Fougères au début du XXe siècle," *Le mouvement social* 98 (Jan.–Mar., 1977), pp. 3–41.

Lehning, James R., "Nuptuality and Rural Industry: Families and Labor in the French Countryside," *Journal of Family History*. 8 (4) (1983), pp. 333–45.

Lequin, Yves, "A propos de la classe ouvrière du Rhône à la fin du XIXe siècle: conscience de classe et conscience urbaine," in *Colloque franco-suisse d'histoire économique et sociale, Genève 5–6 mai 1962* (Genève, Georg et cie. SA, 1969), pp. 207–26.

—— "La formation du prolétariat industriel dans la région lyonnaise au XIX siècle: approches méthodologiques et premiers résultats," *Le mouvement social* 97 (Oct.–Dec., 1976), pp. 121–37.

—— "Labor in the French Economy since the Revolution," in *Cambridge Economic History of Europe*, ed. Peter Mathias and M. M. Postan (Cambridge, Cambridge University Press, 1978), vol. 7, pt 1, pp. 296–346.

Lesthaeghe, Ron, "On the Social Control of Human Reproduction," *Population and Development Review* 6 (Dec., 1980), pp. 527–48.

Levine, A., Sober, E., and Wright, E. O., "Marxism and Methodological Individualism," *New Left Review* 162 (Mar.–April 1987), pp. 67–84.

Limousin, Charles-M., "Une transformation industrielle: l'industrie du ruban et Saint-Etienne," *Journal des Economistes* 46 (3) (juin, 1901), pp. 329–45.

Loefgren, Orvar, "Family and Household among Scandinavian Peasants: An Exploratory Essay," *Ethnologia Scandinavia* (1974), pp. 17–52.

Lorcin, J., "Un essai de stratigraphie sociale: chefs d'ateliers et compagnons dans la grève de passementiers de Saint-Etienne en 1900," *Cahiers d'histoire* 13 (2) (1968), pp. 179–92.

—— "Réaction Stéphanois et la concurrence de Bâle," *Colloque franco-suisse d'histoire économique et sociale, Genève 5–6 mai 1962* (Genève, Georg et cie. SA, 1969), pp. 145–66.

Lynch, Katherine A., "Marriage Age among French Factory Workers: An Alsatian Example," *Journal of Interdisciplinary History* 16 (3) (Winter, 1986), pp. 405–30.

McKendrick, Neil, "Home Demand and Economic Growth: A New View of the Role of Women and Children in the Industrial Revolution," in *Historical Perspectives: Studies in English Thought and Society*, ed. Neil McKendrick (London, Europa, 1974), pp. 152–210.

Magraw, Roger William, "Pierre Joigneaux and Socialist Propaganda in the French Countryside," *French Historical Studies* 10 (4) (Fall, 1978), pp. 599–640.

Maitron, Jean, "Les penseurs sociaux et la famille dans la première moitié du XIXe siècle," in *Renouveau des idées sur la famille*, ed. Robert Prigent (Paris, PUF, 1954), pp. 81–102.

Marec, Yannick, "L'épargne populaire en France au XIXe siècle et au début du XXe siècle: les enseignements d'un exemple Rouennais," *Revue d'histoire économique et sociale* 55 (1977), pp. 271–83.

Mark-Lawson, Jane and Witz, Anne, "From 'Family Labour' to 'Family Wage'? The Case of Women's Labour in Nineteenth-Century Coalmining," *Social History* 13 (May, 1988), pp. 151–74.

Markovitch, Tihomir J., "Le revenu industriel et artisanal sous la monarchie de juillet et le Second Empire," *Economies et sociétés* series AF (4) (April, 1967).

—— "The Dominant Sector of French Industry," in *Essays in French Economic History*, ed. Rondo Cameron (Homewood, Ill., Richard Irwin, 1970), pp. 226–44.

Martinon, J.-F., and Riou, R., "Conditions de travail et de santé au XIXe siècle: les verriers de Rive-de-Gier," *Cahiers d'histoire* 26 (1) (1981), pp. 27–39.

Martourey, Albert, "La famille et le problème de l'enfance dans une ville ouvrière du XIXe siècle: Saint-Etienne," in *Colloque franco-suisse d'histoire économique et sociale Genève 5–6 mai 1967* (Genève, Georg et ci S.A., 1969), pp. 227–41.

Marvel, Howard P., "Factory Regulation: A Reinterpretation of Early English Experience," *Journal of Law and Economics*, 20 (2) (1977), pp. 379–402.

May, Martha, "The Historical Problem of the Family Wage: The Ford Motor Company and the Five-Dollar Day," *Feminist Studies* 8 (2) (Summer, 1982), pp. 399–424.

Medick, Hans, "The Proto-Industrial Family Economy: The Structural Function of Household and Family During the Transition from Peasant Society to Industrial Capitalism," *Social History*, 3 (1976), pp. 291–315.

Mendels, Franklin F., "Agriculture and Peasant Industry in Eighteenth-Century Flanders," in *European Peasants and Their Markets*, ed. William N. Parker and Eric L. Jones (Princeton, New Jersey, Princeton University Press, 1975), pp. 179–204.

—— "Proto-Industrialization: The First Phase of the Industrialization Process," *Journal of Economic History*. 32 (1) (1972), pp. 241–61.

Mercer, A. J., "Relative Trends in Mortality from Related Respiratory and Airborne Infectious Diseases," *Population Studies* 40 (1986), pp. 129–45.

Merley, Jean, "Les élections de 1869 dans le département de la Loire," *Cahiers d'histoire* 6 (1) (1961), pp. 59–93.

—— "Elements pour l'étude de la formation de la population Stéphanoise à l'aube de la révolution industrielle," *Démographie urbaine XVe-XXe siècle, Bulletin* 8, (Centre d'histoire économique et sociale de la région lyonnaise, 1977), pp. 261–75.

Milkman, Ruth, "Redefining 'Women's Work,' The Sexual Division of Labor in the Auto-Industry during World War II," *Feminist Studies* 8 (Summer, 1982), pp. 337–72.

Millward, R., "The Emergence of Wage Labor in Early Modern England," *Explorations in Economic History* 18 (1) (Jan. 1981), pp. 21–39.

Mincer, Jacob, "Labor Force Participation," *International Encyclopedia of the Social Sciences*, vol. 8, (New York: Macmillan and Free Press, 1968), pp. 474–81.

Moch, Leslie Page, and Tilly, Louise, "Immigrant Women in the City: Comparative Perspectives," CRSO working paper 205 (Sept. 1979).

Model, J., Furstenberg Jr, F., and Hershberg, T., "Social Change and Transitions to

Adulthood in Historical Perspective," *Journal of Family History* 1 (Autumn, 1976), pp. 7–32.

Model, John, and Hareven, Tamara, "Transitions: Patterns of Timing," in *Transitions: The Family and the Life Course in Historical Perspective*, ed. Tamara K. Hareven (New York, Academic Press, 1978), pp. 245–69.

Moss, Bernard, "June 13, 1849: The Abortive Uprising of French Radicalism," *French Historical Studies* 13 (3) (Spring, 1984), pp. 390–414.

Moutet, Aimee, "Le mouvement ouvrier à Paris du lendemain de la Commune au premier congrès syndical en 1876," *Le mouvement social* 58 (Jan.–Mar., 1967), pp. 3–39.

Mueller, Eva, "The Economic Value of Children in Peasant Agriculture," in *Population and Development: The Search for Selective Intervention*, ed. Ronald G. Ridker (Baltimore, Johns Hopkins University Press, 1976), pp. 98–153.

Newell, William H., "The Agricultural Revolution in Nineteenth-Century France," *Journal of Economic History*, 33 (4) (Dec., 1973) pp. 697–730.

Nord, Philip G., "The Party of Conciliation and the Paris Commune," *French Historical Studies* 15 (1) (Spring, 1987), pp. 1–35.

Nugent, Jeffrey B., "The Old-Age Security Motive for Fertility," *Population and Development Review* 11 (Mar. 1985), pp. 75–97.

Perrot, Michelle, "Les couches populaires urbaines," in *Histoire économique et sociale de la France*, ed. Fernand Braudel and Ernest Labrousse (Paris, Presses universitaires de France, 1979), vol. 1, pp. 454–82.

Poirier-Coutansias, Françoise, "Analyse d'un rapport sur la situation industrielle du département de la Loire au début du Consulat," in *Colloque franco-suisse d'histoire economique et sociale, Genève 5–6 mai 1962* (Genève, Georg et cie. SA, 1969), pp. 121–8.

Poitrineau, Abel, "Aspects de l'émigration temporaire et saisonnière en Auvergne et la fin du XVIIIe et au début du XIXe siècle," *Revue d'histoire moderne et contemporaine*, 9 (Jan.–Mar., 1962), pp. 5–50.

Poussou, Jean-Pierre, "Les mouvements migratoires en France et à partir de la fin du XVe siècle au début du XIXe siècle: approches pour une synthèse," in *Annales de Démographie Historique – 1970* (Paris, Mouton, 1970), pp. 11–79.

Preston, Samuel H., and van de Walle, Etienne, "Urban French Mortality in the Nineteenth Century," *Population Studies*, 32 (2) (July, 1978), pp. 275–97.

Price, Roger, "The Onset of Labour Shortage in Nineteenth-Century French Agriculture," *Economic History Review*, 2nd series, 28 (2) (1975), pp. 260–79.

Przeworski, Adam, "Proletariat into a Class: The Process of Class Formation from Karl Kautsky's *The Class Struggle* to Recent Controversies," *Politics and Society* 7 (1977), pp. 343–401.

Quick, Paddy, "The Class Nature of Women's Oppression," *Review of Radical Political Economics*, 9 (3) (Fall, 1977), pp. 42–53.

Reid, Donald, "The Role of Mine Safety in the Development of Working-Class Consciousness and Organization: The Case of the Aubin Coal Basin, 1867–1914," *French Historical Studies*. 12 (1) (Spring, 1981), pp. 98–119.

Rist, Charles, "La durée de travail dans l'industrie française de 1820 et 1870," *Revue d'économie politique*, 11 (1897), pp. 371–93.

Robinson, Robert, and Kelley, Jonathan, "Class as Conceived by Marx and Dahrendorf: Effects on Income Inequality and Politics in the United States and Great Britain," *American Sociological Review* 44 (Feb., 1979), pp. 38–58.

Rose, Sonya O., "Proto-Industry, Women's Work and the Household Economy in the Transition to Industrial Capitalism," *Journal of Family History* 13 (2) (1988), pp. 181–93.

Saville, John, "Primitive Accumulation and Early Industrialization in Britain," in *Socialist Register: 1969* (New York, Monthly Review Press, 1969), pp. 247–71.

Schlumbohm, Jürgen, "Seasonal Fluctuations and Social Division of Labor: Rural Linen Production in the Osnabruck and Bielefeld Regions and the Urban Woolen Industry in the Niederlausitz, *c.*1770–*c.*1850," in *Manufacture in Town and Country before the Factory*, ed. Maxine Berg, Pat Hudson, and Michael Sonenscher (Cambridge, Cambridge University Press, 1983), pp. 92–123.

Seccombe, Wally, "Domestic Labor and the Working-Class Household," in *Hidden in the Household: Women's Domestic Labor under Capitalism*, ed. Bonnie Fox (Oshawa, Ontario, Women's Press, 1980), pp. 25–99.

—— "Marxism and Demography," *New Left Review*. 137 (Jan.–Feb., 1983). pp. 22–47.

Seibert, Henri, "The Progress of Ideas Regarding the Causation and Control of Infant Mortality," *Bulletin of the History of Medicine* 8 (4) (April, 1940), pp. 546–98.

Sen, Gita, "The Sexual Division of Labor and the Working-Class Family: Towards a Conceptual Synthesis of Class Relations and the Subordination of Women," *Review of Radical Political Economics* 12 (2) (Summer, 1980), pp. 76–80.

Sjaastad, Larry A., "The Costs and Returns of Human Migration," *Journal of Political Economy* 70 (supp. 5, pt 2) (Oct., 1962), pp. 80–93.

Smailes, Arthur E., "Population Changes in the Colliery Districts of Northumberland and Durham," *Geographical Journal* 91 (Jan.–June 1938), pp. 220–32.

Sonenscher, Michael, "Work and Wages in Paris in the Eighteenth Century," in *Manufacture in Town and Country before the Factory*, ed. Maxine Berg, Pat Hudson, and Michael Sonenscher (Cambridge, Cambridge University Press, 1983), pp. 147–72.

Spagnoli, Paul G., "Industrialization, Proletarianization and Marriage: A Reconsideration," *Journal of Family History* 8 (3) (1983), pp. 230–47.

Spaven, Pat, "Main Gates of Protest: Contrasts in Rank and File Activity among the South Yorkshire Miners, 1858–1894," in *Independent Colliers*, ed. R. Harrison (New York, St Martin's, 1978), pp. 201–31.

Stolnitz, George J., "A Century of International Mortality Trends: I," *Population Studies* 9 (1) (July, 1955), pp. 24–55.

Tabarrah, R., "Toward a Theory of Demographic Development," *Economic Development and Cultural Change* 19 (2) (Jan. 1971), pp. 257–76.

Tarle, Eugène, "La grande coalition des mineurs de Rive-de-Gier en 1844," *Revue Historique* (1936), pp. 249–78.

Thomson, J. K. L., "Variations in Industrial Structure in Pre-Industrial Languedoc," in *Manufacture in Town and Country before the Factory*, ed. Maxine Berg, Pat Hudson, and Michael Sonenscher (Cambridge, Cambridge University Press, 1983), pp. 61–91.

Thuillier, Guy, "En Nivernais: les assurances au XIXe siècle," *Annales – ESC* 19 (4) (July–Aug. 1964), pp. 665–84.

Tilly, Charles, "Demographic Origins of the European Proletariat," CRSO working paper 207 (University of Michigan, 1979).

—— "Migration in Modern European History," in *Human Migration: Patterns and Policies*, ed. William H. McNeill and Ruth S. Adams (Bloomington, Indiana University Press, 1978), pp. 48–72.

Tilly, Louise, "The Family Wage Economy of a French Textile Town: Roubaix, 1872–1906," *Journal of Family History* (Winter, 1979), pp. 381–94.

—— "Individual Lives and Family Strategies of the French Proletariat," *Journal of Family History* 4 (Summer, 1979), pp. 137–52.

—— "Structure d'emploi, travail des femmes et changement démographique dans deux villes industrielles, Anzin et Roubaix, 1872–1906," *Le mouvement social* 105 Nov.–Dec., 1978), pp. 33–58.

Tomas, François, "La démographie Forézienne au XVIIIe siècle." *Bulletin de la Diana* 40 (7) (1968), pp. 279–300.

—— "Géographie sociale du Forez en 1788 d'après les tableaux des propriétaires et habitans," *Bulletin de la Diana* 39 (3) (1965), pp. 80–117.

—— "Problemes de démographie historique: Le Forez au XVIIIe siècle," *Cahiers d'histoire* 13 (4) (1968), pp. 381–99.

Toutain, J. C., "La population de la France de 1700 et 1959," in *Histoire quantitative de l'économie française* (Paris, ISEA, 1963), vol. 3.

Trempé, Rolande, "Travail à la mine et vieillissement des mineurs au XIXe siècle," *Le mouvement social* 124 (July–Sept., 1971), pp. 131–52.

Uselding, Paul, "In Dispraise of the Muckrakers: United States Occupational Mortality, 1890–1910," in *Research in Economic History: An Annual Compilation of Research*, ed. Paul Uselding (Greenwich, Conn., JAI Press, 1976), vol. 1, pp. 334–71.

van de Walle, Etienne, "France," in *European Demography and Economic Growth*, ed. W. R. Lee (New York, St Martin's Press, 1979), pp. 123–43.

van de Walle, Francine, "Infant Mortality and the European Demographic Transition," in *The Decline of Fertility in Europe*, ed. Ansley J. Coale and Susan Cotts Watkins (Princeton, Princeton University Press, 1981), pp. 201–33.

Weiss, John H., "Origins of the French Welfare State: Poor Relief in the Third Republic, 1871–1914," *French Historical Studies* 13 (1) (Spring, 1983), pp. 47–78.

Wright, Eric Olin, and Perrone, Luca, "Marxist Class Categories and Income Inequality," *American Sociological Review* 42 (Feb., 1977), pp. 32–55.

Wrigley, E. A. "Family Limitation in Pre-Industrial England," *Economic History Review* 19 (1966), pp. 82–109.

Yudkin, J., "Some Basic Principles of Nutrition," in *The Making of the Modern British Diet*, ed. Derek J. Oddy and Derek S. Miller (London, Croom Helm, 1976), pp. 214–31.

Zelinsky, Wilbur, "The Hypothesis of the Mobility Transition," *Geographical Review* 61 (2) (April, 1971), pp. 219–49.

UNPUBLISHED DISSERTATIONS

Accampo, Elinor Ann, "Industrialization and the Working-Class Family: Saint Chamond, 1815–1880" (University of California, 1984).

Alter, George Charles, "The Influence of Social Stratification on Marriage in Nineteenth-Century Europe: Verviers, Belgium, 1844–1845" (University of Pennsylvania, 1978.

Blee, Kathleen Marie, "The Impact of Family Settlement Patterns on the Politics of Lake Superior Communities, 1890–1920" (University of Wisconsin, 1982).

Feldblum, Mary Alice, "The Formation of the First Factory Labor Force in the New England Cotton Textile Industry, 1800–1848" (New School for Social Research, 1977).

Jaffe, J. A., "Economy and Community in Industrializing England: The Durham Mining Region before 1840" (Columbia University, 1984).

Lamb, George Jared, "Coal Mining in France, 1873 to 1895" (University of Illinois, 1976).

Liebman, Robert Curtis, "Structures of Solidarity: Class, Kin, Community, and Collective Action" (University of Michigan, 1981).

Pemberton, David Mckinney, "Industrialization and the Bourgeoisie in Nineteenth-Century France: The Experience of Saint-Etienne, 1820–1872" (Rutgers University, 1984).

Potash, Janet Ruth, "The Foundling Problem in France, 1800–1869: Child Abandonment in Lille and Lyon" (Yale University, 1979).

Skluth, Myra L., "To the First International: Beauregard Society, Vienne (Isère)" (Columbia University, 1982).

Weir, David Rangeler, "Fertility Transition in Rural France, 1740–1829" (Stanford University, 1983).

Index

Accampo, Elinor, 138, 157
agricultural economy, 10, 60–4, 76–9
  dairying, 76–9, 156
  grain growing, 60, 76, 78, 156
  in Haute-Loire, 64–6, 76
  in Loire, 65, 76
  in Puy-de-Dôme, 65, 66, 76
Ambert, 60, 64
American Civil War, 45
Amiens, trade union congress (1906),
  198
Anderson, Michael, 134
Anglo-French trade agreements (1860),
  184
apprenticeship, see job training
Arbel, Lucien, 81
Ariès, Philippe, 96
artisans, 2, 31, 46, 47, 208
Assaily, 50
associationism, 12–21, 188, 189,
  199–200
associations, 12–15
Audiganne, Armand, 100, 110–11
Ava-Cottin, Charles, 182–3

Banque de France, 44
Basse Isère, 33
beggars, 3, 138, 188
Bertholon, César, 103, 104, 189–90,
  191, 197
birth control, see fertility, control
birth rate, see fertility
Blanqui, Adolphe, 17–18
boarding houses, 83–5, 141
Bonaparte, Louis Napoleon, see
  Napoleon III
Bonapartists, 184
Bourdelais, Pierre, 153

braidweaving, 38, 39, 148, 162
bread prices, 135–6
Brunons, 40
bureaux de bienfaisance, 137–8
Burke, Edmund, 7

Cabet, Etienne, 12, 13, 14, 15
cafés, 84–5
capital concentration, 6, 29–56, 57
Castaing, 185
censuses,
  sampling, 213–15
  underenumeration of child labor, 142,
    213
  underenumeration of female labor,
    142, 159, 160–1, 214, 215
Chandler Jr, Alfred, 41
charities, religious, 136–7
Charpin-Feugerolles, Comte de, 191–3
Chennan, Pierre, 69
child labor, 9, 35, 99, 142, 147–8, 161,
  165
cholera epidemic (1854), 141, 153
class, 4
class consciousness, 4, 183, 187–93,
  197, 199, 210–12
class formation, 1–28, 208, 211–12
Claudinon, Jacques, 40, 42, 45, 98
coal mining, 2, 7–8, 8–11, 30, 33, 35,
  37–9, 41–5, 95–133
Coale, 106
communism, 13, 16, 17
Compagnie de la marine et des chemins
  de fer, 45
Compagnie des mines de la Loire, 9–11
  41, 49, 112, 115, 119
conscription, 146–7, 148
Coulon, Etienne, 79

Crimean War, 110, 153
Critaud, Louis, 139
Crozet-Fourneyron, Emile, 197
cutlery, 34

de la Platière, Roland, 32
death rates, *see* mortality
Delahante, Gustave, 9
Démocratie Pacifique, La, 12
domestic industry, 2, 34, 142, 147,
    159–62
  rural, 2, 161–2
  urban, 2, 160–1
Dorian, Pierre-Frédéric, 103, 182, 184,
    188, 189–90, 191, 195, 197
d'Osmond, Marquis, 35, 40
du Maroussem, Pierre, 76
Duché, Tristan, 17
Duruy, Victor, 184

Eclaireur, L', 103, 188, 189–90
Ecole des mines, Saint-Etienne, 37
education, 98–104, 182, 184–5, 189,
    190; *see also* job training
election (May–June 1869), 183–7
employers,
  court rulings in favor of (1850s and
    1860s), 121
  dependency on, 3–4, 6
employment,
  in coal mining, 41–5, 95–133
  in industry, 29–56, 95–133, 209
  in metalworking, 41–5, 95–133
engineers, 9
England, 37, 46, 57, 120
enquêtes (1848), 19–20
epidemics, 141, 153–4

family economy, 139–81
  contribution of children, 142–4,
    147–8, 149, 163, 165, 166
  contribution of men, 140, 146–7,
    163–7
  contribution of women, 140–2, 146,
    163, 165, 166
  industrial working class, 1–28,
    104–14, 134–81
family life, and proletarianization, 1,
    3–4, 6–7
family strategies, 138–9, 208–9, 210
  coal miners, 19–20, 21–4, 104–14
  metalworkers, 104–14

Favre, Jules, 185
Faure, Petrus, 84–5
fertility,
  control, 106–7, 149
  differential by occupation, 107–10
  levels, 5, 106–10, 120, 156–8,
    178–81
Firminy, 137, 192, 194
food prices, 10–11; *see also* bread prices
Forcade-Laroquette, Jean de, 194–5
Forges de Couzon 81
Forissier, Antoine, 200–2
foundling hospital, 3
Fourier, François Marie Charles, 12,
    13–15
Fourneyron, Benoît, 37
Franco-Provençal dialects, 70
Franco-Prussian War, 146
Fraternelle, La, 122–3, 185–7, 188, 191,
    192–3
Frèrejean family, 39–40, 44–5
Friedlander, Dov, 120
Furet, François, 100

Gaga, 70
Gambetta, Léon, 182, 191
Gard, 49
Gaudet, Jean-Marie, 40
Gausserand, Captain, 195
Gille, Bertrand, 40
glassmaking, 147–8, 162, 189
goguette, 85
Gordon, David, 16
Goudefer, Louis, 199–200
Gross Reproduction Rate (GRR) for
    married women, 156–7
Guillaumin, Emile, 146–7
gunsmithing, 34

hardware, 34, 35, 49
Hareven, Tamara, 106
Harris, Marvin, 3
Haute-Loire, 59–86
Hennequin, Victor, 13–15
Hervier, Doctor, 153–4
Hollingworth, Dorothy, 156
Holtzer, Jacob, 37, 40, 45, 98, 184
Hôpital de la Charité, Saint-Etienne, 3
hospitals, 3, 120, 137
housing, 154–5
Hufton, Olwen, 3, 50

industrial organization, 8–11, 29–50
  division of labor, 32, 34–5
  mechanization, 32, 35, 39–41, 57
  technological change, 29, 37–41, 46
Industrial Revolution, 30–1, 36–41,
  72–86
industrial workers,
  semi-skilled, 3–4, 29–30, 37, 41–5,
    45–50, 183–202, 208
  skilled, 46, 48, 68
  unskilled, 31, 41–5
insurance, 10, 23
  accident, 118–24, 185, 186, 201, 210
  sickness, 118–24, 135, 201
Italians, 75, 84

Jackson, James, 37, 44, 46
Jackson Brothers, 42, 50, 98
Janin, Jules, 31
Jezierski, Louis, 189, 191
job training, 98–104
  apprenticeship, 19–20, 46–7, 48, 102
  craft controlled, 47
  employer controlled, 46, 47–8, 102,
    209, 210
  informal, 99
  in schools, 47, 98, 101–2

Kerr, Clark, 96

labor, division of, *see under* industrial
  organization
labor force participation, 35–6, 60–72,
  128, 130, 142–9
  female, 159–63, 166
labor movement, rise of the modern,
  196–202
labor recruitment, 5, 9, 46, 47–8, 80, 82
Lamy, Etienne, 104
Lancashire, 134
language, 70
Lappier de Gemeaux, 32
Le Chambon-Feugerolles, 2, 36, 72–3,
  137, 154–5
Le Play, Frédéric, 134–5
Le Puy, 60, 64
Ledru-Rollin, 20
Lehning, James, 78
Leroux, Jules, 12
Leroux, Pierre, 12
life cycle,
  earnings, 96, 97

employment opportunities, 95–133
  family, 14
life expectancy, 149–51
Linossier, François, 70
literacy, 100–1, 110
Loire, 49, 59–86
Louis Napoleon, *see* Napoleon III
Louis-Philippe, 16
Lyon, 3, 12–13, 20
  Congress of (1878), 197–8

MacMahon, 199
Mandon, Daniel, 85
manufacturing (1780–1820), 31–6
Marrel works, 81–2
marriage,
  age of, 83, 144
    coal miners, 158
    in Le Chambon-Feugerolles, 158–9
    in Rive-de-Gier, 158
    in Saint-Chamond, 83, 144
  proportion ever married:
    in Le Chambon-Feugerolles, 83, 145
    in Rive-de-Gier, 83, 145
    in Saint-Chamond, 83, 145
Marseilles, Congress of (1879), 198,
  199, 202
Marx, Karl, 56
Marxism, 198, 199
mechanization, *see under* industrial
  organization
Merley, Jean, 63, 65
Messance, 32, 35, 36
metalworking, 2, 30, 33, 37–8, 40–1,
  41–5, 95–133
Michelet, Jules, 30, 31, 43
migration, 3, 57–94
  international, 75
  seasonal, 3, 32, 60–1, 63
  temporary, 3, 32, 57–9, 63–4, 69, 71,
    79
miners' strike (1844), 10–12
miners' strike (1848), 16–17
miners' strike (1869), 111, 113,
  193–6
miners' strikes (1849–51), 21
miners' strikes (late 1860s), 167
mining concessions, 43
mobility,
  industrial, 100
  social, 101
Montagne family, 66

Montgrand, Benoîte, 79
Montrambert mines, 49, 115, 195
Morels, 40, 45
mortality,
  age-specific, 149–56, 174, 176–7
  child, 149, 151
  epidemic, 141, 152–6
  infant, 149–51, 153, 173
  in Le Chambon-Feugerolles, 149–50,
    157
  occupational, 119
  in Rive-de-Gier, 149–50, 151
  in Saint-Chamond, 149–50, 151
  seasonal, 152, 155
municipal aid, 137–8
mutual aid societies, 119, 122–3, 137,
  185

nail making, 34
Napoleon III, 6, 20–1, 45, 70, 113, 185
Net Reproduction Rate (NRR) for
  married women, 156–8
Neyrand, 40
Nord, 49

Occitan dialects, 70
Oriol, Benoît, 148
Ozouf, Jacques, 100

Pagnal, Damiens, 69–70
Palluat, 40, 44
Paris, 16, 21, 45
Paris Commune, 197
Parkin, Frank, 4
Parti ouvrier français, 202
patois, 70
Pavezin, 59, 76, 78, 79
pensions,
  old age, 114–17, 119, 135, 191, 201,
    210
  widows and orhans, 120, 121, 201
Perkin, Harold, 188
Petin, Hippolyte, 40
Petin–Gaudet works, 42, 44, 45, 98,
  102, 192
Petit Lyonnais, Le, 199
Peyret, Jean-Claude, 192
Phalanges, 14
proletarianization, 3, 31–50, 57, 95–8,
  156
proletariat, 1, 182–202

permanent, 50, 57–94, 95, 156,
  182–202
temporary, 62–72, 95
Proudhon, P. J., 13
Prugnat, Antoine, 122
Prussia, 118
Przeworksi, Adam, 16
public health, 151–6
Puy-de-Dôme, 59–86

Raboulet, Pierre, 140
railways, 39, 41, 43, 44, 45
Raulot, Jean-Yves, 153
receiving communities, 59, 72–3
republicanism, 12–14, 15–21, 182–202,
  210
Reybaud, Louis, 140, 161
ribbon weaving, 32, 34, 45, 49, 160–2,
  186, 187, 208
Richard-Chambovet, Charles-François,
  39, 41
Richarme, Petrus, 197
Richarme glassworks, 189
Ripagérienne, La, 85
Rive-de-Gier, 2, 7–8, 12–13, 15–21,
  36, 71–4, 80–2, 137, 153–4
Rondet, Michel, 113, 114, 115, 118,
  186, 187, 191, 193, 194
Ross, Eric, B., 3
Royet, 40

safety delegates' election, parliamentary
  committee on (1884), 18
Sain, M., 11, 17
Saint-Amant-Roche-Savine, 59, 61–3,
  64, 67
Saint-Chamond, 2, 34, 36, 72–4,
  137–8, 153–4
Saint-Christo-en-Jarez, 59–67, 76, 77
Saint-Etienne, 1, 2, 12–13, 34, 36
Saint-Julien-Chapteuil, 59, 61, 63, 65
Saint-Just-Malmont, 45, 67
Saint-Simon, Claude Henri de, 12, 14
schooling, 98, 101, 147, 201
  religious, 101, 102–3
  secular, 101–2, 104, 184
  vocational, 102, 103
secret societies, 20
sending communities, 58, 65, 68, 72–3
sex ratios, 97
  in Le Chambon-Feugerolles, 142,
    159–62, 163

in Rive-de-Gier, 160–1, 162, 163
in Saint-Chamond, 142, 159–61, 162, 163
Siegel, Abraham, 96
Siemens–Martin process, 111
silicosis, 118
silk weaving, 13, 34, 38, 45
Smailes, Arthur, 158
social classes, 133
social organizations, voluntary, 85–6
socialism, 182–202, 211–12
Société des houillères de Rive-de-Gier, 158
Société musicale de Rive-de-Gier, 85
state intervention, 42–3, 44, 148, 188
state welfare, 137–8
steam power, 38–9, 41, 44
Stedman, Gareth Jones, 8
Stéphanois region, 1–28, 29–56, 139–49, 187–93
population, 1, 36
strike militancy, 182–202
strikes (1870s), 198–9; *see also* miners' strikes
sub-contracting, 9
supervisors, election of, 18

Taylor, Barbara, 14
technological change, *see under* industrial organization
Terrenoire, 38
Thiollière, 40
Thomas–Gilchrist basic, 111
Thompson, Edward, 4

Tiennon, Père, 146–7
Total Fertility Rate (TFR) for married women, 156–7
Tours, Socialist party congress (1920), 198
trade unionism, 122, 186, 187, 189–90, 197, 200
transportation, 33–4
Tristan, Flora, 12, 71
Truvet, Elisabeth, 163
typhoid epidemic (1869), 153–4

urban environment and mortality, 151–6
urban growth, 2, 29–56, 134–81

Velle, Léon, 71
Vinovskis, Maris, 106

wages,
of children, 159
in industry, 10–11, 135–6, 186–7
metalworkers and miners compared, 49–50, 105–6, 111–14, 115, 189
of women, 159–60, 161
Wales, 120
water power, 33, 35, 37, 39
water supply, 155
Watt, James, 39
worker/consumer rations, 163–7

Yssingeaux, 60, 64

Zola, Emile, *Germinal*, 114, 121, 190